Pariis
8-74

D0027464

PRAXIS AND ACTION

Richard J. Bernstein

PRAXIS
AND
ACTION

CONTEMPORARY
PHILOSOPHIES
OF HUMAN
ACTIVITY

University of Pennsylvania Press

Philadelphia

1971

Copyright © 1971 by the University of Pennsylvania Press, Inc.

Second printing 1974

All rights reserved

Library of Congress Catalog Card Number: 77-157048

Copyright information for quoted material

Selections from *Concluding Unscientific Postscript,* by Søren Kierkegaard, trans. by David F. Swenson and Walter Lowrie (copyright 1969 by Princeton University Press; Princeton Paperback, 1968), pp. 71-72, 109, 271, 551, reprinted by permission of Princeton University Press and the American Scandinavian Foundation. Selections from *Writings of the Young Marx on Philosophy and Society,* edited and translated by Loyd D. Easton and Kurt H. Guddat, reprinted by permission of Doubleday & Company, Inc. Selections from G. W. F. Hegel, *The Phenomenology of Mind,* 2d rev. ed., trans. and with an Introduction by J. B. Baillie, reprinted with the permission of Humanities Press, Inc., New York, and George Allen & Unwin, Ltd., London, 1949. A revised version of sections from Richard J. Bernstein, *John Dewey,* New York, 1966. Permission granted by Washington Square Press. A revised version of "Action, Conduct, and Self-Control," from *Perspectives on Peirce,* edited by Richard J. Bernstein, New Haven. With the permission of Yale University Press. Selections from Jean-Paul Sartre, *Being and Nothingness,* trans. by Hazel Barnes, New York, 1956. Permission granted by Philosophical Library.

ISBN (cloth) 0-8122-7640-X
ISBN (paper) 0-8122-1016-6

Designed by
Martyn J. Hitchcock

Printed in the United States of America

FOR CAROL

κοινὰ γὰρ τὰ τῶν φίλων.

Plato's *Phaedrus*

CONTENTS

PREFACE

THE TITLE OF THIS BOOK, "*Praxis* and Action," may seem redundant, but the redundancy is intentional. The Greek term *"praxis"* has an ordinary meaning that roughly corresponds to the ways in which we now commonly speak of "action" or "doing," and it is frequently translated into English as "practice." As Lobkowicz points out, "The verb 'πράσσω' [*prassô*] has a number of closely related meanings such as 'I accomplish (e.g., a journey),' 'I manage (e.g., state of affairs),' 'I do or fare (e.g., well or ill),' and, in general, 'I act, I perform some activity.' "[1]

While these uses are common enough in Greek, *"praxis"* takes on a distinctive and quasi-technical meaning in Aristotle. Aristotle continues to use the expression in a general way to refer to a variety of biological life activities, but he also uses *"praxis"* to designate one of the ways of life open to a free man, and to signify the sciences and arts that deal with the activities characteristic of man's ethical and political life. In this context, the contrast that Aristotle draws is between *"theoria"* and *"praxis"* where the former expression signifies those sciences and activities that are concerned with knowing for its own sake. This contrast is an ancestor of the distinction between theory and practice that has been central to almost every major Western philosopher since Aristotle.

At times, Aristotle introduces a more refined distinction between *"poesis"* and *"praxis."* The point here is to distinguish activities and disciplines which are primarily a form of making (building a house, writing a play) from *doing* proper, where the end or *telos* of the activity is not primarily the production of an artifact, but rather per-

1. Nicholas Lobkowicz, *Theory and Practice: History of a Concept from Aristotle to Marx,* p. 9. (Place and date of all books cited in the text are given in the Bibliography.) This is a good source for a more extensive discussion of the meaning and significance of the distinction between theory and practice in Aristotle and for following the vicissitudes of this distinction through history, culminating in a detailed examination of Marx's thought.

forming the particular activity in a certain way, i.e., performing the activity well: *"eupraxia."*

"Praxis" in this more restricted sense signifies the disciplines and activities predominant in man's ethical and political life. These disciplines, which require knowledge and practical wisdom, can be contrasted with *"theoria"* because their end is not knowing or wisdom for its own sake, but doing—living well. When we add that for Aristotle, individual ethical activity is properly a part of the study of political activity—activity in the *"polis,"* we can say that *"praxis"* signifies the free activity (and the disciplines concerned with this activity) in the *"polis."*[2]

We must be careful not to distort the spirit of Aristotle's distinctions. Although *"theoria,"* the etymological source of our word "theory," is sometimes translated as "contemplation," "contemplation" tends to suggest a receptive and passive state of mind. But for Aristotle, *"theoria"* is a form of life that involves strenuous disciplined activity. It is not entirely accurate to call *"theoria"* and *"praxis"* ways or forms of life, for according to Aristotle they emerge as two dimensions of the truly human and free life.

Already we can detect an important ambiguity revealed by the disparity between Aristotle's meaning of *"praxis"* and the English translation "practice." For "practice" and its cognate "practical" call to mind some mundane and bread-and-butter activity or character. The practical man is one who is not concerned with theory (even anti-theoretical or anti-intellectual), who knows how to get along in the rough and tumble of the world; he is interested in the "practical" or "material" things of life. Consequently, a person with this characteristically contemporary sense of "practical" in mind may be initially perplexed when he realizes that what we now call "practical" has little to do with what Aristotle intended by *"praxis."*

The ambiguity of what we might label the "high" and "low" senses of "practical" has been the source of innumerable confusions, even among philosophers. When, for example, the pragmatists emphasized the role of the "practical" in human life, they were primarily developing a category derived from the "high" sense of practical; they were close in spirit to Aristotle's *"praxis."* But many of their

2. For an ambitious attempt to articulate and revive this Aristotelian meaning of free political activity, see Hannah Arendt, *The Human Condition.*

critics—either out of ignorance or malice—have interpreted them as sanctifying the "low" sense of "practical."

It is not solely with Aristotle in mind that we have introduced the term *"praxis"* into the title of this book, even though we shall see that in modern uses of *"praxis,"* it never loses the distinctive Aristotelian flavor of suggesting that form of truly human activity manifested in the life of the *polis*. In the history of philosophy, there are times when a concept catches the imagination of a group of thinkers. At such periods, the concept can have an almost magical significance, suggesting an entire way of looking at things, or a cluster of issues and problems to be confronted. In Germany among the young left Hegelians in the 1840's, *"praxis"* had this power. These thinkers had plunged deeply into the intricacies of Hegel's thought, but in their own attempts to come to grips with the problems of the time, they felt profoundly that something had gone desperately wrong with the Hegelian system. There was an urgent quest to go "beyond" Hegel. In this quest the concept of *"praxis"* arose on the horizon. Cieszkowski seems to have coined this "new" use of *"praxis"* and declared that the role of philosophy was "to become a practical philosophy or rather a philosophy of practical activity, of *'praxis,'* exercising a direct influence on social life and developing the future in the realm of concrete activity."[3] Among the left Hegelians, the excitement generated by talk of *"praxis"* was equaled only by the vagueness with which they used the expression. Marx was part of this movement and borrowed the idea (as he did with so many of his other key ideas) from his contemporaries. What distinguishes Marx from the other left Hegelians is that he soon grew impatient with vague talk about *praxis* and he went on to develop a thorough, systematic and comprehensive *theory* of *praxis*—a theory, which I shall argue, provides the key for understanding his basic outlook from his early speculations to his mature thought. Until recently, the concept of *praxis* has not played a fundamental role in traditional or "orthodox" interpretations of Marxism. But with the renaissance of interest in Marx since World War II, the concept has once again been revived, and revived with the idea of evoking what is taken to be most vital and basic in a Marxist orientation. The new

3. A. V. Cieszkowski, *Prolegomena zur Historiosophie*, p. 129. This passage is translated and cited by David McLellan, *The Young Hegelians and Karl Marx*, p. 10.

interest in *praxis* is indicated by the fundamental role it plays in Sartre's *Critique de la raison dialectique* and by the appearance of the international journal, *Praxis,* published in Yugoslavia, which has become a vehicle for the revival of humanistic interpretations of Marx and Marxism.

Just as the concept of *praxis* has come to have an enormous power in suggesting a particular reading of Marx and a humanistic interpretation of Marxism, we find, in a very different context, that the concept of action has come to have the same type of evocative significance for analytic philosophers. Among philosophers trained in or sympathetic to analytic philosophy, especially the philosophy of Wittgenstein, the concept of action has become *the* focal point of post-Wittgensteinian investigations. In Part IV, I shall explore how and why this has come to be. Scarcely a month passes without the appearance of an article or a book dealing with some aspect of the concept of action. "Action" in this context has come to signify a complex web of issues in understanding "intention," "motive," "purpose," "reasons," and "teleological explanation" that has dominated analytic investigations for the past two decades. Ironically, although the meanings of *"praxis"* and "action" are very close, few philosophers have even raised the question of whether there is any relation between analytic discussions of the concept of action and the interest in *praxis* among Marxist thinkers. I do not want to suggest that at heart both movements are dealing with the same basic issues. We shall see that they are not. But I do want to claim—this is, in part, the justification for this book—that it is important and fruitful to inquire into the meaning and significance of these central concepts in both traditions.

Consequently, if we ignore the contexts of recent philosophic inquiries, *"praxis"* and "action" may seem redundant, but when we consider the role that these concepts have played in Marxist thought and analytic philosophy respectively, they appear to indicate two independent and unbridgeable intellectual concerns. The use of both these terms in the title of this work is explicitly intended to heighten this tension and to call for a *single* inquiry into these two influential movements.

If we enlarge our horizon to include other philosophic movements that have shaped our modern consciousness, we soon discover that the focus on *praxis* and action is not unique to Marxist thought and contemporary post-Wittgensteinian philosophy, but has a much larger scope. The sentence we quoted earlier from Cieszkowski might have been written by John Dewey. Dewey, like Marx, was overwhelmed early in his intellectual career by Hegel and the Hegelians. Dewey himself called for a philosophy that would "become a practical philosophy or rather a philosophy of practical activity." It is well known that the pragmatic philosophers were preoccupied with the nature of human action and with practice, but there still is a great deal of confusion about what the pragmatists understood by "action" and precisely what role action does or ought to play in understanding human life.

The pragmatic movement has been a disinctively American movement (although recent Anglo-Saxon analytic philosophy is pervaded by pragmatic themes). There has been little appreciation or understanding in Europe of the pragmatist's contribution to philosophic inquiry.[4] If we turn to Europe, however, we discover that in the phenomenological movement, especially in existentialist thought, the central issue again turns out to be the nature of human action. Like Marxism, and Dewey's pragmatism, existentialism can only be properly understood as it emerges out of, and violently reacts to, Hegelianism.

The guiding principle of this study is that the investigation of the nature, status, and significance of *praxis* and action has become the dominant concern of the most influential philosophic movements that have emerged since Hegel. The essential aim of this study is to understand what each of these philosophic movements has been telling us about action, how it is to be characterized, what issues must be confronted in coming to grips with action, and what is the significance of action in the attempt to understand what man is.

The intellectual seeds for this study were planted and cultivated during the decade that I spent at Yale, first as a graduate student

4. There are some very encouraging signs that during the past decade this situation has been changing, especially in Germany. Peirce is the pragmatic philosopher who is being "discovered" by German philosophers. In addition to the translation of Peirce's writings into German, there have been a number of fine and subtle studies of Peirce's philosophy. One German philosopher should be singled out for his serious critical encounter with Peirce's philosophy, Jürgen Habermas. See his *Erkenntnis und Interesse* which has recently been translated into English as *Knowledge and Human Interests* by Beacon Press.

and then as a member of the faculty. It was John E. Smith who first opened my eyes to the richness, vitality, and variety of pragmatic philosophy. During the academic year 1953-1954, I had a chance to participate in a seminar on Hegel's *Phenomenology* given by George Schrader. My immediate philosophic interests were to take other directions, but I have never forgotten my initial traumatic and exciting encounter with Hegel. Even my interest in John Dewey was colored by the way in which I saw Dewey attempting to naturalize Hegel and make him more palatable to the contemporary thinker. Since that time, I have myself given seminars on Hegel and have come to feel more and more that all contemporary philosophy, including analytic philosophy, can best be understood as an outgrowth of, or reaction to Hegel's profoundly presumptuous claims. I had the good fortune to be introduced to analytic philosophy by Rulon Wells and Carl G. Hempel. At a later date, Wilfrid Sellars showed me—by his own example—how analytic tools could be used to deal with the perennial philosophic issues. Charles Hendel, a most humane scholar, had the rare gift of opening up new areas to his students and colleagues. He was the first to initiate me into the discovery of Marxist and existentialist thought. I find it difficult to specify what I learned from Paul Weiss—we have always disagreed about basic philosophic issues—but I know that during the years when I attended his classes, argued fiercely with him as a colleague, and learned daily from him in my capacity as assistant editor of *The Review of Metaphysics,* no one has taught me better than he has what it is to be a philosopher. He first suggested that I write this book.

While the ideas in this book were nurtured at Yale, this study only came to fruition when I joined the faculty at Haverford. Haverford is a rare and fragile institution—especially in these chaotic times—where there is still a delicate balance between intellectual excitement and tranquility that is so necessary for and conducive to scholarly research. I want to express my gratitude to my lively students and colleagues and to a most enlightened and philosophic administration. My wife neither typed this manuscript nor helped with the technical details, but she helped in more ways than I can say by being an intellectual companion. The book is dedicated to her.

Many persons have helped in writing this book. Marcel Gutwirth, Charles Kahn, and my wife, Carol have read and commented on the entire manuscript. Parts of it have been read by Shlomo Avineri,

Stephan Crites, Louis Mackey, and Richard Rorty. I have benefited enormously from their critical comments. Catherine Schweitzer, Judy Perloe, and Bjorg Miehle helped with many technical details. Adeline Taraborelli patiently typed the manuscript. Ann Taraborelli assisted with compiling the index.

Throughout this book I have followed the practice of citing available English translations where the original works have been translated. When more than one translation is available, I use what I consider to be the best or most convenient translation (for example, I quote from Walter Kaufmann's translation of the preface to Hegel's *Phenomenology* rather than Baillie's original translation). I do, however, give original source references for all works cited that have been written in German and French. The one case where I have some misgivings about this procedure is in quoting passages from Hegel. While recent translations of Hegel are adequate, some of the older translations are not. This is especially true for Baillie's translation of the *Phänomenologie des Geistes* which he translates as *"The Phenomenology of Mind."* For reasons which will become clear, I refer to this work as *"The Phenomenology of Spirit."* Baillie undertook the heroic task of translating the *Phenomenology,* and it is through this translation that this book is known to English readers, if it is known at all. By contemporary standards of scholarship, his translation leaves much to be desired in accuracy, readability, and intelligibility. I have been tempted to offer new translations of all passages quoted from the *Phenomenology,* but I have refrained for two reasons. First, because a new translation of the *Phenomenology* is now being prepared and I think it unwise to compound confusion by offering my own translations. Second, because translating Hegel requires making basic decisions about the proper English equivalents for his key concepts. To introduce new terms for some of these concepts without systematically altering the entire terminology is unsatisfactory. In a few cases, I have used the original German expression where no translation captures the richness of the original.

R. J. B.

INTRODUCTION

THIS INQUIRY IS CONCERNED with the themes of *praxis* and action in four philosophic movements: Marxism, existentialism, pragmatism, and analytic philosophy. It is rare that these four movements are considered in a single inquiry, for there are profound differences of emphasis, focus, terminology, and approach represented by these styles of thought. Many philosophers believe that similarities among these movements are superficial and that a close examination of them will reveal only hopelessly unbridgeable cleavages. While respecting the genuine fundamental differences of these movements, this inquiry is undertaken in the spirit of showing that there are important common themes and motifs in what first appears to be a chaotic babble of voices. I intend to show that the concern with man as agent has been a primary focal point of each of these movements and further, that each contributes something permanent and important to our understanding of the nature and context of human activity. But the possibility and legitimacy of such an inquiry requires that I first confront the issues raised by the manifest pluralism of philosophic positions and movements.

These problems may seem more acute in our time because philosophers not only disagree about fundamental issues, they also differ about what are the important philosophic issues, the types of considerations relevant to exploring them, and even about the nature of philosophy itself. Significant disagreement presupposes a common universe of discourse within which men can disagree. One would be hard pressed to specify any common universe of discourse that can encompass the variety of contemporary philosophic orientations. Differences are frequently so extreme that there is virtually no communication among representatives of the various philosophic styles of thought. This is not a new phenomenon in philosophy. When we look back over the past, the history of philosophy seems much more orderly and coherent. But if we look closely at any period of intensive philosophic activity, we will discover a similar pluralistic situa-

1

tion. What are we to make of this phenomenon? What does it tell us about the nature of the philosophic enterprise?

There have been a variety of ways in which philosophers have attempted to come to grips with this manifest pluralism. Perhaps the most typical way, at least in modern philosophy, has been to claim that one has "finally" hit on the right method, approach, or criteria to philosophize correctly. Then one can determine the success or failure of other approaches by measuring them against the newly discovered norm. In different ways, this is the "solution" of Descartes, Hume, Kant, the early logical positivists, Husserl, and many others. Each of these philosophers or movements promises us that we have finally arrived at a point where we can provide a firm and secure foundation for philosophy, that the method has been discovered by which we can distinguish knowledge from mere opinion, truth from falsity, the meaningful from the meaningless. Although it is a typical stance of modern philosophers to wipe the slate clean and start afresh, we have all learned that what has first appeared to be clear and distinct, secure and unassailable, turns out to harbor ambiguities and suppressed premises. But even so, many philosophers continue in this vein. Thus, when analytic philosophers allow themselves to peek into what is going on in continental phenomenology and existentialism, they usually do so with an eye to reassuring us that it is the very epitome of obscurantism and muddled thinking from which analytic philosophy has "finally" liberated us. The compliment is returned on the other side by the claim that analytic philosophy is the epitome of triviality which is of interest only insofar as it shows how alienated modern man has become.

For the skeptic, the pluralism of philosophic positions is sufficient proof of the futility of philosophy. His wisdom consists (he thinks) in seeing that the emperor has no clothes. Philosophers, with all their pretentions of searching for the truth and telling us how it is, are victims of a grand illusion. Their battles are, at best, the battles of competing ideologies or systems of belief without any rational foundation. If there is truth and genuine knowledge, it is to be found someplace else, not in philosophy. The skeptic can rest secure in his skepticism by challenging any philosopher to name a single philosophic proposition that has not been denied or contradicted by some other philosopher.

There are more generous ways of confronting the pluralism of philosophy. A philosopher may come to view conflicting positions as partial approximations of a correct view which need to be understood and properly synthesized. He can do this in a modest manner, as Aristotle does in the first book of his *Metaphysics* where he reviews earlier Greek philosophy with the aim of showing how his doctrine of the four causes encapsulates the insights of earlier philosophers and corrects their one-sidedness. The variety of conflicting claims can be reconciled as approximations of a correct view. Or a philosopher can attempt this unification in a grand manner, as Hegel does. Hegel not only claims that the major philosophic positions that have emerged in the course of Western philosophy form parts of a single coherent rational story, he also claims that the way in which this story develops is through the agency of conflicting and contradictory positions. From his perspective, the pluralism of past philosophy is not a source of despair and frustration, but a virtue and a necessity—it is the means by which the truth becomes manifest.

What is so disturbing about the state of philosophy in our own time is that never before has there been a greater opportunity for communication among philosophers with radically different orientations. At no other time have translations become so rapidly and easily available. Never before has it been so convenient to listen to and speak with philosophers throughout the world. Yet significant communication among representatives of different philosophic movements is minimal. There are awkward conferences and meetings where different types of philosophers are brought together, but rarely does anything productive come from this. Our philosophic journals are filled with articles in which someone suddenly discovers that there are similarities among different approaches or philosophers where it had been thought that there were only differences. But the dominant characteristic of our philosophic age is one of ignorance and suspicion of different philosophic styles and movements, usually mixed with disdain, and a stubborn conviction that one's own way of philosophizing is the only worthwhile way.[1]

1. While I do believe that this ignorance is still the dominant characteristic of our time, there are some outstanding exceptions which (hopefully) indicate the possibility of a much more serious encounter between Anglo-Saxon and European philosophic orientations. Stuart Hampshire, Alaisdair MacIntyre, and Charles Taylor are prominent Anglo-Saxon philosophers primarily trained

Since the issues raised by the pluralistic variety of contemporary philosophic positions are central to the inquiry of this study, it is necessary to articulate my own biases. At this preliminary stage, they can only be stated as biases, but they are not arbitrary prejudices. They will be justified in the course of this inquiry.

There are two extremes that must be avoided. On the one hand, the provincialism that is so fashionable among "true believers" of different philosophic orientations can blind us to a serious, sympathetic understanding of other philosophers who are working in different idioms. The vehement polemics of the proponents of different positions are among the least illuminating, informative, and lasting aspects of philosophic inquiry. The idea that there is *the* correct method of philosophizing is a myth and a delusion. On the other hand, it is false to think that all significant philosophic positions are equally correct, that once we genuinely understand what a philosopher is saying and why he is saying it, then all sharp disagreements disappear. Frequently, different philosophic orientations have more in common than is first apparent, but they also have sharp differences in emphasis, style, and doctrine that cannot be wished away.

While the views expressed above are applicable to any period in the history of philosophy, they have a special significance for coming to grips with the pluralism of contemporary philosophy. It is easier to detect coherence in what is long past than it is to find it in the intellectual turmoil that one is living through. It may therefore

---

in analytic philosophy. Their work displays an awareness and sensitivity to issues that have been foremost in European philosophy. In Germany, Jürgen Habermas and some of his students who have been steeped in nineteenth and twentieth century European philosophy have been attempting to engage in a serious encounter with both pragmatism and analytic philosophy. Habermas, whose work is just beginning to be translated into English is not yet widely known or appreciated in the Anglo-Saxon world. I think his work provides a fresh and exciting basis for a serious intellectual encounter with what have been relatively isolated philosophic interests and movements. The type of philosophic dialogue that Habermas is attempting to foster while speaking primarily to philosophers familiar with European philosophy is close in spirit to what I am modestly trying to encourage among philosophers whose roots are in Anglo-Saxon philosophic traditions. For the relevant works of Hampshire, MacIntyre, Taylor, and Habermas, see the Bibliography.

be helpful to the reader to know something of the intellectual journey that led to the writing of this book.

Like many philosophy students, I was initially excited and confused by the variety of contemporary philosophic orientations. Studying thinkers as different as Hegel, Wittgenstein, Dewey, Marx, and Kierkegaard was both a source of excitement and frustration. While it was possible to be "carried along" by each of these thinkers and to appreciate his distinctive insights, there seemed no way of even beginning to reconcile the conflicting approaches. Gradually, I began to see some order emerging from what appeared to be sheer chaos. At first, it was the common negative stance of contemporary philosophers that most forcefully struck me. Most contemporary philosophers have been in revolt against the Cartesian framework. Descartes is frequently called the father of modern philosophy. If we are to judge by philosophy during the past hundred years, this title can best be understood in a Freudian sense. It is a common characteristic of many contemporary philosophers that they have sought to overthrow and dethrone the father.

We find this strain in the pragmatic thinkers. Peirce's series of articles written in 1868 is still the most brilliant and devastating critique of the Cartesian framework.[2] (I speak of the "Cartesian framework" rather than "Descartes" because there is a serious question whether what is being attacked is really the *historical* Descartes.) In one fell swoop Peirce sought to demolish the interrelated motifs that make up Cartesianism. He attacked the ontological duality of mind and body; the subjective individualism implicit in the ultimate appeal to direct personal verification; the method of universal doubt which was supposed to lead us to indubitable truths; the doctrine that language and signs are an external disguise for thought; the doctrine that vagueness is unreal and that the philosophic endeavor is one of knowing clearly and distinctly a completely determinate reality; and most fundamentally, the doctrine that we can break out of the miasma of our language or system of signs and have direct

2. "Questions Concerning Certain Faculties Claimed for Man"; "Some Consequences of Four Incapacities"; and "Grounds of Validity of the Laws of Logic: Further Consequences of Four Incapacities." These articles are reprinted in *Collected Papers of Charles Sanders Peirce,* ed. by Charles Hartshorne and Paul Weiss, Vol. V.

intuitive knowledge of objects. It is this last claim that Peirce took
to be the heart of Cartesianism and the central dogma of modern
philosophy. The themes that are developed in these articles and the
alternative conception of knowledge and inquiry sketched by Peirce
here, not only preoccupied him throughout his life, but are echoed
and further developed by John Dewey, especially in his *Logic: The
Theory of Inquiry*.

It is striking that with all their differences, the same motifs—the
same attack on intuitionism and what has been called the "myth of
the given"—are to be found in Wittgenstein's *Philosophic Investigations*. Miss Anscombe speaks for many contemporary post-Wittgenstein analytic philosophers who have been influenced by Wittgenstein when she writes:

Certainly in modern philosophy we have an incorrigibly contemplative conception of knowledge. Knowledge must be something that is
judged as such by being in accordance with the facts. The facts, reality,
are prior, and dictate what is to be said, if it is knowledge. And this is
the explanation of the utter darkness in which we found ourselves.[3]

We find a similar criticism and attack on the Cartesian view of
knowledge and philosophy in a thinker who shares little else with
Miss Anscombe—Marx. Marx, of course, was scarcely concerned
with the epistemological and metaphysical disputes of modern philosophy. His famous eleventh thesis on Feuerbach was written more
with Hegel and his disciples in mind than with Descartes. It is, however, perfectly applicable to what Anscombe calls "the contemplative conception of knowledge" and what Peirce calls the "Cartesian
framework." "The philosophers have only *interpreted* the world in
various ways; the point is, to *change* it."[4] In this thesis, Marx is
characterizing what he understands to be the aim of philosophy—an
aim enshrined in the Cartesian tradition—but calling for the need to
go "beyond" philosophy.

Existentialist thinkers are tainted with the subjectivist bias implicit in Cartesianism insofar as, first and last, their concern is with

3. G. E. M. Anscombe, *Intention*, p. 57.

4. Marx's "Theses on Feuerbach," trans. and reprinted in *Writings of the
Young Marx on Philosophy and Society*, ed. by Loyd D. Easton and Kurt
H. Guddat, p. 402; Marx/Engels *Werke*, Bd. 3, p. 7. References to the
German or French text are given immediately after the English reference.

the existing individual, but they are no less vehement in their attack on the Cartesian account of what it is to be an existing individual and the distortion that results from an "incorrigibly contemplative conception of knowledge."

There is common ground in what contemporary philosophers have attacked even though the points of attack, strategies, and emphases are quite different. What do they offer to replace the traditional foundations of modern philosophy? Gradually, it became clearer to me that there are also common positive themes and "family resemblances" among the variety of contemporary philosophic positions. The felt difficulty experienced by many contemporary philosophers with the mainstreams of modern philosophy and even earlier philosophy has been that the conception of man which we have inherited is a distorted one. It has been distorted not only by the preoccupation with man as knower, but by a certain view of what knowledge is or ought to be—one that is "incorrigibly contemplative." To correct this distortion, to achieve a better understanding of just what sort of creature man is and can be, we need to understand him as an agent, as an active being engaged in various forms of practice. It is necessary to be very careful here. There is a tendency to think or expect in a study of this kind, that we will or ought to arrive at some grand synthesis in which everything has its proper place. I do not think there is such a synthesis. Contemporary philosophy, like contemporary life, is fragmentary. But it is not completely chaotic. We will be left with sharp differences and conflicts that do not fit into any neat overall pattern, but perhaps the reader will better understand the basis and significance of these differences.

It should now be apparent what my own attitude is to the manifest pluralism of contemporary philosophy. I reject the view that one of these philosophic perspectives is the true path to understanding, while all others are false, confused, or misguided. Each of the philosophic orientations discussed in this book deserves serious study, not simply because it is the product of thoughtful philosophers, but because each has something important to say to us about what it is to be a thinking and active human being.

The skeptic ultimately may be right in his judgment about philosophy, although I do not think he is. But it is clear that the evaluation of what he claims can come only after careful and patient study, not as an a priori bias based on ignorance. There is more wisdom in the way suggested by Aristotle and Hegel. Most of the truly great philosophers have sought to show us how their own views capture what they *take* to be the insight and "truth" implicit in other views, and they reject what is thought to be misleading and false. Our first task is to try to understand, and to understand in such a way that we can highlight what is important and sound. Consequently, I sharply disagree with Hegel, who in some of his more ambitious moments, wrote as if the problem presented by the pluralism of philosophy were resolved once and for all—that we (Hegel) could now see the inner *logos* of the development of philosophy. What Hegel some-times seems to have taken as an established truth is better under-stood as a heuristic principle—not to be put off by the manifest radical pluralism of competing philosophic positions, but to attempt to understand each, to appreciate both the distinctive contributions and the limitations of each. This is really a very old idea in philoso-phy; giving each man and argument its proper due is central to the Platonic idea of justice. This is the spirit in which this inquiry is undertaken.

In a study of this type there must be drastic selection if one is to do justice to the thinkers and issues studied. There are major philosophers of the nineteenth and twentieth century, including Nietzsche, Husserl, and Heidegger, and Whitehead who are not discussed here. If my primary aim were to give a complete over-view or survey of philosophy during the past 150 years, then these omissions would be inexcusable. Furthermore, I believe that each of these thinkers can also be seen as providing important con-tributions to our understanding of man as agent and actor. But I have tried to strike a balance between dealing with thinkers and issues that are genuinely *representative* of the major currents that have shaped our modern consciousness and becoming overwhelmed by the complexity and variety of contemporary philosophy. It is my hope that this book provides a guide and orientation for coming to grips with other dominant figures who are no less important for tell-ing the full story of philosophy during our time.

In Part I, *"Praxis,"* the primary aim is to understand the role of this concept in Marx's thought, especially against the background of Marx's own dialectical struggles with Hegel. In Part II, "Con-sciousness, Existence, and Action," a very different type of reaction to Hegel is explored in the thinking of Kierkegaard and Sartre. Part

III "Action, Conduct, and Inquiry," deals exclusively with Peirce and Dewey. I do not want to sleight the importance of James and Mead to the pragmatic movement, but my purpose is not to tell the story of pragmatism. I focus on Peirce and Dewey because it was Peirce who most systematically and rigorously developed a logical understanding of the nature of action and conduct, while Dewey's focus is on the social implications of the pragmatic understanding of action. Finally, in Part IV, "The Concept of Action," this concept is investigated in the development of analytic philosophy. Because analytic philosophy has been characterized by an intense dialogue involving many thinkers, I do not deal exclusively with individual thinkers. The aim here is to recreate and interpret the internal dialectic that has led to a concern with action and related concepts, and to explore the various options now open to us. The concluding epilogue is not a summary or a conclusion, but a series of reflections about where our inquiry has led us.

I have refrained from weighing down each part with elaborate cross references and discussions of similarities and differences among the four approaches studied. It is challenging enough to understand in depth each of these approaches. The reader may draw conclusions different from mine, but I hope that the evidence for my reading of the theme of *praxis* and action in contemporary thought will emerge with clarity.

PART ONE

PRAXIS

MARX AND THE HEGELIAN
BACKGROUND

Marx's "Theses on Feuerbach"[1]

(1)

THE CHIEF DEFECT of all previous materialism (including Feuerbach's) is that the object, actuality, sensuousness is conceived only in the form of the *object or perception* [*Anschauung*], but not as *sensuous human activity, practice* [*Praxis*], nor subjectively. Hence in opposition to materialism the *active* side was developed by idealism—but only abstractly since idealism naturally does not know actual, sensuous activity as such. Feuerbach wants sensuous objects actually different from thought objects: but he does not comprehend human activity itself as *objective*. Hence in *The Essence of Christianity* he regards only the theoretical attitude as the truly human attitude, while practice is understood and fixed only in its dirtily Jewish form of appearance. Consequently he does not comprehend the significance of "revolutionary," of "practical-critical" activity.

(2)

The question whether human thinking can reach objective truth— is not a question of theory but a *practical* question. In practice man must prove the truth, that is, actuality and power, this-sidedness of his thinking. The dispute about the actuality or non-actuality of thinking—thinking isolated from practice—is a purely *scholastic* question.

(3)

The materialistic doctrine concerning the change of circumstances and

1. "Theses on Feuerbach" in *Writings of the Young Marx on Philosophy and Society,* ed. by Loyd D. Easton and Kurt H. Guddat, pp. 400-402 (hereafter referred to as *Young Marx*); Marx/Engels *Werke,* Bd. 3, pp. 5-7. For a detailed analysis of Marx's "Theses on Feuerbach," and the philosophic background of these theses, see Nathan Rotenstreich, *Basic Problems of Marx's Philosophy.*

education forgets that circumstances are changed by men and that the educator must himself be educated. Hence this doctrine must divide society into two parts—one of which towers above [as in Robert Owen, Engels added].

The coincidence of the change of circumstances and of human activity or self-change can be comprehended and rationally understood only as *revolutionary practice*.

(4)

Feuerbach starts out from the fact of religious self-alienation, the duplication of the world into a religious and secular world. His world consists in resolving the religious world into its secular basis. But the fact that the secular basis becomes separate from itself and establishes an independent realm in the clouds can only be explained by the cleavage and self-contradictoriness of the secular basis. Thus the latter must itself be both understood in its contradiction and revolutionized in practice. For instance, after the earthly family is found to be the secret of the holy family, the former must then be theoretically and practically nullified.

(5)

Feuerbach, not satisfied with *abstract thinking,* wants *perception*; but he does not comprehend sensuousness as *practical* human-sensuous activity.

(6)

Feuerbach resolves the religious essence into the *human* essence. But the essence of man is no abstraction inhering in each single individual. In its actuality it is the ensemble of social relationships.

Feuerbach, who does not go into the criticism of this actual essence, is hence compelled

1. to abstract from the historical process and to establish religious feeling as something self-contained, and to presuppose an abstract— *isolated*—human individual;

2. to view the essence of man merely as "species," as the inner, dumb generality which unites the many individuals *naturally*.

(7)

Feuerbach does not see, consequently, that "religious feeling" is itself a social product and that the abstract individual he analyzes belongs to a particular form of society.

(8)

All social life is essentially *practical*. All mysteries which lead theory to mysticism find their rational solution in human practice and the comprehension of this practice.

(9)

The highest point attained by perceptual materialism, that is, materialism that does not comprehend sensuousness as practical activity, is the view of separate individuals and civil society.

(10)

The standpoint of the old materialism is civil society; the standpoint of the new is human society or socialized humanity.

(11)

The philosophers have only *interpreted* the world in various ways; the point is, to *change* it.

The eleven theses on Feuerbach jotted down by Marx in 1845 when he was only twenty-seven but published with some revisions only after his death as an appendix to Engels' *Ludwig Feuerbach,* is one of the most remarkable and fascinating documents of modern thought. The theses were written after a period of intensive philosophic study and a deepening interest in politics and economics. They contain the quintessence of Marx's thought at the time, which is articulated in greater detail in the famous 1844 *Paris Manuscripts (Economic and Philosophic Manuscripts),* and *The German Ideology* written less than a year after the theses. This was a period when Marx's diverse studies and interests were developing into a coherent perspective, and the theses can serve as a basis for understanding his later development, including the writing of *Capital.* All of these theses revolve around the meaning and significance of *praxis. Praxis* is the central concept in Marx's outlook—the key to understanding his early philosophic speculations and his detailed analysis of the structure of capitalism. It provides the perspective for grasping Marx's conception of man as "the ensemble of social ✓ relationships" and his emphasis on production; it is the basis for comprehending what Marx meant by "revolutionary practice." The theses have important critical practical consequences; they also have metaphysical and epistemological ramifications. To comprehend these theses in detail, we must look backwards to the origin of *praxis,* and forward to the way in which this concept affects Marx's later development. To understand what Marx meant by *praxis* we must first dig back into Hegel. It was Feuerbach who helped Marx see what was wrong and what was right in Hegel's philosophy. But as the theses made clear, Marx was severely critical of Feuerbach's solution to the "riddle" of Hegel.

Geist[2]

Geist (which is best translated as "spirit," not "mind") is the most fundamental concept in Hegel's philosophy, just as *praxis* is basic in Marx's thought. There is not a theme or subject in Hegel that does not lead us back to the nature and dynamics of *Geist,* and the same can be said about the centrality of *praxis* in Marx. *Praxis,* I intend to show, is itself the result of a dialectical critique of Hegel's *Geist*.

Geist is at once a most elusive and seductive concept. It turns up every place in Hegel's philosophy and plays numerous roles. If we are to gain some grasp of what Hegel means by *Geist,* we must approach it from a variety of partial (Hegel would say, "abstract")

2. Any brief discussion of Hegel is bound to be inadequate, or to use Hegelian idiom, "abstract" and "false." I have explored Hegel's thought only insofar as it is necessary to understand the post-Hegelian thinkers and movements who were reacting against Hegel or stressing one aspect of his thought. Furthermore, I discuss those aspects of Hegel's thought which are most *directly* relevant to their concerns. Marx, Kierkegaard, Sartre, Peirce, and Dewey have all criticized Hegel and in each case there is an important issue of whether they correctly interpreted Hegel. In many instances it is clear that they have not done so. Since my aim is to understand the distinctive character of their thought and this frequently depends on how *they* interpreted Hegel, I have emphasized *their* reading of Hegel and the Hegelians rather than exploring the correctness of their interpretations. There are also complex questions concerning how well acquainted each of these thinkers was with Hegel's writings. While it is clear that Marx had a deep knowledge of the Hegelian corpus, this is less true of the other thinkers. In approaching each of these thinkers from the perspective of their reaction to Hegel, I am not assuming that each self-consciously started with a critique of Hegel. Rather, I think that we can understand the thought of each with reference to a "problematic" which can be located in Hegel's thought.

Until recently, Hegelian scholarship in English has been very sporadic and is quite inferior in sophistication when compared with French and German scholarship where there has been a long tradition of serious interest in Hegel. For a brief bibliography of some of the better works on Hegel see the Bibliography in Walter Kaufmann's *Hegel: Reinterpretation, Texts and Commentary*.

perspectives. Hegel self-consciously attempts to integrate and synthesize in a single concept two independent leading ideas that have shaped Western thought. The first is that of Reason or *Noûs,* especially as this concept emerges from Greek philosophy. The second is that of God as Spirit as this concept emerges from the Judaeo-Christian tradition, where God is conceived of as an omniscient, omnipotent, active Being who makes Himself manifest in history and guides history in the form of Divine Providence.

To appreciate what Hegel intends when he tells us that *Geist* is rational, or is Reason, we must divest ourselves of certain modern conceptions of reason and project ourselves back into the Greek—more specifically—the Aristotelian understanding of *Noûs.* Much of modern thinking about reason has been shaped by the Humean doctrine that separates reason from experience and the passions, and conceives of reason as a faculty of individual men that has no inner *conatus* or dynamic force of its own. Reason is a faculty or instrument for drawing logical consequences. Except for the narrow class of analytic truths (or in Humean terminology, "relations of ideas") reason cannot make any inferences without presupposing premises or starting points that are based on experience. Hume's famous doctrine that "reason is, and ought only to be the slave of the passions"[3] is not intended to be a license for irrationality, but rather a way of calling attention to the impotence of reason when not motivated by the passions. Furthermore, "reason" is actually a predicate and not a subject. Reason, by itself, doesn't *do* anything. To speak of reason is to speak of an abstraction. It is individual men who reason; reason is a faculty possessed by and exercised by individuals. It sounds odd to the modern ear to say, for example, that "Reason knows the world," or that "Reason rules the world." But if we think of the ways in which reason has been understood in the mainstream of Western philosophy, we realize that the Humean conception of reason is a tributary of the mainstream. Philosophers from Anaxagoras to Spinoza felt no intellectual embarrassment in speaking of Reason itself as a subject with its own power and *telos.* From this point of view, *we* are rational insofar as we manifest or participate in universal Reason or *Noûs*—a universal Reason closely associated

3. David Hume, *A Treatise of Human Nature,* ed. by L. A. Selby-Bigge, p. 415.

with the concept of the Divine. For Aristotle as well as for many modern rationalists, we are most godlike when we manifest our Reason. Reason, from the perspective of this tradition, is not merely a faculty, capacity, or potentiality, it is an actuality. When Reason is fully actualized, both the understanding and what is understood are characterized as rational: they are, according to Aristotle, identical. When Reason is understood in this manner, the aim or *telos* of philosophy as the highest form of *theoria* is to *interpret* the world— to grasp its ultimate rational principles and to contemplate the nature of reality. This reality is properly understood when we grasp the rational order inherent in it. It is not a metaphor to speak of Reason pervading the world; it is a literal and fundamental truth. To say that Reason rules the world is to say that there are rational principles, or universal unchangeable laws that govern the world.

For Hegel these general claims about Reason are "abstract," and consequently "false," until we have shown concretely and in detail precisely how Reason is realized in the world. When Hegel comments on Socrates' criticism of Anaxagoras' claim that Reason rules the world, he says: "It is evident that the insufficiency which Socrates found in the principle of Anaxagoras has nothing to do with the principle itself, but with Anaxagoras' failure to apply it to concrete nature. Nature was not understood or comprehended through this principle; the principle remained abstract—nature was not understood as a development of Reason, as an organization brought forth by it."[4] *Geist* for Hegel is Reason or *Noûs* as charac-

---

4. *Reason in History,* trans. with an introduction by Robert S. Hartman, p. 14; *Vorlesungen über die Philosophie der Weltgeschichte,* ed. by J. Hoff-meister, p. 38. Hegel never published a book with the title *"Die Vernunft in der Geschichte,"* or *"Vorlesungen über die Philosophie der Weltgeschichte."* These "Lectures" are essentially lecture notes; so even the German edition is basically an edited version of Hegel's lecture notes. Furthermore, the German text is supplemented by students' notes. Eduard Gans' edition appeared in 1837. A revised and enlarged edition was edited by Hegel's son, Karl, and was published in 1840. Karl Hegel published still another edition in 1843. An entirely new edition of the "Lectures" was prepared by Georg Lasson in four volumes (1917-1920). Since Lasson's original edition, four more editions of Vol. I, *Die Vernunft in der Geschichte: Einleitung in die Philosophie der Weltgeschichte,* have appeared. The most recent is by J. Hoffmeister. It appeared in 1955, reprinted in 1963. Hartman's *Reason in History* is a

terized by the Greeks, but *Geist* is not "abstract" understanding, it is not *Verstand;* it is Reason *(Vernunft)* fully actualized in the world.

The above comment on Anaxagoras, especially the phrase "the development of Reason," reveals an important distinction for Hegel and suggests a second perspective for understanding *Geist.* The distinction is that between nature and spirit. Ultimately, *Geist* is all-comprehensive, but in the course of its development it dirempts itself into a realm of nature and a realm of spirit. "Spiritual life is distinguished from natural, and particularly from animal, life in this, that is does not merely remain *in itself,* but is *for itself.*"[5] Hegel here is making the point that what distinguishes the spiritual from the natural is the development of consciousness, and ultimately self-consciousness. But this diremption of *Geist* into the natural and the

---

pastiche. It is based on Karl Hegel's second edition; but Hartman interpolates passages from other editions as well as some passages of his own.

The above gives a brief idea of the editorial problems involved in quoting from Hegel. Hegel published only four books during his lifetime, some essays and some book reviews. Most of what we today consider to be his *Werke* was published posthumously, some of it reconstructed and supplemented with student notes. Problems are further compounded by the fact that Hegel followed the typical nineteenth-century German practice of extensively revising and rewriting his works when he published subsequent editions of them. While I have made use of the full range of Hegel's works, including the posthumous works and student notes published with them, I believe that every passage cited is a true reflection of his thought and can be supported by passages from those works which are considered to be most authoritative. For an excellent discussion of the state of Hegel's editions and their translations, see Walter Kaufmann, *Hegel: Reinterpretation, Texts, and Commentary,* especially his "Bibliography." See also Otto Pöggler's illuminating discussion of the history of Hegel-editing and its close connection with Hegel research, "Hegel-editing and Hegel Research." This article will be published in a forthcoming volume of papers from the 1970 Hegel Symposium sponsored by Marquette University. For a discussion of the special textual problems involved in *Die Vernunft in der Geschichte,* see the Hoffmeister edition, pp. 272 ff.

5. The translations of this passage and the next passage are by Findlay. J. N. Findlay, *Hegel: A Re-examination,* p. 37. See also William Wallace, *The Logic of Hegel,* pp. 54-55 (hereafter referred to as Hegel's *Logic*); Hegel, *Werke,* Bd. VI, p. 55. Wallace's translation is based on the first part of Hegel's *Encyclopaedia,* and is frequently called "The Lesser Logic" in order to distinguish it from Hegel's *Science of Logic* which has recently appeared in a new translation: *Hegel's Science of Logic,* trans. by A. V. Miller.

spiritual spheres is eventually *aufgehoben*[6] in the full development of *Geist*. "Nature is by no means something fixed and finished for itself, which could also exist without Spirit: rather does it first reach its aim and truth in Spirit. Just so Spirit on its part is not merely something abstractly beyond nature, but exists truly and shows itself to be Spirit, insofar as it contains nature as subjugated in itself."[7]

When Hegel speaks of *Geist* in this manner, he is thinking of *Geist* as God who does not abandon the world to chance and accident but guides it by Providence. "The truth that a Providence, that is to say, a divine Providence, presides over events of the world corresponds to our principle; for divine Providence is wisdom endowed with infinite power which realizes its own aim, that is, the absolute, rational final purpose of the world."[8] *Geist,* according to Hegel, turns out not only to be the final cause of the world, it is also the material, efficient, and formal cause. It is the material cause in the form of the natural and spiritual realms (the spiritual realm is the realm of history). It is the efficient cause, for through the "cunning of Reason" *(List der Vernunft)* which works in devious ways through the passions of men, *Geist* is the agency of historical development. It is the formal cause, for as *Noûs,* it is the source of the rational structure or form of the world. And it is the final cause, because *Geist* guides history to its true and final aim—the complete realization of freedom. Hegel is claiming that if we take a world historical perspective, we will see that there is an inner *logos* to the seemingly chaotic multiplicity of events. This *logos* has a teleological form. There is a narrative or "story" to be discovered in history—this is the epic of the devious ways in which *Geist* is realizing itself, moving from freedom and self-determination as an abstract idea to its concrete embodiment in human institutions.

Hegel is fully aware of the ambitiousness, initial implausibility,

6. There is no English word that captures the distinctive meaning that *"aufheben"* has for Hegel. Baillie's translation "to sublate," and Kaufmann's translation "to sublimate" are pallid substitutes. *"Aufheben"* is to negate, affirm and transcend, or go beyond. These are not necessarily three distinct moments, but can be involved in a single process. Throughout, I use the German expression. Its full meaning for Hegel and Marx will be brought out from the contexts in which it is used.

7. Findlay, op. cit., p. 37; Hegel's *Logic,* p. 180; Hegel, *Werke,* Bd. VI, pp. 190-191.

8. *Reason in History,* p. 15; *Vorlesungen über die Philosophie der Weltgeschichte,* p. 39.

and emptiness of these grand claims. He fully realizes that he is drawing together the two most profound traditions that have shaped Western culture—the classical Greek tradition and the Judaeo-Christian tradition. As he himself emphasizes, these abstract claims are empty, for they neither provide us with a clear meaning of "Geist" nor a proof that it is actually manifest. But if we grasp the import of Hegel's claims, we can already see what he would have to do to make these abstract claims concrete and to validate them. He would have to show us in complete systematic detail how *Geist* manifests itself. This is precisely what he attempted to do. Hegel's entire system can be viewed as an attempt to reveal the meaning and to demonstrate the truth of these claims. This is why in his *Phenomenology of Spirit,* he announces that the time is ripe to show that philosophy can relinquish the name of the *love* of wisdom and finally become actual wisdom; philosophy is finally to be elevated to a science revealing the inner necessity of the truth of *Geist.*[9]

But how does *Geist* realize itself or make itself manifest? Here we have a third perspective for understanding *Geist.* The logic or dynamic structure of *Geist* manifesting itself is not a direct or immediate unfolding of its nature.

The transition of its potentiality into actuality is mediated through consciousness and will. These are themselves first immersed in their immediate organic life; their first object and purpose in this natural existence as such. But the latter, through its animation by Spirit, becomes infinitely demanding, rich, and strong. Thus Spirit is at war with itself. It must overcome itself as its own enemy and formidable obstacle. Development, which in nature is a quiet unfolding, is in Spirit a hard, infinite struggle against itself.[10]

Geist is perpetually alienating itself, dirempting itself, and struggling with itself. But it is not a meaningless struggle. It is by means of this life and death struggle with itself that *Geist* emerges triumphant and realizes itself. Hegel uses and modifies the oriental image

9. See "The Preface to the *Phenomenology,*" translated by Walter Kaufmann, *Hegel: Reinterpretation, Texts, and Commentary,* p. 372; *Phänomenologie des Geistes,* ed. by J. Hoffmeister, p. 12. English quotations from the "Preface" are from Kaufmann's translation in the above-mentioned work, which is hereafter referred to as *Hegel: Reinterpretation.*

10. *Reason in History,* p. 69; *Vorlesungen über die Philosophie der Weltgeschichte,* pp. 151-152.

of the Phoenix to convey his meaning about the nature of the ceaseless activity of *Geist*. The Phoenix prepares its own pyre and consumes itself "so that from its ashes the new, rejuvenated, fresh life continually arises."[11] Hegel goes on to comment:

This picture, however, is Asiatic; oriental, not occidental. The Spirit, devouring its worldly envelope, not only passes into another envelope, not only arises rejuvenated from the ashes to its embodiment, but it emerges from them exalted, transfigured, a purer Spirit. It is true that it acts against itself, devours its own existence. But in so doing it elaborates upon this existence; its embodiment becomes material for its work to elevate itself to a new embodiment.[12]

Lest we think that Hegel is speculatively spinning metaphors, we need to realize how seriously he takes this picture of the eternal self-struggle of *Geist*. We find here the kernel of what Hegel means by "dialectic." There has been a lot of loose talk about Hegel's dialectic being a movement from thesis to antithesis to synthesis. Not only do these concepts play an insignificant role in Hegel's philosophy, they are essentially static concepts and completely misrepresent what Hegel means by "dialectic."[13] The dialectic of *Geist* is essentially a dynamic and organic process. One "moment" of a dialectical process, when it is fully developed or understood gives rise to its own negation; it is not mechanically confronted by an antithesis. The process here is more like that of a tragedy where the "fall" of the tragic hero emerges from the dynamics of the development of his own character. When *Geist* is dirempted, alienated from itself, a serious struggle takes place between the two "moments." Out of this conflict and struggle, out of this negativity, emerges a "moment" which at once negates, affirms, and transcends the "moments" involved in the struggle—these earlier moments are *aufgehoben*. In the course of *Geist* realizing itself, this process which involves a stage of self-alienation that is subsequently *aufgehoben* is a continuous, restless, infinite one. The logic of the development of *Geist* is dialectical where *Geist* struggles with what *appears* to be "other" than it—a limitation, or obstacle which must be overcome. *Geist* "returns to itself" when it overcomes the specific obstacle that it

11. *Reason in History,* p. 89; Hegel, *Werke,* Bd. IX, p. 90.
12. *Reason in History,* p. 89; Hegel, *Werke,* Bd. IX, pp. 90-91.
13. See Gustav Emil Müller, "The Hegel Legend of 'Thesis-Antithesis-Synthesis' " in *Journal of the History of Ideas* 19 (June 1958).

encounters, only to renew the dialectical process again. *Geist finally* "returns to itself" when all obstacles and determinations have been overcome, when everything that has appeared "other" than itself is fully appropriated and thereby subjectivized. This is the final aim or goal of *Geist*. The *negativity* and *activity* of *Geist* come into focus in this dialectical characterization.

Death . . . is what is most terrible, and to hold on to what is dead requires the greatest strength. That beauty which lacks strength hates the understanding because it asks this of her and cannot do it. But not the life that shrinks from death and keeps itself undefiled by devastation, but the life that endures, and preserves itself through death is the life of the spirit. Spirit gains its truth only by finding itself in absolute dismemberment. This power it is not as the positive that looks away from the negative— as when we say of something, this is nothing or false, and then, finished with it, turn away from it to something else: the spirit is this power only by looking the negative in the face and abiding with it. This abiding is the magic force which converts the negative into being.[14]

The self-realization and the self-fulfillment of *Geist* takes place only by self-destruction. This tremendous power of the negative has dramatic consequences for the study of history. History is the scenario of perpetual struggle and self-destruction where all *finite* social institutions are destroyed and *aufgehoben*. History is "the slaughter-bench at which the happiness of peoples, the wisdom of states, and the virtue of individuals have been sacrificed."[15] But the power of negativity does not result in meaningless destruction; it is the means by which the progressive development toward concrete freedom is realized.

It should be manifest that by "negativity" Hegel means an active process. *Geist* is the principle of self-activity itself. "The very essence of spirit is *action*. It makes itself what it essentially is; it is its own product, its own work."[16] This is the dimension of Hegel's *Geist* that most fascinated and deeply influenced Marx. Or again, Hegel tells us the "criterion of Spirit is its action, its active essence."[17] If we keep in mind that it is man, who according to Hegel reflects the develop-

14. *Hegel: Reinterpretation*, pp. 406-408; *Phänomenologie des Geistes*, pp. 29-30.
15. *Reason in History*, p. 27; Hegel, *Werke*, Bd. IX, p. 27.
16. *Reason in History*, p. 89; Hegel, *Werke*, Bd. IX, p. 91.
17. *Reason in History*, p. 51; Hegel, *Sämtliche Werke*, Bd. VIII. 2, p. 93.

ment of *Geist* and is the agent through which *Geist* expresses itself in history, then we can understand what he means when he says "Man is his own action, the sequence of his actions, that into which he has been making himself."[18] *Geist* is what it does, and man *is* what he does. This strain in Hegel's thought has had the profoundest influence on post-Hegelian thinking. We shall see how fundamental this view of man—as a being who is what he does—is for Marx and how this motif stands at the very center of existentialist thought.

But we need to counterbalance the negativity and activity of *Geist* with an opposite image that is just as important and basic for Hegel. This is an image that dates back to the Greeks (and even earlier) and that held a special fascination for Hegel. It is the image of circular or spherical motion. The rotating sphere is at once in continual motion and always at rest. The ceaseless activity of *Geist* corresponds to the way in which the sphere is always in motion. But *Geist* is also eternal, infinite, and unchangeable; *Geist* is always the self-same, always at "rest." Just as Hegel gives a distinctive twist to the oriental image of the Phoenix, he gives a dialectical twist to the occidental image of the sphere. The dialectical activity of *Geist* is more like a spiral than a circle or a sphere. What is potential and implicit in *Geist* becomes actual and explicit. The eternal logical structure of *Geist* is always the same. Appreciating the ceaseless activity of *Geist* is essential for understanding history, the rise and fall of political and social institutions, the development of the stages of consciousness. However, from the perspective of logic, of *Geist* as *Noûs* or Reason, *Geist* displays an eternal, necessary, rational structure. Consequently, when Hegel writes a logic laying bare the fundamental categories of the Concept (*Begriff*); or a phenomenology of the developing stages of consciousness, self-consciousness, and spirit; or a philosophical analysis of world history or the evolution of political society, he is not telling different "stories," but the same basic story of *Geist* from different perspectives.

While we might rebel against what at first appears to be Hegel's mythmaking, we cannot help being impressed with the power of this vision of *Geist* when Hegel deals with specific dialectical movements. This is especially true in following the developments traced for us in the *Phenomenology of Spirit*. The *Phenomenology* presents us with still another prespective for grasping the nature of *Geist*. The

18. *Reason in History*, p. 51; Hegel, *Sämtliche Werke*, Bd. VIII. 2, p. 93.

Phenomenology follows the stages in the development of consciousness from its most primitive stage to its final stage of absolute knowledge. The general movement of the *Weltgeist* is repeated in the individual spirit. "The individual must also pass through the contents of the educational stages of the general spirit, but as forms that have long been outgrown by the spirit, as stages or a way that has been prepared and evened for him."[19] Three angles of vision must be maintained for a correct reading of the *Phenomenology*. It is a phenomenology of *Geist,* and as such it is not merely a study of the stages that each individual spirit passes through. Nevertheless, Hegel maintains an "ontogenetic principle" whereby the stages of *Geist* are repeated in the individual spirit. Finally, we must realize that there is a philosophic "we" that is describing and interpreting the stages of consciousness—a "we" which already knows the end of the story and is able to detect the overall dialectical movement taking place at each stage of development of *Geist.*

Hegel begins his *Phenomenology* with what today we might call an "epistemological" orientation. He examines three stages of our cognitive awareness of objects: sense certainty, perception, and understanding. In each of these progressive stages, consciousness seeks to know directly and immediately the object that it confronts; consciousness seeks to fulfill itself and found itself on a firm foundation. And in each stage, contradictions and conflicts emerge in the quest for immediate certainty that force us to a "higher" stage. We think, for example, that in confronting the mere object denoted by such expressions as "here" and "now" we are directly grasping the particular which stands before us. But Hegel not only seeks to expose the speciousness of this claim to immediate knowledge of particulars and the illusion that sense certainty provides us with the "richest kind of knowledge,"—"a knowledge of endless wealth" (*Phen.*, p. 149; *p. 79*),[20] he wants to show us that the hard objectivity of the "facts" before us dissolves into subjectivity. This forces

19. *Hegel: Reinterpretation,* p. 402; *Phänomenologie des Geistes,* p. 27. For a critical discussion of various interpretations of the "point of view" in the *Phenomenology,* and especially the status of the philosophic "we," see Kenley R. Dove "Hegel's Phenomenological Method," *The Review of Metaphysics* 23 (June 1970).

20. Page references to *The Phenomenology of Mind* are included in the text. Page numbers of the English translation are followed by the page numbers of the German text.

us to a more comprehensive stage of perception where our basic
category is the thing or substance manifesting different properties.
But this stage in turn is unstable and we are led to the next stage
where we postulate entities that are neither sensed nor perceived
in order to account for that which confronts us.[21]

When we (or more properly "we" as the embodiment of *Geist*)
pass through the first three stages of consciousness and come to the
realization that what we know—that which stands as an object for
consciousness, is nothing but another form of consciousness itself,
we reach the stage of "Self-consciousness." Summing up the result
of the first three stages of consciousness, Hegel says:

In the kinds of certainty hitherto considered, the truth for consciousness
is something other than consciousness itself. The conception, however,
of this truth vanishes in the course of our experience of it. What the
object immediately was *in itself*—whether mere being in sense-certainty,
a concrete thing in perception, or force in the case of understanding—
it turns out, in truth, not to be this reality; but instead, this inherent
nature (*Ansich*) proves to be a way in which it is for an other (*Phen.*,
p. 218; *p. 141*).

With this realization that consciousness in its attempt to know an
"other"—an object truly independent of consciousness—is really
knowing *itself*, the journey of *Geist* takes a distinctively practical
turn. The task of *Geist* is to make "itself what it essentially is; it is its

21. The opening section of the *Phenomenology*, "Consciousness," which
deals with "sense certainty," "perception," and "understanding," is rarely
read and discussed by contemporary philosophers. This is a pity because these
sections can be read as a perceptive and incisive commentary and critique of
a dialectical development in epistemology which has been repeated in contemporary analytic philosophy. The stages in contemporary epistemological
investigations which have moved from phenomenalism with its foundation
in "sense data" to the emphasis on a "thing language" as an epistemological
foundation, to the realization of the importance of "theoretical constructs"
and finally the "new" concern with total "conceptual frameworks" or "language games" closely parallels the development that Hegel sketches for us in
the opening sections of the *Phenomenology*. One can find analogues in the
development of epistemology during the past fifty years for the difficulties that
Hegel locates at each dialectical stage. I do not mean to suggest that Hegel
was prophetic, but rather that he had a genuine insight into a dialectical
progression of epistemological positions, which has repeated itself in a
linguistic mode during our time.

own product, its own work."[22] In the stage of "Self-consciousness."
Geist seeks to establish its *own* self-certainty.[23] But self-consciousness cannot fully realize itself, fulfill itself, or know itself unless it is
recognized by another self-consciousness. "Self-consciousness exists
in itself and for itself in that, and by the fact that it exists for another
self-consciousness; that is to say, it *is* only by being acknowledged
or 'recognized' " (*Phen.*, p. 229; *p. 141*). *Es ist ein Selbstbewusstsein
für ein Selbstbewusstsein.* This is the way in which Hegel begins
one of the most famous sections of the *Phenomenology of Spirit,*
"Lordship and Bondage" *(Herrschaft und Knechtschaft).* Only when
self-consciousness reaches that stage when it is fully recognized, acknowledged, and reflected in another self-consciousness will it complete its journey, attain satisfaction and fulfillment by being actually
free and self-determined. At the terminus of this journey all forms
of objectification and alienation are *aufgehoben.* The language
here is distinctively Hegelian, but the insight reflects back to Kant's
concept of a kingdom of ends (where we treat others not as means
but as ends-in-themselves). It also foreshadows Marx's vision of a
humanized society where our labor is a *"free manifestation of life*
and an *enjoyment of life,"* where "our productions would be so
many mirrors reflecting our nature," and where I not only "would
have objectified my *individuality* and its *particularity,* but be affirmed in the thought and love of my fellowmen."[24]

The stage of a fully developed and free self-consciousness that
is recognized and reflected in another self-consciousness is the end of
the story of *Geist*'s journey. In "Lordship and Bondage" Hegel provides a phenomenological description of the first stage of the encounter between self-consciousnesses where the lord or master attempts
to realize himself and gain recognition by dominating the bondsman
or slave. The essential drive of *Geist* in any of its forms is to infinitize
itself, to prove to itself that it is truly infinite and self-sufficient. In
the form of Lordship it seeks to show that "it is fettered to no deter-

22. *Reason in History,* p. 89; Hegel, *Werke,* Bd. IX, p. 91.

23. The first section of "Self-Consciousness" (*Selbstbewusstsein*) deals
with "The Truth of Self-Certainty." For a discussion of this section, see
Part II, pp. 85-86.

24. *Young Marx,* p. 281; Karl Marx/Friedrich Engels, *Historisch-kritische
Gesamtausgabe,* ed. by D. Rjazanov and V. Adoratskij, I.3, p. 546. Hereafter
referred to as *MEGA.*

minate existence" (*Phen.*, p. 232; *p. 144*). Self-consciousness must test and prove itself. The existence of an "other" (another self-consciousness) is initially a threat, a limitation upon the self-sufficiency of the lord. "The relation of both self-consciousnesses is in this way so constituted that they prove themselves and each other through a life-and-death struggle" (*Phen.*, p. 232; *p. 144*). Hegel emphasizes that "it is solely by risking life that freedom is obtained" (*Phen.*, p. 233; *p. 144*). But if one self-consciousness succeeds in literally destroying his opponent, he does not succeed in his project. He does not succeed in gaining the recognition that he demands to assert himself as a fully developed free self-consciousness. Death becomes an "abstract negation, not the negation characteristic of consciousness, which cancels in such a way that it preserves and maintains what is sublated, and thereby survives its being sublated" (*Phen.*, p. 234; *p. 145*). This latter form of negation is one of dominance or subjugation. The one self-consciousness is "independent, and its essential nature is to be for itself; the other is dependent, and its essence is life or existence for another. The former is the Master, or Lord, the latter the Bondsman" (*Phen.*, p. 234; *p. 146*). To be a lord or master requires a bondsman or slave. The slave produces or works for the master; the slave's essential nature is expressed in the things he produces for the master. His essence takes the form of "thinghood." The master's relation to the slave is not only mediated by the things that the slave produces for the master, the slave's life is dependent on the whims of the master. The master is the power dominating the slave and he keeps the slave in thrall by consuming the objects that the slave produces. "In these two moments, the master gets his recognition through another consciousness, for in them the latter affirms itself as unessential, both by working upon the thing, and, on the other hand, by the fact of being dependent on a determinate existence" (*Phen.*, p. 236; *p. 147*). It would seem that the master does achieve his project of affirming himself and negating any limitations, by making the slave subservient and dependent upon him. But ironically (and here we find a typical Hegelian dialectical turn) the more the master succeeds, the more he fails. "Just where the master has effectively achieved lordship, he really finds that something has come about quite different from an independent consciousness. It is not an independent, but rather a dependent consciousness that he has achieved" (*Phen.*, pp. 236-237; *p. 147*). In his desperate attempt to become an independent self-consciousness, a true master, he has actually enslaved himself, made himself dependent on the slave for his own existence *qua* master. It is by virtue of the slave, who was initially taken to be unessential, that the master has achieved lordship. The slave then is not really unessential, he is the essential reality of the master, i.e., he is the essential condition by which the master can be what he is. This is the dialectical movement by which the master's project ends in failure, a failure that results from the process of trying to achieve fully developed lordship. But let us see what happens from the perspective of the bondsman or slave.

As a self-consciousness, the slave initially takes the master to be his (the slave's) essential reality. For the slave is what he is by virtue of the master. The slave lives in fear of his own being, he feels "the fear of death, the sovereign master" (*Phen.*, p. 237; *p. 148*). Furthermore, the slave's essential nature is realized in his labor, the work he does to satisfy the master. He sees his own essential consciousness expressed in the objects that he produces, in the products of his labor. He himself is "nothing," his sole function is to produce. By his labor, the slave shapes and fashions objects and thereby externalizes himself. "The consciousness that toils and serves accordingly attains by this means the direct apprehension of that independent being as its self" (*Phen.*, p. 238; *p. 149*). But at the very moment that the slave is most closely reduced to nothingness, where he empties himself in the form of objects that he labors on and produces for the master, he becomes aware of the fact that he has a "mind of his own"—that he is not simply a thing, that his essential nature is not exhausted in the things that he produces. Only when the slave is shaken by absolute fear, only when his consciousness has been "tottered and shaken" (*Phen.*, p. 240; *p. 150*) does the slave realize that he is not simply an instrument of the master, but is a consciousness in his own right. "In the master, the bondsman feels self-existence to be something external, an objective fact; in fear self-existence is present within himself; in fashioning the thing, self-existence comes to be felt explicitly as his own proper being, and he attains the consciousness that he himself exists in its own right and on its own account *(an und für sich)*" (*Phen.*, p. 239; *p. 149*). This is the beginning of the slave's own freedom. At first it is only an abstract freedom which does not issue in any specific concrete action; it is only the realization that he too is an independent self-consciousness, but this abstract freedom is the seed out of which concrete freedom will emerge. Ironically (or dialectically) it is precisely out of and because of his labor which initially was labor for another (the master) that the slave comes to the realization of his own self-existence and freedom. "Thus precisely in labor where there seemed to be merely some outsider's mind and ideas involved, the bondsman becomes aware, through this re-discovery of himself by himself, of having and being a 'mind of his own' " (*Phen.*, p. 239; *p. 149*).

We have presented Hegel's analysis of the dialectic of lordship and bondage for a variety of reasons. It is a paradigm of what Hegel means by dialectic and it shows what Hegel means by *Geist* realizing itself through its own "negation." This particular dialectical movement is one of the most suggestive and richest in Hegel. In the literature of the twentieth century, there has been a deep fascination with variations on the dialectic of master and slave. We find this theme reverberating in the writings of Marx, Nietzsche, Freud and Sartre in their own attempts to account for the conflicts and paradoxes of the individual psyche and our relations with our fellowmen. There are commentators on Hegel such as Kojève (whose reading of Hegel has exerted an enormous influence on contemporary French philosophers) who see in this dialectical movement the quintessence of Hegel's thought.[25] We must be careful, however, not to read this passage from an exclusively social point of view, for the *Phenomenology* is a study of the stages of the development of *Geist,* and "Lordship and Bondage" is only one brief moment in the realization of *Geist.* As the subsequent sections in the *Phenomenology* ("Stoicism," "Skepticism," and "Unhappy Consciousness") show, the dialectic of master and slave is not exclusively a dialectic that takes place between different individual self-consciousnesses or even between classes of men; it repeats itself within a single "Unhappy Consciousness."[26]

25. See Alexandre Kojève, *Introduction à la lecture de Hegel,* ed. by Raymond Queneau. Excerpts of this book have appeared in an English translation: *Introduction to the Reading of Hegel,* ed. by Allan Bloom.

26. Cf. George Armstrong Kelley's discussion, "Notes on Hegel's 'Lordship and Bondage,' " *The Review of Metaphysics* 19 (June 1966).

Before leaving our preliminary analysis of what Hegel means by *Geist,* we need to explore one more aspect of the nature of *Geist.* This is the issue of Hegel's "idealism," for it has significant consequences for understanding Hegel and for understanding Marx's "materialism." Almost everyone agrees that Hegel is an idealist; *prima facie,* labeling Hegel as an "idealist" appears to be perfectly sound. *Geist* is spirit and is the all-inclusive and all-encompassing reality. The upshot of the *Phenomenology* is to show us that when we think we are encountering something other than consciousness, it turns out that this "other" is really an alienated form of consciousness. Isn't it clear that Hegel is forcefully asserting his idealism when he declares "The spiritual alone is the actual; it is [i] the essence or being-in-itself; [ii] that which relates itself and is determinate, that which is other and for itself; and [iii] that which in this determinateness and being outside itself remains in itself—or, in other words, it is in and for itself"?[27] We find the same type of point made in the *Logic* when Hegel introduces the stage of "Being-for-self" *(Fürsichsein);* for he announces that "In Being-for-self enters the category of Ideality."[28]

Yet despite all this, I want to maintain that it can be extraordinarily misleading to think of Hegel as an idealist.

The classificatory term "idealism" is normally contrasted with "materialism" or "realism." These contrast terms, which have become fashionable in modern philosophy, can best be understood against the background of Cartesian dualism. If one excludes the status of God (who is really the only fully independent substance), Descartes claims that reality consists of two types: thinking substance and extended substance. Mind is thinking substance while body or matter is extended substance. Much of modern philosophy since Descartes has presupposed this dualistic framework. Even philosophers who have denied the ontological reality of one of these types of substance and have argued that everything is *really* mental or everything is *really* material, have basically accepted the dichotomy formulated by Descartes. This ontological contrast generates the idealist/materialist dichotomy. But if we think of idealism in this manner—as the contrast to materialism—then Hegel is certainly *not* an idealist. The whole thrust of his philosophy is toward

27. *Hegel: Reinterpretation,* p. 396; *Phänomenologie des Geistes,* p. 24.
28. Hegel's *Logic,* p. 178; Hegel, *Werke,* Bd. VI, p. 188.

the concrete, toward showing that what may appear to be "other" than *Geist* is really spiritual in its true nature. Thus, for example, when Hegel deals with history, he does not view it as a march of bloodless mental abstractions. "The actions of men spring from their needs, their passions, their interests, their characters, and their talents."[29] History is the drama of the playing out of men's most deeply felt passions. Hegel insists upon the *prima facie* "irrationality" of history more vehemently than any classical materialist. His claim, however, is that men's passions are not something other than *Geist,* they "constitute the tools and means of the World Spirit for attaining its purpose, bringing it to consciousness, and realizing it."[30] So too when we try to comprehend the nature and realization of freedom in the political sphere, we cannot limit ourselves to "abstract" Reason; for the "material" of Geist *consists* of the actual human political institutions that do and have existed. In every sphere of Hegel's thought, the drive is to reach down to the inner recesses of what is taken to be recalcitrant facticity; not to deny its ontological status, but to show how *Geist* operates in and through it. Even this use of the terminology of agency in characterizing the role of *Geist* can be misleading insofar as it suggests a picture of the matter of the world or history as inherently passive, waiting upon the bidding of *Geist. Geist* literally *informs* the matter of the world. What Hegel seeks to achieve is an *Aufhebung* of the dichotomy of ideality and materiality. If we are to discover the working of *Geist,* we must understand its concrete working in the "material" of the world.

This same point—the attempt to achieve an *Aufhebung* of the materialist/idealist dichotomy—can be seen in Hegel's *Logic,* especially the second part dealing with Essence *(Wesen).* Hegel examines the major metaphysical dichotomies which have been fundamental to Western philosophy, including Identity *(Identität)* and Difference *(Unterschied);* Ground *(Grund)* and Existence *(Existenz);* Matter *(Materie)* and Form *(Form);* Content *(Inhalt)* and Form *(Form).* He seeks to show us that if we isolate one of these contrasting concepts from its "other" the result is an unstable contradiction. Ultimately these concepts do not isolate ontological dualities or dichotomies; they are moments in a single unified totality *(Totalität).* Thus the attempt to isolate "pure" materiality or "pure" ideality

29. *Reason in History,* p. 26; Hegel, *Werke,* Bd. IX, p. 26.
30. *Reason in History,* p. 31; Hegel, *Werke,* Bd. IX, p. 32.

results in an empty abstraction. Each demands the "other" to complete itself, to fulfill or to realize what it is in itself. The general point is nicely illustrated in one of the informal additions *(Zusätze)* to the *Logic*.

The various matters of which the thing consists are potentially the same as one another. Thus we get one Matter in general to which the difference is expressly attached externally and as a bare form. This theory which holds things all round to have one and the same matter at bottom, and merely to differ externally in respect of form, is much in vogue with the reflective understanding. Matter in that case counts for naturally indeterminate, but suspectible of any determination; while at the same time it is perfectly permanent, and continues the same amid all change and alteration. And in finite things at least this disregard of matter for any determinate form is certainly exhibited. For example, it matters not to a block of marble, whether it receive the form of this or that statue or even the form of a pillar. Be it noted however that a block of marble can disregard form only relatively, that is, in reference to the sculptor: it is by no means purely formless. And so the mineralogist considers the relatively formless marble as a special formation of rock, differing from other equally special formations, such as sandstone or porphyry. Therefore we say it is an abstraction of the understanding which isolates matter into a certain natural formlessness. For properly speaking the thought of matter includes the principle of form throughout, and no formless matter therefore appears anywhere even in experience as existing.[31]

Rather than simply classifying Hegel as an idealist and thereby grouping him with other philosophers who want to deny that the world has a material substratum, it is more perspicuous to see that he is radically challenging the very framework within which the idealist/materialist dichotomy arises. Hegel's philosophy might just as well be called a form of "materialism," for it is just as true and basic to his view of the world to realize that our access to *Geist* and its dynamics is in and through its concrete manifestations in the world. I do not want to deny that Hegel's *Aufhebung* of the materialist/idealist dichotomy is heavily weighted in the direction of seeing matter as the self-alienation of *Geist*. Hegel means or intends to be an idealist. But I do want to insist that to think of Hegel as a traditional idealist is drastically to misconceive his position. When we examine Marx's thought, we shall see—despite his frequent polemics

31. Hegel's *Logic*, p. 236; Hegel, *Werke*, Bd. VI, pp. 257-258.

about the idealism of Hegel and philosophy—that his materialism makes sense only against the background of the transformation of the idealist/materialist dichotomy effected by Hegel.

The misleading character of the idealist/materialist dichotomy bears on two other dichotomies that have been fundamental to modern philosophy and which can get in the way of understanding Hegel's philosophy. These are the dichotomies of reason and passion or affection; and theory and practice. Our modern consciousness has been shaped by a sharp contrast between reason and the passions. Once again we are reminded of Hume's neat dichotomy. But even in Kant, who is sharply critical of Hume's conception of reason, we find a variation on this dichotomy in the distinction between pure reason and the desires or inclinations of men. We have already noted that Hegel's conception of *Geist* as Reason is close in spirit to Aristotle's universal *Noûs*. Hegel would also agree with the merging of *eros* and *logos* that Plato so beautifully illustrates in the *Phaedrus*. Hegel is challenging the modern dichotomy between reason and passion. Reason without passion is empty and passion without reason is blind. Hegel seeks an *Aufhebung* of the modern dichotomy of reason and passion, and to restore what he takes to be the truth inherent in the classical Greek view of an ultimate organic unity and harmony of the rational and affective dimensions of human life. Once again, to think of *Geist* as a universal Reason which is distinct from the phenomenal world of men's passions, affections, and inclinations would result in an abstract and "false" understanding of *Geist*.

We find this same drive for an *Aufhebung* of *all* dichotomies which modern philosophy has taken as fundamental in Hegel's reflections on theory and practice. From one perspective, Hegel is squarely in the classical tradition that conceives of philosophy as the highest form of *theoria* which has the *telos* of interpreting, understanding, comprehending reality.

To comprehend what is, this is the task of philosophy, because what is, is reason. Whatever happens, every individual is a child of his time; so philosophy too is its own time apprehended in thoughts. It is just as absurd to fancy that a philosophy can transcend its contemporary world as it is to fancy that an individual can overleap his own age, jump over Rhodes. If his theory really goes beyond the world as it is and builds an ideal one as it ought to be, that world exists indeed, but only in his opinions, an unsubstantial element where anything you please may, in fancy, be built.

One more word about giving instruction as to what the world ought to be. Philosophy in any case always comes on the scene too late to give it. As the thought of the world, it appears only when actuality is already there cut and dried after its process of formation has been completed. The teaching of the concept [*Begriff*], which is also history's inescapable lesson, is that it is only when actuality is mature that the ideal first appears over against the real and that the ideal apprehends this same real world in its substance and builds it up for itself into the shape of an intellectual realm. When philosophy paints its grey in grey, then has a shape of life grown old. By philosophy's grey in grey it cannot be rejuvenated but only understood. The owl of Minerva spreads its wings only with the falling of dusk.[32]

This passage from the preface of *The Philosophy of Right* is fascinating. It indicates that Hegel was fully aware of the limitations of philosophy, including his own. And it contains a crucial ambiguity. If it is true—as Hegel sometimes writes—that history is reaching its fulfillment, then philosophy too, as the world "apprehended in thoughts" is also reaching its fulfillment. The end of history as the fulfillment of the *telos* implicit in history also signals the completion of philosophy. But to the extent that one argues that history and culture have not *yet* reached fulfillment, then the task of philosophy still remains to be accomplished.[33]

The above passage also throws into sharp relief Marx's claim that the philosophers have only interpreted the world in various ways. This is not intended (as it is frequently read) as a blanket condemnation of philosophy; it is a characterization of what philosophy is. Ironically, Marx is in perfect agreement with Hegel's own characterization of philosophy. Marx adds a "but" that signals his departure from Hegel. It is as if Marx were saying to Hegel, "Yes, you are right, the *task* of philosophy is to interpret the world, but

32. *Hegel's Philosophy of Right,* trans. with notes by T. M. Knox, pp. 11-13; *Grundlinien der Philosophie des Rechts,* pp. 16-17.
33. For an exploration of the ambiguity of Hegel's conception of time and eternity and its significance for an understanding of the nature of philosophy, see Nathan Rotenstreich, "The Essential and the Epochal Aspects of Philosophy," *The Review of Metaphysics* 23 (June 1970); Alexandre Kojève's discussion of time and eternity in his *Introduction to the Reading of Hegel*.

with your System, that task is now completed and we can now understand philosophy for what it really is and pass beyond or overcome philosophy. Now the point is to change the world. What is needed is an *Aufhebung* of philosophy."

How does the above passage, which seems to signal the impotence of philosophy—the highest form of *theoria*—bear on the issue of practice? Philosophy does not and cannot guide practice. Philosophy's sole task is to comprehend the actual; it is the actual "apprehended in thoughts." But what is the actual? Our discussion of *Geist* provides the answer, for actuality is *Geist* actively realizing itself in the world. The actual is not a static reality, but the process of activity itself manifested in a variety of forms. *Geist* as activity itself is *praxis*. *Theoria*, in its purest form, as philosophy, is nothing but the articulation of the rationality ingredient in *praxis*. There is then an ultimate harmony of theory and practice—*theoria* and *praxis*—not in the sense that philosophy guides action, but rather in the sense that philosophy is the comprehension of what is; it is the comprehension of the *logos* ingredient in *praxis*, i.e., *praxis* as the self-activity of *Geist*. There is an ultimate unity of theory and practice, a unity that becomes intelligible when we understand that *Geist* is at once *praxis*, and in its self-reflective form, *theoria*. And we shall see that Marx *accepts* this unity of *theoria* and *praxis* and dialectically transforms it—in Marx, Hegel's unity of *theoria* and *praxis* is *aufgehoben*.

The Hegelian Origins of Praxis

We know that Marx's early encounter with Hegel's philosophy was traumatic. His discovery of Hegel during his student days at the University of Berlin bears many of the marks of a "religious conversion." Isaiah Berlin eloquently describes this period in Marx's life.

Hegelianism at first repelled his naturally positivist intelligence. In a long and intimate letter to his father he described his efforts to construct a rival system; after sleepless nights and disordered days spent wrestling with the adversary, he fell ill and left Berlin to recuperate. He returned with a sense of failure and frustration, equally unable to work or to rest. His father wrote him a long paternal letter, begging him not to waste his time on barren metaphysical speculation when he had his career to think of. His words fell on deaf ears. Marx resolutely plunged into an exhaustive study of Hegel's work, read night and day, and after three weeks announced his complete conversion. He sealed it by becoming a member of the *Doctorklub* (Graduates' Club), an association of free-thinking university intellectuals, who met in beer cellars, wrote mildly seditious verse, professed violent hatred of the King, the church, the bourgeoisie and above all argued endlessly on points of Hegelian theology.[34]

To speak of Marx's "conversion" can be an overstatement, for Marx was never a slavish disciple of Hegelianism. From his first encounter he struggled with a critique of Hegel; he felt deeply that there was something essentially right and something desperately wrong with Hegelianism. In the course of the next few years he returned over and over again to articulate for himself what was of lasting value in Hegelianism and what had to be rejected as mystification. In rapid succession, he absorbed, utilized, and rejected tools of critique that he picked up from the other young Left Hegelians.[35] Marx's scribblings on Hegel, especially during 1843-1844, reveal his Talmudic temperament. He would copy down texts from Hegel and then proceed to write laborious involuted commentaries on them. Most of this material was never published during Marx's lifetime; they were exercises for sharpening, testing, and formulating his own ideas. But the posthumous publication of these documents reveal the intensity of his struggle with Hegel. Marx began with a critique of Hegel's political philosophy, but soon he also took up the *Phenomenology* and Hegel's *Logic*. An early remark about Feuerbach, who Marx thought was the first to show the way to a thorough critique of Hegel, reveals the direction of Marx's own thought. In a letter to Ruge dated March, 1843, Marx writes the following comment about Feuerbach's provocative *Thesen:* "The only point that I do not like about

34. Isaiah Berlin, *Karl Marx: His Life and Environment*, pp. 67-68. For a description of Marx's early life, see David McLellan, *Marx Before Marxism;* Auguste Cornu, *Karl Marx. Sa vie et son oeuvre* and *Karl Marx et Friedrich Engels: leur vie et oeuvre;* Maximilien Rubel, *Karl Marx: essai de biographie intellectuelle.*

35. David McLellan's recent study, *The Young Hegelians and Karl Marx,* presents a good synopsis of the thought of the various young Hegelians. This study clearly shows how much Marx borrowed (and ultimately rejected) from his contemporaries. See also Sidney Hook, *From Hegel to Marx,* second edition, and William J. Brazill, *The Young Hegelians.*

Feuerbach's aphorisms is that he talks too much about nature and too little about politics. The latter is the only means by which present philosophy can become a reality."[36] This remark is especially revealing because in Marx's first detailed systematic critique of Hegel, it is Hegel's political philosophy that was subjected to devastating criticism. Until recently, Marx's *Critique of Hegel's Philosophy of Right,* which is a commentary on paragraphs 261-313 of Hegel's *Rechtsphilosophie,* has been generally ignored and overshadowed by the more famous 1844 *Paris Manuscripts.* But Shlomo Avineri has brilliantly demonstrated that a careful reading of this document shows the emergence of many of Marx's distinctive themes *before* Marx seriously studied political economy.[37] For example, in Marx's criticism of Hegel's analysis of bureaucracy as the universal class, Marx argues that it is a fraud to think that the bureaucracy has truly universal interests. Bureaucracy identifies the interest of the state with its own private goals. But Marx doesn't reject the idea of a "universal class," he "historicizes the term, and as a dynamic term it looms very large in the evolution of his thought towards the proletariat."[38] As Avineri points out, when Marx mentions the proletariat for the first time in "Toward The Critique of Hegel's Philosophy of Law: Introduction" (1843), Marx's description is dominated by universalistic attributes:

A class must be formed which has *radical* chains, a class in civil society which is not a class of civil society, a class which is the dissolution of *all*

36. Quoted in McLellan, *The Young Hegelians,* p. 113; *MEGA,* I.i.2, p. 308.

37. Shlomo Avineri, *The Social and Political Thought of Karl Marx.* This is now one of the best books in English dealing with Marx's social and political thought. I am not only indebted to Avineri for his demonstration of the importance of Marx's *Critique of Hegel's Philosophy of Right,* but for many other points discussed in this part. See also his "The Hegelian Origins of Marx's Political Thought," *The Review of Metaphysics* 21 (September 1967). For further discussions of the *Critique of Hegel's Philosophy of Right,* see Louis Dupré, *The Philosophical Foundations of Marxism;* Henri Lefebvre, *The Sociology of Marx;* Jean Hyppolite, "Marx's Critique of the Hegelian Concept of the State," *Studies on Marx and Hegel;* J. Barion, *Hegel und die marxistische Staatslehre.* Sections of the *Critique* have been translated in *Writings of the Young Marx on Philosophy and Society,* ed. by L. Easton and K. Guddat. The entire manuscript has been translated by Joseph O'Malley. This translation, which has been published by Cambridge University Press, was unavailable at the time of writing this book.

38. "The Hegelian Origins of Marx's Political Thought," loc. cit., p. 39.

classes, a sphere of society which has a *universal* character because its sufferings are *universal,* and which does not claim a particular redress because the wrong which is done to it is not a particular wrong but wrong in *general*. There must be formed a sphere of society which claims no traditional status but only a *human* status, a sphere which is not opposed to particular consequences but is *totally* opposed to the assumptions of the German political system; a sphere, finally, which cannot emancipate itself without emancipating itself from *all* other spheres of society, without, therefore, emancipating *all* these other spheres; a class which is, in short, a *total* loss of humanity and which can only redeem itself by a *total* redemption of humanity. This dissolution of society, as a particular class, is the *proletariat. . . .*[39]

So too, Avineri shows us how in an obscure section of the *Critique of Hegel's Philosophy of Right* we can detect the origins of Marx's conception of private property. By dialectically twisting Hegel's defense of the right of primogeniture, Marx sketches for us what was to become a major thesis for him, that under a system of private property, it is an illusion to think that man is truly a master of his property. Man is himself made into an object of property and his own products master and enslave him.[40] One by one, Marx subjects Hegel's claims in the *Philosophy of Right* to the same sort of dialectical critique.

Marx's procedure in this unpublished manuscript may strike a contemporary reader as perverse. Why dedicate all this energy to the critique of another philosopher's work in order to arrive at a correct analysis of existing political institutions. To understand what Marx is doing, we need to realize how seriously Marx takes Hegel's pro-

39. Quoted in "The Hegelian Origins of Marx's Political Thought," p. 41; *Frühe Schriften,* I, p. 503. McLellan has recently suggested that Marx's understanding of the proletariat at this time is "empirically based" and that "Marx's proclamation of the key role of the proletariat is a contemporary application of the analysis of the French Revolution he had outlined earlier in his article, when he talked of a particular social sphere having to 'stand for the notorious crime of society as a whole so that emancipation from this sphere appears as general self-emancipation.' " (David McLellan, *Marx Before Marxism,* pp. 156 ff.) I do not think that this lessens the significance of the Hegelian origins of Marx's thought. The issue is not primarily whether Marx had empirical evidence for his concept of the proletariat but rather how he *interpreted* this evidence. The above passage makes clear that at this early stage of his career, Marx's understanding of the proletariat is shaped by Hegelian categories.

40. "The Hegelian Origins of Marx's Political Thought," pp. 42 ff.

ject. The *Philosophy of Right* cannot be viewed as an afterthought or an appendix to Hegel's system. If one takes the Hegelian impulse toward concreteness with full earnestness, then the crucial test of the system is its ability to explain and comprehend existing political institutions. This is a demand entailed by Hegel's most central convictions about what philosophy is. Marx doesn't reject the claim that a correct theoretical understanding can and ought to explain what is. But the cumulative result of his critique of Hegel is that Hegel has failed—completely and in detail—to comprehend the nature and meaning of existing political institutions; Hegel glosses over real and fundamental contradictions in these institutions. Marx is, in effect, applying Hegel's own criterion to the evaluation of Hegel's political philosophy. Hegel would be the first to insist that if one discovers unresolved conflicts and contradictions, this is a sure sign that one has not yet arrived at a true rational account of what is. Marx's attack in the *Critique of the Philosophy of Right* is an immanent dialectical critique of the master himself; it could only be performed by one who identified himself with the Hegelian project of rational comprehension.

The method that Marx uses in his manuscript is one that he took over from Feuerbach—the transformative method. According to Feuerbach, Hegelian philosophy is a "mystification" because it inverts the subject-predicate relation. "It is important that Hegel always converts the Idea into the subject and the particular actual subject, such as 'political sentiment,' into the predicate" (*Y.M.*, p. 159; *I, p. 266*).[41] *Geist* or *Reason* is not a subject; it is not a source of agency. It is a predicate, the result of real, active, subjects. But Hegel, so Marx claims, has mistaken these real subjects as mere consequences, effects, or predicates of *Geist*. Over and over again, Marx attempts to show how Hegel's detailed analyses are guilty of this reversal and this mystification. The transformative method may at first seem like a logical gimmick, and it is too simple to say that either Feuerbach or Marx "merely" reverses the roles of subject and predicate in Hegel. But one should not underestimate the powerful overtones of this transformation. What Feuerbach noted—and what Marx took over from Feuerbach—was that the

41. Page references to passages cited from the *Young Marx* (*Y.M.*) are given in the text followed by the reference to the German source in *Frühe Schriften*, I.

grand dialectic of *Geist* is basically a myth. Like powerful myths it contains a latent truth, one which needs to be uncovered. The story of the development of *Geist* with all its divine attributes which ends in the realization of freedom is nothing but the story of the development of man with his ideal human attributes. And the successive forms of the self-alienation of *Geist* turn out to be nothing but the forms of *human* alienation. In the 1844 *Paris Manuscripts*, Marx writes:

Feuerbach is the only one who has a *serious, critical* relation to Hegel's dialectic, who has made genuine discoveries in this field, and who above all is the true conqueror of the old philosophy. The magnitude of Feuerbach's achievement and the unpretentious simplicity with which he presents it to the world stand in strikingly opposite inverse ratio.

Feuerbach's great achievement is: (1) proof that philosophy is nothing more than religion brought to and developed in reflection, and thus is equally to be condemned as another form and mode of the alienation of man's nature;

(2) the establishment of *true materialism* and *real science* by making the social relationship of "man to man" the fundamental principle of his theory;

(3) opposing to the negation of the negation, which claims to be the absolute positive, the self-subsistent positive positively grounded on itself (*Y.M.*, pp. 316-317; *I, p. 639*).

Once Marx made this breakthrough in understanding and "conquering" Hegel, his eyes were open to a new reading of the *Phenomenology*—a reading that brings us close to the role that *praxis* was to serve for Marx.

The *Phenomenology* is thus concealed and mystifying criticism, unclear to itself, but inasmuch as it firmly grasps the *alienation* of man—even though man appears only as mind—*all* the elements of criticism are implicit in it, already *prepared* and *elaborated* in a manner far surpassing the Hegelian standpoint.

The great thing in Hegel's *Phenomenology* and its final result—the dialectic of negativity as the moving and productive principle—is simply that Hegel grasps the self-development of man as a process, objectification as loss of the object, as alienation and transcendence of this alienation; that he thus grasps the nature of *work* and comprehends objective man, authentic because actual, as the result of his *own work*. The *actual*, active relation of man to himself as a species-being or the confirmation

of his species-being as an actual, that is, human, being is only possible so
far as he actually brings forth all his *species-powers*—which in turn is
only possible through the collective effort of mankind, only as the result
of history—and treats them as objects, something which immediately is
again only possible in the form of alienation (*Y.M.*, pp. 320-321; *I,
pp. 644-645*).

This passage, written under the dominating influence of Feuerbach,
especially in its reliance on the concept of "species-being," prefigures Marx's own analysis of *praxis* and shows the direction he was
taking in his dialectical critique of Hegel. Marx's "depth" reading
of Hegel shows that the *Phenomenology* is not properly a phenomenology of *Geist,* but of *man.* The point here is the way in which
Marx transforms the meaning of the activity of *Geist,* of its self-
realization in history. This is in reality a concealed way of describing
and criticizing the "development of man as a process." "Process" is
not a general vague term: it refers to human activity in the form of
work. Just as the objectifications of *Geist* are to be properly understood, according to Hegel, as the ways in which *Geist* congeals itself,
objectifies itself and thereby alienates itself, so too the products that
a man produces are not just accidental by-products; they are the
objectification, the concrete expression of what he is. And under
prevailing conditions of political economy, it is the very process of
objectification, production, that results in human alienation. Human
alienation is the true latent content of Hegel's myth of *Geist.*
Nevertheless human alienation finds its expression in the actual
social and political institutions that encompass man. There exist
practical contradictions in the world; contradictions which have the
consequence of dehumanizing man and of separating him from his
true species-being. And just as in Hegel there is an incessant drive
to overcome *(aufheben)* all contradictions, so too Marx sees the
demand for an *Aufhebung* of the practical contradictions that really
exist. It is only a short step to the demand for "revolutionary *praxis*"
as the way of overcoming the forms of human alienation which have
existed until now and of achieving a humanistic society in which man
reappropriates his own essence, his own species-life.

   If Marx's dialectical critique of Hegelianism had stopped here, he
might have had the same status and significance that the other Left
Hegelians have for us today. Much of what we have thus far attrib-

uted to Marx was said by other young Hegelians and intellectuals of the day. We have already noted that Marx was not the first to emphasize *praxis*. But where others were content to stop, Marx relentlessly dug deeper. "To be radical," Marx declared, "is to grasp things by the root" (*Y.M.*, p. 257; *I, p. 497*). By 1845, Marx was already far beyond most of his contemporaries. The intellectual journey that began with the critique of Hegel culminated in a critique of political economy. Along with his contemporaries, Marx engaged in the critique of philosophy, the critique of the state and the law, and the critique of religion. But the criticism of religion results in the demand for unmasking "human self-alienation in its *unholy forms* . . ." (*Y.M.*, p. 251; *I, p. 489*). "*Religious* suffering is the expression of real suffering and at the same time the *protest* against real suffering" (*Y.M.*, p. 250; *I, p. 488*). "The criticism of religion ends with the doctrine that *man* is *the highest being for man,* hence with the *categorical imperative to overthrow all conditions* in which man is a degraded, enslaved, neglected, contemptible being . . ." (*Y.M.*, p. 257-258; *I, p. 497*). There is a direct dialectical continuity from the critique of Hegel to the critique of political economy to (as we shall see) the diagnostic analysis of the contradictions inherent in capitalism.[42]

42. It should be clear from what I have said already that I share the view of those interpreters of Marx who emphasize the dialectical continuity of his development. By this I mean that Marx was engaged in a continuous process of self-criticism in which he sought to extract the "truth" implicit in his earlier hypotheses, reject what he took to be vague, inadequate, and misleading, and pass beyond to new insights and hypotheses. This is a characteristic that pervades Marx's thinking from his earliest gropings to the latest fragments. Reading Marx in this way demands that we be sensitive to what is absorbed and refined as well as what is rejected in the course of his intellectual development. To demonstrate that this is a correct reading of Marx would require a detailed and exhaustive study of his intellectual development which neither exaggerates nor denigrates any stage of that development. The reader, at least, may be alerted that I reject those interpretations of Marx which claim to find sharp and radical breaks in his development where some early phase of development is *totally* rejected as false. The most sophisticated recent reading of Marx which emphasizes the sharp breaks in his thought is Louis Althusser, *For Marx.* For a critical discussion of Althusser, see Gajo Petrović, "The Development and Essence of Marx's Thought," *Praxis* 3/4 (1968).

Praxis *as human activity and human alienation*

We have already detected in Marx's comment on the *Phenomenology* the seeds of Marx's concept of *praxis*. This provides us with a background for understanding Marx's first thesis on Feuerbach.

The chief defect of all previous materialism (including Feuerbach's) is that the object, actuality, sensuousness is conceived only in the form of the *object or perception* [*Anschauung*], but not as *sensuous human activity, practice* [*Praxis*], not subjectively. Hence in opposition to materialism the *active* side was developed by idealism—but only abstractly since idealism naturally does not know actual, sensuous activity as such.[43]

Marx develops the theme we have already encountered in his critique of Hegel's *Phenomenology*. Idealism (here Marx has in mind not only Hegel but Fichte) did emphasize the essential active dimension of human life. "Activity" here has the same over-tones as the activity of *Geist* described by Hegel, where *Geist* produces, objectifies, and thereby alienates itself, only to be engaged in a powerful struggle to overcome the forms of alienation. Hegel mystified this essential truth by conceiving it primarily in terms of "thought objects"—or at least so Marx claims. The great contribution of materialism has been to locate properly this dimension of *Geist,* to see it for what it really is, "*sensuous human activity.*" Nothing could be further from Marx's meaning than the classical mechanistic materialist doctrine that reality consists exclusively of basic discrete particles or atoms in motion—matter regulated by mechanical laws. The failure of classical materialism has been the failure to understand that the basic actuality is *active,* not passive. No end of confusion has resulted from the misconception that when Marx characterizes his own position as "materialism," he means some variety of mechanistic materialism.[44] Even in Marx's shrillest polemics against "idealism," the contrast he has in mind is not that of mechanism versus teleology. Marx's materialism is essentially teleological, not in the sense that teleology commits us to the fantastic notion that a final cause precedes in time an actual event and somehow directs it, but in the empirical sense of teleology where we want

43. *Young Marx,* p. 400; Marx/Engels *Werke,* Bd. 3, p. 5.
44. See Jürgen Habermas' discussion of Marx's "materialism," *Theorie und Praxis,* p. 269.

to distinguish goal-directed activity from the mechanical regularity of matter in motion. Even when Marx is most explicit about his materialism—in *Capital*—he characterizes human activity in the form of labor as directed by *purposes*.

We pre-suppose labor in a form that stamps it as exclusively human. A spider conducts operations that resemble those of a weaver, and a bee puts to shame many an architect in the construction of her cells. But what distinguishes the worst architect from the best of bees is this, that the architect raises his structure in imagination before he erects it in reality. At the end of every labor-process, we get a result that already existed in the imagination of the laborer at its commencement. He not only effects a change of form in the material on which he works, but he also realises a purpose of his own that gives the law to his *modus operandi,* and to which he must subordinate his will. And this subordination is no mere momentary act. Besides the exertion of bodily organs, the process demands that, during the whole operation, the workman's will be steadily in consonance with his purpose.[45]

From its origins in the 1840's through its later development, Marx's materialism is properly understood as a synthesis of both traditional materialism and idealism. Earlier we indicated that Hegel stresses that *Geist* is manifested in its material forms of life and our access to *Geist* is through these concrete manifestations. Hegel did not *intend* to give a materialistic emphasis to these claims. But this is the very aspect of Hegel's philosophy that Marx is stressing. Marx's materialism can best be understood as an *Aufhebung*—in precisely the sense in which Hegel used this concept—of previous materialistic and idealistic doctrines; he at *once* negates, affirms, and goes beyond these polar "moments."

One extremely important consequence of this "synthesis" which is already suggested by the first thesis on Feuerbach is Marx's relocation or reinterpretation of "consciousness." "Consciousness" is not something other than "sensuous human activity" or *praxis*. It is to be understood as an aspect or moment of *praxis* itself. Furthermore the forms that "consciousness" takes in society are to be understood within the context of the forms of social *praxis*.

There is another aspect of Marx's conception of human activity

45. Karl Marx, *Capital,* ed. by Friedrich Engels and trans. by Samuel Moore and Edward Aveling, Three volumes, I, p. 178; Marx/Engels *Werke,* Bd. 23, p. 193.

or *praxis* that needs to be recognized from the outset. From the perspective of common sense categories, it may seem that talk of *Geist* objectifying itself, or human activity objectifying itself is, at best, "merely" metaphorical. If we accept a view of the world—which is fashionable among some contemporary analytic philosophers—that the basic entities in the world are persons and things, we are inclined to think of a person working on a thing, shaping it, or using it in some way. But we will say that the person and the thing that he shapes are distinct, they belong to different ontological categories. To think of a person and a thing under the same category would be the grossest sort of "category mistake."

But both Hegel and Marx are challenging this ontological division. The object or product produced is *not* something "merely" external to and indifferent to the nature of the producer. It is his activity in an objectified or congealed form. We have encountered this idea in Hegel's claim that *Geist* continually objectifies itself and we have seen a particular representation of this idea in the description of the bondsman whose essence is expressed in the form of "thinghood." Everything that is of fundamental importance in Marx's outlook depends on grasping this manner of viewing the relation of the objects that a man produces and his activity: it is essential for understanding what *praxis* means, the precise significance of human alienation, the concept of a "humanized nature," and even the labor theory of value that dominates *Capital*. Echoing the Hegelian claim that the self is what it does, Marx maintains that a man is what he does. Consequently the very nature or character of a man is determined by what he does or his *praxis,* and his products are concrete embodiments of this activity. In an alienated society, man is not only alienated from the products he shapes, but the very activity by which he produces these objects is itself alienated. Man is alienated from his fellow men as well as from himself. More perspicuously, all alienation can be understood as a form of self-alienation. Alienation does not result from the fact that man objectifies himself, produces objects—this is man's distinctive character. Alienation results when he produces in such a way (conditioned by the political economy in which he finds himself) that his products are at once an expression of his labor-power and at the same time are not a true expression of his potentialities—what Marx, following Feuerbach, called man's "species-being." His products become hostile to him; they negate and dehumanize him. In short, to understand Marx, we must grasp the sense in which a product can both *be and not be* an expression of the producer (just as for Hegel, the slave *is* and *is not* his products). It *is* the producer in the sense that in it is a congealed form of his most distinctive attribute—activity. But in an alienated society, it *is not* he in the sense that the product assumes an independent, hostile dimension which dehumanizes the producer.

In order to clarify further what alienation means for Marx and to see where he departs from Hegel, it is necessary to discriminate between objectification *(Vergegenständlichung)* and alienation *(Entfremdung)*. Objectifications for Hegel represent the finite stages in the development of *Geist* dirempting itself and overcoming these diremptions. All forms of objectification must be overcome, *aufgehoben.* "According to my view, which must justify itself by the presentation of the system, everything depends on this, that we comprehend and express the true not as substance but just as much as subject."[46] Even nature for Hegel is a congealed form of *Geist* and must be thoroughly subjectivized when *Geist* comes to full realization. But Marx sharply distinguishes objectification and alienation and accuses Hegel of confusing the two.[47] Objectification is the condition for human material existence. Dropping the Hegelian idiom, man simply cannot survive without producing, without working and using his products. Marx tells us in *The German Ideology,* "Man can be distinguished from the animal by consciousness, religion, or anything else you please. He begins to distinguish himself from the animal the moment he begins to *produce* his means of subsistence, a step required by his physical organization. By producing food, man indirectly produces his material life itself."[48] Marx makes essentially the same point in *Capital* in his characterization of "labor-power." "Labor-power exists only as a capacity, or

46. *Hegel: Reinterpretation,* p. 388; *Phänomenologie des Geistes,* p. 19.

47. The distinction between "objectification" (*Vergegenständlichung*) and "alienation" (*Entfremdung*) which represents a historical form of "objectification" is an extremely important distinction for Marx. This is the basis of his conviction that an alienated condition can be overcome by revolutionary *praxis.* But Marx's claim that Hegel failed to make such a distinction is very dubious, for Hegel never claims that all forms of objectification are forms of alienation. This is one more example of where Marx is interpreting (or misinterpreting) Hegel in order to make his own position clear.

48. *Young Marx,* p. 409; Marx/Engels *Werke,* Bd. 3, p. 21.

power of the living individual. Its production consequently presupposes his existence. Given the individual, the production of labor-power consists in his reproduction of himself or his maintenance. For his maintenance he requires a given quantity of the means of subsistence."[49] Furthermore, Marx ridicules the Hegelian notion that nature is objectified or congealed spirit. Nature is rather the source of the objects that man employs or consumes in order to satisfy his needs and desires. There is nothing about the *intrinsic* nature of production or objectification that results in alienation. But alienation is a *form* of objectification. Objectification becomes alienation only in a given historical social setting. When man exists in a social situation where the objects that he produces and the "system" in which these are exchanged is such that his products gain a mastery over him and dehumanize him, then *this* form of objectification is alienation. Alienation has no fundamental ontological status, it is a historical condition, and one of Marx's chief endeavors was to lay bare the structures of the historical social situations in which objectification becomes alienation.[50] Marx characterizes this process as it occurs in a capitalist society in the 1844 *Paris Manuscripts*.

49. *Capital*, I, p. 171; Marx/Engels *Werke*, Bd. 23, p. 185.

50. For a further discussion of the significance of the distinction between objectification (*Vergegenständlichung*) and alienation (*Entfremdung*) see Avineri, *The Social and Political Thought of Karl Marx*, pp. 97 ff.; Jean Hyppolite, *Studies on Marx and Hegel*, trans. by John O'Neill, pp. 70 ff.; Jean-Paul Sartre, *Search For a Method*, trans. by Hazel E. Barnes, pp. 150 ff.

One of the most explicit statements of the import of the distinction between "objectification" and "alienation" appears in the writings of the "mature" Marx. In the *Grundrisse*, he writes: "The stress is not on being objectified, but on being *alienated*, externalized, estranged; on the fact that the immense objective power *set up by social labor*, as one of its moments, *over against itself*, does not belong to the worker but to the personified conditions of production, i.e., to capital. Inasmuch as at the standpoint of capital and wage-labor the production of this objective body of activity unfolds in opposition to direct labor-power—this process of objectification appears in fact as a *process of alienation* from the standpoint of labor and as *appropriation of alien labor* from the standpoint of capital—this perversion and overturning is real, not imagined; it does not merely exist in the mind of the workers and capitalists. But obviously this process of overturning is only a historical necessity; it is a necessity for the development of the productive forces from a certain point of departure, or basis, but by no means an absolute necessity of production as such; rather it is a disappearing necessity, and the

The *increase in value* of the world of things is directly proportional to the *decrease in value* of the human world. . . . The object which labor produces, its product, stands opposed to it as an *alien thing*, as a *power independent* of the producer. The product of labor is labor embodied and made objective in a thing. It is the *objectification* of labor. The realization of labor is its objectification. In the viewpoint of political economy this realization of labor appears as the *diminution* of the worker, the objectification as the *loss of and subservience to the object*, and the appropriation as *alienation* [*Entfremdung*], as externalization [*Entäusserung*].[51]

But unlike many existentialists who have focused on this aspect of Hegel, Marx is perfectly clear that it is not objectification *per se* that results in alienation. The contrast to an alienated society is *not* one in which objectification no longer takes place—this is impossible. Rather, a radically different form of objectification takes place—one in which the objects that a man produces are no longer the chains for alienating him, but the means by which there is a free, social, and human expression of him in the very activity he performs and in the products that he produces. An unalienated society is one in which it is no longer the case that "the process of production has mastery over man"[52] but the process is controlled by him to satisfy and give expression to his human needs and desires. Among Marx's unpublished notes written in 1844 there is an almost euphoric description of what such an unalienated society would be like.

---

result and end which is immanent in this process is the supersession of this basis and this particular form of objectification. Bourgeois economists are so tied to the representations of a determinate historical stage of social development that in their eyes the necessary objectification of labor's social powers is inseparable from the latter's necessary *alienation from living labor*. However, with the supersession of the direct character of living labor as merely individual—or as merely internally, or only externally universal—labor, with the constitution of the individual's activity as *directly universal, i.e., social activity*, the objective moments of production will be freed of this *form of alienation;* they will be constituted as property, as the *organic body of society* in which individuals reproduce themselves as individuals, but *as social individuals."* *Grundrisse der Kritik der politischen Ökonomie* (*Rohentwurf*), p. 716. The above translation is given by I. Mészáros, *Marx's Theory of Alienation*, p. 329.

51. *Young Marx*, p. 289; *MEGA*, I.3, pp. 82-83.

52. *Capital*, I, p. 81; Marx/Engels *Werke*, Bd. 23, p. 95.

Suppose we had produced things as human beings: in his production each of us would have *twice affirmed* himself and the other. (1) In my *production* I would have objectified my *individuality* and its *particularity,* and in the course of the activity I would have enjoyed an individual *life;* in viewing the object I would have experienced the individual joy of knowing my personality as an *objective, sensuously perceptible,* and *indubitable* power. (2) In your satisfaction and your use of my product I would have had the *direct* and conscious satisfaction that my work satisfied a *human* need, that it objectified *human* nature, and that it created an object appropriate to the need of another *human* being. (3) I would have been the *mediator* between you and the species and you would have experienced me as a redintegration of your own nature and a necessary part of your self; I would have been affirmed in your thought as well as your love. (4) In my individual life I would have directly created your life; in my individual activity I would have immediately *confirmed* and *realized* my true *human* and *social* nature.[53]

We can now draw a number of consequences which will help us pinpoint what Marx means by "alienation" and thereby rescue this concept from the way in which it has been abused and vulgarized in recent times. First, alienation is clearly, for Marx, a social category —a category for understanding "political economy," not an ontological category rooted in the nature of man. Alienation is no more and no less fundamental than the reality of the determinate set of political and economic institutions and practices.[54] If these are radically transformed (and they can be so transformed) then alienation can and will be overcome *(aufgehoben).*

Secondly, in recent times "alienation" has widely been used to designate some sort of psychological condition in which the individual feels frustrated, unsatisfied, and unfulfilled. However, the psychological dimension of alienation is not primary for Marx, it is sec-

53. *Young Marx,* p. 281; *MEGA,* I.3, pp. 546-547.

54. The most comprehensive discussion in English of the theme of alienation in Marx is to be found in I. Mészáros, *Marx's Theory of Alienation.* The bibliography of this book is a fine guide to the voluminous literature on this subject. In addition to a detailed analysis of the meaning of alienation in Marx's early writings, Mészáros shows how this concept pervades Marx's "mature" writings. One limitation of Mészáros' study is that he doesn't explore in detail the ways in which the theme of alienation is transformed and given greater specificity in Marx's later works. See also Jean-Yves Calvez, *La Pensée de Karl Marx.*

ondary and derivative. One can be in an alienated condition and accept it without full consciousness of man's alienated condition. This is what Marx takes to be the condition of the working class of his time. The issue is not primarily how one—or even a class of people—feel or think of themselves. The issue is rather one of the *objective* conditions and relations under which men labor and produce. Marx is unmoved by the "fact" that those who have been exploited in a capitalist society may be content with their lot. We recall that in Hegel's dialectic of master and slave, there is a moment when the slave sees his reality and essential nature as being a slave for a master. This is one of the major reasons why Marx is sharply critical of those who think that amelioration of the basic frustrations of the working class gets at the political and economic roots of alienation. On the contrary, the chief task of revolutionary leaders, "the educators who must be educated," is to foster and develop the consciousness of the basic alienated condition of the exploited. In an early letter to Ruge, Marx spells this out for us, "The reform of consciousness exists *merely* in the fact that one makes the world aware of its consciousness, that one awakens the world out of its own dream, that one *explains* to the world its own acts. Our entire purpose consists in nothing else (as is also the case in Feuerbach's criticism of religion) but bringing the religious and political problems into the self-conscious human form" (*Y.M.*, p. 214; *I, pp. 449-450*).

Thirdly, the technology that has resulted and continues to be developed by capitalism is neither the *intrinsic* source nor cause of human alienation. Here, too, Marx's concept must be carefully distinguished from those contemporary prophets of doom who look upon advanced technology as the source of all human ills and alienation. Marx is not only completely unsentimental about technology, he sees in technology the sole means for overcoming alienation. With the development of technology, man for the first time in history can gain a mastery over nature; he has the means for satisfying basic human needs. The communist or humanist society that Marx sees as emerging from the womb of advanced technological capitalism is a post-industrial and technological society, not a pre-industrial pastoral utopia. This is why Marx condemns all "utopians" and "sentimental socialists" who are fixated on an imaginary past golden age, rather than on what is emerging from present conditions.

Our initial attempt to clarify the meaning of *praxis* has led us to an appreciation of *praxis* as human activity, with the realization that this human activity is for Marx the most basic and distinctive characteristic of man. We have also seen how this view of man helps us to understand the sense in which classical mechanistic materialism and idealism are *aufgehoben* in Marx. We have begun to see how Marx's concept of *praxis* is a dialectical transformation of Hegel's *Geist;* it would be impossible to make sense of *praxis* without the Hegelian background. But just as *Geist* must be understood as an active unifying principle and as the power of negativity bringing about its own alienation, so too must *praxis* be understood in this double perspective. *Praxis* in its present historical form is alienating activity. But Marx's very analysis of alienation, and the way in which it must be distinguished from the generic concept of objectification, already begins to point the way to the real historical overcoming of alienation. But thus far, I (and Marx) have been exceedingly vague about how this overcoming is to be realized. It is necessary to take a closer look at the development of Marx's thinking about the meaning of *praxis*.

From "Relentless Criticism" to "Revolutionary Practice"

Among the young Hegelians there was a heady sense that they were living in a time of great crisis, a time when the old world and the old philosophy were on the verge of collapse, and they were to be the *avant garde* of a new, radical, exciting era. Their enthusiasm for the great changes that they believed were about to take place frequently blinded them to considering the more mundane matter of how and what changes would actually take place. They agreed that as intellectuals their weapon was to be "criticism," but when it came to specifying what was to be criticized and how such criticism would be effective, there was a good deal of polemic but not much illumination.

One of the earliest places where Marx speaks directly to this issue is in an exchange of letters with Ruge written in the spring and fall of 1843 which was published in the first and last issue of *Deutsch-Französische Jahrbücher* in February 1844. Ruge, who for

a short time had served as Marx's mentor, expressed his deep pessi-
mism about the prospects of a revolution in Germany. Marx took up
the challenge directly; he was much more optimistic about the
prospects of revolution—not because he detected the beginnings of
a revolutionary class, but because he thought that conditions in
Germany were rapidly deteriorating. He was self-conscious about
the task that "we intellectuals" must play in bringing about the
revolution. "It is true," Marx affirms, "the old world belongs to the
Philistine" (*Y.M.*, p. 205; *I, p. 432*). "Freedom, the feeling of man's
dignity, will have to be awakened again in these men. Only this feeling, which disappeared from the world with the Greeks and with
Christianity vanished into the blue mist of heaven, can again transform society into a community of men to achieve their highest purposes, a democratic state" (*Y.M.*, p. 206; *I, p. 433*). Marx still
speaks here in the language of German radical liberalism. But
exactly how is this new sense of "man's dignity" to be awakened?
What is the role that the intellectual is to play? In a subsequent
letter, Marx spells this out. "We wish to find the new world through
criticism of the old." Marx goes on to say—expressing convictions
that were central to him throughout his life—"Even though the
construction of the future and its completion for all times is not
our task, what we have to accomplish at this time is all the more
clear: *relentless criticism of all existing conditions,* relentless in the
sense that the criticism is not afraid of its findings and just as little
afraid of the conflict with the powers that be" (*Y.M.*, p. 212; *I,
p. 447*).

Many young Hegelians would have championed this manifesto,
but there was an enormous difference between what they meant by
it and what Marx intended. In the main, the young Hegelians thought
of "relentless criticism" as criticism of religion and philosophy. For
Marx this was only the beginning, not the end of criticism. Criticism
of philosophy, religion, and even the political state led inevitably to
the roots of all criticism—the forms of alienation and the practical
contradictions inherent in the actual institutions of political economy. "Our slogan, therefore, must be: Reform of consciousness,
not through dogmas, but through analysis of the mystical consciousness that is unclear about itself, whether in religion or politics"
(*Y.M.*, p. 214; *I, p. 450*).

Marx's remarks help us to appreciate his life-long preoccupation with understanding *present* institutions rather than speculating about the future. Projecting future possibilities, speculating about the nature of utopian future societies, is idle and irrelevant. One must understand the tendencies inherent in present institutions. At many stages of his career Marx insisted that it is only by understanding and criticism of what is now taking place that we can successfully come to understand what are the real possibilities for society. These reflections also indicate Marx's view of ideology, the general outlook of the world accepted by men. Ideology does not conform to the way things really are, although it tells us something important about social reality. It is not accidental that men conceive of social reality in the ways that they do. Their "thought forms" are a reflection of this reality, only they do not yet understand this. In a passage that is frequently quoted and misinterpreted, Marx illustrates what he means by ideology.

Religious suffering is the *expression* of real suffering and at the same time the *protest* against real suffering. Religion is the sigh of the oppressed creature, the heart of a heartless world, as it is the spirit of spiritless conditions. It is the *opium* of the people.

The abolition of religion as people's *illusory* happiness is the demand for their *real* happiness. The demand to abandon illusions about their condition is a *demand to abandon a condition which requires illusions.* The criticism of religion is thus in *embryo a criticism of the vale of tears* whose *halo* is religion (*Y.M.,* p. 250; *I, pp. 488-489*).

Criticism, then, is not a matter of arbitrarily *condemning* an institution or a belief, but of *understanding* it. Marx doesn't view religion as an accidental stupidity of men, a hoax perpetrated by a priestly class. Religion is an illusion, but one rooted in existing social reality, one which is a reflection of the real alienation that man suffers. It is also a protest against this condition. The criticism of religion leads to an understanding of the meaning, causes, and the ultimate resolution of the "latent" content of "manifest" religious suffering. The program that Marx projects in these early writings is one in which a similar critique would be performed of law, philosophy, theology, politics, and political economy.[55]

55. "Political economy" (politische Ökonomie) has a distinctive meaning for Marx. He characteristically uses the expression to refer to actual bourgeois economy or to the theories and explanations of this economy by the "classical

The most important feature of these early reflections is that they indicate what *praxis* originally meant for Marx. Although his ideas were rapidly developing, he never abandoned the view that the task of the revolutionary intellectual—"the educator"—is in the first instance "relentless criticism of all existing institutions," a criticism that demands a correct *theoretical* analysis of existing institutions and the contradictions inherent in them. Throughout his life, Marx heaped scorn on those who were ready to plunge into action without such a critical understanding. This is the gist of his condemnation of "true socialists" and his devastating attack on the Gotha Program.[56] The latter represented sentimental sloganizing. Marx went through the document line by line, exposing its lack of "relentless criticism" and suggesting how such a program should have been written when based on a critical understanding of social reality.

But how could such a program of criticism be efficacious? What reason is there to believe that even a "correct" critical understanding of existing institutions would lead to a transformation of these institutions? Marx turned against his fellow young Hegelians who frequently wrote and acted as if their intellectual posturing would shake worlds. We detect here a second "moment" in Marx's development of the concept of *praxis*. In his article "Toward the Critique of Hegel's Philosophy of Law: Introduction" written in 1843, Marx says, "The weapon of criticism obviously cannot replace the criticism of weapons. Material force must be overthrown by material force. But theory also becomes a material force once it has gripped the masses. Theory is capable of gripping the masses when it demonstrates *ad hominem,* and it demonstrates *ad hominem* when it becomes radical" (*Y.M.*, p. 257; *I, p. 497*). "Theory is actualized in a people only insofar as it actualizes their needs" (*Y.M.*, p. 259; *I, p. 498*). No more than Hegel, did Marx believe that men are primarily motivated by conscious rational considerations.

---

economists." Already in his essay, "On the Jewish Question" (1843), Marx distinguishes between the level of "politics" and the more basic level of "political economy." He criticizes Bauer for the superficiality of his thinking in restricting himself to political emancipation. Real emancipation—human emancipation—demands a transformation of political economy.

56. "Critique of the Gotha Program" in *Marx and Engels: Basic Writings on Politics and Philosophy,* ed. by Lewis S. Feuer; Marx/Engels *Werke,* Bd. 19.

For both of them history is the playing out of men's deepest passions. The reason why criticism can be efficacious is that it speaks directly to these passions. It has the power *not* of delineating some utopian ideal which is to be striven for, but of revealing to men a critical understanding of what they are suffering. Unless criticism does this, it becomes idle speculation; the test of the correctness of a radical critique is its ability to bring genuine human problems suffered by men to a "self-conscious human form." This is the meaning of the second thesis on Feuerbach: "The question whether human thinking can reach objective truth—is not a question of theory but a *practical* question. In practice man must prove the truth, that is, actuality and power, this-sidedness of his thinking."[57]

The union of theory and practice that Marx develops for us is the culmination of his various lines of inquiry. His early *Critique of Hegel's Philosophy of Right* indicates Marx's acceptance of the Hegelian principle that a correct theoretical analysis of politics and political economy—the pay-off of The System—leads to a critical understanding of existing institutions. His sharp critique of Hegel does not challenge this principle, but attacks the adequacy of Hegel's theoretical analysis of politics. Hegel was guilty of the worst of all possible Hegelian sins, of rationalizing instead of providing true understanding. But if it is true, as Marx claimed, that the real locus of conflicts and contradictions is in these very existing institutions, then these must be *aufgehoben* by radical transformation. This is the conclusion that all of Marx's early critiques were pointing toward.

Marx still speaks as a philosopher, calling for a new direction in philosophy. He states as much when he declares, "As philosophy finds its *material* weapons in the proletariat, the proletariat finds its *intellectual* weapons in philosophy. And once the lightning of thought has deeply struck this unsophisticated soil of the people, the *Germans* will emancipate themselves to become men" (*Y.M.,* pp. 263-264; *I, p. 504*).

But even in the article in which Marx expresses this interplay of philosophy and the proletariat, he was already moving beyond this view to a third "moment" in the understanding of *praxis.* He speaks of transcending philosophy and warns, *"you cannot transcend [aufheben] philosophy without actualizing it"* (*Y.M.,* p. 256; *I,*

57. *Young Marx,* p. 401; Marx/Engels *Werke,* Bd. 3, p. 5.

p. 495). By the time he wrote the eleventh thesis on Feuerbach, this aspect of Marx's view of *praxis* had crystallized. "Practical-critical" activity becomes "revolutionary practice." Marx's own critique of philosophy had led him beyond philosophy—this is the point of the last thesis; it is not a call for a new direction in philosophy. Philosophy, which had reached its culmination in Hegel, had led to the full articulation of the demand for freedom to be realized—not the freedom of *Geist,* but the freedom of human sensuous individuals. But philosophy was impotent to bring about this freedom, impotent to bring about revolution. This had been revealed by philosophy itself. The critique of philosophy had dialectically led Marx to the conclusion that only a correct, detailed understanding of existing social reality could effect such a revolution. The root of all critique is the critique of political economy. After the 1840's Marx no longer has much to say about philosophy—the task had now become to change the world. But even this declaration was not a call for "direct action," but for the concrete theoretical knowledge that could guide revolutionary *praxis*.

Praxis *as Labor-Power*

One of the most popular and sterile issues in Marxist scholarship during the past few decades has been the debate about the "early" Marx versus the "mature" Marx. The debate starts from the fact that Marx's early writings are much more philosophical and speculative in tone than his later detailed, technical investigation of capitalism. The problem then is one of "reconciling" these two aspects of Marx. The variations on this attempt at reconciliation are numerous. At one extreme there are those who think that the early Marx is the *true* humanistic Marx and the Marx of *Capital* represents a rigidified, degenerate position. At the other end of the spectrum there are those who scorn the early works as immature speculations which are superseded by the mature "scientific" position developed in *Capital*. We have already suggested that this is a pseudo-issue, that the claim that there are "two" Marxes is a fiction. There is the development and dialectical continuity of a single total perspective which cannot be understood unless we appreciate its Hegelian origins and the ways in which Marx continually refined, specified, and criticized his own investigations.[58] It is ironic that so many Marxist scholars have failed to appreciate the dialectical character of Marx's own development—dialectical in the precise sense in which he and Hegel used the concept where a stage is *aufgehoben:* negated, affirmed, and transcended. But advocates of this specious dichotomy or break in Marx's thought are likely to charge us with basing our interpretation primarily on Marx's early work. They will point out that not only the concept, but the term *"praxis"* virtually disappears in Marx's mature thought.[59] To meet this challenge and

58. Although Avineri is not primarily concerned with attacking the myth of the "two" Marxes, his book, *The Social and Political Thought of Karl Marx* cogently demonstrates the speciousness of this myth. See also I. Mészáros, *Marx's Theory of Alienation.*

59. An entire library of literature has already been published on the problem of the "early Marx" and the "late Marx," and the debate is rapidly becoming "scholastic" where almost every possible variation on this theme has been advanced. Until recently, one scandal in this debate has been a neglect of Marx's *Grundrisse der Kritik der politischen Ökonomie (Rohentwurf).* This is an enormous volume of Marx's writings from 1857-1858. These writings were first published in two parts by the Marx-Engels-Lenin Institute in Moscow in 1939 and 1941. But this edition was little known and almost unavailable. In 1953 the Dietz publishing house in Berlin republished the two volumes together with some excerpts from Marx's notebooks of 1850-1851. This edition is now out of print. A fragment from the *Grundrisse* was translated into English under the title *Pre-Capitalist Economic Formations* with an introduction by E. B. Hobsbawm. The title indicates the way in which the *Grundrisse* has frequently been read—as notes toward the writing of *Capital.* A distorted French translation which minimizes the Hegelian cast of this work was published in Paris in 1967-1968. An English translation of selections is promised for 1971 and a complete translation of the whole work is now planned. Despite the fragmentary and repetitious character of this work, I believe that when it is better known and more carefully studied, it will emerge as one of Marx's major works—if not his major work. Concerning the issue of the "young Marx" vs. the "old Marx," the availability of the *Grundrisse* will place this discussion on a new level of sophistication. For what is so clearly evident in the *Grundrisse* is the ease with which Marx moves from a "Hegelian" idiom to a more "scientific" idiom. It conclusively shows the falsity of the claim that Marx dropped all significant discussion of "alienation" and *"praxis"* after the 1840's.

The *Grundrisse* has much greater significance than simply helping to clarify the issue of Marx's intellectual development. We are only beginning to discover how rich a source it is in seeing Marx working out hypotheses concerning the nature of class conflict, the theory of surplus value, the significance of production in understanding capitalism, and an understanding of the "Asiatic

to further our understanding of *praxis,* it is therefore essential that we show its development in *Capital.*

Three very fashionable claims have been made about Marx's "mature" outlook in *Capital.* First, that Marx rejects his early philosophical speculations—and with them, the terminology so dominant in his early writings, including the concepts of *"praxis"* and "alienation." Secondly, that with *Capital,* Marx's "reduction" of all basic categories to economic categories is clear and explicit. Thirdly, that the image of man that emerges from *Capital* is that of a class animal swept along by a web of impersonal forces that have a law-like regularity—laws that determine what man is and over which he has no control.

All three of these interrelated claims are false. On the contrary, one cannot make much sense of *Capital* unless one is sensitive to how earlier themes dialectically emerge in it, especially the concepts of *praxis* and alienation. Furthermore, it is extremely misleading to think of *Capital* as a study in economics where "economics" is understood in the *contemporary* sense of the term. We normally think of economics as one of the social sciences, along with political science, sociology, anthropology, psychology, etc. Economic categories pre-

---

mode of production." The scope of the *Grundrisse* is much broader than that of *Capital.* It becomes clear that the three volumes of *Capital* represent only a small fragment of the comprehensive theory projected in the *Grundrisse.* Rather than the *Grundrisse* representing a fragmentary groping toward the doctrines of *Capital, Capital* represents a small part of the total theory outlined in the *Grundrisse.* Three recent articles in English discuss enthusiastically the significance and content of the *Grundrisse.* See Martin Nicolaus, "The Unknown Marx," *The New Left Reader,* ed. by C. Ogelsby; and "Proletariat and Middle Class in Marx: Hegelian Choreography and the Capitalist Dialectic," *For A New America,* ed. by J. Weinstein and D. W. Eakins. See also David McLellan's "The Missing Link," *Encounter* 35 (November 1970). I. Mészáros cites numerous passages from the *Grundrisse* that discuss alienation. George Lichtheim has discussed the theory of the "Asiatic mode of production" as it is developed in the *Grundrisse* and says, "I express a mere personal opinion when I say that the argument outlined in pp. 375-396 of the *Grundrisse* seems to me to be among the most brilliant and incisive of Marx's writings," George Lichtheim, "Oriental Despotism," *The Concept of Ideology and Other Essays,* p. 85. For other appreciations of the *Grundrisse,* see Maximilien Rubel, "Contribution à l'histoire de la genèse du 'Capital,'" *Revue d'historie economique et sociale,* 2 (1950); André Gorz, *Strategy for Labor,* pp. 128-130; and Herbert Marcuse, *One-Dimensional Man,* pp. 35-36.

sumably locate only one *aspect* of human activity. But the thrust of
Capital is to reveal that under seemingly abstract, impersonal, economic categories, a great *human* drama is taking place. Economy,
or to use Marx's term, "political economy" is not a single, selective
dimension of human life; it is a congealed or crystallized form of
human activity—of *praxis*. To think of economic categories as
referring to a single, abstract dimension of human life is to be guilty
of what Marx himself called "fetishism." The third claim above is
the most misleading. It is certainly true for Marx that economic
systems, and capitalism in particular, exhibit a regularity and law-
likeness that shapes those who function in them. And it is also true
that Marx is attempting to lay bare and understand the fundamental
dynamic mechanisms operating in capitalist society. But these are
not eternal, immutable mechanisms; they arise and will pass away
in history. They are historical tendencies that manifest one of the
forms that human *praxis* has taken. A major, if not the major aim,
of Marx's analysis of capitalism is to unmask the forms of mystification in capitalist ideology—the ways in which we can all too easily
lose sight of the basic fact that underlying the complex interrelationships in a capitalist society are various forms of congealed
human labor. The apologists for capitalism have sought to justify
capitalism by an appeal to rigid, economic laws; and this is what
Marx is attacking and criticizing. Emerging from the study in
Capital is not a sanctification or reification of economic laws, but the
very opposite—a demonstration of the mutability of all so-called
economic laws, the ways in which they arise, the internal dynamic
contradictions they harbor, and the ways in which they pass away.
Marx is uncovering for us the "long and painful process of development" by which men have not controlled their own activity and have
been controlled by the process of production in which they find
themselves. The critical understanding of this process opens up the
real possibility of a society of "freely associated men" in which their
production "is consciously regulated by them in accordance with
a settled plan."[60] The thrust of *Capital,* and all of Marx's thinking,
is *not* to affirm the impotence of man in the face of impersonal
forces but rather to affirm the *real* possibility of a critical understanding of the world which allows man's eventual mastery of his
own fate.

60. *Capital,* I, p. 80; Marx/Engels *Werke,* Bd. 23, p. 94.

In order to substantiate our counterclaims to the three widely held prejudices that we have listed, let us begin by recalling Marx's comment on Hegel's *Phenomenology* in his 1844 *Paris Manuscripts.*

The great thing in Hegel's *Phenomenology* and its final result—the dialectic of negativity as the moving and productive principle—is simply that Hegel grasps the self-development of man as a process, objectification as loss of the object, as alienation and transcendence of this alienation; that he thus grasps the nature of *work* and comprehends objective man, authentic because actual as the result of his *own work.*[61]

This "great truth" became the kernel of what Marx meant by *praxis.* In the process of *praxis* as human activity, the products men produce are congealed or crystallized forms of their activity or their labor. When the product gains an independent hostile power, when the system of political economy in which men produce and work is such that their practical activity is in conflict with itself—i.e., their activity is essentially "forced" activity and not free activity, then men are alienated from their products, their fellow men, and themselves.

This concept of *praxis* provides the orientation needed for understanding the most fundamental category in *Capital,* the concept of value, or more specifically, labor value. The value of a product that a man produces is a crystallized form of labor-power.[62] In our

61. *Young Marx,* p. 321; *MEGA,* I.3, p. 156.

62. In the two articles by Martin Nicolaus previously mentioned, he describes in detail the shift that takes place in the *Grundrisse* from an economics of "competition" to an economics of "production." This shift is reflected in the importance that Marx assigns to the concept of labor-power (*Arbeitskraft*) as contrasted with labor (*Arbeit*). This new category enables Marx to explain how "surplus-value" comes into existence. "What the worker sells is not 'labor' but *labor-power* (*Arbeitskraft*); not a commodity like any other, but a commodity which is unique. Labor alone has the capacity to create values where none existed before, or to create greater values than those which it requires to sustain itself. Labor alone, in short, is capable of creating *surplus-value.* The capitalist purchases control over this creative power, and commands this power to engage in the production of commodities for exchange during a specified number of hours. The worker's surrender of control over his creative power is called by Marx exploitation," Martin Nicolaus, "The Unknown Marx," p. 98.

While I think that Nicolaus is correct in emphasizing this shift to the concept of *Arbeitskraft* as the key for understanding surplus-value, he overstates his case when he says that the shift from the concept of *Arbeit* to *Arbeitskraft*

advanced forms of exchange economies, we think and act in relation to the commodities we exchange and use as if these were impersonal physical things. According to Marx, this is a form of fetishism.[63] We fail to realize that these commodities are social products and that the value they possess (the labor value) is nothing but a *materialized form of labor activity*.

Hence, when we bring the products of our labor into relation with each other as values, it is not because we see in these articles the material receptacles of homogeneous human labor. Quite the contrary: whenever, by an exchange, we equate as values our different products, by that very act, we also equate, as human labor, the different kinds of labor expended upon them. We are not aware of this, nevertheless we do it. Value, therefore, does not stalk about with a label describing what it is. It is value, rather, that converts every product into a social hieroglyphic. Later on, we try to decipher the hieroglyphic, to get behind the secret of our social products; for to stamp an object of utility as a value, is just as much a social product as language. The recent scientific discovery, that the products of labor, so far as they are values, are but material expressions of the human labor spent in their production, marks, indeed, an epoch in the history of the development of the human race, but, by no means, dissipates the mist through which the social character of labor appears to us to be an objective character of the products themselves. The fact, that in the particular form of production with which we are dealing, viz., the production of commodities, the specific social character of private labor carried on independently, consists in the equality of every kind of that labor, by virtue of its being human labor, which character, therefore, assumes in the product the form of value—this fact

---

is "the crucial difference on which may be said to hinge the entire distinction between Marxist and non-Marxist economics—as well as the distinction, perhaps, between the 'young Marx' and the 'mature Marx.' " (Martin Nicolaus, "Proletariat and Middle Class in Marx: Hegelian Choreography and the Capitalist Dialectic," p. 267.) Nicolaus suggests but fails to make explicit that the "mature" emphasis on production and labor-power as the source of surplus-value is in harmony with and develops Marx's early understanding of the concept of *praxis*. Indeed without such an understanding of *praxis*, whereby the object produced is understood as a congealed form of the activity, it would be impossible to make sense of the rationale for claiming that labor alone creates values where none existed before or that labor creates greater values than those necessary to sustain it.

63. See the section, "The Fetishism of Commodities and the Secret Thereof" in *Capital*, I, pp. 71-83; Marx/Engels *Werke*, Bd. 23, pp. 85-98.

appears to the producers, notwithstanding the discovery above referred to, to be just as real and final, as the fact, that, after the discovery by science of the component gases of air, the atmosphere itself remained unaltered.[64]

The conception of labor value articulated in the above passage functions as a leitmotif throughout *Capital*. As Marx methodically introduces more and more complex analytic distinctions in order to understand critically the complexities of a capitalist society, as he explicates the concepts of money, constant capital, variable capital, surplus value, profit, interest, etc., he argues that while they appear to the participants in a capitalist society as impersonal entities and forces, they are in reality—when demystified from their reified and fetishistic appearances—various forms of social *praxis* or social labor.

The subtitle of *Capital* is *A Critique of Political Economy* and there is a dialectical continuity between the sense of "critique" as it is used here and the sense in which it was used in Marx's first "critique," *The Critique of Hegel's Philosophy of Right*. Just as Marx sought to demystify Hegel's *Philosophy of Right*, he now seeks to demystify political economy; to reveal to us what is really going on underlying the elaborate forms of reification of the world of economic "things" within which we operate. And just as the earlier critique led us to the idea of *praxis* as the "secret" for understanding Hegel, so now Marx is spelling out in detail what human *praxis* concretely means as human labor and production. "The life-process of society, which is based on the process of material production, does not strip off its mystical veil until it is treated as production by freely associated men, and is consciously regulated by them in accordance with a settled plan. This, however, demands for society a certain material ground-work or set of conditions of existence which in their turn are the spontaneous product of a long and painful process of development."[65]

Capital is the drama of *praxis* as labor or production in modern society. It is a drama because the cumulative effect of Marx's apparently dry and technical analysis is the unmasking of the alienated forms of labor—the ways in which the worker is exploited.

64. *Capital*, I, p. 74; Marx/Engels *Werke*, Bd. 23, p. 88.
65. *Capital*, I, p. 80; Marx/Engels *Werke*, Bd. 23, p. 94.

While alienation or exploitation reaches its apogee in advanced capitalist society, the dynamic contradictions inherent in capitalism provide the "material groundwork" for passing beyond capitalism, the stage in which the exploitation and alienation of a capitalist society are finally *aufgehoben*. Capitalism, then, is only one historical form that human *praxis* has taken, and *Capital* is concerned with the origins of the historical set of conditions and the passing beyond this alienated form of *praxis* or labor.

The above considerations significantly qualify a narrow "economic" reading of *Capital,* but Marx is quite explicit about what he intends by the use of economic categories. In the *Grundrisse der Kritik der politischen Ökonomie,* Marx takes issue with Proudhon's narrow conception of "economic" and his claim that property has an *"extra-economic"* origin. In criticizing Proudhon, Marx remarks:

> But to claim that pre-bourgeois history and each phase of it, has its own *economy* [Ökonomie] and an *economic base* of its movement, is at bottom merely to state the tautology that human life has always rested on some kind of production—*social* production—whose relations are precisely what we call economic relations.
>
> *The original conditions of production cannot* initially be *themselves produced*—they are not the results of production. (Instead of original conditions of production we might also say: for if this reproduction appears on one hand as the appropriation of the objects by the subjects, it equally appears on the other as the moulding, the subjection, of the objects by and to a subjective purpose; the transformation of the objects into results and repositories of subjective activity.) What requires explanation is not the *unity* of living and active human beings with the natural, inorganic conditions of their metabolism with nature, and therefore their appropriation of nature; nor is this the result of a historic process. What we must explain is the *separation* of these inorganic conditions of human existence from this active existence, a separation which is only fully completed in the relationship between wage-labor and capital.[66]

The outlines of what we might call Marx's "anthropology" should now be clear. Man is by nature an active, productive animal. "By nature" simply means that man is a creature who cannot survive unless he produces—exercises labor-power—in order to maintain

66. Karl Marx, *Pre-Capitalist Economic Formations,* trans. by Jack Cohen; ed. and with an introduction by E. J. Hobsbawm, pp. 86-87; Marx, *Grundrisse der Kritik der politischen Ökonomie,* pp. 388-389.

himself. This essential productive dimension of human life is *praxis*. But the social *forms* that this labor takes are historically conditioned. In the course of history, a variety of different and successively more complex social forms of production have evolved. Moreover, the succession of these modes of production has a rationale or *logos* in the sense that we can discover how one mode of production when fully developed (especially in Western societies) tends to undermine the very conditions that have given rise to it and eventually provides the basis for a new mode of production. In this process there is an increasing "*separation* of these inorganic conditions of human existence from this active existence," a separation that reaches its culmination in capitalist society. Just as all previous forms of production (in Western forms of production as distinguished from "Asiatic" production)[67] have in the course of their full development destroyed themselves, Marx in *Capital* is showing us how this same instability is inherent in a capitalist mode of production. However, with the passing away of capitalism, there is a real possibility (not a logical necessity), that the "separation" or "alienation" which has been characteristic of the development of man thus far will be overcome, *aufgehoben,* and human *praxis* will achieve its full, positive, creative, actualization. In another passage from the *Grundrisse,* where Marx sharply distinguishes the present potentialities of *praxis* from a nostalgia for some ancient "golden age," he writes:

Thus the ancient conception, in which man always appears (in however narrowly national, religious or political a definition) as the aim of production, seems very much more exalted than the modern world, in which production is the aim of man and wealth the aim of production. In fact, however, when the narrow bourgeois form is peeled away, what is wealth, if not the universality of needs, capacities, enjoyments, productive powers, etc., of individuals, produced in universal exchange? What, if not the full development of human control over the forces of nature—those of his own nature as well as those of so-called "nature"?

67. Marx's views on the Asiatic mode of production not only have intrinsic importance, they help to overthrow the myth that Marx had a rigid historical theory of economic development applicable to all societies. For excellent discussions of Marx's reflections on the Asiatic mode of production, see George Lichtheim, "Oriental Despotism," *The Concept of Ideology and Other Essays,* and Shlomo Avineri's "Introduction" to *Karl Marx: On Colonialism and Modernization.*

What, if not the absolute elaboration of his creative dispositions, without any preconditions other than antecedent historical evolution which makes the totality of this evolution—i.e., the evolution of all human powers as such, unmeasured by any previously established yardstick—an end in itself? What is this, if not a situation where man does not reproduce himself in any determined form, but produces his totality? Where he does not seek to remain something formed by the past, but is in the absolute movement of becoming? In bourgeois political economy—and in the epoch of production to which it corresponds—this complete elaboration of what lies within man, appears as the total alienation, and the destruction of all fixed, one-sided purposes as the sacrifice of the end in itself to a wholly external compulsion. Hence in one way the childlike world of the ancients appears to be superior; and this is so, insofar as we seek for closed shape, form and established limitation. The ancients provide a narrow satisfaction, whereas the modern world leaves us unsatisfied, or, where it appears to be satisfied with itself, is *vulgar* and *mean*.[68]

This passage further articulates a point which we have previously emphasized—that Marx sees modern bourgeois capitalist society as developing the material conditions required for the full development of man. It shows how the concept of "alienation" is still fundamental to Marx's "mature" thought. Furthermore, the claim that the "complete elaboration of what lies within man, appears as the total alienation," is fundamental (as we shall see in the next section) for understanding Marx's primary concern with the present and why he scorned speculation about future societies which was not rooted in a systematic critique of present institutions. But this passage further substantiates our claim that in order to appreciate and understand Marx's use of "economic" categories, we must view them as encapsulating the fundamental modes of human production—*praxis*.

We have now set the stage to justify our third counterclaim— that the point of *Capital* is not to sanctify the immutability of "economic laws" but to reveal their mutability in history. Capitalist society has brought about the most complete and thorough form of alienation that has yet existed. Or to use the distinctive language of *Capital*, capitalism is based upon and increases exploitation and the "rational" efficient use of surplus value to increase capital. Without surplus value—the value of products appropriated by the

68. *Pre-Capitalist Economic Formations*, pp. 84-85; Marx, *Grundrisse der Kritik der politischen Ökonomie*, pp. 387-388.

capitalist which is over and above the portion of value needed to sustain the producers and the means of production—there is no capitalism. But the story that Marx tells through the three volumes of *Capital* is of an economic mode of production that is inherently unstable and contradictory. The more capitalism succeeds in achieving its aim of increasing capital, the more it succeeds in undermining itself. Near the end of Vol. III of *Capital* (a passage taken from fragments of Marx's writings and published posthumously by Engels) Marx reflects on where his complex, intricate investigation of capitalism has led him. Even the language of this section ("The Trinity Formula") echoes the language of Marx's "early" writings.

In the case of the simplest categories of the capitalist mode of production, and even of commodity-production, in the case of commodities and money, we have already pointed out the mystifying character that transforms the social relations, for which the material elements of wealth serve as bearers in production, into properties of these things themselves (commodities) and still more pronouncedly transforms the production relation itself into a thing and money. All forms of society, insofar as they reach the stage of commodity-production and money circulation, take part in this perversion. But under the capitalist mode of production and in the case of capital, which forms its dominant category, its determining production relations, this enchanted and perverted world develops still more.[69]

Marx proceeds to review "the complete mystification of the capitalist mode of production" whereby it becomes perfectly natural "for the actual agents of production to feel completely at home in these estranged and irrational forms of capital-interest, land-rent, labor-wages, since these are precisely the forms of illusion in which they move about and find their daily occupation."[70] For Hegel, the end of history, the *telos* of *Geist,* is the concrete realization of freedom. In order to achieve this freedom, *Geist* must pass through a long and painful process. So too for Marx, the long painful history of *praxis* in the forms of modes of production which culminate in the capitalist mode of production is the necessary condition for freedom whereby the "economic laws" of capitalist society are *aufgehoben.* Freedom "can only consist in socialized man, the associated producers,

69. *Capital,* III, pp. 826-827; Marx/Engels *Werke,* Bd. 25, p. 835.
70. *Capital,* III, p. 830; Marx/Engels *Werke,* Bd. 25, p. 838.

rationally regulating their interchange with Nature, bringing it under their common control, instead of being ruled by it as by the blind forces of Nature; and achieving this with the least expenditure of energy under conditions most favorable to, and worthy, of their human nature."[71] The end of history—or as Marx claimed, the end of prehistory and the beginning of human history—comes when man finally triumphs over the "blind forces of Nature" and the economic regularities and laws which have determined what he has been thus far, not in the sense that man is finally free *from* all law-like regularity, but in the sense that he rationally and freely regulates his life in a way that is most favorable and worthy of his human nature.

Species-Being, Praxis, *and Alienation*

Throughout our discussion thus far we have uncritically followed Marx in his appeal to the concepts of "species-being" and "human nature." But the problems posed by these concepts are central ones for Marx and for understanding *praxis*. Marx's early use of the concept of "species-being" and his subsequent criticism of this concept is a typical instance of his own progressive dialectical development in which he negates, affirms, and passes beyond an earlier stage in his thinking. Marx relies heavily on this concept in his writings during the early 1840's. Species-being is man's true or ideal nature and it becomes fully manifest only when human alienation is overcome. Already in 1845, in his sixth thesis on Feuerbach, Marx is critical of this concept.

> Feuerbach resolves the religious essence into the *human* essence. But the essence of man is no abstraction inhering in each single individual. In its actuality it is the ensemble of social relationships.[72]

Feuerbach is compelled "to view the essence of man merely as species, as the inner, dumb generality which unites individuals *naturally*."[73] Marx is not only criticizing Feuerbach, he is also criticizing himself. While Marx used the concept of "species-being" in the

71. *Capital,* III, p. 820; Marx/Engels *Werke,* Bd. 25, p. 828.
72. *Young Marx,* p. 402; Marx/Engels *Werke,* Bd. 3, p. 6.
73. *Young Marx,* p. 402; Marx/Engels *Werke,* Bd. 3, p. 6.

1844 *Paris Manuscripts* to refer to man's *historical* nature, he did not pin down the precise meaning and justification of this concept. Let us review the stages in Marx's own acceptance and subsequent rejection of the concept of "species-being."

Feuerbach played the role of helping Marx to see that once Hegel's philosophy is demystified—once we uncover the latent content of Hegel's great "myth," we realize that *Geist* is nothing more than a disguised way of referring to man or humanity. Echoing, but at the same time transforming, Hegel's story of the journey of *Geist*, Marx writes in his 1844 *Paris Manuscripts:* "Since for socialist man, however, the *entire so-called world history* is only the creation of man through human labor and the development of nature for man, he has evident and incontrovertible proof of his *self-creation*, his own *formation process*."[74] In order to understand the dynamics of *Geist* (and consequently *praxis*) a double perspective is needed. *Geist* is concretely realized in the actual stages of history and is also the dynamic potential to overcome all forms of alienation. Without this double perspective, it would not make any sense to claim that *Geist* is not "satisfied" or "fulfilled" in any of its determinate forms. Nor would we be able to say that *Geist* continually "strives" to overcome all determinations or objectifications and to infinitize itself. The same double perspective is needed to account for Marx's own analysis of *praxis* as human alienation. The very meaning of "alienation" seems to presuppose a vision, ideal, or norm of what man can become when his creative potential is fully and freely developed.

For Feuerbach, this ideal of what man can become (and will become) is expressed in the concept of species-being—this is the truth implicit in the Hegelian notion of *Geist* once the transformative method is applied to it. The idea of a "species" *(Gattung)* which had been popularized by D. F. Strauss was taken over by Feuerbach. Feuerbach's *The Essence of Christianity* begins by telling us that man is distinguished from the animals because he alone is conscious of himself not only as an individual but as a species.[75] God, for Feuerbach, is a projection and reification of the human species. When man acts so that he is conscious of himself as a species-being,

74. *Young Marx*, p. 314; *MEGA*, I.3, p. 125.
75. Ludwig Feuerbach, *The Essence of Christianity*, trans. by George Eliot, p. 1.

his acts are qualitatively different from those when he acts as a single individual. The idea of a human species is that of all human perfections concretely realized.

Marx was initially impressed by the underlying humanism of *The Essence of Christianity*. We can detect its influence in his essay "On the Jewish Question" and the 1844 *Paris Manuscripts* where he adopted Feuerbach's concept of "species being" as the background for analyzing human alienation. In "On the Jewish Question," where Marx criticizes the notion of political emancipation which is not yet full human emancipation, he says:

Political democracy is Christian in that it regards man—not merely one but every man—as *sovereign* and supreme. But this means man in his uncivilized and unsocial aspect, in his fortuitous existence and just as he is, corrupted by the entire organization of our society, lost and alienated from himself, oppressed by inhuman relations and elements—in a word, man who is not yet *actual* species-being (*Y.M.*, p. 231; *I, p. 468*).

Or again in the 1844 *Paris Manuscripts,* Marx, repeating Feuerbach, says:

Man is a species-being (*Gattungswesen*) not only in that he practically and theoretically makes his own species as well as that of other things his object, but also—and this is only another expression for the same thing— in that as present and living species he considers himself to be a *universal* and consequently a free being.[76]

But for all the importance that species-being plays for Marx in these early writings, there is no serious attempt to analyze and justify this crucial concept. When Marx criticizes this concept in the sixth thesis on Feuerbach and says that the essence of man is "in its actuality the ensemble of social relationships," he is already foreshadowing his concept of class as the appropriate social category for understanding what man is. What first appeared to be a move away from Hegel to concreteness (from *Geist* to species-being) turns out to be another form of misplaced concreteness. This is the sort of criticism that Marx was developing of all the young Hegelians (including his own earlier efforts). They were not being radical enough; they were not getting at the "roots."

By the time that Marx wrote *Capital,* he was quite explicit about

76. *Young Marx*, p. 293; *MEGA*, I.3, p. 87.

the abandonment of species-being and its replacement by the concept of class. Early in *Capital,* when Marx introduces the concept of exchange, he says: "The persons exist for one another as representatives of, and, therefore, as owners of, commodities. In the course of our investigation we shall find, in general, that the characters who appear on the economic stage are but the personifications of the economic relations that exist between them."[77]

But the critique of the concept of species-being would appear to create a serious intellectual problem for Marx. Throughout his writings in the 1840's there is a strong moralistic tone. The sharpness with which Marx describes the varieties of alienation and dehumanization only serves to highlight his positive vision of what man can and "ought" to become—man as actual species-being. How can it make any sense to speak of the "dehumanization" of man unless we have some viable ideal or norm of what it is to be a human being? The very notion of alienation with its pejorative overtones seems to presuppose some positive view of what it means to be unalienated, and this positive view needs to be articulated and justified. Many critics and some defenders of Marx have interpreted him as being primarily a moralist, a prophet holding before us a vision of what man is to become. Many have claimed that it is at this crucial point that we can detect the essential confusion of Marx's position. Marx, so the criticism runs, is constantly confusing descriptive and evaluative claims—evaluative claims which he never justifies. The issues raised by this line of criticism are so central to our understanding of Marx and the concept of *praxis* that we must confront them squarely.

I want to challenge the claim that Marx *presupposes* an ideal of what man can and ought to become and condemns existing social reality by measuring it against some ideal norm. This way of "interpreting" Marx distorts the main thrust of his work. Marx's central thought is that a correct understanding of present political economy and its historical origins provides the sole basis for revealing genuine human potentialities. This point is nicely expressed by Lobkowicz when he says, "Neither Hegel nor Marx measures man's 'alienated state' either against a transhistorical human nature or against a 'logically predetermined' future. Rather, they measure it against a human potentiality revealed by the very phenomenon of alienation—against a human potentiality which though at first it emerges in an alienated

77. *Capital,* I, pp. 84-85; Marx/Engels *Werke,* Bd. 23, pp. 99-100.

state, allows one to envisage a previously unknown possibility of ultimate human self-actualization."[78]

Such an orientation cuts at the very heart of the modern dogma that there is an unbridgeable gap between the descriptive and the prescriptive, or between fact and value, or between the "is" and the "ought." For Marx, human alienation is an *objective* social condition. On the basis of a critical understanding of the roots and causes of this alienation, we can come to discover real human potentialities and "envisage a previously unknown possibility of ultimate human self-actualization." The metaphysical and epistemological implications of his position echo a more classical Greek, especially Aristotelian, view of man that maintains that it is only by understanding what man is—his actuality—that one can appreciate what he can become—his potentiality. Just as there is no clear "fact-value" or "is-ought" dichotomy in Aristotle, so there is none in Marx. This similarity should not blur the sharp differences that exist between Marx's and Aristotle's understanding of "actuality" and "potentiality." The most dramatic difference is that for Marx both man's actuality and his potentiality change in the course of man's historical development. Genuinely new potentialities arise as a result of human *praxis*. Marx's understanding of human potentialities as rooted in history foreshadows themes that have been central to contemporary phenomenology with its insistence that the basic reality that man encounters is his *Lebenswelt,* and that it is only by sensitively understanding this *Lebenswelt* that one discovers new human potentialities.

The essential thrust of Marx's dialectical development throws into relief another common objection to his thought and resolves a perplexity which many readers have felt. It is frequently pointed out that Marx provides us with only the sketchiest outlines of what a future communist or humanist society will be like. Some readers have been perplexed by Marx's relentless scorn of utopian thinking. For Marx as for Hegel, speculation about future possibilities which is not rooted in a critical understanding of present institutions is idle and unrealistic. Marx is in complete agreement with Hegel when he says in the Preface to the *Philosophy of Right* that "if . . . theory really goes beyond the world as it is and builds an ideal one as it ought to be, that world exists indeed, but only in his opinions,

78. Lobkowicz, op. cit., p. 315.

an unsubstantial element where anything you please may, in fancy, be built."[79] On many occasions, Marx warns that he is concerned with communism and socialism only as they emerge from the womb of capitalism—from present political and economic institutions. Marx does not begin with a vision or norm of what ought to be and then proceed to criticize what is, in light of this norm. His position (and Hegel's) is severely critical of this Kantian bias. It makes eminently good sense—from the perspective of this dialectical development in Marx's thought—that *Capital* and his other writings after the 1840's are dedicated almost exclusively to a critical understanding of present institutions and developments.

The above sketch not only reveals the direction of Marx's thought, it has important metaphysical and epistemological implications. Marx's central concepts such as alienation and *praxis* demand a radical rethinking of the most fundamental epistemological concepts that have preoccupied modern philosophers. Marx was not only aware of this: we can find in his writings hints of such a radical epistemology, one which challenges what I have called the main epistemological dogma of modern philosophy.

It is not by any superficial or careless reasoning that most modern thinkers have been led to maintain dichotomies between the is and the ought, the descriptive and the prescriptive, fact and value. In a variety of ways, philosophers have argued that whatever status we assign to values, norms, and ideals, they are not objective phenomena to be discovered in *nature*. Science, our most powerful and successful means for exploring nature, can tell us only what is; it can describe, explain, predict, but it cannot tell us in any categorical sense what ought to be. If we want to find the philosophic arguments in support of such a position, we need only study the works of most of the major figures or movements in philosophy since Descartes. Hume (in some of his moods), Kant, classical materialism, logical positivism and empiricism are all agreed about this "dogma." But it is precisely this dogma that is the focal point of Marx's (and Hegel's) attack.

In a soul-searching letter written to his father in 1837 when Marx was nineteen—he announces this concern: " . . . I was greatly disturbed by the conflict between what is and what ought to be. . . . In

79. *Philosophy of Right*, p. 11; *Grundlinien der Philosophie des Rechts*, p. 16.

the concrete expression of the living world of thought—as in law, the state, nature, philosophy as a whole—the object itself must be studied in its development; there must be no arbitrary classifications; the rationale of the thing itself must be disclosed in all its contradictoriness and find its unity in itself" (*Y.M.*, pp. 42-43; *I, p. 9*). Marx's thought here is still inchoate but the direction is clear. What Marx found in Hegel is an attempt, indeed the most ambitious attempt in post-Kantian philosophy, to overcome the dichotomy of the "is" and the "ought," and throughout his life, Marx's polemics against those who insisted on some version of this dichotomy were no less vehement than Hegel's similar critiques.

To sharpen our sensitivity to the issues involved, consider again the passage cited from Lobkowicz, in which he says that Hegel and Marx measure man's alienated state "against a human potentiality which, though at first it emerges in an alienated state, allows one to envisage a previously unknown possibility of ultimate human self-actualization." From the bias of modern philosophy, this claim is at best misleading and at worst false or nonsensical. Human alienation is, strictly speaking, not an objective phenomenon. It is not something that is directly or even indirectly observed. Strictly speaking, we should say that we observe certain value-free characteristics and when we label these "alienation" we are making a logically independent value judgment. The very concept of potentiality is suspect from the perspective of a tough-minded empiricism; it is a posit or construct based upon what is directly observable. It is this antiseptic notion of observation—and more generally—the view that our cognitive categories are value neutral that Marx (and Hegel) are attacking as false. In his own way, Marx is attacking the notion of the "myth of the given"[80]—the idea that we can sharply distinguish that which is immediately given to us in cognition from what is constructed, inferred, or interpreted by us. In this respect there is a strong family resemblance between what Marx is claiming and what has been claimed by many of the most sophisticated contemporary philosophers, whether of an analytic or phenomenological orientation. Marx would agree that all observation is "theory-

80. This expression has been recently popularized by Wilfrid Sellars. His own philosophic investigations represent a sustained critique of "the myth of the given" in its multiple forms. See *Science, Perception and Reality*, especially Chapter 5, "Empiricism and the Philosophy of Mind."

laden,"[81] and that the reality we know and encounter is conditioned by the "forms of life" that have evolved in human social institutions.

The central motif here can be traced back to Kant who emphasized the constructive, categorical aspect of judgment. But unlike Kant, Marx does not believe there is any *Ding-an-sich* that stands apart from human knowing, and furthermore, Marx would maintain that our basic categories change and develop in history. Nor is Marx sympathetic with those thinkers who interpret man's cognitive perspective as an act of individual will or arbitrary convention. What is distinctive about Marx's reflections on human cognition is the way in which he relates it to the evolution of man's practical needs as manifested in his social life. It is *praxis* that turns out to be the key for understanding the full range of man's developing cognitive activities.

Georg Lukács first underscored this aspect of Marx's thought and more recently Leszek Kolakowski has articulated the epistemology implicit in Marx's early writings—one that shows us that man's practical relation to the objects and the world he confronts is the basis for understanding man's cognitive relationship to the world.[82]

Human consciousness, the practical mind, although it does not produce existence, produces existence as composed of individuals and divided into species and genera. From the moment man in his onto- and phylogenesis begins to dominate the world of things intellectually—from the moment he invents instruments that can organize it and then expresses this organization in words—he finds that world already constructed and differentiated, not according to some alleged natural classification but according to a classification imposed by practical need for orientation in one's environment.[83]

The world that man encounters, attempts to dominate, finds satisfaction in, and wants to know is not a world that exists in and of itself independently of man's relation to it. We must be careful here.

81. See N. R. Hanson, *Patterns of Discovery;* Paul Feyerabend, "Explanation, Reduction, and Empiricism," *Minnesota Studies in the Philosophy of Science,* Vol. 3.

82. Georg Lukács, *Geschichte und Klassenbewusstsein;* Leszek Kolakowski, "Karl Marx and the Classical Definition of Truth," in *Toward a Marxist Humanism,* trans. by Jane Zielonko Peel. Sartre, in a very perceptive footnote, points out the epistemological implications of the concept of *praxis: Search For a Method,* pp. 32-33; *Critique de la raison dialectique,* I, pp. 30-31.

83. Kolakowski, op. cit., p. 46.

For while Marx is appropriating an insight central to idealism, he rejects Hegel's notion that nature is externalized *Geist*. There is always a nonhuman "natural substratum" or "stuff" that man works upon and shapes. He is a natural being among other natural beings. And there "exists a reality that is common to all people, and that remains forever in a state of incipience."[84] But Kolakowski is dead right when he characterizes Marx's basic idea as follows:

that man as a cognitive being is only part of man as a whole; that that part is constantly involved in a process of progressive autonomization, nevertheless it cannot be understood otherwise than as a function of a continuing dialogue between human needs and their objects. This dialogue, called work, is created by both the human species and the external world, which thus becomes accessible to man only in its humanized form.[85]

But how do these epistemological considerations bear on the issue of the dichotomy between description and prescription, fact and value? The very roots of this dichotomy are misconceived. This dichotomy is based on a false understanding of man's practical-cognitive relation to the world. "The values and practical preferences we have put into this world are concealed within it, we no longer see the mark we have stamped upon the world and upon its permanent human coefficient."[86] When Marx describes the condition of man as an alienated one, he is *not* imposing arbitrary value judgments on a value neutral world; he is uncovering and revealing the *social* reality in which we find ourselves. But this social reality is not man's fixed permanent human reality. It is itself the resultant of the dynamics of human social *praxis* congealed into a world of "things" and alienated institutions. This is what Marx means when he says that "In bourgeois political economy—and in the epoch of production to which it corresponds—this complete elaboration of what lies within man, appears as the total alienation, and the destruction of all fixed, one-sided purposes as the sacrifice of the end in itself to a wholly external compulsion."[87] It is this under-

84. Kolakowski, p. 56.

85. Kolakowski, p. 66.

86. Kolakowski, p. 63.

87. Karl Marx, *Pre-Capitalist Economic Formations,* p. 85; Marx, *Grundrisse der Kritik der politischen Ökonomie,* p. 387.

standing of our present objective alienated condition that reveals the possibility of a humanized nature—one in which the reality that man shapes and works upon no longer has the status of an alien, hostile character, but is a world in which

man appropriates to himself his manifold essence in an all-sided way, thus as a whole man. Every one of his *human* relations to the world— seeing, hearing, smelling, tasting, feeling, thinking, perceiving, sensing, wishing, acting, loving—in short, all the organs of his individuality, which are immediately communal in form, are an appropriation of the object in their *objective*-relation [*Verhalten*] or their *relation to it*. This appropriation of *human* actuality and its relation to the object is the confirmation of human actuality.[88]

But if it is true that man's present reality and world is an objectively alienated one, then the abstract possibility of a "humanized world" only becomes a real possibility through a radical transformation of this objectified alienated condition—by revolutionary *praxis*.

I want to be as explicit as I can in clarifying what I am and am not claiming concerning Marx's basic orientation—one which emerges from his understanding of *praxis*. I am not claiming that Marx solved, once and for all time, the so-called problem of fact and value or the "is-ought" dichotomy. I am claiming, however, that to approach Marx from the perspective of these dichotomies is to distort what he *sought* to achieve. Marx was only incidentally interested in metaphysical and epistemological issues—and after his early writings they receded into the background for him. We find, at best, hints and suggestions, not a well-developed theory. Nevertheless, one cannot overemphasize the change of perspective on social reality that Marx was attempting to bring about—one which would justify an understanding of man where it could be legitimately claimed that "In bourgeois political economy—and in the epoch of production to which it corresponds—*this complete elaboration of what lies within man, appears as the total alienation . . .* " (italics added).

The complex issues involved here are not only fundamental for an understanding of Marx—his scorn of utopian thinking, his relentless criticism of existing institutions of political economy, his attacks on Kantians of all varieties—they have formed the essential prob-

88. *Young Marx*, p. 307; *MEGA*, I.3, p. 118.

lematic of much of the history of Marxist thought since Marx. Some have read Marx as a crypto-moralist and some as a crypto-positivist announcing the coming of the new and final science of man. Both extremes, and the many variations on them, neglect the ways in which Marx's understanding of *praxis* and alienation presents a basic challenge to the dichotomy of the descriptive and the prescriptive which has shaped so much of modern thought and is presupposed by so much of contemporary "social science." For those who seek to develop a Marxist perspective, the most central and difficult task is to further develop, explore, and justify Marx's radical "anthropology."

We have now attempted to justify our claim that *praxis* is the central concept of Marx's outlook and to articulate what he means by *praxis*. What might at first seem to be a chaotic array of meanings —*praxis* as human activity, production, labor, alienation, relentless criticism, and revolutionary practice—are aspects of a single, comprehensive and coherent theory of man and his world. Our primary emphasis thus far has been to develop an interpretation of the meaning and centrality of *praxis* for Marx, but we must now ask in a more direct manner, just what Marx and Marxism have contributed to our understanding of human action.

But first let us consider the recent revival of interest in Marx. During the past few decades, no other intellectual figure has received so much discussion and has so deeply influenced men's thinking throughout the world. Marx's influence is not sufficient to justify the correctness of his orientation, but it can provide clues to the power and insight of his thought. The revival of interest that I have in mind has little to do with the dogmatics of Marxist interpretation that has become a form of scholasticism in many Communist countries and for many Communist parties. It is a revival that represents a counter-movement and challenge to Communist dogmatics. Roughly speaking, we can classify the revival of interest in Marx into three groupings: scholarly, religious, and political.

Recently there has been a tremendous scholarly interest in interpreting and rediscovering the "historical" Marx. In part this has been stimulated by the publication of Marx's early writings which have become available only since the 1930's. Scholars from almost every country in the East and West have participated in this study

and in the problems and conflicts generated by the variety of interpretations. Even though we can bracket this aspect of the Marxist
revival as an "objective" scholarly interest, there is frequently an
underlying motivation or rationale for the "new" scholarly interpretation of Marx. It is too simple to think that the concern for
Marx is sufficiently explained by the fact that Marx is taken as the
"official" philosopher or intellectual spokesman of existing Communist societies. The Marx that is being "rediscovered" is drastically
different from the "official" Marx of Communist ideologists. As so
frequently happens in the history of scholarship, the examination
of a thinker becomes a central concern because there is a deep belief
in the relevance of his ideas to our present situation. Certainly this
motivation is manifest in much of the best writing on Marx in our
time. Although the historical scholar can and must abide by the
canons of historical research and objectivity, he can and often does
select his subject because he feels a special empathy with it, because
he thinks that we can not only learn about the past but about ourselves from a proper understanding of a great thinker's thought. But
what is it about Marx that still "speaks" to so many intellectuals?
We can approximate a partial answer by considering the "religious"
interest in Marx.

At first, it might seem surprising that Marx, who was so critical
of religion and theology, should have a special significance for religious thinkers. But some of the best interpretation and discussion
of Marx in France, Germany, and even America has been by religious thinkers. Perhaps one might think this is simply a matter of
knowing "one's adversary," but again I think this is too superficial
an answer. We have seen in our discussion of *praxis* and human alienation that Marx can be read as developing a systematic and comprehensive "philosophical" anthropology. The more one penetrates
to the quintessence of Marx's thought, the more one can see the
presence of themes (in a secularized form) that have preoccupied
religious thinkers throughout the ages—the severity of human
alienation, the apocalyptic sense of the imminence of the coming
revolution, and the messianic aspiration that infuses much of Marx's
thinking. Even the temperament and outlook of Marx are in the
direct vein of the Biblical prophets. Ironically, just as Marx sought
to uncover the latent truth in religious suffering, so now many contemporary religious interpreters of Marx seek to uncover the religious

significance of his secular thought. Contemporary theologians claim
that Marx speaks much more directly to man's religious condition
than do acknowledged "religious thinkers." Marx, especially the early
Marx, has come to be *used* as a basis for critique of more superficial
theological and religious beliefs. Marx's thought not only expresses
the dominant themes of the history of Western culture, it also speaks
to our deepest aspirations and hopes—that the day will come when
man will be freely and creatively fulfilled.

The third aspect of the revival of interest in Marx is, I believe,
the most interesting and important. Although it is often disguised
behind the façade of scholarly interest—especially in Eastern Communist countries—it has explosive political significance. In countries such as Poland, Czechoslovakia, and Yugoslavia, the redis-
covery of "authentic" Marxism has been the primary intellectual
weapon for the criticism of the totalitarian and bureaucratic tendencies of existing Communist regimes. Implicitly—and sometimes explicitly—the basic argument emerging is that Communist societies
do not represent the historical realization of Marxism, but its be-
trayal. This underlying political concern finds its counterpart in the
West. Two outstanding thinkers who look to an enriched Marxism
as providing the viable context for coming to grips with present
political, economic, and social problems are Jean-Paul Sartre and
Maurice Merleau-Ponty. In West Germany and even in unofficial
circles in East Germany, Ernst Bloch has served to stimulate this
dimension of the contemporary interest in Marxism. The "Frankfurt
school," including Adorno, Horkheimer, Marcuse, and Habermas
represents one of the most creative developments of Marxist thought.
In Italy the work of Gramsci is being rediscovered. For most European Marxists, both in Eastern and Western countries, the pivotal
figure for the new humanistic reading of Marx has been the Hun-
garian Marxist, Georg Lukács. Even in America, which has never
been hospitable to Marxism as a viable political orientation, we find
that the basic themes that have played such a dominant role in the
recent European revival of Marxism have elicited a similar response
among a small but articulate group of radical thinkers groping for a
political orientation with which to confront and criticize existing
institutions.

What is common to the variety of types of interest in Marx—

scholarly, religious, and political—and the great diversity of thinkers deeply influenced by Marx is not any fundamental agreement about what tenets of Marxism are correct or even most important. Pervading this revival is a general sense that Marx and Marxism still provide a fund of insight, challenges, hypotheses, and suggestions for understanding what man is, for confronting existing problems, for carrying on "relentless criticism of all existing conditions." While there isn't a single claim or thesis articulated by Marx that does not demand significant critical rethinking, starting with Marx's reflections on *praxis* provides us with some of the most fruitful leads in understanding and criticizing our *present* social reality, for coming to a better grasp of what man is and can become.

One way of judging the value and significance of an intellectual orientation is by the problems it uncovers, the challenges it forces us to confront, the hypotheses it suggests, and the insight that it brings to bear on a variety of issues—by what Whitehead once called the "sense of importance." On these grounds, Marxism—and in particular the Marxist conception of *praxis*—must be judged to be one of the richest and most vital intellectual orientations of our times. Marxism has been pronounced "dead" many times, but it would be difficult to specify another intellectual orientation that has elicited so much original thought.

As we follow out the themes of *praxis* and action in the other thinkers and movements to be explored, we will see more vividly how Marx's thought functions as a corrective and a challenge (while it also needs to be complemented by these other views). In tracing the "logic" of existentialist thought, we will see how it faces the danger of resulting in a form of romantic solipsism where the obsessive concern for the existing individual is in danger of losing all contact with social reality. This tendency is poignantly illustrated in the intellectual biography of Sartre, who after developing a thoroughgoing ontology in which the individual is virtually isolated from his fellowmen (despite Sartre's counter claims), has been for the last thirty years desperately trying to fight his way out of this impasse. It is no accident that in his systematic attempt to come to grips with social reality and its complex facticity and dynamics, Sartre has turned to Marx—and, in particular, to Marx's concept of *praxis*—for illumination.

We shall see too that when we discuss pragmatism, there are striking similarities and differences with Marxism. The pragmatists have been especially sensitive to the epistemological and metaphysical consequences of the shift in orientation that focuses on man as an active being who is shaped by and shapes existing practices. The dominance of the category of the practical, the emphasis on social categories for understanding man and the ways in which man functions in a community, and even the understanding of man's cognitive activities from the perspective of his practical activity, pervade the pragmatists' investigations. Although Peirce was almost totally indifferent to the concrete problems of social and political philosophy, Dewey considered these to be central to a reconstructed philosophy. Paradoxically, Dewey—of all the thinkers considered—is the closest and furthest away from Marx. *Au fond,* Dewey was a reformer. He was deeply skeptical of the demand for revolution as understood by Marx. Dewey's advocacy of liberal amelioration would have been seen as the greatest threat to genuine revolutionary *praxis,* and I have no doubt that Marx would have attacked Dewey in the same ruthless manner in which he attacked all "true socialists." The dialectic that can take place between Marx and Dewey is the political dialectic of our time. On the Marxist side, there is the sharp criticism that liberalism can be self-defeating and sanction what it seeks to change. From a Marxist point of view, reformist liberalism of Dewey's variety doesn't get at roots and fails to appreciate the extent to which conditions of political economy as they now exist in advanced capitalist societies (including the state capitalism of many so-called Communist countries) continues to perpetuate the alienation and exploitation of man. If we are honest about the inadequacy of Dewey's faith in creative intelligence, in his fundamental belief that through the educational process we can create a new type of man and a new type of society, we cannot be insensitive to the Marxist critique. The crises that we are now confronting in America in race relations, in the crumbling of our cites, in the failures of our school system, in the realization of how impotent government controls are in the face of increasing pollution, are indications of inability of reformist liberalism to come to grips with the social problems and crises that confront us all. But on the side of Dewey and the pragmatists, we cannot forget how easily a demand for absolute humanism and human emancipation can turn into its opposite—absolute totalitarianism. Radicalism, not simply as a professed intellectual ideal but as actual political practice, is double-edged. It can and has at times ended in destroying the basic ideals professed by the most thoroughgoing radicals. We can, from the vantage point of scholarly objectivity, say that the crimes committed in the name of "orthodox" Marxism are the greatest perversion of the letter and spirit of Marx's work, that the Marxism represented by a Stalin is an absolute distortion of Marx. But such a claim, which is all too common today, tends to be naive about those elements in Marxism which allowed for such a perversion and misinterpretation. I recognize that we cannot condemn Marx for the barbaric practices carried out in his name. But I believe that we must be sensitive to those elements in Marx's own thought which have allowed for this perversion. Here I think that the pragmatists can be heplful. For they had a more thoroughgoing understanding of what must be the norms of objective, self-correcting inquiry. Epistemologically and practically, they have been aware of how any theory, hypothesis, or doctrine, can all too easily pass into dogma. Marx himself practiced what the pragmatists preached about self-corrective inquiry. Although he announced and defended his theses boldly and attacked his foes with stinging polemic and sharp criticism, he was always ready to turn this critique on himself and reject what he took to be vague, misleading, and superficial. But it cannot be said that this ongoing critique has always been practiced by those who have called themselves "Marxists." Too frequently, and with tragic results, they have turned Marxism into a new form of uncritical dogmatism. I do not think that there is any neat solution to the claims and counterclaims of a Marx and a Dewey, but I do believe that the issues that arise from this confrontation are the central issues of social philosophy in our time.

The issues and orientation that are characteristic of Marx and Marxism and those of analytic philosophy are extremely remote from each other. As a historical comment, this is undeniable. But here too there is the real possibility of a creative dialectic. On the side of analytic philosophy, perhaps no other movement in the history of philosophy has placed such a high priority on clarity, rigor, and subtlety. It has made us self-conscious of intellectual standards that must be placed on any legitimate intellectual position, includ-

ing Marxism. It places upon Marxism the challenge to seriously
encounter the insights, distinctions, and claims that have been the
fruit of analytic investigations. To condemn the whole of the analytic
movement as nothing but a faulty outcropping of an idealistic bourgeois superstructure is to be guilty of the worst sort of intellectual
provincialism. It is to betray what was so fundamental to Marx
himself, the willingness and ability to carry on a careful critique of
alternative intellectual orientations. But analytic philosophy has
paid a heavy price for this clarity and rigor. It is itself guilty of har-
boring suppressed premises and convictions. To a greater extent
than is warranted, analytic philosophy has isolated itself from the
practical concerns of men, from what Dewey called the "problems
of men." Its contribution to political and social philosophy has been
virtually nonexistent, and analytic ethics has tended to become an
arid, scholastic jungle. Analytic philosophers, and especially younger
students of analytic philosophy, are growing restless with the artificial, self-imposed limitations of the movement. I am not making the
fashionable but false charge that analytic philosophy fails to treat
the "big, important" issues of life. We will see that this is not true.
My quarrel is an immanent one, which can be justified only when
we examine analytic philosophy in detail, but which can be briefly
indicated here. From a variety of angles, analytic philosophy has
affirmed the importance of social practices and institutions in understanding man—his language, his morals, and especially his activity.
But analytic philosophers tend to stop the inquiry just where Marx
and the Marxists begin to ask questions. There has been virtually no
attempt among analytic philosophers to press further, to ask critical
questions about the origin and development of these social institutions
and practices which shape what we are. In principle, analytic philosophers are open to such questions. In fact, they have not seriously
asked them. Marx thought he had discovered an overall pattern that
could explain and throw critical light on all existing social institutions,
not just well-recognized political and economic ones, but institutions
that affect every aspect of human life and activity. Whatever our
reservations and conclusions about Marx's theory, it cannot be denied that he showed the possibility and the importance of asking
and trying to answer questions which analytic philosophers have
scarcely begun to ask—questions concerning the origin and nature

of social institutions that pervade and shape human life. These questions cannot be conveniently assigned to some other approach or discipline; they are questions that must be confronted in pursuing the very issues central to analytic philosophy. The richness, the variety of possible directions for explorations, the challenges presented to every other contemporary intellectual orientation, the profundity of Marx's reflections on *praxis* continue to provide a matrix for us in coming to an understanding of what it is to be an active human being.

PART TWO

CONSCIOUSNESS, EXISTENCE, AND ACTION

KIERKEGAARD & SARTRE

I ARGUED in Part I that Marx's distinctive orientation emerges from a radical critique of Hegel's philosophy. The dominant concept of *praxis* in Marx represents a dialectical transformation of Hegel's *Geist,* and Marx's own analysis of the conflict of classes can be read as a critical commentary on Hegel's brief, but penetrating, analysis of the dynamics of Lordship and Bondage.

In this part, I want to show how another major strain in contemporary philosophy can also be interpreted as a dialectical critique of Hegel. The leading ideas of existentialist thought can be interpreted as a critical commentary on another stage in the *Phenomenology,* viz., Unhappy Consciousness *(Das Unglückliche Bewusstsein).* Unhappy Consciousness, like Lordship and Bondage, is but one stage in the grand progressive self-development of *Geist*—a stage that must, like the other stages of the actualization of *Geist,* be *aufgehoben.* But many post-Hegelian thinkers have claimed that the transition in the *Phenomenology* beyond Unhappy Consciousness is specious. Much more is at stake than a matter of scholarly interpretation. The dialectic of Unhappy Consciousness has been taken as a portrayal of *the* basic existential human condition—not a stage of *Geist* to be *aufgehoben.* I want to show that both Kierkegaard's and Sartre's essential visions of what it is to be an existing human being are variations of Hegel's phenomenological description of Unhappy Consciousness.

Hegel is not simply describing possible forms of consciousness from an external point of view. The stages in the *Phenomenology* are forms of consciousness that *Geist* (and concretely, men) have lived through. Kierkegaard and Sartre are not only talking about

84

Unhappy Consciousness; their own life projects and their most intimate intellectual struggles exemplify Unhappy Consciousness. But if Unhappy Consciousness and its essential self-divisiveness is not a passing phase in the development of mankind, but the inescapable existential situation of human life, then there are drastic consequences for understanding the nature and significance of human freedom and action. Out of the novel twist that these thinkers have given to the Hegelian dialectic arises a new perspective on human action.

Unhappy Consciousness

We begin our journey in the *Phenomenology* with the conviction that what is immediately before us is not only the secure foundation of all knowledge, but is also the "richest kind of knowledge." In each of the developing stages of Consciousness, we are initially convinced that we have finally discovered something genuinely other, independent, fixed, and secure. But the culmination of the dialectic of Consciousness reveals that what was taken as "other" than us and truly objective turns out to be nothing but a congealed form of consciousness itself. With this realization, viz., that the subject-object distinction does not apply to consciousness and to something other than consciousness, but to two moments within consciousness we arrive at the stage of Self-consciousness *(Selbstbewusstsein)*.

Underlying the *Phenomenology* is the drive of the self to discover itself, fulfill itself, to actualize its potential freedom, and to know itself. Hegel now describes the ways in which the *self* (as self-consciousness) seeks to achieve this project. The first stage of Self-consciousness, is The Truth of Self-certainty *(Die Wahrheit der Gewissheit seiner selbst)*. We discover here a typical dialectical movement whereby in the very attempt of the self to affirm itself, contradiction and failure emerge. The self at this initial stage of Self-consciousness is represented as pure desire and the self seeks to affirm its autonomy by the gratification of and satiation of its desires. From the internal perspective of this stage, the world is viewed solely as a source of gratification, as existing only for the desiring self. The self seeks to prove itself by "negating" all objects—by taking them as objects for itself, for its own gratification. An excellent concrete representation of the attitude that Hegel is representing here is developed in complete sensuous detail by Kierkegaard in the first half of *Either/Or* where the "aesthetic personality" is intimately and graphically portrayed. The project of A, the anonymous aesthete of *Either/Or* ingeniously seeks to gratify all his sensuous desires. He also seeks to heighten his satisfaction by reflecting on the pleasures of gratification.[1] But as Kierkegaard shows us and Hegel tells us, the project of complete self-sufficient immediate gratification ends in failure and despair. "Desire and the certainty of its self obtained in the gratification of desire, are conditioned by the object; for the certainty exists through cancelling this other; in order that this cancelling may be effected, there must be this other (*Phen.,* p. 225; *p. 139*).[2] The aesthete is caught in a dialectical trap. He seeks to assert his autonomy by cancelling or negating the world, by treating it solely as a source for his gratification. But he comes to the realization that he is not truly autonomous and independent. He is dependent in his essential being as pure desire on the existence of objects which are other than he is and which condition him. He discovers that his form of consciousness is really a dependent consciousness.

The conclusion of the dialectic of Self-certainty where the self has tried and failed to achieve genuine autonomy through gratification of desire is the realization that the self (as self-consciousness) needs to be recognized by another self-consciousness in order to achieve genuine freedom and autonomy. The dialectic of master and slave is introduced at this stage to clarify the dynamics of the "first" encounter between independent self-consciousnesses.

Hegel maintains that each "higher" stage of a dialectical process contains the truth implicit in earlier stages as well as the dynamics of these earlier stages that have been *aufgehoben*. Presumably, we could read the *Phenomenology* backwards, and read out of the final stage all the preceding ones. However, while this relation between earlier and later stages must be true according to Hegel's conception of dialectic, he is not always explicit about the precise way in which a "lower" stage is contained in a "higher" one. In Unhappy Con-

1. S. Kierkegaard, *Either/Or.*
2. Page references to *The Phenomenology of Mind* are included in the text. Page numbers of the English translation are followed by page numbers of the German text.

sciousness, which is the final stage of Self-consciousness, we do have one of the clearest examples of how a later stage encompasses earlier ones. Consequently, it is important that we carefully follow Hegel's dialectic from the primitive stage of Self-consciousness as desire to its culmination as Unhappy Consciousness.

Earlier, we followed in detail the dialectic of master and slave. We now need to pick up the story of the development of Self-consciousness where the dialectic of master and slave ends. The slave, at the very moment when he is most oppressed, when he comes closest to being reduced to mere "thinghood," when the entire content of his natural consciousness has been "tottered and shaken" comes to the realization that he has a "mind of his own," that he is not a mere thing, but an independent consciousness that cannot be reduced to "thinghood" (*Phen.*, pp. 237 ff; *pp. 147 ff*). This is the beginning of his freedom. But it is freedom in a very primitive and abstract mode, a freedom that manifests itself first in the form of consciousness that Hegel calls "Stoicism."

"The essence of this [stoical] consciousness is to be free, on the throne as well as in fetters, throughout all the dependence that attaches to its individual existence, and to maintain that stolid lifeless unconcern which persistently withdraws from the movement of existence, from effective activity as well as from passive endurance, into the simple essentiality of thought" (*Phen.*, p. 249; *p. 153*). The project of stoical consciousness is to acheive its freedom by the attempt to identify itself with the "simple essentiality of thought." Stoical consciousness seeks to remove itself from the trial and contingency of determinate existence and dwell in the abstract, pure realm of thought itself—the realm which is the proper sphere of freedom. Hegel calls this form *(Gestalt)* of consciousness, "Stoicism" because he believes that this conception of freedom "can come on the scene as a general form of the world's spirit only in a time of universal fear and bondage, a time, too, when mental cultivation is universal, and has elevated culture to the level of thought" (*Phen.*, p. 245; *p. 153*). This is an attitude that can be shared by a master (Marcus Aurelius) and a slave (Epictetus). But the more this form of consciousness tries to identify itself with the realm of pure thought, the more manifest becomes its essential failure. "Freedom of thought takes only pure thought as its truth, and this lacks the concrete filling of life. It is, therefore, merely the notion of freedom, not living freedom itself; for it is, to begin with, only thinking in general that is its essence, the form as such, which has turned away from the independence of things and gone back into itself" (*Phen.,* p. 245; *pp. 153-154*). When Hegel makes such a claim, he is speaking from the perspective of the philosophic "we"—what he calls *"für uns"*—who are witnessing and comprehending the dialectical movement of the stages of *Geist*. But we must not forget that each moment of the *Phenomenology* is not only a stage to be grasped externally by us, but is a stage that the *Geist* (and consequently man) has "lived through." Stoical consciousness begins to "crack" when it realizes that it can never succeed in completely denying and ignoring the contingent determinate reality from which it is trying to escape.[3]

However we may assess the relation between Hegel's description of stoical consciousness and actual historical Stoicism (I think the connection is slight), we must admit that he has succeeded in portraying brilliantly a basic mode of consciousness—or in more mundane language—a typical human response to the painful contingency of the world. This is the response that seeks to escape the pain and frustration of the facticity of life by denying its reality, by withdrawing into a realm of pure thought untouched by this contingency. As Hegel so penetratingly sees, this project is self-defeating, for the effort required to try to escape from contingency and to identify oneself with the rarified realm of pure thought implicitly acknowledges the particularity, individuality, and contingency that stoical consciousness finds so offensive.

Emerging out of Stoicism is the form of consciousness that Hegel calls "Skepticism": "*Skepticism* is the realization of that of which Stoicism is merely the notion, and is the actual experience of what freedom of thought is; it is in itself and essentially the negative, and must so exhibit itself" (*Phen.,* p. 246; *pp. 154-155*). (Here too, it is more illuminating to pay close attention to what Hegel says about skeptical consciousness than to think of historical Skepticism.) Hegel describes the transition from Stoicism to Skepticism as follows:

3. It is ironic that many of Hegel's critics, especially Kierkegaard, have accused Hegel of the failure which Hegel himself so incisively describes in "Stoicism." It is a malicious and false criticism of Hegel to claim that he gets lost in the speculative realm of "pure thought," which "lacks the concrete filling of life."

This thinking consciousness, in the way in which it is thus constituted, as abstract freedom, is therefore only in complete negation of otherness. Withdrawn from existence solely into itself, it has not there fully vindicated itself as the absolute negation of this existence. The content is held indeed to be only thought, but is thereby also taken to be determinate thought, and at the same time determinateness as such (*Phen.*, p. 246; *p. 154*).

Skepticism is the mode of consciousness that seeks to deny or negate the "independent existence or permanent determinateness" which has for stoicism "dropped as a matter of fact out of the infinitude of thought." "Thought becomes thinking which wholly annihilates the being of the world with its manifold determinateness, and the negativity of free self-consciousness becomes aware of attaining, in these manifold forms which life assumes, real negativity" (*Phen.*, p. 246; *p. 155*). Hegel does not think of the skeptical consciousness as limited to a philosophical epistemological attitude. It is a way of life, or a basic attitude that pervades all experience. It sets out to prove itself by its versatility in denying or negating anything that it encounters.

Once we penetrate the Hegelian idiom, we can concretely grasp what Hegel is describing. Skeptical consciousness is the representation of negative freedom—a fundamental attitude that many have flirted with, especially in recent times. One becomes aware of one's power and freedom only in the act of denying and negating—freedom is exclusively freedom against something. All institutions, all objects, anything that appears to be permanent, fixed, determinate, must be destroyed. It is anarchy carried to the extreme. This is "the giddy whirl of a perpetually self-creating disorder" (*Phen.*, p. 249; *p. 157*). This attitude too is caught in self-contradiction. The more it succeeds in negating everything that is external to it and even turning against itself and negating any determinate form that such a consciousness takes, the more it succeeds in affirming itself as "universal self-sameness." The point that Hegel is making about the dilemma of skeptical consciousness carried to its extreme is nicely illustrated by Hume when he writes:

When I enter most intimately into what I call *myself,* I always stumble on some particular perception or other, of heat or cold, light or shade, love or hatred, pain or pleasure. I never catch *myself* at any time without a perception, and never can observe anything but a perception.[4]

What is the "I" here that is doing the looking and the perceiving, that remembers that it has never found anything in itself that is not a perception, that can compare and contrast successive perceptions, and that affirms this truth? The more systematically and thoroughly I deny that there is anything fixed or permanent in me, and the more I affirm that I am nothing but an aggregate of "successive perceptions," then, consequently, the more I succeed in affirming that there is "something, I know not what" that is "looking" into myself. This is the type of paradox that skeptical consciousness comes to acknowledge, but it continues to live within this contradiction.

This form of consciousness is, therefore, the aimless fickleness and instability of going to and fro, hither and thither, from one extreme of the self-same self-consciousness, to the other contingent, confused and confusing consciousness. It does not itself bring these two thoughts of itself together. It finds its freedom, at one time, in the form of elevation above all the whirling complexity and all the contingency of mere existence, and again, at another time, likewise confesses to falling back upon what is unessential, and to being taken up with that. It lets the unessential content in its thought vanish; but in that very act it is the consciousness of something unessential. It announces absolute disappearance but the announcement is, and this consciousness is the evanescence expressly announced. It announces the nullity of seeing, hearing, and so on, yet *itself* sees and hears. . . . Its deeds and words belie each other continually . . . (*Phen.*, pp. 249-250; *p. 157*).

Skepticism, like Stoicism, exemplifies what Sartre so aptly calls "bad faith" *(la mauvaise foi)*. In both of these forms of consciousness there is at once a recognition of the failure of the project they have sought to achieve—freedom by escape into pure thought, freedom by escape into an "absolutely fortuitous imbroglio"—and an inability to accept and come to grips with this failure.

Skepticism lives in a self-contradictory condition, but it is not yet fully self-conscious that *this* is its condition. "Its talk, in fact, is like a squabble among self-willed children, one of whom says A when the other says B, and again B, when the other says A, and who, through being in contradiction with themselves, procure the joy of remaining in contradiction with one another" (*Phen.*, p. 250; *p. 158*).

4. *A Treatise of Human Nature*, p. 252.

Unhappy Consciousness arises when there is a movement toward becoming *aware* of the contradictory condition that characterizes Skepticism. More generally, we become painfully aware of the essential self-contradictoriness of all the stages of Self-consciousness. Even the condition which was divided into two individual self-consciousnesses in the dialectic of master and slave is now internalized in a *single* self-consciousness. Unhappy Consciousness arises when an individual is fully aware of himself as a contradictory being. It is "the Alienated Soul which is the consciousness of self as a divided nature, a doubled and merely contradictory being" (*Phen.*, p. 251; *p. 158*).

In each stage of Self-consciousness—Desire, Lordship and Bondage, Stoicism, and Skepticism—*we,* the observers of this development, have been aware of failure and internal contradiction. We have witnessed the "highway of despair." All of these stages have been attempts by the self to fulfill itself and assert its own autonomy, and each of these ends in failure. But in Unhappy Consciousness, the self that experiences this dialectic is itself aware of its own inner diremption and failure. All the stages of Self-consciousness are now replayed in Unhappy Consciousness, but they are replayed with a significant difference. Unhappy Consciousness—or the individual experiencing this form of consciousness—is now itself self-conscious of what we have been witnessing from the outside—that it is an alienated soul.

This unhappy consciousness, divided and at variance within itself, must, because this contradiction of its essential nature is felt to be a single consciousness, always have in the one consciousness the other also: and thus must be straightaway driven out of each in turn, when it thinks it has therein attained to the victory and the rest of unity. . . . It is itself the gazing of one self-consciousness into another, and itself is both, and the unity of both is also its own essence; but objectively and consciously it is not yet this essence itself—is not yet the unity of both (*Phen.*, p. 251; *pp. 158-159*).

This is the epitome of what Hegel means by alienation. Alienation is not simply a splitting apart, a duplicity, or even an awareness that something is hostile and alien to us. It is the awareness by a single consciousness, or an undivided consciousness that it itself consists of two opposing, contradictory "selves." Both of these are essentially what the alienated soul is. While it desparately seeks to harmonize, reconcile, synthesize (*aufheben*) this inner duplicity, the self in its alienated condition has not yet succeeded in overcoming its own inner contradiction. This "not yet" is all important. For Hegel and Marx, this "not yet" signifies only a stage, a transition in the development of *Geist* (Hegel), or in revolutionary *praxis* (Marx). But for Kierkegaard and Sartre, it is a fraud to think that this "not yet" can be *aufgehoben*. For them, this "not yet" signifies the ontological chasm that characterizes human existence and demands decisive action.

The dialectic of Unhappy Consciousness is described in great detail by Hegel and his argument is extremely complicated. (This section is about as long as the four preceding sections of Self-consciousness.) Although Hegel doesn't explicitly mention Christianity, he cannot resist the temptation to make various allusions to different aspects of Christian consciousness. The wealth of detail in this section can divert us from appreciating its essential content. As in the sections on Lordship and Bondage, Stoicism, and Skepticism, Hegel's historical allusions are of incidental value. In the *Phenomenology,* Hegel is not primarily concerned with doing justice to actual historical movements. Hegel uses historical material heuristically in order to illustrate the developing forms of consciousness. The insights gained from the description of each of these stages transcend actual historical movements. Unhappy Consciousness does describe an attitude that has been illustrated in Christianity, but Unhappy Consciousness can also assume secular forms. These points need to be emphasized in order to distinguish what is incidental in this section (the allusions to God as Judge, Christ, and the Religious Communion) from what is essential—the dialectical movement of an alienated consciousness which is self-conscious of its own inner duplicity.

The general structure of Unhappy Consciousness is that of a single consciousness that is aware of itself as being both unchangeable or universal and radically contingent or particular. Hegel describes three ways in which Unhappy Consciousness seeks to overcome this internal opposition: Unhappy Consciousness seeks to negate itself as particular and contingent; it negates itself as unchangeable; and finally it attempts to harmonize this opposition by "discovering" the unchangeable in the form of its particularity.

Here, then, there is a struggle against an enemy, victory over whom really means being worsted, where to have attained one result is really to lose it in the opposite. Consciousness of life, of its existence and action, is merely pain and sorrow over this existence and activity; for therein consciousness finds only consciousness of its opposite as its essence—and of its own nothingness. Elevating itself beyond this, it passes to the unchangeable. But this elevation is itself this same consciousness. It is, therefore, immediately consciousness of the opposite, viz., of itself as single, individual, particular. The unchangeable, which comes to consciousness, is in that very fact at the same time affected by particularity, and is only present with this latter. Instead of particularity having been abolished in the consciousness of immutability, it only continues to appear there still (*Phen.*, pp. 252-253; *pp. 159-160*).

The above passage describes the first two major movements by Unhappy Consciousness in the attempt to confront its self-divisiveness—attempts which unsuccessfully seek to negate one moment of this tension. In the very process of carrying through this negation, Unhappy Consciousness succeeds in affirming or recognizing what it seeks to deny. The result of this struggle is an intensified awareness that Unhappy Conciousness is both unchangeable and radically contingent. We now struggle to reconcile the internal oppositions not by denying one moment of this opposition, but by finding some way of positively joining and reconciling our particularity and universality.

We seek to preserve the "truth" of Stoicism which affirms the reality of pure universal thought and "turns away from particulars altogether," as well as the "truth" of Skepticism which has culminated in mere "particularity in the sense of aimless contradiction and the restless process of contradictory thought" (*Phen.*, p. 256; *p. 163*). Unhappy Consciousness has therefore gone beyond both these stages for

it brings and keeps together pure thought and particular existence, but has not yet risen to that level of thinking where the particularity of consciousness is harmoniously reconciled with pure thought itself. It rather stands midway, at the point where abstract thought comes in contact with the particularity of consciousness *qua* particularity. Itself *is* this act of contact; it is the union of pure thought and individuality; and this thinking individuality of pure thought exists as object for it, and the unchangeable is essentially itself an individual existence. But that this

its object, the unchangeable, which assumes essentially the form of particularity, is *its own self*, the self which is particularity of consciousness
—this is *not* established *for it* (*Phen.*, pp. 256-257; *p. 163*).

Despite Hegel's seemingly "abstract" language here, he is describing a form of suffering consciousness that has been central to Western thought in both its religious and secular manifestations. It is this
desperate attempt to reconcile, to overcome the condition of the
alienated self that Kierkegaard calls "Sickness unto Death," and
Kierkegaard's book of the same title is a commentary on the devious
ways in which the self seeks to effect such a reconciliation of its
inner oppositions, attempts which end only in despair. And when
Sartre examines the varieties of "bad faith," we discover how consciousness unsuccessfully seeks to deceive itself into thinking that
it has effected a successful synthesis of itself.

Hegel's own description of the ways in which Unhappy Consciousness struggles with itself "hints" at the reconciliation which
is, eventually, to be achieved. In the last sentence of this section, he
declares that in the course of the various attitudes of Unhappy Consciousness "has arisen the idea of Reason, of the certainty that consciousness is, in its particularity, inherently and essentially absolute,
or is all reality" (*Phen.*, p. 267; *p. 171*). Presumably, it is through
the mediation of Reason that the internal opposition that the self
so deeply experiences in Unhappy Consciousness will be *aufgehoben*.

The transition that Hegel now makes from Self-consciousness to
Reason is one that is so vital for the *Phenomenology* and for grasping Hegel's conception of the nature and role of Reason, that it is
worth quoting in its entirety.

With the thought which consciousness has laid hold of, that the individual consciousness is inherently absolute reality, consciousness turns
back into itself. In the case of the unhappy consciousness, the inherent
and essential reality is a "beyond" remote from itself. But the process of
its own activity has in its case brought out the truth that individuality,
when completely developed, individuality which is a concrete actual
mode of consciousness, is made the negative of itself, i.e., the objective
extreme;—in other words, has forced it to make explicit its self-existence,
and turned this into an objective fact. In this process it has itself become
aware, too, of its unity with the universal, a unity which, seeing that the
individual when sublated is the universal, is no longer looked on *by us*
as falling outside it, and which, since consciousness maintains itself in

this its negative condition, is inherently in it as such its very essence. Its truth is what appears in the process of synthesis—where the extremes were seen to be absolutely held apart—as the middle term, proclaiming to the unchangeable consciousness that the isolated individual has renounced itself, and to the individual consciousness that the unchangeable consciousness is no longer for it an extreme, but is one with it and reconciled to it. This mediating term is the unity directly aware of both, and relating them to one another; and the consciousness of their unity, which it proclaims to consciousness and thereby to itself, is the certainty and assurance of being all truth.

From the fact that self-consciousness is Reason, its hitherto negative attitude towards otherness turns round into a positive attitude. So far it has been concerned merely with its independence and freedom: it has sought to save and keep itself for itself at the expense of the world or its own actuality, both of which appeared to it to involve the denial of its own essential nature. But *qua* reason, assured of itself, it is at peace so far as they are concerned, and is able to endure them; for it is certain its self is reality, certain that all concrete actuality is nothing else but it. Its thought is itself *eo ipso* concrete reality; its attitude towards the latter is thus that of *Idealism*. To it, looking at itself in this way, it seems as if now, for the first time, the world had come into being. Formerly, it did not understand the world, it desired the world and worked upon it; then withdrew itself from it and retired into itself, abolished the world so far as itself was concerned, and abolished itself *qua* consciousness—both the consciousness of that world as essentially real, as well as the consciousness of its nothingness and unreality. Here, for the first time, after the grave of its truth is lost, after the annihilation of its concrete actuality is itself done away with, and the individuality of consciousness is seen to be in itself absolute reality, it discovers the world as its own new and real world, which in its permanence possesses an interest for it, just as previously the interest lay only in its transitoriness. The subsistence of the world is taken to mean the actual presence of its own truth; it is certain of finding only itself there.

Reason is the conscious certainty of being all reality. This is how Idealism expresses the principle of Reason (*Phen.*, pp. 272-273; *pp. 175-176*).

Hegel's unbounded optimism breathes through the heaviness of this passage. All the struggles of Consciousness and Self-conciousness —from Sense Certainty to Unhappy Consciousness—have contributed toward bringing to light this revelation that "Reason is the conscious certainty of being all reality." We have arrived at that point announced in the more famous passage of the *Philosophy of Right: "What is rational is actual and what is actual is rational."* [*Was vernünftig ist, das ist wirklich; und was wirklich ist, das ist vernünftig.*][5] From this point on, *Geist* is certain of itself as Reason —Reason which is all embracing—and *Geist* now turns its attention to proving this truth to itself, to making this "abstract" truth concrete, and thereby bringing us to ever higher stages of spiritual self-development. Hegel's Idealism—the principle that what is rational is actual and what is actual is rational—is now manifest.

It is here that Kierkegaard and Sartre protest: the transition described above is fraudulent.

If Hegel is wrong here then one must rethink basic categories to see how and why he is wrong, why man never gets "beyond" Unhappy Consciousness, how the mediation of Reason which is the copingstone of Hegel's philosophy is nothing but a grand illusion. If we cannot get "beyond" Unhappy Consciousness, then we must authentically confront the challenge that this situation presents for living one's life as an existing individual—an individual whose inescapable human condition is to be alienated. When this challenge is met, then, consciousness, existence, and action become all important in ways that Hegel (so Kierkegaard and Sartre claim) never really understood.

Kierkegaard: "The Poetry of Inwardness"[6]

Any attempt at reading and interpreting Kierkegaard is fraught with dangers and traps. Kierkegaard is a supreme ironist, equaled only by that other great ironist whom he so deeply admired, Socrates. Many of the works that have served as the basis for understanding Kierkegaard were published under pseudonyms. A close reading of these

5. *Hegel's Philosophy of Right*, p. 10; *Grundlinien der Philosophie des Rechts*, p. 14.

6. The expression, "The Poetry of Inwardness" is taken from Louis Mackey's article with this title in *Existential Philosophers: Kierkegaard to Merleau-Ponty*, ed. by George Alfred Schrader, Jr. I am primarily concerned with Kierkegaard's reflections as they bear on the nature of human action, but Mackey's eloquent interpretation of Kierkegaard is the best general introduction to the range of Kierkegaard's thought. I want to acknowledge my great debt to Mackey's writings on Kierkegaard. See also his "Kierkegaard

works reveals that the pseudonymous authors play different roles in different works. If we are not to be misled, we must pay close attention to what is being said, who is saying it, and what is the relation between the poetic character created and Kierkegaard himself. It is disastrous to think that the pseudonymous works are direct vehicles by which Kierkegaard expresses his ideas.

There is another distracting presupposition that affects Kierkegaardian scholarship. Frequently, there is an implicit assumption that through the various masks, one can discover the secret or key to Kierkegaard's real beliefs—beliefs which, with care and caution, can be expressed in propositions. But Kierkegaard himself warns against reading him in this way—one of the dramatic effects of his writings is to challenge this typical mode of understanding. Even thinking of Kierkegaard as a philosopher, or as expressing a philosophic outlook can mislead us, although Kierkegaard certainly *uses* philosophy and dialectical argument. If we think of philosophy as a discipline that is committed to articulating an objective truth—no matter how remote this may be from common sense or ordinary beliefs—and that the primary function of philosophy is to explicate and defend this objective truth, then Kierkegaard's main preoccupation was *not* philosophical. While he doesn't deny that there is objective truth— he insists upon it—he seeks to understand the role that it plays in human life. He shows how the "lure" of objective truth can be a temptation which blinds us to the realization of what it is to be an existing individual. Kierkegaard uses philosophic devices along with a variety of poetic devices to show us what he is talking about. The phrase "what he is talking about" can also be a trap, for Kierkegaard is constantly trying to force us—his individual readers—and to force himself to face up to the painful existential dilemmas that confront every one of us as unique individuals.

In the *Tractatus,* Wittgenstein draws a sharp, unbridgeable gap

---

and the Problem of Existential Philosophy," *The Review of Metaphysics* 9 (March, June, 1956). Although Josiah Thompson's approach to Kierkegaard's pseudonymous writings is quite different from that of Mackey's, and at points in conflict with it, I have also benefited from his extremely sensitive analysis. Although I suspect they would disagree with my interpretation, I think both Mackey and Thompson contribute to an acute awareness of how Kierkegaard's life and works exemplify the dialectic of Unhappy Consciousness. See Josiah Thompson, *The Lonely Labyrinth: Kierkegaard's Pseudonymous Works.*

between what can be said and what can be shown. What can be shown cannot, strictly speaking, be said. Kierkegaard would have been sympathetic with this distinction and his comments on "indirect communication" and "double reflection" (*C.U.P.*, pp. 67 ff.)[7] reveal an awareness of this chasm—and of the problem of using language to say what cannot be said, but can be only directly and intimately encountered.

We suspect, when someone speaks or writes in this way, that he is playing games with us, and that if we are careful and clever enough we can *say* what the author takes to be ineffable. We might try to sum up Kierkegaard's outlook by claiming, as many have done (following Johannes Climacus, the pseudonymous author of the *Concluding Unscientific Postscript*), that "Truth is Subjectivity," or "Truth is Inwardness." But Kierkegaard himself was acutely sensitive to this temptation—a temptation which has seduced many existential philosophers who have sought to build a "new" philosophy on Kierkegaard's (especially Climacus') claims.

Suppose that someone wished to communicate the following conviction: Truth is inwardness; there is no objective truth, but the truth consists in personal appropriation. Suppose him to display great zeal and enthusiasm for the propagation of this truth, since if people could only be made to listen to it they would of course be saved; suppose he announced it on all possible occasions, and succeeded in moving not only those who perspire easily, but also hard-boiled temperaments: what then? Why then, there would doubtless be found a few laborers, who had hitherto stood idle in the market-place, and only after hearing this call went to work in the vineyard—engaging themselves to proclaim this doctrine to all. And then what? Then he would have contradicted himself still further, as he had contradicted himself from the beginning; for the zeal and enthusiasm which he directed toward the end of getting it said and heard, was itself a misunderstanding. The matter of prime importance was, of course, that he should be understood; the inwardness of the understanding would consist precisely in each individual coming to understand it by himself. Now he had even succeeded in obtaining town criers of inwardness, and a town crier of inwardness is quite a remarkable species of animal. Really to communicate such a conviction would require both art and self-control: self-control to understand in-

7. Page references to the *Concluding Unscientific Postscript* are included in the text.

wardly that the God-relationship of the individual man is the thing of prime importance, and that the busy intermeddling of third parties constitutes lack of inwardness, and an excess of amiable stupidity; art enough to vary inexhaustibly the doubly reflected form of the communication, just as the inwardness itself is inexhaustible (*C.U.P.*, pp. 71-72).

This passage, put into the mouth of Johannes Climacus (who does not himself fully understand what he is saying) provides a clue about how we are to read and understand Kierkegaard. If "inwardness" which is itself inexhaustible is the focus of our concern, then what is required is a form of *art* that can illuminate and point us towards this inwardness. "The greater the artistry, the greater the inwardness" (*C.U.P.*, p. 72). The variety of Kierkegaard's writings and the multifarious devices and techniques he uses are sketches toward an art form. Its essential aim is to reveal what is at once hidden from us and yet always before us—our own inwardness. Louis Mackey's apt expression, "The poetry of inwardness" captures what is distinctive about Kierkegaard's writings.

Kierkegaard's poetic is a rhetoric designed to coerce its reader to freedom. By the impassioned detachment with which it marshals the resources of spirit, it lays on him the necessity to act and deprives him of any warrant for action except his own freedom. The Kierkegaardian corpus can neither be "believed" nor "followed": it is and was meant to be—poetically—the impetus, the occasion, and the demand for the reader's own advance to selfhood and to a solitary meeting with the divine. Not by exhorting him to this or that line of conduct, not by offering him the chance to let knowledge or admiration go proxy for decision, but by vividly summoning before him the richness and the risk ingredient in his freedom. Kierkegaard's works impart to "that individual" who is their true reader the opportunity and the need of achieving himself in the sight of God.[8]

If we read Kierkegaard's works in this manner as "the poetry of inwardness" which "drive their reader through the calm of contemplation into the passion of personal appropriation,"[9] we must nevertheless try to grasp (no matter how approximately) what Kierkegaard means by "freedom," "inwardness," "selfhood,"

8. "The Poetry of Inwardness," loc. cit., p. 105.
9. "The Poetry of Inwardness," loc. cit., p. 105.

"risk,"—in sum, what it means to be an "existing individual" and its consequences for understanding human action. To do this, we will use some of the philosophic discussions that appear in his works, but with the warning that these must be taken tentatively and with a touch of irony.

The Confrontation with Hegel[10]

The first part of *Sickness Unto Death: A Christian Psychological Exposition for Edification and Awakening* (published under the pseudonym, Anti-Climacus and "edited" by S. Kierkegaard) begins with a passage that comes close to being a parody of Hegel.

> Man is spirit. But what is spirit? Spirit is the self. But what is the self? The self is a relation which relates itself to its own self, or it is that in the relation [which accounts for it] that the relation relates itself to its own self; the self is not the relation but [consists in the fact] that the relation relates itself to its own self. Man is a synthesis of the infinite and the finite, of the temporal and the eternal, of freedom and necessity, in short it is a synthesis. A synthesis is a relation between two factors. So regarded, man is not yet a self.[11]

After continuing with dialectical twists and turns of this formula, Anti-Climacus concludes:

> The disrelationship of despair is not a simple disrelationship but a disrelationship in a relation which relates itself to its own self and is constituted by another, so that the disrelationship in that self-relation reflects itself infinitely in the relation to the Power which constituted it.
>
> This then is the formula which describes the condition of the self when despair is completely eradicated; by relating itself to its own self

10. I want to reiterate what I have already suggested. In approaching Kierkegaard from the perspective of Hegel I am *not* claiming that Kierkegaard explicitly began his reflections with a criticism of Hegel's philosophy, nor am I *endorsing* Kierkegaard's criticism and parody of Hegel. Rather I think that approaching Kierkegaard in this manner enables us to get to the heart of his thought, especially his conception of action as inwardness. We know that the primary object of Kierkegaard's polemical remarks was the Danish Hegelians, rather than Hegel himself. For a discussion of Kierkegaard and the Hegelians see Niels Thulstrup, *Kierkegaards forhold til Hegel og til den speculative idealisme intil 1846* (Copenhagen: Gyldendal, 1967). I am indebted to Josiah Thompson for telling me about this discussion.

11. *The Sickness unto Death,* trans. by Walter Lowrie, p. 146.

and by willing to be itself the self is grounded transparently in the Power which posited it.[12]

A reader encountering these passages for the first time could hardly resist thinking that they are sheer gibberish. Anti-Climacus certainly doesn't go on to give us a philosophic explication of what he means. Instead we proceed to a discussion of despair and sin, their universality, and the various forms they can assume.

But Kierkegaard's own readers could hardly have missed the Hegelian overtones of these passages. A "good" Hegelian might even have accused Anti-Climacus of plagiarizing from Hegel, for these passages are remarkably close to Hegel's own style in Unhappy Consciousness. After all, it is Hegel who tells us that man is spirit, and that the spirit is the self. But the self, in the course of its development, is dirempted, split apart from itself, alienated. In Unhappy Consciousness we have discovered a stage of self-consciousness in which the self is aware of its own inner contradictoriness. We cannot fully identify the self with the "self" that is aware of this duplicity, nor can we identify it with either of the two "selves" that constitute this duplicity—"the self is not the relation but [consists in the fact] that the relation relates itself to its own self." Man or the self is, therefore, only potentially a synthesis of the infinite and the finite, of the eternal and the temporal, of freedom and necessity. Man is not yet a fully developed or actual self. Our Hegelian commentator might go on to point out that it was Hegel and not Anti-Climacus or Kierkegaard who first pointed out that the self in its alienated condition suffers a variety of forms of despair. The *coup de grâce* of his *explication de texte* would be that Anti-Climacus, like Hegel before him, recognizes that the very formula for understanding the structure of despair, suggests a stage beyond "when despair is completely eradicated."

But if our Hegelian commentator reads further, he will be disturbed at what he discovers. Instead of finding the transition, the movement beyond despair, the indication that Reason arises to mediate the self's alienation, he discovers that Anti-Climacus is obsessed with Unhappy Consciousness and the varieties of despair. We never seem to get "beyond" despair. Instead of showing us how to overcome the despair resulting from the self's alienated condition,

12. *The Sickness unto Death,* p. 147.

the synthesis of the self as infinite and finite, eternal and temporal, freedom and necessity becomes more and more impossible. If the Hegelian peeks at the last page of the book in the hope of finding some sign of the coming of Reason, he may be jolted when Anti-Climacus declares the opposition of sin and faith, and concludes by saying, "this opposition is affirmed in the whole of this work, which straightway in the first section . . . constructed the formula for the situation where no offence at all is to be found: 'By relating itself to its own self and by willing to be itself, the self is grounded transparently in the Power which constituted it.' And this formula again, as has often been noted, is the definition of faith."[13]

Still, a Hegelian, intent upon reading Kierkegaard in terms of Hegelian categories might gloss over this "conclusion." Anti-Climacus has simply neglected to emphasize the mediating role of Reason in overcoming the alienation of the self and in effecting a genuine synthesis. Since Hegel has already demonstrated the ultimate harmony and compatibility of Reason and Faith, we need only give Reason its proper due to arrive at a "correct" reading of what Anti-Climacus and Kierkegaard are saying. But this "happy resolution" is a bit too easy. Faith and Reason are not so easily reconciled. Faith turns out not to be a form of knowledge and not an act of will. Faith is a miracle; it is paradoxical and has the Absolute Paradox as its Object. Faith stands in radical opposition and is an offense to Reason.

What might disturb a perceptive Hegelian—one who is not so blinded by his own categories that he fails to see anything but Hegel's reflection—is not the highly polemical attacks and caricatures of Hegel that one discovers in almost every work by Kierkegaard, but something much more profound. Kierkegaard, or rather the pseudonymous authors such as Anti-Climacus and Johannes Climacus, seem to be starting with concepts and categories that are similar to Hegel's starting points and yet end up—like *Sickness unto Death*—with very different "conclusions"; conclusions that are the dialectical opposites of Hegel's. Something seems to have gone desperately wrong. The Hegelian may begin to suspect that he is the victim of a malicious parody.

Consider another place where Hegelian dialectic seems to take a

13. *The Sickness unto Death*, p. 262.

perverse turn. In the "Interlude" of the *Philosophical Fragments,* Johannes Climacus analyzes the relations among the three modalities: possibility, actuality, and necessity. An Hegelian knows how important and central these categories are and may at first welcome Johannes Climacus' appreciation of their centrality. Climacus asks, "Can the necessary come into existence?" Coming into existence is a change, but the necessary by its very nature is that which is unchangeable, which *is;* it cannot suffer change. Since all coming into existence is suffering a change, the necessary cannot, therefore, come into existence. "Everything which comes into existence proves precisely by coming into existence that it is not necessary, for the only thing which cannot come into existence is the necessary, because the necessary *is.*"[14] Climacus asks again, "Is not necessity then a synthesis of possibility and actuality? What could this mean? Possibility and actuality do not differ in essence but in being; how could there from this difference be formed a synthesis constituting necessity, which is not a determination of being but a determination of essence, since it is the essence of the necessary to be?"[15]

To elucidate Climacus' meaning, consider such a possibility as a plan to marry. There is all the difference in the world between such a plan as a possibility and as an actuality—actual wedlock. But the difference is not one of *essence,* it is a difference in *being;* both the possibility and the actuality share the same essence. If there were a difference of essence, it would not make sense to say that the possibility of marriage had now been realized or actualized. The essence of the possibility and that of the actuality are identical. A possibility has come into existence; "the change involved in coming into existence is actuality. . . ."[16]

But can we say that necessity is a synthesis of possibility and actuality? This is absurd. What distinguishes a specific possibility from its actualization is its "coming into existence," but the necessary can never (by its very nature) come into existence. Climacus calls the transition from possibility to actuality "freedom," and tells us that "all coming into existence takes place with freedom, not by necessity. Nothing comes into existence by virtue of a logical ground,

14. *Philosophical Fragments,* trans. by David F. Swenson, 2nd ed., p. 91.
15. *Philosophical Fragments,* pp. 91-92.
16. *Philosophical Fragments,* p. 93.

but only by a cause. Every cause terminates in a freely effecting cause."[17]

All this may seem like a fanciful playing with "abstract categories" (and in a certain sense it is), but we will see that it has dramatic, concrete, practical consequences for understanding what it is to be an existing human being, especially when it is compared with Hegel's treatment of the modalities.

Hegel makes a similar point in his *Logic* about the similarity and difference between possibility and actuality; they do not differ in their essential nature. Hegel notes that "our picture-thought is at first disposed to see in possibility the richer and more comprehensive, in actuality the poorer and narrower category. Everything, it is said, is possible, but everything which is possible is not on that account actual. In real truth, however, if we deal with them as thoughts, actuality is the more comprehensive, because it is the concrete thought which includes possibility as an abstract element."[18] So far, Climacus and Hegel seem to be in basic agreement; both insist upon the identity of structure or essence between possibility and actuality; and both agree that actuality is the richer and more comprehensive category in the sense that it "contains" the relevant possibility, but actuality is something "more" than a mere possibility. But now there is a sharp divergence. Hegel goes on to claim that "if all the conditions are at hand, the fact (event) *must* be actual; and the fact itself is one of the conditions. . . . Developed actuality, as the coincident alternation of inner and outer, the alternation of their opposite motions combined into a single motion, is Necessity."[19] According to Hegel, necessity is precisely the union of possibility and actuality; it *is* the transition itself from possibility to actuality. We have arrived at contradictory conclusions from what appeared to be similar starting points.

What Hegel takes to be the quintessence of *Geist*, of Reason concretely realizing itself—the *necessary* transition from possibility to actuality—is according to Climacus, impossible and absurd. Once again, something seems to have gone desperately wrong. Our hypothetical Hegelian interpreter of Kierkegaard has been "taken in."

17. *Philosophical Fragments*, p. 93.
18. Hegel's *Logic*, p. 261; Hegel, *Werke*, Bd. VI, p. 285.
19. Hegel's *Logic*, p. 267; Hegel, *Werke*, Bd. VI, p. 292.

Neither Johannes Climacus nor Anti-Climacus reflect Hegel's thought—they are personifications of the Anti-Hegel! Hegel's profoundest "insight" has been parodied. The union and reconciliation of freedom and necessity, the infinite and the finite, the universal and the particular—a mediation which is the work of *Reason*—is exactly the way in which Johannes Climacus characterizes the Absurd, the Absolute Paradox. Climacus' discussion of the Absolute Paradox is like a Black Mass where everything is at once the same and the opposite. For the Absolute Paradox, the eternal becoming temporal, or the infinite becoming finite—that most absurd and logically contradictory thought which offends Reason—is precisely what Hegel has taken to be the distinctive character of Reason.

If we return to the passage that we cited earlier where Hegel describes the transition beyond Unhappy Consciousness, we can draw together the threads of Climacus' own whimsical use of dialectic. It is not the "idea of Reason" that emerges from the dialectic of Unhappy Consciousness, an idea that promises a rational mediation of the self-alienation that is so deeply experienced by Unhappy Consciousness, but rather the idea of the utter impossibility of any rational mediation of this alienated condition. The dialectic of Unhappy Consciousness leads us to the threshold of The Absolute Paradox.

But what do these reversals, these parodies of Hegelian dialectic portend? What is the suggested alternative to which we are being directed? To speak of a suggested alternative is perfectly appropriate because Johannes Climacus does not directly *argue* for an alternative position. He suggests it, offers it as a *possibility,* speaks in the language of "what if. . . ." The more closely we attend to this hypothetic mode of speech, the more we understand that Kierkegaard in the guise of his various created "authors" is not presenting us with a philosophy in any traditional sense, but "vividly summoning before [us] the richness and the risk ingredient in [our] freedom."[20] Parody, specifically parody of the Hegelians, is one of Kierkegaard's sharpest weapons in this task.

20. "The Poetry of Inwardness," loc. cit., p. 105.

Existence

In the *Concluding Unscientific Postscript,* Johannes Climacus declares:

> Two ways, in general, are open for an existing individual: *Either* he can do his utmost to forget that he is an existing individual, by which he becomes a comic figure, since existence has the remarkable trait of compelling an existing individual to exist whether he wills it or not. (The comical contradiction in willing to be what one is not, as when a man wills to be a bird, is not more comical than the contradiction of not willing to be what one is, as *in casu* an existing individual; just as the language finds it comical that a man forgets his name, which does not so much mean forgetting a designation, as it means forgetting the distinctive essence of one's being.) *Or* he can concentrate his entire energy upon the fact that he is an existing individual. It is from this side, in the first instance, that objection must be made to modern philosophy; not that it has a mistaken presupposition, but that it has a comical presupposition, occasioned by its having forgotten, in a sort of world-historical absent-mindedness, what it means to be a human being. Not indeed, what it means to be a human being in general; for this is the sort of thing that one might even induce a speculative philosopher to agree to; but what it means that you and I and he are human beings, each one for himself (*C.U.P.,* p. 109).

Why is the first alternative "comical"? What is the "comical presupposition" that it makes? The clue to understanding this charge is to be found in Climacus' reflections on possibility, actuality and necessity in the *Philosophical Fragments.* Climacus claims that while possibility and actuality do not differ in essence, there is a radical difference in being—a difference only palely indicated by saying that a possibility has "come into existence." But existence is that mode of being which is incommensurate with any thought, with anything universal, with anything abstract. Existence is not something that we can prove (not God's existence or even my own existence). We reason *from* existence, not *to* existence. Existence can never be *aufgehoben* by thought and reason.

Let us see how much Climacus takes from Hegel and how much he rejects. Hegel's idealism, the principle announced at the conclusion of Unhappy Consciousness, seeks to establish that thought and being are ultimately identical, that the actual is rational and the rational is actual. When *Geist* is fully actualized, the essence and existence of *Geist* are identical. Hegel's system, insofar as it purports to be a demonstration of the actuality of *Geist,* is a grand ontological argument. The essence of *Geist* (as God) necessitates its own existence. Insofar as the essence of man is *Geist,* there is also an ultimate unity and harmony of man's essence and his existence. In the course of arguing to this grand conclusion, indeed in the very first chapter of *Phenomenology*, Hegel argues that although we (as the form of consciousness of sense certainty) may *think* we are directly grasping or encountering what exists in its particularity and uniqueness, in truth, we only grasp and know what is universal. Climacus agrees with this claim about the object of a knowing consciousness. But at this initial point, Hegel ridicules those who want to claim that there is something left over, some surd, some irreducible existential element that is not captured by the categories of thought, but which nevertheless has authentic reality. "If they really wanted to *say* this bit of paper which they 'mean,' and they wanted to *say* so, that is impossible, because the This of sense, which is 'meant,' cannot be reached by language, which belongs to consciousness, i.e., to what is inherently universal. In the very attempt to say it, it would, therefore, crumble in their hands. . . . Consequently what is called unspeakable is nothing else than what is untrue, irrational, something barely and simply 'meant' " (*Phen.,* pp. 159-160; *p. 88*). Climacus does not really disagree with Hegel here, but he gives a slight twist that makes all the difference in the world. It is true that existence *per se,* whether the existence of "this bit of paper" or my own existence, eludes the categories of thought and language—categories which are essentially universal. It is also true that existence *per se* is "unspeakable." But this does *not* mean that it is nothing! Existence is that mode of being which is at once beyond and presupposed by all understanding, abstraction, thought, and language. This is what Hegel, the Hegelians, and modern philosophers have forgotten. Hegel's dialectic moves only in the realm of thought and language. As a dialectic of thought it is unimpeachable. But Hegel's grand mistake, or rather, his comical presupposition, is that he forgets that he himself is an existing individual who can never succeed in identifying himself with pure thought. In its infatuation with the world-historical, the universal, and reason, modern philosophy forgets this "small point." It is this "small point" that hangs and condemns modern philosophy which has done its utmost to "forget" that we are existing individuals. All of Kierkegaard's writings are ultimately directed toward shaking us out of our "forgetfulness" and directing us toward the consequences to be confronted when we confront our own existence. Hegel's philosophy then, is a comedy because it forgets what it is to be a human being, it forgets that it is not merely a very difficult task for an existing human being to identify himself with the results of speculative philosophy and with pure Reason— it is impossible.

But even if existence in itself is ineffable, it is not yet clear what Climacus intends by the concept of existence. As in the endeavor of negative theology, we can best approximate what existence means by becoming clearer about what it is not. Climacus is not primarily interested in developing a general metaphysics, but in understanding existence as it pertains to an existing human being. Existence is not a static, fixed character of something. If it were, then there would be no reason why existence could not be fully grasped by language and thought. The world in which we live is characterized neither by a realm of static pure possibilities nor by an unchangeable necessity. It is a world in which possibilities are constantly becoming actual, in which time is real, and is consequently a world in which there is genuine becoming—"coming into existence." This transition, this becoming "takes place with freedom," a freedom that excludes all necessity.

But surely, there is necessity in history. What has happened has happened, and cannot be undone; it does not admit of change. Here too a cardinal Hegelian doctrine is being called into question, for the aim of philosophy as the System is to show the inner necessity of historical development of *Geist*. Climacus' point is that Hegel is confusing the immutability of the past with the immutability of necessity. Looking backwards, there is, of course, no change that *now* takes place in the past. The past itself has "come into existence," and "coming into existence is the change of actuality brought about by freedom."[21] The historical, whether past, present, or future, is properly the realm of becoming, of "coming into existence," and as such it is the realm of freedom, not necessity.

21. *Philosophical Fragments,* p. 96.

These reflections are abstract, and if we are to penetrate further, we must try to understand what it means for a human being to exist. A human being is not just an existing entity like a stone. A human being is distinguished by the fact that he has consciousness; he can think, he can imagine and project possibilities for himself. Man is an existing *spiritual* being. But as a thinking being, the content of what he thinks is abstract and universal. Even when he tries to think of himself as an individual existing being, he is confronted (as Hegel has shown) with what is universal. He may *mean* to think about his unique existence, but he cannot do it because of the very nature of his consciousness. The "divine nature" of language and thought betrays him "directly turning the mere 'meaning' right round about . . . " (*Phen.*, p. 160; *p. 89*).

The paradox of being a man is expressed by saying that he is an existing spiritual being. As spirit, he is a thinking being capable of abstract thought, and even capable of striving to comprehend the eternal. But as an individual existing being, he can never completely identify himself with the intent or content of his thought. He may try to do this, but the results are comical (and sometimes tragic), because he is trying to escape from what is inescapable, his unique existence, "for existence has the remarkable trait of compelling an existing individual to exist whether he wills it or not." Louis Mackey has succinctly summed up the results of Climacus' dialectical exercises:

the relation of thought and being, in the sense of the objective idea and the realm of essence, is a simple identity. But the relation of actual thinking and actual existence to essential being and the objective idea is a problem. It is a problem which cannot be solved in terms of objective ideas and essences, since as Kierkegaard [Climacus] perceives, it does not even arise at this level. . . . The problem of the relationship between two distinct modes of being cannot even be formulated, much less settled, by a thinking which operates solely in terms of one of the modes involved. Kierkegaard's [Climacus'] metaphysical opposition to Hegel is just this, that he "explained" existence in terms of pure thought—the dialectic of mediation and reconciliation—when the real problem lay elsewhere. The Hegelian explanation of existence is in reality a suppression of existence, and his answer to the problem of the relation of thought and being is a pseudo-answer to a pseudo-problem. The real question for a philosopher is not, How is the eternal truth to be understood by eternal beings? but, How is the eternal truth to be apprehended temporally by one who exists in time?[22]

This is the problem that obsessed Kierkegaard throughout his life, and each time that he or one of his pseudonymous authors comes close to approximating an answer that would be conceptually satisfying, we find the brilliant, sharp Kierkegaardian irony exposing the temptation. Even Climacus, as we shall see, becomes a comical figure; he is not the vehicle for Kierkegaard's "true beliefs." Kierkegaard was not only obsessed with trying to comprehend this condition of Unhappy Consciousness, his life-long struggle with his own inwardness was a living out of the dialectic of Unhappy Consciousness.[23]

But what is the existential problem of an existing spiritual being, the problem that cannot be "formulated, much less settled in terms of the objective categories of thought and essence"? We can now finally grasp the distinctive role of decisiveness and action in human life.

Decisiveness and Action

As we proceed in following the labyrinth to what Kierkegaard, and even Climacus, are forcing us to confront, we see, at each step, how much and how little is granted to Hegel and the Hegelians. As long as we confine ourselves to the realm of Hegelian Reason—the realm of objective thought—"the difficulty inherent in existence and confronting the existing individual never really comes to expression.

22. "Kierkegaard and the Problem of Existential Philosophy," loc. cit., pp. 412-413.

23. Kierkegaard's struggle with the "disease of consciousness" has been perceptively explored by Josiah Thompson in *The Lonely Labyrinth*. The theme that Thompson discovers in Kierkegaard's journals and pseudonymous works is that: "Buried at the heart of Kierkegaard's struggle toward health lies hidden a subtle truth concerning the dialectic of consciousness with itself. His struggle is not an idiosyncratic one, nor is his sickness a perculiarity for the self of psychopathology. His struggle and his sickness have rather a universal basis, springing up as they do from the mere fact of being conscious. Kierkegaard's struggle is with no less an adversary than consciousness itself, for it is finally consciousness which supplies both the source of his estrangement as well as the pressure to overcome it. His awareness of the world as alien and 'infected' is only one specification of that more general distinction between self and the world which is necessary to consciousness. For what is

. . . Hegel is utterly and absolutely right in asserting that viewed eternally, *sub specie aeterni*, in the language of abstraction, in pure thought and pure being, there is no either-or" (*C.U.P.*, p. 270). If we really were "divine beings," if we really could live our lives *sub specie aeterni,* then all contradictions would ultimately be *aufgehoben* and mediated by Reason. But Climacus continues that "Hegel is equally wrong when, forgetting the abstraction of his thought, he plunges down into the realm of existence to annul the double *aut* with might and main. It is impossible to do this in existence, for in so doing the thinker abrogates existence as well" (*C.U.P.*, p. 271). But why is existence abrogated? Climacus suggests an answer and thereby indicates what is the problem of existence when he asks a series of questions of the speculative philosopher.

Is he himself *sub specie aeterni,* even when he sleeps, eats, blows his nose, or whatever else a human being does? Is he himself the pure "I am I"? This is an idea that has surely never occurred to any philosopher; but if not, how does he stand existentially related to this entity, and through what intermediate determinations is the ethical responsibility resting upon him as an existing individual suitably respected? Does he in fact exist? And if he does, is he then not in process of becoming? And if he is in process of becoming, does he not face the future? And does he ever face the future by way of action? And if he never does, will he not forgive an ethical individuality for saying in passion and with dramatic truth, that he is an ass? But if he acts *sensu eminenti,* does he not in that case face the future with infinite passion? Is there not then for him an either-or (*C.U.P.*, p. 271)?

The pieces of the "alternative" picture that Climacus is leading us toward begin to fall into place. The abstract thinking of an existing spiritual being confronts him with alternative existential possibilities, alternative ways of living his life, of facing his future. With imagination, wit, and dialectical skill, he can sketch these alternatives in the

---

the state of 'being conscious' if it is not this distinction between subject and object, self and the world? And what finally supports this distinction other than the mere awareness of it? Thus the estrangement Kierkegaard feels is only an intensification of one term of the dialectic of consciousness—of that fissure between self and world which consciousness requires." op. cit., p. 46. Compare this description of Kierkegaard's struggle with the analysis of Unhappy Consciousness as "the sick soul" in J. Lowenberg's *Hegel's Phenomenology*, pp. 97 ff.

minutest detail. But thinking, no matter how concrete it becomes, is not *choosing* or *deciding*, nor is it even a sufficient condition for a choice. The existential possibilities that an individual thinker entertains may very well be compatible in the abstract realm of thought. But they are not compatible in actuality, in existence. An individual existing being, self-conscious of his condition, is constantly faced with an *aut-aut*, an either-or. How he is to live his own individual life—in each moment of his becoming—is never determined for him by thought alone or by any of the conditions that make up his past. He must choose and act among competing possibilities—and such a choice is radically contingent and free. Nothing makes him what he is to become—there is no necessity here—except his own radically free choice. Yet everything that is momentous and important for him as an existing individual depends on this choice; his own decisiveness determines what he is to become. This terrible freedom is the condition of an existing individual at every moment of his life. As long as he is alive, he is constantly "coming into existence."[24]

But before we pass too quickly to this "conclusion," we must pause to consider an ambiguity of "existence." After all, if it is true

24. The existential locus of the either/or provides an orientation for reading Kierkegaard's pseudonymous works, including the book with the title *Either/Or*. They present us with existential possibilities—*possible* life projects or styles. As possibilities, they are abstract; they exist in the realm of thought, and despite the vividness of portrayal, they are impersonal. The title *Either/Or* only makes sense when we realize that there is a "third term" implicated in the disjunction, namely, the existing individual who reads and understands the book. If he reads the book (or any of the pseudonymous works) as solely a sketch of various possible life projects, or even as a grand argument between adversaries of different alternatives, he misses the point. Insofar as he does this, he limits himself to the realm of abstract thought where there is no either/or. But insofar as he reads the book as presenting *him* with live existential possibilities, calling forth *his* decision and passionate subjective appropriation, then he is reading the book as an existing individual who struggles with and is forced to choose among existential alternatives. For him there is a genuine *aut-aut*. Speaking of *Either/Or,* Climacus says, "It is a fundamental confusion in recent philosophy to mistake the abstract consideration of a standpoint with existence, so that when a man has knowledge of this or that standpoint he supposes himself to exist in it; every existing individuality must precisely as existing be more or less one-sided. From the abstract point of view there is no decisive conflict between the standpoints, because abstraction precisely removes that in which the decision inheres: *the existing subject*" (*C.U.P.,* p. 262).

that a man is an existing individual, then regardless of what a man does, he is always existing. What is the special role that decisiveness and passion play? Climacus is aware of the "loose" or "ordinary" sense of existence. "Existing is ordinarily regarded as no very complex matter, much less an art, since we all exist; but abstract thinking takes rank as an accomplishment" (*C.U.P.*, p. 273). Most men do exist in this sense—they lack any awareness of what it is to be an existing human being. Most of our "decisions," "actions," and "strivings," take place without reflection, without painful self-consciousness of what it means *really* to exist. "But really to exist, so as to interpenetrate one's existence with consciousness, at one and the same time eternal and as if far removed from existence, and yet also present in existence and in the process of becoming: that is truly difficult" (*C.U.P.*, p. 273). Really to exist—to live authentically—is to "interpenetrate one's existence with consciousness"; it is to heighten one's awareness of the existential possibilities that constantly confront one and to heighten one's awareness that choice is demanded, a choice that is never necessitated by any prior conditions. Man is, or rather becomes, what he himself chooses to become, and the problem of choice confronts a man at every moment of his life.

It is impossible to exist in this heightened sense in which consciousness interpenetrates our existence without passion. It is this heightened consciousness of our condition that stimulates "passionate enthusiasm." "All existential problems are passionate problems, for when existence is interpenetrated with reflection it generates passion. To think about existential problems in such a way as to leave out the passion, is tantamount to not thinking about them at all, since it is to forget the point, which is that the thinker is himself an existing individual" (*C.U.P.*, p. 313).

The alternative emerging from Climacus' inquiry is that of an existential dialectic which at once plays upon and drastically diverges from Hegel's dialectic of *Geist*. The accusation against Hegel is that he neglected to consider one essential moment of life's dialectic—the moment of existence—or rather that since Hegel understands existence only as it is reflected in thought and reason, he thereby abstracts from, and "forgets" concrete existence. Once this step is taken, a step that Climacus calls a "lunatic postulate" (*C.U.P.*, p. 279), everything then makes eminently good sense. In the realm of thought and Reason, contradictions can be mediated and *aufgehoben*. But suppose

Hegel is wrong. Suppose that Climacus comes closer to portraying what our human condition really is. Then we are forced to confront drastically anti-Hegelian "conclusions." The locus of dialectic that a man experiences is not in the realm of pure thought, but between himself as an existing individual and himself as a conscious thinking being. There can be no mediation, no higher synthesis in which existence and thought are happily reconciled. Each man is solitary and he finds no comfort in being carried along by a world-historical spirit—such a thought is only a temptation to escape from what is inescapable. A man is in constant tension with himself—he can never escape the condition of Unhappy Consciousness by any of his *own* efforts. His task as a human being is not to "think" himself out of this condition: such an attempt is pathetic and comic. His task is to *become* an existing human being, and this means to become subjective, not objective, to passionately appropriate and identify himself with the existential possibilities that confront him. In the task of becoming subjective, man is constantly confronted with an either/or. At the very juncture where Hegel indicates the possibility (and the necessity) of Reason as mediating the self-divisiveness of the Alienated Soul, Climacus points to the need for passion, decisiveness, and action. But we should not think that the passionate choice of an existential possibility is formally analogous to the mediating role of Reason. There is no resolution of the alienated condition of an existing individual in the sense in which Reason resolves the tension of Unhappy Consciousness. The passionate appropriation of an existential possibility or life style does not *once and for all* overcome the tension and diremption between existence and consciousness of an existing spiritual being. It is existentially impossible successfully and finally to bridge this gap. Insofar as a man continues to "come into existence," he faces the situation of existential choice and decision over and over again. This is the profoundest difference between the existential dialectic suggested by Climacus and Hegelian dialectic. It provides the essential perspective for grasping what Kierkegaard is showing us, especially in his pseudonymous writings. These writings not only present in vivid detail the various kinds of existential possibilities that confront a man, they show us how the passionate attempt to live out these possibilities results in despair. This is true for the individual who tries to live the aesthetic life and the ethical life. It is also true for the individual who leads the religious life. The self-conscious awareness that every project that an individual passionately appropriates is doomed to failure can drive an individual to the highest intensity of despair, to the consciousness of sin, and ultimately to the very brink of madness. But is there any way "out" of this hopeless situation? Like the Book of Job in which the Voice of the Whirlwind speaks to Job, Kierkegaard gives us an answer that is not an answer.

The question that sets the context for Climacus' investigations in the *Concluding Unscientific Postscript* is "How may I, Johannes Climacus, participate in the happiness promised by Christianity?" In asking this question, Climacus himself is confronting Christianity as an existential possibility. However, we already know that when the question is put in this way, it cannot be answered.

How, then, does a man become a Christian? Johannes Climacus— "John the Climber"—cannot vouch for the reality. His name and his testimony reveal that he himself is only on the way up, not yet arrived. But the condition—the possibility—of becoming a Christian is well within his bailiwick: First become a man, and when you are driven by this exertion into the narrows of despair, when you have become spirit by the recognition that absolute freedom is identical with absolute dependence, when you are alone in fear and trembling, without sustenance of nature, knowledge, or community, with no recourse but God—then and only then may the threat and promise of Christianity surge redemptively from the abyss.[25]

The action involved in passionately choosing an existential possibility is not measured by any external criteria; it is the decisiveness and action of inwardness. Although Climacus could agree with the Hegelian and Marxist formula that a man is what he does, Climacus' specification of what this formula means is anti-Hegelian and anti-Marxist. "The real action is not the external act, but an internal decision in which the individual puts an end to mere possibility and identifies himself with the content of his thought in order to exist in it. This is the action" (*C.U.P.*, pp. 302-303). This is what it means to become an existing individual. But this conception of action is not a throwback to an "ethics of intention." "The real action often tends to be confused with all sorts of notions, intentions, approximations to a decision, and so forth, and that it is seldom that anyone really

25. Mackey, "The Poetry of Inwardness," *loc. cit.*, p. 91.

acts, is not denied. . . . But let us take an act *sensu eminenti,* where everything stands out quite clearly. The external element in Luther's action consists in his appearance before the Diet of Worms; but from the moment that he had committed himself with entire subjective passion to his decision, so that every mere relationship of possibility to this action was interpreted by him as a temptation—from that moment he had acted" (*C.U.P.,* p. 304). In a typical pedantic fashion, Climacus adds the following footnote.

In general, the difference between the action as conceived and the action as inwardly real, consists in the fact that while in the case of the former every additional consideration is welcome, in connection with the latter it is to be regarded as a temptation. If in spite of this, some additional consideration reveals itself as of sufficient importance to command respect, this means that the way to a new resolve goes through repentance. When I am deliberating, it is my task to think every possibility; but when I have decided, and consequently acted inwardly, a change takes place so that it is now my task to ward against further deliberation, except in so far as something requires to be undone. The external decision is but a jest; but the more sluggishly an individual lives, the more does the external decision become the only one he knows anything about. Often people have no notion of the eternal decision that the individual may make inwardly; but they believe that when a decision has been registered on a piece of stamped paper it is really decided, but not before (*C.U.P.,* pp. 304-305).

All the themes that we have been tracing in Kierkegaard's writings culminate in this conception of action as inward decision and the demand that each of us must choose what he is to become. The confrontation with Hegel, the portrayal of the human condition as one of inescapable Unhappy Consciousness, the alternative of an existential dialectic to the dialectic of *Geist,* the reflections on the relations of possibility, actuality and necessity, the claim that all "coming into existence" excludes any necessity, lead us to the realization that to become an existing individual—that most difficult of all human tasks—demands passionate inward decisiveness and action.

But let us be careful here. It is all too easy to misread and misinterpret Kierkegaard at this crucial point. We have seen how the threads of Kierkegaard's thought lead to a heightened significance of human action as inward decisiveness. This is the basic human existential problem, a problem that confronts a man at every moment of his existence. And we have seen too that human action is not to be "confused" with social *praxis,* or indeed any of its external manifestations. Action here is a form of inwardness. Furthermore this is not an "accidental" conclusion, it is the heart of what Kierkegaard has been pointing us toward. But it is all too easy —as so many interpreters of Kierkegaard have done—to read this as an exuberant "theory" of individual action. After all, isn't Kierkegaard telling us that there is nothing that makes us into what we are to become? All appeals to past circumstances, social conditions, etc. can only be deceptive excuses. We are completely and radically free to choose what we are to become. We are never really shackled by any past decisions. It may be terrifying and momentous to face up to our fundamental freedom, but it is also exhilarating.

Such a reading of Kierkegaard can miss what is so crucial in his insight. For we can too easily forget that the problem of choice is an impossible one. Kierkegaard is not telling us to stand before our existential possibilities and courageously and authentically choose what we are to become. He is not telling us that we are free to choose the aesthetic life, the ethical life, or even the religious life. On the contrary, Kierkegaard seeks to show us that all choice, decisiveness, and action leads to despair. We can never succeed in identifying ourselves with any existential possibility, for we are always beyond it, we are always "coming into existence." And the dialectic of an existing conscious or spiritual being is such that he becomes increasingly self-conscious of this failure, this impossibility. The more we try to become subjective, the more we try to passionately appropriate an existential possibility, the more we try to *act,* the more we become aware of the impossibility to do so. Kierkegaard's "existential dialectic" leads in a curious and desperate way to an overwhelming sense of our own impotence, of the emptiness of "the eternal decision that the individual may make inwardly." Indeed, as Kierkegaard so brilliantly saw, those who think we can escape from despair by authentically and passionately committing ourselves to some existential possibility are guilty of being seduced by a temptation—a temptation which is only another variation of the Hegelian temptation to identify ourselves once and for all with an abstract possibility. It is not just the Hegelians who are guilty of making a "lunatic postulate," for this is the condition of the existential philosopher who deceives himself into thinking that passionate commitment is ultimately the way to escape from despair and Unhappy Consciousness. Ironically, Kierkegaard's point of view does not lead to a celebration of acting inwardly, but rather to the utter despair that overcomes one when he realizes the impossibility of this situation. There is no escape from this despair except a "miracle"—the miracle of faith, but faith itself is only given to those who are saved by God's grace.

Postscript

In "A First and Last Declaration," included at the very end of *Concluding Unscientific Postscript,* Kierkegaard, writing under his own name, acknowledges that he is the pseudonymous author of the *Postscript* as well as the other books he published under a variety of pseudonyms. He explains his pseudonymous authorship as follows:

My pseudonymity or polynymity has not had a casual ground in my *person* (certainly it was not for fear of a legal penalty, for in this respect I am confident that I have committed no misdemeanor, and at the time the books were published, not only the printer but the Censor, as a public functionary, was officially informed who the author was), but it has an *essential* ground in the character of the *production,* which for the sake of the lines ascribed to the authors and the psychologically varied distinctions of the individualities poetically required complete regardlessness in the direction of good and evil, of contrition and high spirits, of despair and presumption, of suffering and exultation, etc., which is bounded only ideally by psychological consistency, and which real actual persons in the actual moral limitations of reality dare not permit themselves to indulge in, nor could wish to. What is written therefore is in fact mine, but only in so far as I put into the mouth of the poetically actual individuality whom I *produced,* his life-view expressed in audible lines. For my relation is even more external than that of a poet, who poetizes characters, and yet in the preface is himself the author. For I am impersonal, or am personal in the second person, a *souffleur* who has poetically produced the *authors,* whose preface in turn is their own production, as are even their own names. So in the pseudonymous works there is not a single word which is mine, I have no opinion about these works except as third person, no knowledge of their meaning except as a reader, not the remotest private relation to them, since such a thing is impossible in the case of a doubly reflected communication. One single

word of mine uttered personally in my own name would be an instance
of presumptuous self-forgetfulness, and dialectically viewed it would
incur with one word the guilt of annihilating the pseudonyms (*C.U.P.*,
p. [551]).

Surely, we may protest, this is an overstatement. What can it mean
to say "there is not a single word which is mine," and I have "not the
remotest private relation to them"? The *Concluding Unscientific
Postscript* is not to be interpreted as an argument for a philosophic
position, but rather as a presentation of an existential possibility,
the possibility articulated in the person of Climacus, not Kierkegaard. If we understand the import of what even Climacus has been
telling us, then we the readers should realize that our existential
problem as unique individuals cannot be spoken to in terms of
anyone else's thought. This is not a problem that can be resolved or
confronted by any thought, no matter how convincing and ingenious.
We are called upon to "doubly reflect" on this form of communication, to appropriate subjectively for ourselves, to confront our own
freedom and thereby act inwardly. Kierkegaard is not playing games
with us, modestly declining responsibility for his own pseudonymous
works. He is calling our attention to what he has been showing us all
along. Communication concerning our own inwardness must be
indirect because no one can presume to usurp our own radical freedom, no one can fill the abyss that confronts every individual in
decisively acting and passionately choosing his own existential possibilities. To do so would be an instance of "presumptuous self-
forgetfulness."

Kierkegaard in "The First and Last Declaration" goes on to
request, "My wish, my prayer, is that, if it might occur to anyone to
quote a particular saying from the books, he would do me the favor
to cite the name of the respective pseudonymous author . . ." (*C.U.P.*,
p. [552]). Yet despite all these warnings, there is almost an irresistible
temptation to take the pseudonymous authors—especially Johannes
Climacus—as mouthpieces of Kierkegaard's "true beliefs." After all,
Climacus does develop a point of view, he uses dialectic and argument—sometimes brilliantly—to suggest an alternative to Hegel.
But throughout our explication of this point of view, we have referred
to his dialectic as playful and have suggested that he fails to
understand some of the things he says. It may come as a jolt to some
readers that Johannes Climacus in an "Appendix" declares that he

is not a Christian, but that "he is a *humorist*; content with his situation at this moment, hoping that something higher may be granted him, he feels himself singularly fortunate, if the worse must come to worst, in being born precisely in the speculative, theocentric century" (*C.U.P.*, p. [545]). What kind of trick is this? It is Hegel who has been characterized as a comedian. His system has been called a comedy because Hegel forgets he is an existing individual and takes flight into pure speculative philosophy. One would have thought that if Hegel's project is comical then Climacus is eminently serious. What can it mean from Climacus to declare himself to be a humorist? The issue is of enormous importance.

To read the *Concluding Unscientific Postscript* as a straightforward development of a new existential philosophy, or as the basis for a new existential approach to theological issues (which is the way that many admirers of Kierkegaard have read this book) is to fail to appreciate just how deep Kierkegaard's irony cuts. What is Climacus doing here? Johannes Climacus, the outsider, the self-declared non-Christian, wants to understand Christianity, and especially how he can share in the eternal happiness promised by Christianity. Despite all his criticisms of speculative philosophy, his attacks on Hegel and the Hegelians, Climacus is really a *mirror image* of the speculative philosopher. In his parody of Hegel and speculative philosophy, he is offering us an alternative way of becoming a Christian and thereby achieving salvation. If we pay close attention to his *own* words, it should dawn on us that this is precisely what cannot be done. Besides Kierkegaard, who has "poetically produced" Climacus, and Johannes Climacus, who develops a point of view for us, there is a third person involved in *Concluding Unscientific Postscript,* namely, the reader. And the reader can detect the discrepancy between what Climacus says and his own understanding of what he says. There is a double irony here; an ironical relation between Kierkegaard and Climacus and an equally important ironical relation between Climacus and *us.* The "philosophy" that Climacus offers us is even a greater temptation than the objective philosophy of Hegel.[26] It is a temptation to avoid confront-

26. Several commentators are particularly sensitive to this "double irony" of *Concluding Unscientific Postscript* and have noted the ways in which Climacus' "philosophy" is a parody. See Louis Mackey, "The Poetry of Inwardness," loc. cit., p. 89, where he says that *Concluding Unscientific Post-*

ing the predicament that our own existence presents to us. We are seduced into thinking that Climacus is offering us the "true" point of view. We can, all too easily, go away thinking we have understood Climacus and Kierkegaard when we pronounce the new philosophical truth that we live in a condition of Unhappy Consciousness and that there can be no successful mediation of ourselves as existing individuals. We can easily fall into the trap of becoming town criers of inwardness. We can deceive ourselves by being assured that Christianity is paradoxical, but that if we are concerned with our eternal happiness, it is better to take the risk of faith. We may even think that the leap of faith is like the caricature of a leap that Climacus suggests. "You shut your eyes, you seize yourself by the neck . . . and then—and then you stand on the other side, on the other side of sound common sense, in the promised land of systematic philosophy [or Christian faith]" (*C.U.P.*, p. 91). In short, we may put down this book thinking we have arrived at a new objective truth, one which declares that truth is inwardness or subjectivity. We thereby neutralize Kierkegaard, just as he himself (and Climacus) have prophesied. Kierkegaard himself well understood how deep this tendency is in all of us, especially *those most eager to comprehend. We seek to avoid reading *Concluding Unscientific Postscript* as a poetic exercise in indirect communication whose essential aim is to force each of us to confront his own inwardness, to make his own existential decision. Kierkegaard and Climacus have already warned us that these decisions cannot be justified, recommended, or dictated by anyone else—not even by such a "clever" dialectician as Johannes Climacus.

Kierkegaard himself was possessed and driven by this existential dialectic. As one reads through his works, including those where he acknowledges that he is "quite literally the author . . . and of every word of them" (*C.U.P.*, p. [552]), and his journals, it becomes more and more manifest than the inwardness, decisiveness, and action demanded by Christian faith become his central obsessive preoccupa-

---

script "is a whimsical book with a frighteningly sober purpose: to lead its reader down a path of merriment to the brink of the bottomless pit of freedom and to surprise him with the awful responsibility he bears for his own life." See also Henry Allison, "Christianity and Nonsense," *The Review of Metaphysics* 19 (March 1966), and Herbert Garelick, *The Anti-Christianity of Kierkegaard.*

tion. All illusions, all tricks of the imagination, all attempts to deceive himself that he has faced up to this momentous decision are ruthlessly stripped away. Kierkegaard himself went far "beyond" the whimsical dialectical playfulness of Johannes Climacus. A few months before his death in 1855 he wrote in his journal:

To be Christian

Of all torments, being a Christian is the most terrible; it is—and that is how it should be—to know hell in this life.

What is a human being most terrified of? Most likely of dying, and most of all of the death-agony, therefore wishing it to be as brief as possible.

But to be a Christian means to be in a stage of dying—(you must die off, hate yourself)—and yet, after that you live on, maybe for 40 years, in that state! (We shudder to read about the sufferings a beast undergoes when it is used for vivisection; yet this gives only a glimmering of the pain involved in being a Christian: to be kept alive in a state of death.)[27]

The more closely one tries to follow Kierkegaard into the depths of despair, the more one becomes aware of the morbidity, perversity and paradoxicality of his Unhappy Consciousness. Even the inwardness, decisiveness, choice, and action which stand at the center of his vision of what it is to be an existing individual, turn into their opposite. We may have thought that "to be a Christian" along with other existential possibilities that Kierkegaard has poetically presented, demands inward action on *our* part. But in the end, the faith demanded to be a Christian is not what it appears to be, it is not something of our own doing. Only those "kept alive in a state of death" are "ripe for Eternity,"[28] only they—and this is the most incomprehensible of all human paradoxes—are prepared to be saved by God's grace.

Sartre: Phenomenological Ontology

I have hesitated to call Kierkegaard a "philosopher," and to look upon his writings as developing a new point of view concerning the human condition. The reasons for this should now be clear. Kierke-

27. Quoted in *The Lonely Labyrinth,* p. 212.
28. Quoted in *The Lonely Labyrinth,* p. 212.

gaard's fundamental project is not to develop a new philosophic perspective. He warns us against reading him in this way. To do so is to divert us from confronting the existential either/or of our own inwardness. Like Marx, but in a drastically different way, Kierkegaard wants to force us "beyond" philosophy. Kierkegaard would agree with Marx that the philosophers have interpreted the world only, but he would add, the point is for each of us as unique individuals to change *ourselves*.

But even after we add all the necessary qualifications about "indirect communication," and "double reflection," these latter concepts themselves become intelligible only in light of the alternative picture of the human condition suggested by Kierkegaard and his pseudonymous authors. To be a human being is to be an individual whose existence is that of an Unhappy Consciousness that is never *aufgehoben*. Concretely this means that each of us faces his own future as an either/or where we must make existential choices—act inwardly—in committing ourselves to the existential possibilities that confront us. This demands the highest pitch of subjectivity and passion. But we can never succeed in identifying ourselves with the impersonal possibilities that we choose. We are always, as existing individuals, "beyond" any possibility. We are always in the process of becoming and choosing what we are to become. To be alive is to face the abyss of the future with the full self-conscious realization that nothing makes us what we are to become; we face the future with radical freedom. Any life project in which we seek fulfillment, satisfaction, identification with the possibility we have chosen, whether aesthetic, ethical, or *religious,* inevitably results in failure and despair. We have no reason to hope that we can ever escape from this predicament. The only hope is an absurd and paradoxical one. Only those individuals who suffer the extremities of despair, who, "brought to this point of *taedium vitae,* are able to hold fast to the thought that God acts from love, so that, in their soul, not even in its innermost recesses, there is left a hidden doubt that God is indeed love: only those are ripe for Eternity."[29]

Kierkegaard and his pseudonymous authors suggest this picture of the human condition: they do not assert it. It is presented as a "what if . . . ," not as "this is the way things really are." But with those thinkers in the existential tradition who come after Kierke-

29. Quoted in *The Lonely Labyrinth,* p. 212.

gaard, this possibility of what it is to be a human being haunts their reflections. With Sartre, who differs temperamentally and intellectually in so many ways from Kierkegaard, the "what if . . ." of Kierkegaard is no longer conceived of as a possibility, but as the ontological condition of what it is to be a human being. In this respect, Sartre fits much more easily into the main philosophical tradition. *Being and Nothingness* is "an essay on phenomenological ontology."[30] Its object is to demonstrate that "human reality . . . is

30. This is the subtitle of *Being and Nothingness* (*L'être et le néant: Essaie d'ontologie phénoménologique*). Our treatment of Sartre's phenomenological ontology will deal almost exclusively with its development in *L'être et le néant*. A comprehensive examination of Sartre would, of course, have to take account of his literary work, his popular essays, and his other giant tome, *Critique de la raison dialectique*. The differences of emphasis and doctrine between Sartre's two major philosophical works, the explicit turn to Marxism, and especially Sartre's claim, "I consider Marxism the one philosophy of our time which we cannot go beyond . . . and I hold the ideology of existence and its 'comprehensive' method to be an enclave inside Marxism, which simultaneously engenders it and rejects it" (*Search For a Method*, p. xxxiv; *Critique de la raison dialectique*, I, pp. 9-10) provides plenty of opportunity for scholars to dispute about the relation of the "early" to the "late" Sartre. My primary reason for focusing on *L'être et le néant* is that I believe Sartre has developed a powerful vision of what it is to be a human being and what it means for man to choose and act—a vision which has *not* been directly challenged or superseded by his later work. Although I will not discuss the *Critique* here, I would argue that the uneasy synthesis of existentialism and Marxism that Sartre suggests above and attempts to justify in his *Critique* is a failure. If we take seriously the phenomenological ontology developed in *L'être et le néant*, then Sartre's philosophical investigations since this book are to be viewed as exemplifications of his own category of "bad faith"— attempts to escape from the nothingness that lies at the heart of man's being. Sartre has sought to escape from the nihilistic conclusions that emerge from *L'être et le néant*, but he has never taken up the challenge of rethinking his own ontological claims. This is precisely what such a synthesis requires.

The best overall survey of Sartre's intellectual career in English is Joseph H. McMahon, *Humans Being: The World of Jean-Paul Sartre*. McMahon, however, is more sensitive to the literary dimensions of Sartre's thought than he is to the philosophic dimensions. His bibliography is a good guide to works by and about Sartre. For the most complete annotated bibliography of Sartre's works, see Michael Contat and Michel Rybalka, *Les ecrits de Sartre*. For a bibliography of works by Sartre translated into English and for books in English about Sartre, see Allen J. Belkind, *Jean-Paul Sartre in English: A Bibliographical Guide*.

by nature an unhappy consciousness with no possibility of surpassing its unhappy state" (*B.N.*, p. 90; *p. 34*),[31] to establish the onto-logical basis for this condition, and to draw out the phenomeno-logical consequences of this ontology.

In the analyses of Marx and Kierkegaard, I argued that the dis-tinctive thrust of their reflections represents a dialectical encounter with Hegel. I now want to show how this is also true for Sartre. Hegel was not the primary historical influence on Sartre; Husserl and Heidegger were his intellectual mentors. But hovering over Sartre's phenomenological ontology is the spectre of Hegel. He is the intel-lectual giant who is to be directly confronted and overthrown.

Just as Kierkegaard's title "Concluding Unscientific Postscript" is an ironic comment on Hegel and the Hegelians, so too is Sartre's "Being and Nothingness." Being and Nothingness are the first two concepts introduced in Hegel's *Logic*.[32] From the dialectic gener-ated by these concepts, Hegel seeks to show the necessity of *all* the concepts of logic and thereby to demonstrate the inner necessity and completeness of the System. Like Marx and Kierkegaard, Sartre knows that if one is successfully to criticize Hegel, then one must attack him at his beginning point.

The procedure I shall follow in discussing Sartre is the same that I have followed for Marx and Kierkegaard. After a statement of Hegel's position, Sartre's critique of it will be examined. Once again, the discussion begins with what at first appears to be very abstract and remote considerations. But they have powerful consequences for understanding human action. Hegel's beginning point in the *Logic* is under attack in Sartre's phenomenological ontology, but Sartre's critique of the *Logic* converges with his critique of the *Phenomenology*.

31. Page references to *Being and Nothingness* are included in the text. Page numbers of the English translation are followed by page numbers of the French text.

32. In her translation of *L'être et le néant,* Hazel E. Barnes has translated "le néant" as "Nothingness." William Wallace in his translation of Hegel's *Logic* translates "Nichts" as "Nothing." Since we use both translations, we will sometimes use the noun "Nothing" and sometimes, especially when refer-ring to Sartre, "Nothingness." Both expressions are used to refer to the same concept.

Being and Nothing

The Doctrine of Being forms the first division of Hegel's *Logic*. "Being," we are told, "is the notion [*Begriff*] implicit only" (*Logic,* p. 156; *Bd. VI, p. 163*).[33] "Being itself and the special sub-categories of it which follow, as well as those of logic in general, may be looked upon as definitions of the Absolute, or metaphysical definitions of God . . ." (*Logic,* p. 156; *Bd. VI, p. 163*). As we follow the stages of the *Logic,* we are tracing the logical development of the *Begriff*. This development starts with the emptiest and poorest concepts and proceeds to concepts that are increasingly more determinate. The whole of the *Logic* is intended to lay out for us and establish the completeness of the System of thought and being. According to Hegel there are "three grades" (*drei Stufen*) of Being: quality, quantity, and measure (*Logic,* p. 157; *Bd. VI, p. 164*). It is in the first grade, quality, that Hegel discusses the relation of Being and Nothing.

"Pure *Being* makes the beginning: because it is on the one hand pure thought, and on the other immediacy itself, simple and indeterminate; and the first beginning cannot be mediated by anything, or be further determined" (*Logic,* p. 158; *Bd. VI, p. 165*). Pure Being is the emptiest of all concepts. As an abstract moment in the development of the *Begriff,* it lacks any determination or negation. Pure Being is completely indeterminate (lacking any determinate features or characters). "The indeterminate, as we here have it, is the blank we begin with, not a featurelessness reached by abstraction, not the elimination of all character, but the original featurelessness which precedes all definite character and is the very first of all" (*Logic,* p. 159; *Bd. VI, p. 166*). If pure Being lacks any character whatsoever, then all we can say about pure being is that it *is*. Furthermore, "is" here lacks any specificity or determinateness. This means that we really are not saying anything at all (i.e., anything determinate) when we say that pure Being *is*. Pure Being turns into its opposite: it is Nothing.

Hegel is fully aware of the oddity of this identification of Pure

33. Page references to Hegel's *Logic* are included in the text. Page numbers of the English translation are followed by the page numbers in Hegel's *Werke*. References are to the "Lesser Logic" included in Hegel's *Encyclopaedia*. For the corresponding sections in the "Greater Logic," see *Hegel's Science of Logic,* trans. by A. V. Miller, pp. 79 ff.

Being and Nothing. "If the opposition in thought is stated in this immediacy as Being and Nothing, the shock of its nullity is too great not to stimulate the attempt to fix Being and secure it against the transition into Nothing" (*Logic,* p. 161; *Bd. VI, p. 169*). In the history of philosophy we find attempts to identify Being with something that does not evaporate into Nothing, e.g., the identification of Being with prime matter which persists amid all change. Any attempt to fix Being with some characteristic "causes Being to lose that integrity and simplicity it has in the beginning" (*Logic,* p. 161; *Bd. VI, p. 169*). We, of course, *intend* to distinguish pure Being from Nothing; we do not think that they are identical, but we are at a loss to find any way to make this distinction; the distinction is "only meant" (*nur gemeint*).

The distinction between Being and Nought is, in the first place, only implicit, and not yet actually made: they only *ought* to be distinguished. A distinction of course implies two things, and that one of them possesses an attribute which is not found in the other. Being however is an absolute absence of attributes, and so is Nought. Hence the distinction between the two is only meant to be; it is a quite nominal distinction, which is at the same time no distinction (*Logic,* p. 163; *Bd. VI, p. 170*).

If we remain with this first or immediate "opposition," then there is nothing more that can be said than that Being and Nothing are the same; they are "both" empty, and lack any determination. Hegel now passes to one of his famous transitions, for we are told: "Nothing, if it be thus immediate and equal to itself, is also conversely the same as Being is. The truth of Being and of Nothing is accordingly the unity of the two: and this unity is *Becoming*" (*Logic,* p. 163; *Bd. VI, p. 171*).

But how do we arrive at this conclusion? How does Hegel manage to derive Becoming from the unity of Being and Nothing? What does this mean? Hegel's point in this "logical" transition is similar to that of Plato when he characterizes Becoming as a "mixture" of what is real and what is not, of being and nonbeing. We are not asserting an empty contradiction in claiming that Becoming is and is not. We are distinguishing Becoming from a rigid, static conception of Being. Becoming is not Being, but neither is it sheer nothingness. Hegel claims that we find this idea of Becoming even earlier than in Plato. "In the history of philosophy, this stage of the logical Idea finds its analogue in the system of Heraclitus. When Heraclitus says, 'All is flowing' . . . , he enunciates Becoming as the fundamental feature of all existence, whereas the Eleatics . . . saw the only truth in Being, rigid processless Being" (*Logic,* p. 168; *Bd. VI, pp. 176-177*). The "first concrete thought" is that of Becoming.

Becoming is the first concrete thought, and therefore the first notion: whereas Being and Nought are empty abstractions. The notion of Being, therefore, of which we sometimes speak, must mean Becoming; not the mere point of Being, which is empty Nothing, any more than Nothing, which is empty Being. In Being then we have Nothing, and in Nothing Being: but this Being which does not lose itself in Nothing is Becoming. Nor must we omit the distinction, while we emphasize the unity of Becoming: without that distinction we should once more return to abstract Being. Becoming is only the explicit statement of what Being is in its truth (*Logic,* p. 167; *Bd. VI, pp. 175-176*).

We must not read more into the concept of Becoming than Hegel has made explicit. We are still at a very abstract level of analysis. "Becoming . . . is an extremely poor term" (*Logic,* p. 168; *Bd. VI, p. 177*). It would be misleading to identify Becoming with change, because change presupposes some substratum or determinate entity that changes.[34] Thus far, no category corresponding to a determinate entity has been made explicit. This is the next stage in Hegel's dialectic.

In Becoming the Being which is one with Nothing, and the Nothing which is one with Being, are only vanishing factors; they are and they are not. Thus by inherent contradiction Becoming collapses into the unity in which the two elements are absorbed. This result is accordingly *Being Determinate* (Being there and so) [*Dasein*] (*Logic,* p. 169; *Bd. VI, p. 177*).

Dasein is not only positive Being, it is "Being with negation or determinateness." Insofar as we think of a category as involving both inclusion and exclusion, we can say that *Dasein* is the first genuine category of the *Logic.* For to be determinate entails "exclusion" or what Hegel calls "negation." Quoting Spinoza, Hegel affirms *Omnis determinatio est negatio.*

The unreflecting observer supposes that determinate things are merely positive, and pins them down under the form of being. Mere being how-

34. For a discussion of this point, see McTaggart's *A Commentary on Hegel's Logic,* pp. 17 ff.

ever is not the end of the matter:—it is, as we have already seen, utter emptiness and instability besides. Still, when abstract being is confused in this way with being modified and determinate, it implies some perception of the fact that, though in determinate being there is involved an element of negation, this element is at first wrapped up, as it were, and only comes to the front and receives its due in Being-for-self [*Fürsichsein*] (*Logic,* pp. 171-172; *Bd. VI, pp. 180-181*).[35]

If one were to single out the most important step in Hegel's *Logic,* it would be this introduction of *Dasein.* And from Sartre's point of view this is Hegel's most fundamental error. The culmination of the logical development from pure Being, Nothing, and Becoming is to be found in *Dasein* (Being Determinate). *Dasein* is intrinsically positive and negative. Negativity lies at the very heart of being as *Dasein.* *Dasein* is not set over against, or contrasted with pure Being, or Being-in-itself. *Dasein* is the *truth* of pure Being: it is what pure Being is "discovered" to be when we make explicit what is implicit in pure Being. As Hegel proceeds to develop further categories in the *Logic* there is a working out of the negativity that lies at the heart of being. The third major stage of the Doctrine of Being, Being-for-itself, is already implicit in Hegel's characterization of *Dasein.* This is the moment that Hegel calls Ideality. Consequently if we accept Hegel's claims about the character of *Dasein,* we are already committed to Idealism.

Being-for-self [*Fürsichsein*] may be described as ideality, just as being-there-and-then [*Dasein*] was described as reality. It is said, that besides reality there is *also* an ideality. Thus the two categories are made equal and parallel. Properly speaking, ideality is not somewhat outside of and beside reality: the notion of ideality just lies in its being the truth of reality. That is to say, when reality is explicitly put as what it implicitly is, it is at once seen to be ideality (*Logic,* pp. 179-180; *Bd. VI, p. 190*).

At this point in our explication of the opening moves of Hegel's *Logic,* it is difficult to see where Hegel is leading us and what possible significance this intricate dialectic of concepts has for understanding

35. Once again we run afoul of the variations in English translations. Sartre adopts the expression *"l'être pour soi"* for Hegel's *"Fürsichsein."* However, Wallace translates *"Fürsichsein"* as "being-for-self," while Barnes translates *"l'être-pour-soi"* as "being-for-itself." When not quoting from Wallace, we will use the expression "being-for-itself" to indicate the parallelism with *"l'être-en-soi"* and *"Ansichsein"* ("being-in-itself").

human reality. We can, however, anticipate the thrust of Hegel's dialectic by realizing that the introduction of Being-for-itself parallels the stage reached at the conclusion of Unhappy Consciousness in the *Phenomenology*. For there, too, Hegel announces the emergence of Ideality.[36] Whether we are concerned with the categories of being in the *Logic* or with the forms of consciousness in the *Phenomenology*, the introduction of ideality holds forth the promise that the deepest divisions in being or the deepest divisions in consciousness will be successfully mediated, reconciled, *aufgehoben*. If we descend from the lofty heights of the Doctrine of Being and the development of *Geist* to the more mundane realm of human reality, we realize that Hegel is leading us to the idea of the possibility, and indeed the necessity, of a stage when human reality no longer suffers the pain of self-alienation, a stage when the dialectic of Being is completed and Being is in-itself and for-itself. It is difficult to resist the theological overtones of this view of human reality. The promise of the successful mediation of alienation is the promise of salvation. Hegel follows those Christian thinkers who claim that the fall of man is already implicit in the act of creation, as is the promise of redemption. The beginning is in the end, and the end is in the beginning.

Despite Marx's vehement critique of theology and his attack on Hegel's principle of ideality, he nevertheless shares with Hegel the theme of the real possibility of overcoming alienation. For Marx, this is the achievement of a humanistic society in which freedom and self-determination are finally realized. But Kierkegaard has already questioned the possibility of such a successful mediation of the suffering of human existence. With Sartre's ambitious phenomenological ontology, we find a systematic attempt to expose the principle of ideality and its promise of an escape from Unhappy Consciousness. Since the principle of ideality is already implicit in Hegel's dialectic of Being and Nothing, a systematic refutation of Hegel must start afresh with the analysis of Being and Nothing.

Being-in-Itself

The main thrust of the opening sections of Hegel's *Logic* is to show that negativity lies at the very heart of Being. Once this has been

36. See my discussion of this point, pp. 94-96.

established, the *Logic* follows the working out of this negativity, i.e., the various forms of determination that Being assumes. But as the *Logic* unfolds we realize that negativity is primarily a characteristic of consciousness or, more fundamentally, of Being-for-itself. Consequently, for Hegel, Being-for-itself is already implicit in pure Being. The realization that at the heart of being there is consciousness or Being-for-itself is what Hegel means by the principle of Ideality. Where Hegel argues that the distinction between Being-in-itself and Being-for-itself is progressively mediated, Sartre claims that there is an ontological chasm that cannot be mediated.

Sartre uses three formulae to characterize Being-in-itself: "being is itself" or "being is in itself" (*"l'être est soi"* or *"l'être est en soi"*); "being is what it is" (*"l'être est ce qu'il est"*); and "being-in-itself-is" (*"l'être-en-soi est"*) (*B.N.,* p. 1xiv ff.; *p. 30 ff.*). The first formula is intended to call attention to being as uncreated. Being-in-itself is neither created by God, nor self-created. All creation, properly speaking, is human creation, and we will see that human reality is not being-in-itself; it is being-for-itself. Furthermore, being-in-itself is beyond all passivity and all activity; it is beyond affirmation and negation. Being-in-itself is filled with itself, and opaque to itself, "it is full positivity" (*il est pleine positivité*), "it is solid" (*massif*) (*B.N.,* p. 1xviii; *p. 33*). Sartre follows the Parmenidean tradition of thinking of being-in-itself as a self-contained plenum.

The second formula develops this point, for "if being is in itself, this means that it does not refer to itself as self-consciousness does. . . . That is why being is at bottom beyond the self . . ." (*B.N.,* p. 1xvii; *p. 33*). Being-in-itself exhausts itself in being. It is completely and exclusively identical with itself; it contains no inner tension, no inner negativity. "Transition, becoming, anything which permits us to say that being is not yet what it will be and that it is already what it is not—all that is forbidden on principle" (*B.N.,* p. 1xviii; *p. 33*).

The final formula is intended to emphasize that "being can neither be derived from the possible nor reduced to the necessary."

This is what consciousness expresses in anthropomorphic terms by saying that being is superfluous (*de trop*)—that is, that consciousness absolutely can not derive being from anything, either from another being, or from a possibility, or from a necessary law. Uncreated, without reason for being, without any connection with another being, being-in-itself is *de trop* for eternity (*B.N.,* p. 1xviii; *p. 34*).

Against the background of Hegel's analysis of Being, Sartre's claims take on a forceful significance. They are a direct ontological assault on Hegel. The upshot of Sartre's claims about Being-in-itself is to deny Hegel's central claim that nothingness (negativity) lies at the heart of Being. For Sartre, Being-in-itself completely excludes any negativity, and consequently any becoming, transition, change, activity and determination. If Sartre had left us here and claimed that being-in-itself is all inclusive, he would have been the spiritual offspring of Parmenides. Furthermore, he would be open to the Hegelian charge that his position involves a self-contradiction, for by his own admission, consciousness—the locus of negativity—is excluded from being-in-itself. But Sartre's ontology is a *phenomenological* ontology. His starting point is not being-in-itself, but our *consciousness* of being-in-itself. Sartre adopts the phenomenological starting point of Husserl and Heidegger who claim that the "primal fact" is the intentionality of consciousness—all consciousness is consciousness of something. This, of course, is also the starting point of Hegel's own *Phenomenology*. If we take seriously what Sartre has said about being-in-itself, then we are confronted with a paradox. There seems to be no place for consciousness. If being-in-itself were all that *is*, then we would be forced to the conclusion that consciousness *is not*. Consciousness is Nothing or Nothingness. This is not an inadvertant consequence of Sartre's ontological reflections; it is exactly the point he wants to make. But what does this paradoxical conclusion mean? What is the point of declaring that consciousness—our phenomenological starting point—is its own Nothingness?

When Sartre claims that consciousness is "its own Nothingness" (*B.N.*, p. 23; *p. 59*), he does not mean that consciousness is the empty abstraction, Nothing, that Hegel identified with pure Being. Consciousness itself is a mode of being, but it is not and can never be identical with being-in-itself. But now the paradoxicality of Sartre's claims deepens. How can consciousness be a mode of being and its own nothingness? The formula that Sartre uses to express this peculiar characteristic of consciousness is to say that it *is* if only in the manner of "a being which is not what it is and which is what it is not" (*B.N.*, p. 79; *p. 121*). To give this abstract formula phenomenological content, Sartre analyzes experiences which he calls *négatités*. These include questioning, destruction, missing someone, distance, "absence, change, otherness, repulsion, regret, distraction, etc." (*B.N.,* p. 21; *p. 57*). The common characteristic of these experiences is that we directly experience what is negative—nothingness. If I come into a café looking for Pierre and discover that he is not there, I directly experience his absence.

I myself expected to see Pierre, and my expectation has caused [*a fait arriver*] the absence of Pierre *to happen* as a real event concerning this café. It is an objective fact at present that I have *discovered* this absence, and it presents itself as a synthetic relation between Pierre and the setting in which I am looking for him. Pierre absent haunts this café and is the condition of its self-nihilating organization as ground (*B.N.,* p. 10; *p. 45*).

The experience of discovering that someone is missing is certainly common enough. But what special significance does it have? Sartre is showing us in this example, as well as other *négatités,* that we do have genuine experiences of lacks, deficiencies, absences, etc. The experience of a lack is not an intellectual judgment based on what is exclusively positive. When we consider these experiences in light of what Sartre has said about being-in-itself, we realize that something radically new has been introduced. We have here a new type of being, a being which can encounter nothingness, a being-for-itself. Sartre's phenomenological description of *négatités* is a stepping-stone in clarifying the structure of consciousness as being-for-itself. Klaus Hartmann, who has meticulously reconstructed Sartre's argument, succinctly summarizes the direction of Sartre's reflections.

Nothingness is encountered in the world of objects. It cannot, however, be referred to being-in-itself since this is pure positivity. Nor can it proceed from a nothingness since this is not. It can, therefore, proceed only from a being, but a being subject to the qualification that it maintains a nothingness. Such a being has to constitute a unity with a nothingness, and such nothingness must not "befall" being because, otherwise, the problem would only be pushed back to that being which performs this feat on the former. We end in a regress because nothingness can never issue from a positive being. But even if being maintained nothingness within itself, this might be a "transcendent in the very heart of immanence." Being and nothingness have to be so unified that being is concerned for its nothingness; such being "must be its own nothingness." That is, we are not dealing once more with a negation, a nihilating act, issuing from a positive being—which is impossible—but with a type of being of its own: a being which forms a unity with nothingness in such a way that it is "its own nothingness". . . . Being of the type now discovered is the disjunct of being-in-itself. The opposite of being-in-itself is not simply nothingness but a unity of being and nothingness.[37]

For Sartre then, there is a great ontological divide between being-in-itself and being-for-itself. The former is characterized by its fullness, self-identity, plenitude, and solidity. The latter, which is a unity of being and nothingness, is itself essentially a lack, a deficiency, a being which lacks the fullness and positivity of being-in-itself. When we add that human reality or consciousness *is* that being which is being-for-itself, we realize how Sartre repudiates Hegel's principle of ideality. The unity and mediation of being-in-itself and being-for-itself which for Hegel is the culmination of the dialectic of Being, is an impossible synthesis. Being-for-itself can never become or "return" to being-in-itself, no matter how desperately it strives to attain this unity. This ontological chasm provides the context for grasping the distinctive nature and role of human action.

Being-for-Itself

Being-for-itself is a unity of being and nothingness in the sense of a being which is concerned with its own nothingness; it is a being "which is not what it is and is what it is not." To explicate this paradoxical-sounding expression, I will first explore more fully how being-for-itself is the dialectical opposite of being-in-itself. I will then break down the formula in order to show what it means to say (i) that the for-itself is a "being in the manner of a being which is not what it is . . ." and (ii) that it is "a being in the manner of a being which is what it is not."

Being-for-itself is a *lack of being* (*défaut d'être, manqué*) (*B.N.*, pp. 85, 87; *pp. 128 f.*). But it is not a static lack or emptiness. It is a lack that strives for gratification, completeness, and fulfillment. Sartre's thought here closely parallels the first stage of self-conscious-

---

37. Klaus Hartmann, *Sartre's Ontology*, p. 50. Hartmann's study is a systematic treatment of Sartre's ontology and a comprehensive discussion of the relation of Sartre and Hegel.

ness in Hegel's *Phenomenology* where the self takes the form of desire seeking fulfillment. The for-itself as consciousness not only lacks the completeness of being-in-itself, it is profoundly aware of this lack. (This is what Sartre means when he says the for-itself is concerned with its own nothingness.) The structure of the for-itself is to be a lack or desire seeking fulfillment. The only being which is a being-for-itself is human being, and Sartre tells us:

Human reality is its own surpassing toward what it lacks; it surpasses itself toward the particular being which it would be if it were what it is. Human reality is not something which exists first in order afterwards to lack this or that; it exists first as lack and in immediate, synthetic connection with what it lacks. Thus the pure event by which human reality rises as presence in the world is apprehended by itself as *its own lack*. In its coming into existence human reality grasps itself as an incomplete being. It apprehends itself as being in so far as it is not, in the presence of the particular totality which it lacks and which it is in the form of not being it (*B.N.*, p. 89; *p. 132*).

Hegel could agree with everything that Sartre says here. An appeal to Hegel's *Phenomenology* can help to bring out Sartre's own meaning. For according to Hegel, Sartre is locating the very feature of *Geist—Geist* in the form of human consciousness—which is the motive force for the progressive dialectic of consciousness and self-consciousness. As the *Phenomenology* shows us, it is at the very moment when the self apprehends that it is a lack, that it is not yet fulfilled and consequently not yet autonomous that it drives on to the next "higher stage" of dialectic. But while there is a basic similarity between Sartre and Hegel in their characterization of human reality as a lack seeking fulfillment, there is a radical divergence in assessing the ontological possibility of such a fulfillment. Sartre goes on to claim:

Let no one reproach us with capriciously inventing a being of this kind; when by a further movement of thought the being and the absolute absence of this totality are hypostasized as transcendence beyond the world, it takes the name of God. Is not God a being who is what he is— in that he is all positivity and the foundation of the world—and at the same time a being who is not what he is and who is what he is not— in that he is self-consciousness and the necessary foundation of himself? The being of human reality is suffering because it rises in being as perpetually haunted by a totality which it is without being able to be it, precisely because it could not attain the in-itself without losing itself as for-itself (*B.N.*, p. 90; *pp. 133-134*).

The portrayal of God that Sartre presents—the hypostatization of being and absolute absence—is precisely what Hegel has said about God, the Absolute, *Geist* as concretely realized. For Hegel, however, this is no hypostatization, but the fundamental reality. Human reality is identical with this reality; it becomes this reality when it reaches fulfillment. But according to Sartre, although human reality is haunted by this dream of totality and completeness, it can never become such a totality; it can never mediate itself as in-itself and for-itself. All the lines of Sartre's complex thought lead us to this conclusion. They are stages in a grand argument to demonstrate the impossibility of this synthesis, of this mediation of the for-itself and the in-itself. Human reality desperately seeks fulfillment: to become finally what it seeks *to be*. But while human reality cannot escape this condition, neither can it ever hope to find fulfillment, completeness, totality. It is not that such self-identity is extremely difficult; it is ontologically impossible. Sartre's ontological and phenomenological investigations converge here. The attack on Hegel's *Logic* and Sartre's analysis of being-in-itself and being-for-itself is the basis for the conclusion that "human reality therefore is by nature an unhappy consciousness with no possibility of surpassing its unhappy state" (*B.N.*, p. 90; *p. 134*).

But what does it mean to say that the for-itself is a being which is not what it is? The clue to answering this question is to be found in Sartre's analysis of facticity.

The for-itself is its own foundation in so far as it makes itself the failure of the in-itself to be *its* own foundation. But for all that the for-itself has not succeeded in freeing itself from the in-itself. The surpassed in-itself lives on and haunts the for-itself as its original contingency. The for-itself can never reach the in-itself nor apprehend itself as *being* this or that, but neither can it prevent itself from being what it is—at a distance from itself. This contingency of the for-itself, this weight surpassed and preserved in the very surpassing—this is *Facticity*. But it is also the past. "Facticity" and "Past" are two words to indicate one and the same thing (*B.N.*, p. 118; *p. 162*).[38]

38. Although, I am approaching Sartre's thought by attempting to show how it arises from and can be understood as a reaction to a "problematic" in

Here too, Hegel's analysis of Unhappy Consciousness sheds light on this obscure passage. In Unhappy Consciousness there is a split or division within a single self-consciousness and the painful awareness of this split. I am aware of myself as finite and infinite, and at once of being both of these, but not self-identical with either of these. I am aware of myself as having a certain determinate, finite nature or self, and at the same time of being not this self, of being the power to transcend any determinate self that I have been. Facticity corresponds to the finitude of my being. The things that I have done, the choices I have made, the roles that I have played are *me*; I have a self, an ego, a personality. But I am not and can never be wholly identical with this self that I have been. Facticity is the being-in-itself that I have been. The use of the past tense is crucial here, for it emphasizes that I am and I am not my own facticity. I am it in the sense that it constitutes my past. It is a weight preserved even in the very surpassing of it. But I am not my facticity, past, self, or ego in the sense that I am never completely exhausted or identical with the self that I have been. If such self-identity were possible then I would be in the mode of being-in-itself. It is in death only that we *are*. "By death the for-itself is changed forever into an in-itself in that it has slipped entirely into the past" (*B.N.,* p. 115; *p. 159*). But as a for-itself, I am beyond—I surpass—whatever I have been. I stand in relation to my own facticity at a distance and in such a manner that it never determines what I am to become. On the contrary, I determine the meaning that my facticity is to have for me. As a for-itself, I am radically free and spontaneously determine what I am to become. The reflective awareness of this freedom is anguish (*angoisse*); it is the heightened consciousness that there is no foundation or ground for what I am to become other than myself. It is always false to say that I was caused or determined to do so-and-so. There cannot be any excuses for what I do. I am completely and solely responsible as a for-itself for the way in which I choose to react to any situation including my own past and facticity. We will soon see how far Sartre carries this

---

Hegel, it cannot be underestimated how much of Sartre's thought and even his selection of basic categories was shaped by his reading (misreading?) of Husserl and Heidegger. The concepts of "facticity" and "authenticity" are both directly taken over from Heidegger's *Sein und Zeit*.

line of thought, for he challenges the traditional doctrine that man passively experiences emotions. Even the emotions that I experience are the results of choices.

Thus whatever I can be said to *be* in the sense of being-in-itself with a full, compact density (he is quick-tempered, he is a civil servant, he is dissatisfied) is always *my* past. It is in the past that I am what I am. But on the other hand, that heavy plentitude of being is behind me, there is an absolute distance which cuts it from me and makes it fall out of my reach, without contact, without connections. . . . The past is the in-itself which I am, but I am this in-itself as *surpassed* (*B.N.*, pp. 117-118; *pp. 161-162*).

Or again, stressing the radicalness of my freedom and the way in which my existence is forever beyond my essence, Sartre writes:

For the for-itself, to be is to nihilate the in-itself which it is. Under these conditions freedom can be nothing other than this nihilation. It is through this that the for-itself escapes its being as its essence; it is through this that the for-itself is always something other than what can be *said* of it. For in the final analysis the for-itself is the one which escapes this very denomination, the one which is already beyond the name which is given to it, beyond the property which is recognized in it. To say that the for-itself has to be what it is, to say that it is what it is not while not being what it is, to say that in it existence precedes and conditions essence or inversely according to Hegel, that for it "Wesen ist was gewesen ist"— all this is to say one and the same thing: to be aware that man is free. Indeed by the sole fact that I am conscious of the causes which inspire my action, these causes are already transcendent objects for my consciousness; they are outside. In vain shall I seek to catch hold of them; I escape them by my very existence. I am condemned to exist forever beyond my essence, beyond the causes and motives of my act. I am condemned to be free. This means that no limits to my freedom can be found except freedom itself, or, if you prefer, that we are not free to cease being free. To the extent that the for-itself wishes to hide its own nothingness from itself and to incorporate the in-itself as its true mode of being, it is trying also to hide its freedom from itself (*B.N.*, pp. 439-440; *p. 515*).

Although Sartre has taken a very different route from Kierkegaard, the above passage indicates the convergence of their insights concerning the human condition. For Kierkegaard too it is by virtue of being an existing individual that I am always beyond my essence. As an existing individual I am never identical with anything that I have been or with any of the possibilities that I have chosen. I am radically free in the sense that at every moment of existing, I choose what I am to become, whether I do this reflectively or unreflectively. I may, like Johannes Climacus, try to hide from my own nothingness and freedom and thereby avoid the momentous either/or that confronts every individual, but I cannot escape from this freedom: "I am condemned to be free." Kierkegaard's poetically created authors beautifully illustrate this condition of bad faith—the attempt to escape from one's own nothingness.

We have already anticipated the sense in which the for-itself is a "being which is what it is not." The for-itself is its own facticity and past, but also it is not this facticity. The for-itself nihilates its own past. "The Present is a perpetual flight in the face of being" (*B.N.*, p. 123; *p. 168*). But toward what is the for-itself fleeing? Sartre answers—and this has been implicit in his analysis of the for-itself as a lack—"it is a flight toward *its being,* that is toward the self which it will be by coincidence with what it lacks" (*B.N.*, p. 125; *p. 170*). The for-itself is a flight toward the future self which it is "not yet." The fundamental project of the for-itself is to strive to achieve a coincidence with what it lacks. Combining the three temporal moments of the for-itself, Sartre says "at present it is not what it is (past) and it is what it is not (future)" (*B.N.*, p. 123; *p. 168*). The very structure of the for-itself is to be future oriented: it seeks fulfillment and attempts to achieve this fulfillment by projecting possibilities of what it is to be. This projecting is not a contemplative process, it is an active one. An act is a projection of the for-itself toward what is not. The for-itself chooses its own future, although its choices are not primarily reflective. While the for-itself can never escape from choosing, it must necessarily fail in its fundamental desire to identify itself with the future self that it chooses to be. This doesn't mean that the for-itself must always fail to achieve the specific project that it has set for itself. But in the very success of achieving its aim, the for-itself does not and ontologically cannot identify itself with the achieved possibility. At the very moment of "success," the for-itself is already beyond itself, it surpasses itself, it nihilates what it has become. Suppose it is my fundamental project to become a brilliant politician. Everything that I do—the way I treat my family and friends, allow myself to express my emotions, attend to my physical appearance, etc.—may be conditioned by this project. I may succeed in becoming a brilliant politician. But I will not and cannot succeed in completely identifying myself with this possibility. At the very moment of realizing it, I am condemned as a for-itself to be "beyond" it. I can never simply *be* anything, for I am separated by an absolute distance from whatever I become.

Sartre would affirm that Hegel, better than anyone else, understood the fundamental project of the self—to become in-itself-for-itself. Hegel's entire philosophy, whether his logic, his phenomenology, his philosophy of right, his philosophy of history, etc. is directed toward this goal of completeness, a goal that Hegel never doubts can be realized. However, Sartre argues—and this is at once the basic theme and the grand conclusion of *Being and Nothingness* —that the goal of achieving totality by becoming in-itself-for-itself is ontologically impossible.

Everything happens as if the world, man, and man-in-the-world succeeded in realizing only a missing God. Everything happens therefore as if the in-itself and the for-itself were presented in a state of disintegration in relation to an ideal synthesis. Not that the integration has ever *taken place* but on the contrary precisely because it is always indicated and always impossible (*B.N.*, p. 623; *p. 717*).

Consciousness as Action

In Sartre's ontological investigations, the concepts of nothingness, consciousness, freedom, and the for-itself converge. All of these are ways of approaching the same basic human reality. The convergence of these concepts enables us to sketch the outlines of the image of man and human action that emerges from Sartre's phenomenological ontology. Man is that being who is never completely identical with what he has been or with what he strives to be; he is always at a distance from himself, whether we focus on his past, present, or future. To be a consciousness—to be a for-itself—is to make choices at every moment while we are conscious. In making such choices we are choosing what we are to become. "One must be conscious in order to choose, and one must choose in order to be conscious. Choice and consciousness are one and the same thing" (*B.N.*, p. 462;

p. 539). "The for-itself is the being which is defined by action" (*B.N.*, p. 431; *p. 507*). We may make these choices reflectively, with self-consciousness of what we are doing, or prereflectively, but we are always choosing and thereby always acting. Even our pre-reflective choices are conscious, for Sartre argues that the notion of an unconscious choice is an absurdity. In acting, we "modify the *shape* of the world" within which we live (*B.N.*, p. 433; *p. 508*). In choosing—acting—we *are* radically free. We *are* freedom. There are no limits on our freedom in the sense that nothing determines what we are to become except our own spontaneous choices. While these choices are made on the basis of prereflective or reflective assessment of the situation in which we find ourselves, there is no basis or ground for these choices except our own nothingness. "No factual state whatever it may be (the political and economic struc-ture of society, the psychological 'state,' *etc.*) is capable by itself of motivating any act whatsoever. For an act is a projection of the for-itself toward what is not, and what is can in no way determine what is not" (*B.N.*, p. 435; *pp. 510-511*). Our existence is always beyond our essence. Our essence is what we are, or more perspicuously, what we have been. But at every moment of our existence, we are beyond this essence, nihilating it, projecting toward what is not. For con-sciousness there is "the permanent possibility of effecting a rupture with its own past, or wrenching itself away from its past so as to be able to consider it in light of a non-being and so as to be able to con-fer on it the meaning which *it has* in terms of the project of a meaning which it *does not have*" (*B.N.*, p. 436; *p. 511*). Even our own fac-ticity is not a dead weight upon us or a limitation upon our freedom, for we choose what *meaning* this facticity is to have for us. I may be (have been) a stable, responsible, upstanding citizen. But this charac-ter does not determine what I will do in the future. If I continue to exhibit this same character, it is because I have chosen to do so. "For human reality, to be is to *choose oneself*; nothing comes to it either from the outside or from within which it can *receive or accept*. Without any help whatsoever, it is entirely abandoned to the intoler-able necessity of making itself be—down to the slightest detail" (*B.N.*, pp. 440-441; *p. 516*). By an "intolerable necessity," we are free, and the reflective apprehension of this freedom—our own nothingness—is anguish. The desperate attempt to escape this freedom, the attempt to *be* something (and thereby achieve the impossible unity of the in-itself-for-itself) is bad faith. The existential condition of life is itself bad faith, for in being condemned to freedom we are also condemned to the impossible task of trying to identify ourselves with the possibilities we have chosen, of seeking to become the in-itself-for-itself. "Man is a useless passion" (*B.N.,* p. 615; *p. 708*) because he can never achieve what he lacks and most desperately desires—to become identical with himself, to achieve an integration and harmony with himself as a for-itself and the ideal self that he projects.

At times, Sartre hesitates in drawing the conclusion that the existential condition of life is bad faith. He argues that the project of being sincere is itself a form of bad faith because we deceive ourselves in thinking that we can fully express and identify ourselves with what we are. However, there is a tantalizing footnote in *Being and Nothingness* where Sartre alludes to a possible condition of authenticity.

> If it is indifferent whether one is in good or in bad faith, because bad faith reapprehends good faith and slides to the very origin of the project of good faith, that does not mean that we can not radically escape bad faith. But this supposes a self-recovery of being which was previously corrupted. This self-recovery we shall call authenticity, the description of which has no place here (*B.N.,* p. 70; *p. 111*).

In *Being and Nothingness,* Sartre does not take up an analysis of authenticity, and it is difficult to see why authenticity does not itself slide into bad faith. How can we radically escape bad faith if we are condemned to seek an impossible integration and fulfillment? Even the self-awareness that this is our condition does not enable us to escape from bad faith because as a for-itself, we still must choose and consequently act as if we could become an in-itself-for-itself.

The extreme radicalness of Sartre's claim that the for-itself is defined by its action becomes manifest when we realize that acting and choosing are not modes of consciousness, but characterize consciousness in *all* its modes. In common sense and in traditional philosophy we distinguish between passions and volitions, the former being states of mind or body which *happen* to us, the latter being something that we actively do. We may be sad, depressed, elated, afraid, etc. Normally we think that these are conditions or states of mind in which we find ourselves. It is frequently within our power to choose how we will react to these emotional states. We may try to hide our depression and be cheerful or allow ourselves to manifest this depression. We may try to suppress our emotions or even deceive others by pretending that our emotions are more violent than they really are. However we may make the distinction, we generally assume that there are some emotional states that happen to us or overcome us and we contrast these with states, attitudes, dispositions, etc., that are within our control. Sartre challenges the basis for this distinction, and it is a challenge that has its roots in the ontology he has developed. In an early essay on the emotions, Sartre tells us that emotion "is a transformation of the world. When the paths traced out become too difficult, or when we see no path, we can no longer live in so urgent and difficult a world. All the ways are barred. However, *we must act.* So we try to change the world, that is, to live as if the connection between things and their potentialities were not ruled by deterministic processes, but by magic," (*italics added*).[39] Or again, in *Being and Nothingness,* Sartre says "we have shown elsewhere that emotion is not a physiological tempest; it is a reply adapted to the situation: it is a type of conduct, the meaning and form of which are the object of an intention of consciousness which aims at attaining a particular end by particular means" (*B.N.,* pp. 444-445; *p. 521*). The most forceful statement of this position appears in his essay on existentialism. "The existentialist does not believe in the power of passion. He will never agree that a sweeping passion is a ravaging torrent which fatally leads a man to certain acts and is therefore an excuse. He thinks that man is responsible for his passion."[40]

But in what sense do we "choose" our passions? Sartre does not mean that we make a reflective and voluntary decision; he distinguishes between such reflective decisions and the generic notion of choice which is a characteristic of all consciousness. Sartre explores the subtle gradation of choices moving from prereflective ones through those that are the result of impure reflection, to fully

39. *The Emotions: Outline of a Theory,* pp. 58-59; *Esquisse d'une théorie des émotions,* p. 43.

40. *Existentialism,* trans. by Bernard Frechtman, pp. 27-28; *L'Existentialisme est un humanisme,* pp. 37-38.

reflective decisions.[41] Nevertheless, choosing a passion is something that we *do,* not something that *happens* to us. It is a selective response to a situation, one whose meaning for me is shaped by my own projects. And such a response is not causally determined by anything which *is* or has been. The passions which I choose are themselves the results of free spontaneous acts of consciousness. Although this position may seem extreme, it is entailed by Sartre's analysis of the structure of the for-itself. Suppose I am sad. If I *am* sad then this is already part of my past, my facticity, my personality. But at every moment of existence, I am also "beyond" whatever I am (have been). As I face the future, it is not what I am that determines what I will be. As a for-itself I select or choose what I will be. If I continue to be sad, it is because I have consciously chosen this possibility for myself (*B.N.,* pp. 60-61; *pp. 100-101*).

Or suppose I am faced with a threatening situation. I may flee in fear or stand firm and confront the situation. My own projects or aims give this situation its character or meaning. A situation has the meaning it does for me because I have chosen to give it this meaning. Another consciousness may not perceive the "same" situation as threatening. But if I flee from the situation because of fear, this is not something that happens to me; it is something that I have chosen to do. I am never overcome by passion; I *allow* myself to become overwhelmed by passion. Sartre develops this example in greater detail, emphasizing how choice determines the way in which I perceive and react to the situation.

If I am threatened, I can run away at top speed because of my fear of dying. This passional fact nevertheless posits implicitly as a supreme end the value of life. Another person in the same situation will, on the contrary, understand that he must remain at his post even if resistance at first appears more dangerous than flight; he "will stand firm." But his goal, although better understood and explicitly posited, remains the same as in the case of the emotional reaction. It is simply that the methods of attaining it are more clearly conceived; certain of them are rejected as dubious or inefficacious, others more solidly organized. The difference here depends on the choice of means and on the degree of reflection and of making explicit, not on the end. . . . Human reality can not receive its

41. For a fine discussion of this point and a general interpretation of Sartre's theory of emotions, see Joseph P. Fell, III, *Emotion in the Thought of Sartre.*

ends . . . either from outside or from a so-called inner "nature." It chooses them and by this very choice confers upon them a transcendent existence as the external limit of its projects. . . . Human reality in and through its very upsurge decides to define its own being by its ends. It is therefore the positing of my ultimate ends which characterizes my being and which is identical with the sudden thrust of the freedom which is mine. And this thrust is an *existence* . . . (*B.N.,* pp. 443-444; *pp. 519-520*).

Human reality chooses its ends as well as its means. An emotional response to a situation represents, according to Sartre, a choice of means for achieving certain ends which are not given to us, but freely chosen. When a situation, which has the specific meaning that it does for me because of my freely chosen projects, is too difficult for me, when I cannot bear to confront it, I choose to flee or escape it by "magical means." Our common sense categories tend to break down in such extreme situations. If a person panics or becomes hysterical in a crisis situation, we will sometimes excuse his behavior because of our belief that he could not help doing what he did: he was overcome by passion. In some cases, we do hold a person responsible for irrational behavior because we believe that he could have done otherwise. Normally, we think that the category of choice is appropriate in those cases where an individual confronts his situation and chooses among various alternatives, various courses of action. But for Sartre, "reacting" to a situation in a state of panic or confronting it in a more coldly deliberative manner *already* represents a basic choice.

In fear, fainting and cataplexie aim at suppressing the danger by suppressing the consciousness of the danger. There is an *intention* of losing consciousness in order to do away with the formidable world in which consciousness is engaged and which comes into being through consciousness. Therefore we have to do with magical behavior provoking the symbolic satisfactions of our desires and revealing by the same stroke a magical stratum of the world. In contrast to this conduct voluntary and rational conduct will consider the situation scientifically, will reject the magical, and will apply itself to realizing determined series and instrumental complexes which will enable us to resolve the problems. . . . But what will make me decide to choose the magical aspect or the technical aspect of the world? It can not be the world itself, for this in order to be manifested waits to be discovered. Therefore it is necessary that the for-itself in its project must choose being the one by whom the world is revealed as magical or rational; that is, the for-itself must as a free project of itself give to itself magical or rational existence. It is responsible for either one, for the for-itself can *be* only if it has chosen itself. Therefore the for-itself appears as the free foundation of its emotions as of its volitions. My fear *is* free and manifests my freedom; I have put all my freedom into my fear, and I have chosen myself as fearful in this or that circumstance. Under other circumstances I shall exist as deliberate and courageous, and I shall have put all my freedom into my courage. In relation to freedom there is no privileged psychic phenomenon. All my "modes of being" manifest freedom equally since they are all ways of being my own nothingness (*B.N.*, p. 445; *p. 521*).

The same type of analysis and the same strategy that Sartre employs to show that I choose my emotions, is also used to show that I choose my values. Values themselves are not given to me either by some external source or by an inner nature. The values that I adopt are chosen by me and my values are revealed by the way in which I act. The fact that all of us—regardless of what we profess—do exhibit value preferences in our actions can prevent us from recognizing that these values are not "given" to us but are chosen by us.

Furthermore, it is my freedom that is the foundation of any values that I choose. When we understand what Sartre means by freedom, we realize that ultimately there is no ground or justification for the values that I choose.

. . . my freedom is the unique foundation of values and that *nothing,* absolutely nothing, justifies me in adopting this or that particular value, this or that particular scale of values. As a being by whom values exist, I am unjustifiable. My freedom is anguished at being the foundation of values while itself without foundation. It is anguished in addition because values, due to the fact that they are essentially revealed to a freedom, can not disclose themselves without being at the same time "put into question," for the possibility of overturning the scale of values appears complementary as *my* possibility (*B.N.*, p. 38; *p. 76*).

It may seem from what we have said that every choice and act is absolutely gratuitous. There is a sense in which this is true but there is an important sense in which it is false.

At every moment of existence we are living out projects by which we choose what we are to be. But the projects which define a for-itself form a complex organic totality in which there are "fundamental," "initial," "ultimate" projects, and less fundamental ones whose characters shape and are shaped by ultimate projects. I may be striving to be a brilliant politician, but at each moment of my life I will be engaged in certain lesser projects toward more restricted possibilities involving my physical appearance, my treatment of others, the emotions I allow myself to express in private and in public, etc. The distinctive intentional thrust of an individual's projects and their organic interconnections enable us to predict the ways in which he is likely to act in the future. In this sense acts are not gratuitous and freedom is not "pure capricious, unlawful, gratuitous, incomprehensible contingency" (*B.N.*, p. 453; *p. 530*). Because most of us are so caught up and hemmed in by our fundamental projects, a large measure of what we do is perfectly predictable. We know what an upright, solid, citizen is likely to do in a given situation, just as we can predict what a "free" hippie is likely to do. The common argument of the behavioristically oriented social scientist that human behavior is determined because it is predictable is really a *non sequitur*. In Sartrean terms, behavior is predictable precisely because of the fixity of human projects, but this does not mean that the choosing of a project or its reaffirmation at every moment of our existence is any less radically free. In any particular situation, it is always possible that I might have done or chosen otherwise. But the key issue is at what price. Any choice can involve "a radical conversion of my being-in-the-world; that is, by an abrupt metamorphosis of my initial project" (*B.N.*, p. 464; *p. 542*). Such a modification is always a possibility for me. In *this* respect, all choices are ultimately gratuitous, for at any moment of my existence I can choose such a "radical conversion."

The anguish which, when this possibility is revealed, manifests our freedom to our consciousness is witness of this perpetual modifiability of our initial project. In anguish we do not simply apprehend the fact that the possibles which we project are perpetually eaten away by our freedom-to-come; in addition we apprehend our choice—i.e., ourselves —as *unjustifiable*. This means that we apprehend our choice as not deriving from any prior reality but rather as being about to serve as foundation for the ensemble of significations which constitute reality. Unjustifiability is not only the subjective recognition of the absolute contingency of our being but also that of the interiorization and recovery of this contingency on our own account. . . . Thus we are perpetually engaged in our choice and perpetually conscious of the fact that we ourselves can abruptly invert this choice and "reverse steam"; for we project the future by our very being, but our existential freedom perpetually eats it away as we make known to ourselves what we are by means of the future but without getting a grip on this future which remains always possible without ever passing to the rank of the *real*. Thus we are *perpetually threatened* by the nihilation of our actual choice and perpetually threatened with choosing ourselves—and consequently with becoming—other than we are (*B.N.*, pp. 464-465; *pp. 542-543*).

We are led back once again to Sartre's claim that human reality is an unhappy consciousness with no possibility of surpassing this condition. It is our very nature to be alienated from ourselves, to be a divided self-consciousness desperately seeking to escape this condition and to achieve self-identity. Unhappy Consciousness is not a brief moment in the grand development of *Geist* realizing itself. It is our permanent, ontological, human condition. Once this ontological conclusion is held firm, there are enormously significant consequences for understanding human choice and action. We are choosing what we are to become at every moment of our existence. These choices are ultimately grounded in our own nothingness. When we strip away all illusions, all attempts to deceive ourselves, all attempts to escape from our own freedom and nothingness, we realize that nothing can serve as a ground or justification of our choices. But even this reflective "lucidity" about our human reality, this realization of the impossibility of ever becoming an in-itself-for-itself does not help us to escape from the perpetual attempt to seek some form of self-identity. We are condemned to seek for what is impossible.

Bad Faith

In focusing on the fundamentals of Sartre's ontology and its consequences for understanding human choice and action, I have not been able to discuss many other aspects of Sartre's philosophy. I have not examined Sartre's analysis of "Being-for-others" which forms a major part of *Being and Nothingness,* nor have I considered Sartre's phenomenological investigation of the human body. These are important topics, but Sartre's explanation of them does not alter what I have said about the for-itself as that being which defines itself by its own action. They further develop Sartre's central theme. There is one topic, however, that needs fuller discussion—bad faith. It will enable us to make the transition to an evaluation of Sartre's philosophy.

"Bad faith" *(la mauvaise foi)* is probably Sartre's best-known concept. The section in which it is discussed in *Being and Nothingness* serves the purpose of unfolding the structure of the for-itself. Even those who have balked at Sartre's ontology have been impressed with the acuteness and sensitivity of Sartre's phenomenological description of the varieties of bad faith. Sartre describes a number of situations in which we are engaged in projects of self-deception, attempts to escape from our own freedom. There is a danger that in the vividness of Sartre's descriptions we can lose sight of his main ontological point. We tend to think of "bad faith" as a pejorative term, the opposite of good faith, sincerity, or authenticity. I have already noted that Sartre argues that the projects of good faith and sincerity are themselves forms of bad faith. The attempt to escape from our own nothingness, the attempt of the for-itself to *be* something, i.e., to be finally self-identical with itself, is bad faith. This is what we attempt to achieve in being sincere.[42]

But the question arises, can we ever escape the condition of bad faith? Sartre suggests that we can, although he does not show this in *Being and Nothingness*. The force of Sartre's ontological analysis has been to lead us to the conclusion that bad faith is the inescapable human condition. Sartre's ambivalence plagues him until the very end of *Being and Nothingness*. In the final pages he tells us:

Many men, in fact, know that the goal of their pursuit is being; and to the extent that they possess this knowledge, they refrain from appropriating things for their own sake and try to realize the symbolic appropriation of their being-in-itself. But to the extent that this attempt still shares in the spirit of seriousness and that these men can still believe that their mission of effecting the existence of the in-itself-for-itself is written in things, they are condemned to despair; for they discover at the same time that all human activities are equivalent . . . and that all are on principle doomed to failure. Thus it amounts to the same thing whether

42. For the details of Sartre's analysis of sincerity *(sincerité)*, see *B.N.*, pp. 62 ff.; *pp. 102 ff*.

one gets drunk alone or is a leader of nations (*B.N.*, p. 627; *p. 721*).[43]

This is the conclusion that ought to follow if we take seriously the claim that all choices are ultimately unjustifiable.

But this is not where Sartre finally leaves us. He concludes by holding out some possibility of an escape from bad faith. He tells us that "a freedom which wills itself freedom is in fact a being-which-is-not-what-it-is and which-is-what-it-is-not, and which chooses as the ideal of being, being-what-it-is-not and not-being-what-it-is" (*B.N.*, p. 627; *p. 722*).

This freedom chooses then not to *recover* itself but to flee itself not to coincide with itself but to be always at a distance *from itself*. What are we to understand by this being which wills to hold itself in awe, to be at a distance from itself? Is it a question of bad faith or of another fundamental attitude? And can one live this new aspect of being? In particular will freedom by taking itself for an end escape all *situation*? Or on the contrary, will it remain situated? Or will it situate itself so much the more precisely and the more individually as it projects itself further in anguish as a conditioned freedom and accepts more fully its responsibility as an existent by whom the world comes into being? All these questions, which refer us to a pure and not an accessory reflection, can find their reply only on the ethical plane. We shall devote to them a future work (*B.N.*, pp. 627-628; *p. 722*).

Sartre never wrote this "future work," although his writings after *Being and Nothingness* are dominated by ethical reflections. But this closing passage of *Being and Nothingness* with its rhetorical flourishes, is itself written in bad faith—and I mean this precisely in the sense in which Sartre has characterized bad faith. Sartre is attempting to escape from the stern lesson of his own ontological investigations. If it is true that "all human activities are equivalent,"

43. Sartre's ambivalence is indicated in the sentence that immediately follows this passage: "If one of these activities takes precedence over the other, this will not be because of its real goal but because of the degree of consciousness which it possesses of its ideal goal; and in this case it will be the quietism of the solitary drunkard which will take precedence over the vain agitation of the leader of nations." But why should any activity take precedence over another? Why is the "degree of consciousness" a *reason* for one act taking precedence over another act? Here Sartre is implicitly affirming his own fundamental value—authenticity. But it is as unjustifiable as any other value.

and that none of our choices or acts are justifiable and consequently there is no ultimate sense in saying that one project, choice or act is better than another, then what possible *ethical* significance can be attached to the choice of freedom as "the ideal of being"? Hasn't Sartre—in the main plot of *Being and Nothingness*—already answered the question that there is no other "fundamental attitude" than that of bad faith?

The natural reply at this point is that there is one and only one way of escaping the condition of bad faith—and this is by reflective lucidity. When we lucidly grasp the nature, dilemmas, and traps of our human reality, we can escape the "spirit of seriousness" which tempts us into the false belief that we can become an in-itself-for-itself. It is certainly true that in *Being and Nothingness* the one *value* that really functions as supreme is the value of self-understanding. Sartre is in the classical Socratic tradition where the highest aim of man is to know himself. We are tempted to say that the individual who is no longer caught in the maze of self-deception, which ensnares us at every turn, is the individual who lives authentically. But ironically, Sartre, who throughout his career has in his actions affirmed the value of reflective lucidity as the highest value, has provided an ontological analysis that undermines this value. If all values are ultimately unjustifiable, then there is no reason to suppose that it is any better or any more valuable to be lucid than to be involved in self-deception. The individual in bad faith chooses his being—just as the individual who attempts to escape from bad faith. Both choices are "grounded" in one's nothingness. Both fundamental projects are ultimately gratuitous. There is no reason to value one rather than the other: this is Sartre's own grand conclusion.

We might try to fight our way out of this impossible situation by declaring that values and ends are not given to us but that we choose our values. This is, of course, what Sartre has told us. But does it help us here? When we reflectively choose one course of action rather than another, one life project rather than another, we do so because we believe that one course of action is "better" or "more appropriate" or "more desirable" than another. I may not affirm that reflective lucidity is a universal value, but *I* value it, *I* want to be lucid, *I* choose this as my end. But why? It is no answer to say that I choose because of my assessment of the situation in which I find myself. This pushes the issue back one step further. The concept of value makes no sense if there are no criteria—no matter how vague or subjective they may be—for distinguishing values, for saying that x is better than y. And yet if we hold fast to Sartre's ontological analysis, we can never justify any criteria, we can never ultimately say that one thing is more valuable than another. It doesn't even make sense to say that x is more valuable for *me*. "*All* human activities are equivalent."

Furthermore, what sense can it make to speak, as Sartre does in the final paragraph of *Being and Nothingness,* of choosing freedom? How can we choose that which defines our very human condition and from which we can never escape? Let us not be taken in by the rhetoric. If freedom is our own nothingness, then in choosing freedom we are choosing our own nothingness. We can't even say that we choose to affirm our own nothingness and freedom, for this already introduces a value that has no ontological basis. Here too, we may be tempted to introduce a distinction between freedom as a possibility and freedom as an actuality, freedom as the basic condition of every man and freedom as that state of affairs in which men can "exercise" their freedom without external hindrances. But again, this distinction doesn't help. According to Sartre there are never any limitations on our ontological freedom, and this is just as true for the man living in a free humanistic society as it is for the men enslaved in a concentration camp. The conventional distinction between these two situations which we normally describe as the contrast between freedom and slavery has no ontological foundation. If we take Sartre literally, we simply have no ultimate reason for valuing or preferring one rather than the other. We should have the courage to admit that the consequence of Sartre's analysis of human reality is not only despair, but nihilism in the coldly technical sense. There never is nor can be any basic reason or justification for one value, end, choice, or action rather than another.

The dilemma implicit in Sartre's philosophy as expressed in *Being and Nothingness* becomes even more poignant when we consider Sartre's own life. From beginning to end, Sartre has been a moralist in the great tradition of French moralists. I do not mean that he has been moralistic. But he has been a person outraged with stupidity and injustice, who has dedicated himself to rooting out self-deceit and hypocrisy wherever it exists. He has felt called upon to take a stand on the great political issues of the day and he has done so with courage and lucidity. Sartre has *been* the epitome of the engaged contemporary intellectual.

But who better than Sartre has condemned himself in the very seriousness of this life project? Who better than Sartre has shown us that ultimately, such a life project is no better or worse, no more or less valuable than any other life project? Who better than Sartre illustrates the life of bad faith—the desperate attempt to escape from the nothingness that lies at the heart of one's being?

At times, Sartre has shown remarkable acuteness in grasping the paradoxicality of his own existence, but together with his self-irony, there is also the attempt to escape the consequences of this self-irony.[44] In his popular pamphlet, *L'Existentialisme est un humanisme,* Sartre made a feeble attempt to outline the ethics he promised at the end of *Being and Nothingness.* In declarations that exhibit more rhetoric than substance, Sartre declares "The ultimate meaning of the acts of honest men is the quest for freedom as such. . . . We want freedom for freedom's sake and in every particular circumstance. And in wanting freedom we discover that it depends entirely on the freedom of others, and that the freedom of others depends on ours. . . . I can take freedom as my goal only if I take that of others as a goal as well."[45] We naturally respond to these stirring Kantian slogans. But we have come a long way—without any clear signposts —from the ontological solipsism of *Being and Nothingness.* In choosing, I am choosing an ideal self which I seek to become. But this is the condition of every man; I cannot possibly choose for others just as they cannot choose for me. Why should I or any other man choose freedom and what possible meaning can this have? Even if we can make sense of this paradoxical claim, there seems to be no reason why in choosing my own freedom, I am also taking the freedom of others as my end. "Freedom" no longer has the "neutral" ontological significance that it has in *Being and Nothingness.* It is clearly a moral concept, but the chasm between the ontological and

44. This is beautifully illustrated in the first volume of his "autobiography," *Les mots.*

45. *Existentialism,* p. 54; *L'Existentialisme est un humanisme,* pp. 82-83.

the moral is an unbridgeable one—this is the logical conclusion of Sartre's own complex argument.[46]

Perhaps because Sartre himself detected the shallowness of the position developed in *L'Existentialisme est un humanisme,* we do not find this quasi-Kantian line of thought followed up. When he detected this strain in his once close friend Albert Camus, he turned

46. Cf. Iris Murdoch's discussion of this point, *Sartre: Romantic Rationalist,* pp. 45 ff. Several interpreters of Sartre have attempted to defend him by distinguishing several senses of "freedom." But I don't think any commentator has successfully shown how we can bridge the gap between the ontological or existential sense of freedom and the moral or political senses of freedom. See, for example, Norman McLeod, "Existential Freedom in the Marxism of Jean-Paul Sartre," *Dialogue,* 7 (1968). McLeod distinguishes "existential freedom" from "authenticity." "Existential freedom is a quality which we *are,* and no-one can escape it: it is an ontological reality." "Authenticity refers to a lucid recognition of one's existential freedom and concomitant responsibility . . . and Sartre clearly implies, especially in his novels and plays, that one *should* live an authentic existence." But McLeod adds that "Sartre nowhere gives any reason for this moral imperative; it remains . . . a covert value-judgement" (p. 28). I think everything McLeod *says* is essentially correct. But what he does not say—and this is the point of our claim that Sartre is himself in bad faith—is that the force of Sartre's analysis of "existential freedom" is that it is impossible to justify this or any other moral imperative.

I find the same tendency to blunt the dichotomy between ontological and moral freedom in other commentators on Sartre. Frederick A. Olafson has written a sympathetic and lucid "ethical interpretation of existentialism" in his *Principles and Persons,* and the interpretation he offers conflicts with the above analysis of Sartre. Because Olafson self-consciously attempts to present a composite picture of what the existentialists have been saying, he is able to avoid some of the "awkward" consequences that follow from *Sartre's* own analysis. For example, he says, "but just as Sartre's attempt to think of freedom as a categorical and degree-less attribute of human beings generates difficulties I have already noted, so this attempt to think of total choice as a kind of super-choice that in some measure controls subordinate choices is extremely difficult to reconcile with our sense of psychological reality. In fact, however, such a view is by no means essential to existentialism and has not been adopted by Merleau-Ponty, for example" (p. 171). Perhaps "such a view is by no means essential to existentialism," but it is essential (and central) for Sartre.

The most forceful and complete attempt to answer the objections which I and others have brought against Sartre concerning his conception of freedom is by Thomas C. Anderson, "Is a Sartrean Ethics Possible?" *Philosophy Today* 14 (Summer 1970). But Anderson's argument rests on an appeal to what is "strictly coherent," and what man "wants" which I find very feeble. He says, "Since freedom is the source of all value, it is only logical ('strictly coherent')

all his critical acumen to attacking it.[47] It is as if Sartre were aware of the impasse that his own ontological analysis had led him to and he sought to escape this dead end. In Sartre's Marxist turn, we find still another attempt to escape, another study in bad faith. In his *Critique de la raison dialectique,* Sartre declares that existentialism is an ideology and that Marxism is the only philosophy for our time. The emphasis, concern, direction of Sartre's philosophy are now changed. He not only seeks a synthesis of existentialism and Marxism: he now more meticulously considers the ways in which our social facticity and situations are shaped by "material" conditions of scarcity. But in the hundreds of pages of the *Critique,* or in any other place in Sartre's writings, we never find him squarely confronting the ontological analysis of *Being and Nothingness* which leads to a dispassionate nihilism.[48]

---

that it be taken by man as his supreme value" (p. 121). Anderson realizes that according to Sartre's ontology, the decision to be *logical* already represents a choice which itself is a manifestation of man's freedom. In answer to the question "why choose to be logical," Anderson remarks, "It is worth noting that strictly speaking Sartre himself does not say that man is *obliged* to choose freedom; rather he says that if one becomes aware that he imposes values, he can only 'want' freedom" (p. 121). Sartre does indeed make this claim in *L'Existentialisme est un humanisme,* but his analysis in *L'être et le néant* shows how misleading this claim is. The thrust of his analysis is to show that man *wants* to *escape* from his freedom.

47. See "Reply to Albert Camus," *Situations; Situations,* IV.

48. These brief remarks about Sartre's *Critique* should not be taken as a dismissal of the value of the *Critique.* Although turgid and long-winded, it is important not only for following Sartre's intellectual development, but for its attempt to develop categories to come to grips with *praxis.* Sartre does not himself see the *Critique* as repudiating his early work, but rather as correcting and amplifying it. As in the case of Marx, an enormous body of literature has been addressed to the issue of the "early" and "late" Sartre, focusing on the issues of whether Sartre's two main philosophic works represent a radical break or a continuous development. It has become fashionable to stress that already in *L'être et le néant,* Sartre appreciates the role of the "Other"—our relations with other men—and the situational nature of human freedom i.e., that freedom only becomes manifest in relation to some resisting facticity and is shaped (although not fettered) by concrete situations. The next move is to show that these "understressed" elements of *L'être et le néant* are the elements that become dominant in Sartre's later work, and especially his *Critique.* The argument for the continuity of Sartre's development and the happy synthesis of existentialism and Marxism gets muddied because there is lots of

When I began my examination of Sartre, I suggested that he shrewdly perceived that if Hegel and the Hegelian outlook is to be attacked, then one must get back to its "beginnings," to its roots. The analysis and dialectical interplay of being-in-itself and being-for-itself does develop a radical alternative to Hegel. But we have also seen that if we hold fast to the logic of Sartre's argument—then this analysis has powerful nihilistic conclusions. These are not accidental consequences of Sartre's philosophy; they are already implicit in his characterization of the structure of the for-itself. This nihilism is in existential conflict with the seriousness of the moral and political stance that Sartre has taken throughout his life and which he claims is grounded in existentialism. Sartre himself might well be a character in one of his own novels—a portrait in the study of bad faith, an attempt to escape from his own nothingness. But *if* this nihilism is to be overcome or refuted, then it is essential to make a *new* beginning, to return to the analysis of the structure of being-for-itself in order to show how we might escape the romantic nihilistic solipsism that it entails. Sartre has never done this. Sartre has never fully succumbed to the nihilism that follows from *Being and Nothingness*. However, he has never returned to the ontology of *Being and Nothingness* to show us what is wrong with it or to show us how any moral or political attitude which is not professed in the boldest self-irony (and thereby undercuts itself) is compatible with the groundlessness of our existence.

---

evidence in Sartre's published work where he says that this is his *own* conception of his intellectual development and progress. But the claims and counter claims which have become the preoccupation of commentators frequently tend to obscure the central issues. For the question here is not what Sartre says he is doing, but rather whether his later work provides an answer or "way out" of the nihilistic impasse which is the main thrust of *L'être et le néant*.

For an angry and polemical defense of the continuity of Sartre's development, see James F. Sheriden, Jr., *The Radical Conversion*. But even Sheriden admits, "For Sartre, as many who bear the title of existentialist, an encounter does not legislate the response. Response there must be. Even to persist as before is to respond. But which response is selected is a matter of a commitment which is *ultimately unjustifiable*" [italics added], p. 77. For a helpful exposition of the *Critique de la raison dialectique,* see Wilfred Desan, *The Marxism of Jean-Paul Sartre*. For criticisms of the *Critique,* see George Lichtheim, *Marxism in Modern France,* and "Sartre, Marxism, and History," *The Concept of Ideology*. See also Claude Lévi-Strauss, *La Pensée savage* pp. 324-338.

In making these claims about Sartre, in showing how his analysis leads to nihilism, how he undermines the seriousness of any value position which he or anyone else takes, how his own life is a study in bad faith, I do not want to gloat in moral superiority. To do so is to miss what I think is most admirable and important in Sartre's work. It is no condemnation of *Being and Nothingness* to say that it leads to nihilistic conclusions. This would only be a condemnation if one had good reason for thinking that such a nihilism is mistaken. There is something deep in each of us (including Sartre) that cries out against this possibility. But we cannot ignore that powerful arguments leading us to this conclusion have been developed by continental philosophers for the past hundred years. This is not only true for the tradition that encompasses Kierkegaard and Sartre, we find it also in Wittgenstein.

Taking a very different philosophic route, Wittgenstein relentlessly pushes us to the same conclusion that follows from *Being and Nothingness*:

6.4   All propositions are of equal value.
6.41   The sense of the world must lie outside the world. In the world everything is as it is, and everything happens as it does happen: *in* it no value exists—and if it did, it would have no value.
       If there is any value that does have value, it must lie outside the whole sphere of what happens and is the case. For all that happens and is the case is accidental. . . .
6.42   And so it is impossible for there to be propositions of ethics. Propositions can express nothing of what is higher.[49]

Wittgenstein, in a passage that concludes his "Lecture on Ethics," poignantly develops this point.

You will say: Well, if certain experiences constantly tempt us to attribute a quality to them which we call absolute or ethical value and importance, this simply shows that by these words we *don't* mean nonsense, that after all what we mean by saying that an experience has absolute value *is just a fact like other facts* and that all it comes to is that we have not yet succeeded in finding the correct logical analysis of what we mean by our ethical and religious expressions. Now when this is urged against me I at once see clearly, as it were in a flash of light, not only that no description that I can think of would do to describe what I mean by

49. Ludwig Wittgenstein, *Tractatus Logico-Philosophicus,* trans. by D. F. Pears and B. F. McGuinness.

absolute value, but that I would reject every significant description that anybody could possibly suggest, *ab initio,* on the ground of its significance. That is to say: I see now that these nonsensical expressions were not nonsensical because I had not yet found the correct expressions, but that their nonsensicality was their very essence. For all I wanted to do with them was just *to go beyond* the world and that is to say beyond significant language. My whole tendency and I believe the tendency of all men who ever tried to write or talk Ethics or Religion was to run against the boundaries of language. This running against the walls of our cage is perfectly, absolutely hopeless. Ethics so far as it springs from the desire to say something about the ultimate meaning of life, the absolute good, the absolute valuable, can be no science. What it says does not add to our knowledge in any sense. But it is a document of a tendency in the human mind which I personally cannot help respecting deeply and I would not for my life ridicule it.[50]

I believe that the Sartre of *Being and Nothingness* would agree with everything that Wittgenstein says. Wittgenstein, in describing the situation of the absolute hopelessness of our "running against the walls of our cage" is describing what it means to say that "man is a useless passion." But the most important statement for understanding the basic attitude of both Wittgenstein and Sartre (and we can now add, Kierkegaard) is the final one. Neither Wittgenstein nor Sartre "ridicules" this deep tendency in the human mind. Neither flinches from the results of their intellectual probings: "all propositions have the same value"; "all human acts are equivalent." Both have struggled with this thought which is at once terrifying and liberating and have sought to reconcile it with the inescapability of human choice. I do not think that Sartre has succeeded in reconciling his own deeply felt moral and political convictions with the nihilistic results of his ontological investigations. But more profoundly and passionately than most, Sartre has grappled with what has been and continues to be the profoundest moral dilemma of our time.

In the opening section of the *Phenomenology,* "Sense Certainty," Hegel develops a type of argument that is the key for understanding the point of this section and is repeated throughout the *Phenomenology.* It is fundamental to Hegel's use of dialectic. Hegel is fully aware that the advocate of sense certainty intends to single out "actual things, external or sensible objects, absolutely individual,

50. Ludwig Wittgenstein, "Lecture on Ethics," *The Philosophical Review* 74 (1965).

real, and so on" (*Phen.,* p. 160; *p. 88*). But while we intend to isolate the particular in its essential particularity and to exclude all
mediation, all generalization, anything which goes "beyond" the
immediate, we cannot do this. We (in the stage of Sense Certainty)
say about these particulars "what is simply universal" (*Phen.,*
p. 160; *p. 88*). The point that Hegel is making is similar to one
which has been repeated by analytic philosophers and is expressed
by Wittgenstein in the opening sections of his *Philosophical Investigations.* Wittgenstein shows us that although we may think that
ostensive definition is the foundation for our learning of language,
we must already master a language game in order to understand
ostensive definitions. We may *intend* to establish a foundation for
language, but we succeed in showing that this foundation already
presupposes the mastery of a language.

This type of argument—the disparity between what we intend
(mean) and what we actually succeed in accomplishing—is basic
to Hegel's use of dialectic. The philosophic "we" comprehends this
disparity from the "outside," and Hegel also maintains that in the
developing stages of consciousness in the *Phenomenology* there is
a moment when the individual himself becomes aware of the failure
of what he has sought to achieve. This is the "highway of despair."
Thus the master intends to achieve autonomy and recognition of
himself as a free self-consciousness in his mastership; but although
this is what he intends, he actually achieves a form of slavery—he
becomes dependent on the slave. Or again, we have seen that in
Hegel's *Logic,* we intend to distinguish pure Being from Nothing, but
in the first stage of this dialectic, we are unable to single out any
characteristic whereby we can effectively make this distinction. This
is a necessary consequence of the insistence that pure Being lacks
any determination whatsoever.

The same type of argument that Hegel uses can be used to bring
out the basic instability and self-contradiction of the dialectic of
Kierkegaard and Sartre. Despite all their differences, the felt difficulty that lies at the heart of Kierkegaard's and Sartre's reflections
is that something has gone wrong with the Hegelian system. More
generally, both sense that something has gone wrong with the main
tradition of Western philosophy. Philosophers have lost sight of, or
smothered in misleading abstractions, the human individual who
must choose and act, and who defines himself by his action. Kierke-

gaard incisively criticized the Hegelians and the theologians who were guilty of this "forgetfulness." And Sartre develops the same type of criticism in his attack on the Marxists (as distinguished from Marx himself). Both Kierkegaard and Sartre intend to do justice to the paradoxes and dilemmas that confront each of us as existing individuals. Both focus on the ultimate ontological (existential) isolation of the individual. In their penetrating psychological analyses, they seek to smash the false idols that each of us is so willing to believe in. Both are masters at exposing the varieties of self-deception. And both see in the structure of consciousness the source of our alienated condition. For Kierkegaard, we can all too easily lose ourselves in the search for an "objective truth" that will serve as a foundation for our existence and give "meaning" to our lives. For Sartre, there are no excuses and there never can be any excuses for what we choose to do. Their intention is to heighten our sense of the fear and trembling or the anguish that results when we confront our radical freedom and nothingness. But their dialectic carries us further. Both see the necessary failure and depair that results from making existential choices. If we are always "coming into existence," as Climacus tells us, then we are always "beyond" any existential possibility that we passionately appropriate. This is also Sartre's conclusion. Man is that being who seeks to become a god, to become an in-itself-for-itself, and this goal is ontologically impossible. We always surpass anything we have chosen to be. For Kierkegaard and Sartre, man is an Unhappy Consciousness, an "Alienated Soul" with no possibility of surpassing this situation.

It is at this point that the logic of their arguments turns against itself. There is a disparity between their intentions and what they have succeeded in showing us. What has been so appealing in these two thinkers and has influenced many religious and secular thinkers is the emphasis that they place on the existing individual who, in order to live authentically, must passionately commit and engage himself. Kierkegaard's artful discourse is intended to force us to confront the radical freedom which characterizes our existence. And Sartre's phenomenological ontology is intended to demonstrate that this is what it means to be a human being. But if we stop here, as many admirers and sympathizers have done, we fail to follow out the thrust of their argument. In discussing "bad faith," we have already begun to see the disparity between Sartre's intention of affirming the authentic life of reflective lucidity and the nihilism of his ontological analysis. If everything we choose and do is a manifestation of our radical freedom which is "grounded" in our own nothingness, then there never is or can be any good reason for choosing one course of action rather than another. If we think that lucidity "takes precedence" over self-deceit, if we think it is "better" to affirm the freedom of every man rather than some other condition, if we think that we have some objective reason for working toward a humanistic society, then we are ourselves trapped in our own bad faith. If "all human actions are equivalent," then we must not flinch from the conclusion that ultimately it makes no (ethical) difference what we do. We have no reason to admire the philosopher who laboriously struggles to understand the nature of human reality more than the vain leader of nations or the drunkard. But if all this is true, and I have argued that this is the inevitable conclusion of Sartre's ontology, then there is no reason to admire, respect, or value (either implicitly or explicitly) the individual who lives "authentically." Sartre might have intended to isolate this as the most basic or important human attitude and value, but his own analysis undermines this value. A philosophical investigation that intends to dramatize the significance of individual choice and action ends up in showing its utter insignificance.

Ironically, I think it is Kierkegaard who is much more honest and lucid about where his own labyrinth leads him. I say "ironically," because a frequent charge made by atheistic existential thinkers is that Kierkegaard's concern (obsession) with God and salvation through God's grace is itself a form of bad faith or intellectual suicide. Kierkegaard is unable, so the argument goes, to face the absurdity of the human situation and its utter meaninglessness. Faith can only be bad faith. While this charge may be appropriate for existential theologians who have claimed Kierkegaard as their mentor, it certainly is not true of Kierkegaard. Kierkegaard lucidly saw that his investigations led to a single terrifying conclusion: life is a form of despair from which there is no escape. Kierkegaard realized that the attempt of Climacus in the *Concluding Unscientific Postscript* to show us a "way out" by the passionate subjective appropriation of an existential possibility ends in failure and despair. The thrust of Kierkegaard's dialectic is to show us the absolute absurdity of Faith and Christianity. This is the most absurd of all human thoughts.

Kierkegaard, unlike the town criers of "inwardness," does not cheat. He does not tell us that Christianity is absurd but that it is "better" to have faith if we are concerned with our own salvation. Nor does he give any comfort to those who think that once they have "demonstrated" the absurdity of Christianity, they can rest content in this knowledge and proclaim this as "new" objective truth. Few thinkers have ever sought more relentlessly than Kierkegaard to strip away the devious masks by which we attempt to hide from our own nothingness. Kierkegaard (as distinguished from his pseudonymous authors) perceived that ultimately there is no more reason to "really" exist than to "merely" exist; or to engage in the world-historical speculations of the Hegelian philosopher than to outline, as Climacus does, an "alternative" existential solution. Kierkegaard was painfully aware of the disparity of his intention and what he actually achieved in showing.

Sartre, on the other hand, does cheat. He draws back from the nihilism that lies at the heart of his ontological analysis. He seeks to smuggle in some value as the supreme value—whether it be living one's life authentically, or affirming that one's freedom is bound up with the freedom of every man, or declaring that existentialism is an "ideology" that is basically compatible with a Marxist analysis of the dynamics of *praxis*.

Although this judgment of the failure of both Kierkegaard and Sartre may seem harsh, it must not be taken as a total condemnation. Once again, we can learn from Hegel. For although Hegel notes that the disparity between intention and what is actually shown reveals the failures of the developing stages of consciousness, Hegel better than anyone else has taught us that we must attempt to preserve the truth inherent in each of these stages. To comprehend the failure of a position is also to understand its positive contribution. There are few thinkers who have been as penetrating and incisive as Kierkegaard and Sartre in opening up for us the complexities, paradoxes, and dilemmas involved in human existence. More perceptively than most thinkers, they have shown us how easy it is to lose ourselves in self-deception, to seek excuses for what is inevitably our own responsibility. There is an important dialectical confrontation that can take place between Kierkegaard and Sartre on one side, and the Marxists or the pragmatists on the other. Both of these latter two movements intend to bring about a state of affairs in which freedom is actualized and human activity becomes truly individualized and creative. But we know all too well from the fate of these respective movements in history how easily and subtly they can pass into their opposites: how Marxism can become an ideology for repressive totalitarianism, and pragmatism an excuse for repressive tolerance. The threats and temptations of "forgetfulness," of losing sight of existential individuality of each man in the appeal to the mass, the group, or the class, are genuine threats to human existence. However much we emphasize the need for effective social *praxis* to balance the onesidedness of Kierkegaard and Sartre, we must not lose sight of what they have taught us about the individual existential dilemmas of choice and action. Kierkegaard and Sartre stand as a penetrating challenge to all easy solutions to the problems of human alienation.

Finally, despite all the real differences in style, concern, technique, mode of argument, and claims between existential thinkers and analytic philosophers, there are important similarities which must not be ignored. The concern with choice and action in Sartre and Kierkegaard are not isolated topics. In order to articulate what is distinctive and characteristic about these concepts they have had to work through a philosophical psychology—one which has consequences for the whole range of phenomena of the life of the mind (and body). We have briefly explored Sartre's claims about emotions and volitions. A systematic investigation of his philosophical psychology would examine the function of the imagination as well as the role that our body plays in human choice and action.

It is clear that both Kierkegaard and Sartre are challenging the traditional pictures of the life of the mind which we have inherited from the empiricist and rationalist traditions. Sartre's approach to consciousness and human reality involves a critique of Freudianism and behaviorism. For different reasons and in different ways (as we shall see in Part IV), recent analytic philosophers have also criticized the philosophy of mind of traditional empiricism and rationalism. They have also carried out a sustained critique of Freudian psychoanalysis and behaviorism. But there is not only a similarity in what both of these independent movements have been criticizing. In continental phenomenology which has been closely linked with existentialism and in post-Wittgensteinian philosophical psychology, a much more complex and subtle understanding of the life of mind and body has been emerging. Both of these movements are suspicious of the reductivist tendencies that have characterized many philosophies of man. Both have as a goal an attempt to describe meticulously the *Lebenswelt* or the forms of life that are characteristic of human action. It would be misleading to claim that both movements are converging in their claims, but there are many signs of the beginnings of a universe of discourse in which there can be a genuine dialectical encounter between these two relatively isolated philosophic movements.

ACTION, CONDUCT, AND INQUIRY

PEIRCE AND DEWEY

IN MY DISCUSSIONS of Marx, Kierkegaard, and Sartre, I began by first exploring relevant aspects of Hegel's thought which set the "problematic" for their own investigations of human action. In the case of Marx, this approach enabled me to clarify the dialectical context of his theory of *praxis*. Marx himself had engaged in a close study and critique of Hegel. Even more important than Marx's explicit critique, we could see how deeply he was influenced by a Hegelian orientation and how his successive analyses of *praxis*, labor, and production represent attempts to overcome what he took to be radical deficiencies in Hegel's understanding of the world. With Kierkegaard and Sartre, I have noted that it would be artificial and misleading to suggest that they first studied Hegel and then set out to develop an alternative point of view. Both were sensitive to the insights, claims, and the power of Hegelianism, but both felt that something had gone desperately wrong with the System. By sketching what it was in Hegel that they were reacting against, we could better understand their distinctive understanding of human existence and action. When we examine the pragmatists, the connection with Hegel is much less obvious (with the striking exception of Dewey), but no less important and revealing.

Although Peirce came to recognize basic affinities with his version of pragmatism and Hegelianism, it cannot be said that Peirce was ever a serious student of Hegel. He deplored some of the developments in logic that were carried out by those who considered themselves Hegelians. It was Kant and the medieval philosophers that were the chief source of Peirce's philosophic stimulation. There is, however, a parallel to Hegel insofar as Peirce started developing his own intellectual point of view by reflecting upon and criticizing what he took to be inadequacies in Kant, especially in Kant's understanding of logic. But late in his career when Peirce adopted the term "pragmaticism"—a name "ugly enough to keep it from kid-nappers" (5.414)[1] in order to distinguish his doctrine from other versions of pragmatism, he wrote, "The truth is that pragmaticism is closely allied to Hegelian absolute idealism, from which, however it is sundered by its vigorous denial that the third category (which Hegel degrades to a mere stage of thinking) suffices to make the world, or is even so much as self-sufficient. Had Hegel, instead of regarding the first two stages with his smile of contempt, held on to them as independent or distinct elements of the triune Reality, pragmaticists might have looked upon him as the great vindicator of their truth" (5.436).

James had a deep aversion, and even a hostility toward "German" philosophy—especially Hegel and what he took to be the pernicious influence of Hegel on American and English forms of absolute idealism. The picture of Hegel that emerges from *A Pluralistic Universe* is clearly a caricature; Hegelianism represented intellectualism, obscurity (in the name of profoundity), loss of contact with the tangled reality of life itself, and commitment to a "block universe monism." James was not the first to make such criticisms of Hegel, but he probably did more than any other philosopher in America to create and perpetuate the Hegel myth which continues to prevent many American philosophers from taking a serious look at Hegel. *A Pluralistic Universe,* which is based on lectures that James delivered in England, is tinged with an evangelical fervor in which James sought to "save" British philosophers from the aberration of absolute idealism and to call them back to their healthy empiricist roots. There are several ironies in the caricature of Hegel that James created for us. If we look at what James did—and not so much at what he said he was doing—we discover that James is much closer to Hegel (at least the Hegel of the *Phenomenology*) than he realized. By no stretch of the imagination could James be

1. I have followed the practice of referring to passages from the *Collected Papers* of Peirce by giving the volume and paragraph number. *Collected Papers of Charles Sanders Peirce,* Vols. I-VI, ed. by Charles Hartshorne and Paul Weiss; Vols. VII-VIII, ed. by Arthur W. Burks. The discussion of Peirce is based on my articles, "Action, Conduct and Self-Control," *Perspectives on Peirce,* ed. by Richard J. Bernstein; and "Peirce's Theory of Perception," *Studies in the Philosophy of Charles Sanders Peirce, Second Series,* ed. by E. C. Moore and R. S. Robin.

considered an Hegelian, but there are thematic similarities between Hegel's detailed analyses of the forms of consciousness in the *Phenomenology* and James' own extraordinary perceptive treatments of consciousness.[2]

It is ironical too, that what James found so lacking in Hegel is precisely what Dewey claimed to have discovered in Hegel—a sense of life, process, and the concreteness of experience itself. In a revealing autobiographical sketch that Dewey wrote in 1930, he characterized his early interest in Hegel in the following way:

It supplied a demand for unification that was doubtless an intense emotional craving, and yet was a hunger that only an intellectualized subject-matter could satisfy. It is more than difficult, it is impossible, to recover that early mood. But the sense of divisions and separations that were, I suppose, borne in upon me as a consequence of New England culture, divisions by way of isolation of self from the world, of soul from body, of nature from God, brought a painful laceration. My earlier philosophic study [prior to his discovery of Hegel] had been an intellectual gymnastic. Hegel's synthesis of subject and object, matter and spirit, the divine and the human, was, however, no mere intellectual formula; it operated as an immense release, a liberation. Hegel's treatment of human culture, of institutions and the arts, involved the same dissolution of hard-and-fast dividing walls, and had a special attraction for me.[3]

Not only did Hegel have a "special attraction" for the young Dewey, the legacy of what Dewey took from Hegel became a permanent aspect of his outlook. It was the sense of the dynamic and fluid interaction of life, its organic quality, and the ways in which all philosophic distinctions and dichotomies were "dissolved" and properly

2. A number of recent studies have stressed the phenomenological dimension of James' thought. While James is normally compared with Husserl, the types of phenomenological descriptions that James developed for the varieties of experience are very much in the spirit of Hegel's descriptions of the forms of consciousness. For recent studies of James' phenomenological leanings, see Herbert Spiegelberg, *The Phenomenological Movement;* Hans Linschoten, *On the Way Toward a Phenomenological Psychology: The Psychology of William James,* trans. by Amedeo Giorgi; Bruce Wilshire, *William James and Phenomenology: a Study of* The Principles of Psychology; and, John Wild, *The Radical Empiricism of William James.* See also James Edie's fine critical review of this literature, "William James and Phenomenology," *The Review of Metaphysics* 23 (March 1970).

3. "From Absolutism to Experimentalism," reprinted in *John Dewey: On Experience, Nature, and Freedom,* ed. by Richard J. Bernstein, pp. 10–11.

understood as functional distinctions within the context of experience that Dewey discovered in Hegel and attempted to integrate into his own naturalism and pragmatism.

While many sympathizers and critics of pragmatism recognize the Hegelian origins of at least Dewey's thought, there is another myth that has grown up about the significance of these origins. Dewey's Hegelian "period" represents an early stage of his intellectual development which he eventually outgrew and discarded. When we turn to the study of Dewey, we will see how false this myth is and how pervasive Hegelian themes were in his "mature" philosophy. More generally, it has been thought (and is still thought by many philosophers) that the entire pragmatic movement was a rather fuzzy-minded philosophic movement. The pragmatists had some "good insights," but these were embedded in a muddled and idiosyncratic philosophic context. The pragmatists—so this myth goes—lacked the technical and analytic ability to express what they were trying to say clearly and rigorously. It is a complicated chapter in the history of ideas to account for the origin and basis of this myth, but the influence of the positivists in America during the 1930's played a significant role in fostering this myth. Many students of pragmatism were sympathetic to positivism and logical empiricism and saw in this philosophic movement—especially in the centrality of the verifiability criterion of meaning—an attempt to state rigorously what the pragmatists were supposedly groping toward. What they failed to see is that positivism harbored an atomistic epistemological doctrine which had consistently been one of the main targets of attack by the pragmatists. A number of studies of pragmatic thinkers written in the past two decades have helped to recover the thought of the pragmatists and to show the striking differences between pragmatism and positivism. Many of the criticisms that analytic philosophers themselves have directed against positivism and epistemological phenomenalism are essentially pragmatic criticisms. But myths die hard, and I suspect that most young philosophers trained in analytic philosophy still accept some version of the myth whereby pragmatism is taken as a "doctrine" which saw through a glass darkly what we now presumably see so clearly.

In addition to folklore about the meaning and significance of the pragmatic movement, many American philosophers are totally ignorant of the origins of American philosophy. This type of "historical" understanding is relegated to students of American culture and is not thought to be of much interest or relevance to serious philosophic inquiry. This ahistorical (and even antihistorical) attitude also has its distorting consequences. Philosophy in America has become so entrenched as an "academic" discipline, requiring a very specific and rigorous professional training, that we tend to forget how recent this academic phenomenon is. Philosophy in nineteenth-century America functioned in a very different context and the sharp lines that we draw today between "professional" philosophy and "amateur" philosophy simply did not exist.

We are discovering that throughout America there were "Hegel clubs," "Kant clubs," and other informal groups where men who were not in universities and were not "professional" philosophers met to discuss texts and issues. And we are discovering how widespread and alive an interest there was in Hegel in these various groups.[4] Few philosophers today are aware, for example, that Henry Conrad Brokmeyer (1826–1906), who was a German immigrant, lawyer, and lieutenant-governor of Missouri, spent his life working and reworking a translation of *Hegel's Larger Logic*—a translation which was never published and circulated only in manuscript form to be recopied by others interested in Hegel. Better known, perhaps, is William T. Harris who was a U.S. Commissioner of Education (1889–1906) and a deeply committed Hegelian. Harris is best known today as the founder of the *Journal of Speculative Philosophy,* the first journal in America dedicated primarily to philosophic studies. While Harris conceived of the *Journal* as a means for spreading the influence of Hegelianism, he published some of the important original articles of Peirce, James, and Dewey, among many others. It was Harris who encouraged the young Dewey to pursue

4. See Loyd D. Easton, *Hegel's First American Followers,* and the forthcoming article by John O. Reidl, "The Hegelians of Saint Louis, Missouri, and Their Influence in the United States," which is to be published in the forthcoming proceedings of the 1970 Hegel Symposium sponsored by Marquette University. The bibliographical note in this article gives extensive references to the literature on the Saint Louis Hegelians. For discussions of Dewey's Hegelian origins, see *Morton G. White, The Origin of Dewey's Instrumentalism* and Chapter 2, "From Hegel to Darwin" of my book, *John Dewey.*

his philosophic studies when Dewey sent him some of his first philosophic articles and asked for advice concerning his future as a philosopher.

The point in mentioning some of these facts about the philosophic climate of nineteenth-century America is not to dredge up idle curiosities. Rather, I want to suggest something of the openness and mood of philosophic activity in the period after the Civil War. The informality, the "amateurism," the openness to a variety of influences had a creative and substantive effect on the character and direction of American philosophy. We can too easily forget today, that, as far as philosophy is concerned, both Peirce and James were essentially autodidacts. They were never formally trained in philosophy. Dewey himself was among the first students in an American graduate school when he went to Johns Hopkins. Thomas Kuhn has made us sensitive to the dominant role that existing paradigms can play in the teaching and training of scientists. The same is true for any "professional" training. But the early pragmatists neither benefited nor suffered from the constricting influences of such training. They had, in a sense, to create their own philosophic tradition from which they could develop their own insights. The latter part of the nineteenth century was consequently one of the most creative and fruitful periods of philosophic activity in America. Each of these three philosophers also benefited immensely from their deep interests in areas other than philosophy. James was trained as a medical doctor, Peirce was a practicing scientist for most of his life, and Dewey had a strong interest in the emerging social sciences and in education.

Each of these thinkers was saved from the provincialism that can so easily affect "academic" philosophy. They each exhibited in their life's work a trait that they took to have cosmic significance—novelty and openness.

America has always been hospitable to "foreign" intellectual currents. The interest in Hegelianism was stimulated by the influx of German immigrants in the nineteenth century. It found sympathetic soil in America, in part because of the native American concern with transcendentalism. Just as today it is common for the bright young philosophy student to spend some time at Oxford, so in the last decades of the nineteenth century the place "to go" to cultivate one's philosophic training was Germany.[5] One of the first "professional" Hegelians in America was G. S. Morris, Dewey's teacher at Johns Hopkins, and the man who exerted the greatest influence on Dewey's philosophic orientation during the years he spent as a graduate student at Johns Hopkins. What Dewey said about Morris' interest in Hegel might well have been said about Dewey himself.

I should say that he was at once strangely indifferent to and strangely preoccupied with the dialectic of Hegel. Its purely technical aspects did not interest him. But he derived from it an abiding sense of what he was wont to term the organic relationship of subject and object, intelligence and the world. . . . When he talked as he was wont to do, of the mechanical and the organic, it was this contrast which stood forth. It was a contrast between the dead and the living, and the contrast was more moral and spiritual than physiological, though biology might afford adumbrative illustrations. His adherence to Hegel (I feel quite sure) was because Hegel had demonstrated to him, in a great variety of fields of experience, the supreme reality of this principle of living unity maintaining itself through the medium of differences and distinctions.[6]

The above passage and the previous one that we cited from Dewey's autobiographical sketch provide the clue to what attracted and influenced the young Dewey. It was the category of the organic as a fundamental concept for understanding the variety of human life. This meant that to understand man we must approach him in the complex ways in which he dynamically interacts in the world about him. Just as we approach an organism by appreciating the complex changing functions it can perform, so this provides a point of view for approaching all dimensions of human life. Dewey, too, reacted against the "mechanical," the "merely formal," and the "abstract"; it is concreteness that he demanded and Hegel provided the "intellectualized subject-matter" in which the organic unity of life could

5. Although I do not discuss Josiah Royce in this part, he was, of course, the most famous American convert to German philosophy and absolute idealism. His own late interest in Peirce and his attempt to incorporate Peirce's insights into the nature of "community" into his own idealism is further evidence of the affinity between pragmatism and Hegelianism.

6. From a letter published in Robert Mark Wenley, *The Life and Work of George Sylvester Morris*, pp. 316–317.

be understood. Dewey even claimed that Hegel's understanding of the world was closer to capturing the quintessence of the scientific spirit than other alternative philosophic positions.

This, then, is why I conceive Hegel—entirely apart from the value of any special results—to represent the quintessence of the scientific spirit. He denies not only the possibility of getting truth out of a formal, apart thought, but he denies the existence of any faculty of thought which is other than the expression of fact itself. His contention is not that "thought," in the scholastic sense, has ontological validity, but that fact, reality is significant. Even, then, if it were shown that Hegel is pretty much all wrong as to the special meanings which he finds to make up the significance of reality, his main principle would be unimpeached until it were shown that fact has not a systematic, or interconnected, meaning, but is a mere hodgepodge of fragments.[7]

What so attracted Dewey to Hegel is what eventually led him away from Hegel, for as Dewey's own concern with understanding and extending the "scientific spirit" developed, he turned more directly to scientific analogies for illumination. Darwin supplanted Hegel as an authority. What persisted and even shaped his sensitivity to the new "biology" and the "sciences of life" was his concern and appreciation of the organic unity of life. Dewey's understanding of experience as a series of organic coordinations—including man's cognitive functions—and his typical philosophic approach to problems in which he attempted to show how conflicting viewpoints could be reconciled and synthesized show the persistent influence of what he had discovered in Hegel.

But just as Marx grew restless with Hegel and especially his dominant emphasis on intellectual comprehension, so also did Dewey. Dewey too came to feel an increasing conviction that Hegel had underplayed and misunderstood the practical aspects of life and what it meant to be an active human being shaping the world. Dewey, like the Young Hegelians in Germany, sought to "go beyond" Hegel, and it was in the realm of practice that Hegelianism clearly demanded correction. For Dewey, the primary intellectual project became the attempt to change the world, although this had a very different meaning for him than it did for Marx. Unlike Marx,

7. "The Present Position of Logical Theory," *The Monist* 2 (October 1891) 10.

Dewey did not think it was necessary to abandon philosophy or "go beyond" philosophy, but rather to *reconstruct* philosophy so that it would become a guide to enlightened *praxis*.

Peirce, as we shall see, was unmoved and even suspicious of this practical turn. But it was Peirce who explored and articulated the new conception of inquiry that became so fundamental for Dewey's own conception of philosophy as the guide to social reconstruction. Peirce, concerned primarily with logical issues and with coming to grips with what he called the "experimental habit of mind," traveled an independent route, but he was led to a conception of language, universals, knowledge, and inquiry that bore some basic similarities (as well as some striking differences) to Hegelianism.[8] For both Peirce and Dewey, the role of human conduct and action became central and provided the basis for an understanding of man's place in the world.

The concept of action has been closely associated with the pragmatic movement ever since the term "pragmatism" gained philosophic popularity during the last decade of the nineteenth century. In the opinion of many critics, pragmatism is little more than the pernicious slogan that all inquiry, knowledge, and thought is for the sake of action—where action is understood in some extremely mundane or vulgar manner. Pragmatists have been accused of holding the doctrine that something is meaningful or true only if it works or is useful. The reasons and causes for this bias are complex—in part, pragmatists and especially their popularizers are at fault for this caricature. But it is perfectly clear to anyone who reads the pragmatic thinkers carefully that the accusations are false and misleading. They were vigorously and persistently denied by the major pragmatic thinkers. In a paper published in 1905, Peirce explicitly takes up the various accusations and objections raised by critics. Written in the form of a dialogue, the Questioner asks: "Well, if you choose so to make Doing the Be-all and End-all of human life, why do you not make meaning to consist simply in doing?" And the Pragmaticist answers: "It must be admitted, in the first place, that if pragmaticism really made Doing to be the Be-all and the End-all of

8. For a discussion of these similarities and differences see John F. Boler, *Charles Peirce and Scholastic Realism* and Vincent G. Potter, S. J., *Charles Peirce: On Norms and Ideals.* See also my article "Peirce's Theory of Perception," *Studies in the Philosophy of Charles Sanders Peirce, Second Series.*

life, that would be its death. For to say that we live for the mere sake of action, as action, regardless of the thought it carries out, would be to say that there is no such thing as rational purport." (5.429).

While it is easy to say what pragmatism is not, it is more difficult to say just what pragmatism is and what is the role that action plays. If one considers pragmatism in perspective as a movement that has its beginnings with Peirce and is today manifested in the work of Quine, Sellars, Popper, Feyerabend, Hampshire, Nagel, and many others, we discover the outlines of a new approach to knowledge, inquiry, and conduct.[9] This "new" approach is a reaction to the Cartesian framework that has dominated so much of modern philosophy.

Peirce directly attacks what has been called the "foundation metaphor" of knowledge and the "spectator" view of the knower. The conception of knowledge that Peirce criticizes as mistaken is one that claims that knowledge does—indeed must—have a basic fixed foundation. The character of this foundation is an issue that has divided many modern philosophers—whether it consists of impressions, simple matters of fact, sense data, universals, a priori truths, etc. But in such diverse philosophic positions as rationalism and empiricism, there is an underlying conviction that there is such a rock bottom foundation. From the perspective of this paradigm the task of the philosopher is to discover just what this foundation is or ought to be, and then to show precisely how more complex knowledge rests on this foundation. If we can know what this foundation is (in fact or in principle) as well as the proper procedures for basing more complex knowledge on this foundation, then we will be in a position to "legitimize" our knowledge claims. We will have criteria for distinguishing what we can know from what we cannot know or to distinguish what is meaningful from what is meaningless. From this perspective too, man as knower is a "spectator." He views the world aright, or has legitimate knowledge when he penetrates the vagueness, indeterminacy and confusion of ordi-

9. The historical influence of the pragmatic movement on contemporary philosophers should not be exaggerated. But pragmatic themes pervade recent contemporary Anglo-Saxon philosophy. Amelie Rorty's anthology, *Pragmatic Philosophy,* exhibits this continuity, especially in part three of her book, "Recent Reactions and Adaptations." See also the appendix to my "Peirce's Theory of Perception," *Studies in the Philosophy of Charles Sanders Peirce, Second Series,* where I discuss some fundamental similarities between Peirce and recent epistemological investigations.

nary or common thought and opinions and sees clearly the foundation of legitimate knowledge.[10]

The logically primary elements cannot be inferred or deduced from other elements—for then they would not be primary. Instead, they must be grasped directly, known by acquaintance, immediately perceived, or rationally intuited. It is this cardinal doctrine of immediate knowledge or knowledge by intuition that Peirce attacks directly in his 1868 papers.[11] (These papers have been discussed in the Introduction, pp. 5-6.)

Peirce's immediate objective is to expose the errors of the various sorts of arguments adduced to show that there is or must be such intuitive knowledge. Peirce also argues that the quest for such an epistemological foundation is misguided. Knowledge and inquiry neither have nor need such a foundation. It is certainly true that in any inquiry, there are starting points, procedures, methods, rules, etc. that are taken as fixed and unquestioned. This is the "truth" in the foundation metaphor which is stated by Aristotle in the very beginning of the *Posterior Analytics*: "All instruction given or received by way of argument proceeds from pre-existent knowledge."[12] But it does not follow from this claim that there are absolute logical starting points that are grasped directly by some intuitive faculty. The alternative paradigm of inquiry or knowledge that Peirce begins to develop in these papers and which he refined and modified throughout his career is a view of inquiry as a self-corrective process which has no absolute beginning or end points and in which any claim is subject to further rational criticism, although we cannot question all claims at once. Our claims to knowledge are legitimized not by their origins—for the origins of knowledge are diverse and fallible—but rather by the norms and rules of inquiry itself.[13] These

10. The discussion of reductionism and constructionalism in Part IV indicates the way in which the "foundation metaphor" influenced early analytic philosophy. See pp. 239 ff.

11. "Questions Concerning Certain Faculties Claimed for Man"; "Some Consequences of Four Incapacities"; and "Grounds of Validity of the Laws of Logic: Further Consequences of Four Incapacities." These articles are included in Vol. V of the *Collected Papers*.

12. *Posterior Analytics*, Book I, Chap. 1, p. 110, in *The Basic Works of Aristotle*, ed. by Richard McKeon.

13. For contemporary criticisms of the "foundation metaphor" which echo and develop Peirce's critique, cf. W. V. O. Quine, "Two Dogmas of Empiri-

very norms, rules, and standards are themselves open to rational criticism. The fallibility of all knowledge is not a sign of its deficiency but rather an essential characteristic of knowledge, for every knowledge claim is part of a system of signs that is open to further interpretation and has consequences that are to be publicly tested and confirmed. In the continuous process of inquiry we may be called upon to revise our knowledge claims, no matter how certain and indubitable they may appear. In opposition to the subjectivistic turn in philosophy implicit in the Cartesian framework, Peirce argues that all language, signification, and consequently all inquiry and its end product, knowledge, are essentially social in character. The very meaning of our concepts depends on the role that they play in a social context of rules and norms. Even the concept of reality involves the notion of community.

The real, then, is that which, sooner or later, information and reasoning would finally result in, and which is therefore independent of the vagaries of me and you. Thus the very origin of the conception of reality shows that this conception essentially involves the notion of a COMMUNITY, without definite limits, and capable of a definite increase of knowledge. And so these two series of cognitions—the real and the unreal—consist of those which, at a time sufficiently future, the community will always continue to reaffirm; and those which, under the same conditions, will ever after be denied. Now, a proposition whose falsity can never be discovered, and the error of which therefore is absolutely incognizable, contains, upon our principle, absolutely no error. Consequently, that which is thought in these cognitions is the real, as it really is. There is nothing, then, to prevent our knowing outward things as they really are, and it is most likely that we do thus know them in numberless cases, although we can never be absolutely certain of doing so in any special case. (5.311)[14]

---

cism," *From a Logical Point of View;* Karl Popper, "On the Sources of Knowledge and of Ignorance," *Conjectures and Refutations;* Wilfrid Sellars, "Empiricism and the Philosophy of Mind," *Science, Perception and Reality;* Paul Feyerabend, "Explanation, Reduction, and Empiricism," *Minnesota Studies in the Philosophy of Science,* Vol. 3, ed. by Herbert Feigl and Grover Maxwell.

14. In his later writings Peirce makes it clear that he is not claiming that at some finite future, there will be complete agreement among a community of inquirers. This is an ideal limit, a regulative principle for inquiry. See 8.112 ff.

The shift of orientation from the foundation paradigm to that of inquiry as a continuous self-corrective process requires us to re-think almost every fundamental issue in philosophy. Peirce carries out this fundamental change of orientation by systematically explor-ing many of the technical issues that need revision, including per-ception, the nature of inference, the theory of signs, and the nature of truth and reality. Man as inquirer, as a participant in a com-munity of inquiry, is no longer viewed as "spectator," but rather as an active participant and experimenter. Man as agent comes into the foreground here because human agency is the key for under-standing all aspects of human life, including human inquiry and knowledge.

By exploring the status of conduct, and in particular self-con-trolled conduct, we can penetrate to the heart of Peirce's under-standing of man as an active inquirer. The concept of conduct is one of Peirce's central notions and is systematically related to almost every aspect of his philosophy. Since the exploration of conduct is deeply embedded in Peirce's categorial scheme, let us first take a brief look at this scheme.

Peirce's Categories

Writing to Lady Welby in 1904, Peirce tells us "I was long ago (1867) led, after only three or four years' study, to throw all ideas into the three classes of Firstness, of Secondness, and of Thirdness. This sort of notion is as distasteful to me as to anybody: and for years, I endeavored to pooh-pooh and refute it; but it long ago conquered me completely. Disagreeable as it is to attribute such meaning to numbers, and to a triad above all, it is as true as it is dis-agreeable" (8.328). Peirce uses this categorial scheme in multi-farious and sometimes inconsistent ways, but throughout his writ-ings he maintains that these categories designate elements manifested in all phenomena; that these categories are nonreducible in the sense that we cannot adequately account for the phenomena without refer-ence to all of them; and that we need no further categories to give a comprehensive, coherent, adequate account of experience, reality, and being. Peirce did think that he could "prove" the necessity and nonreducibility of the categories, but it is never quite clear what he has "proven" (cf. 5.469; 1.345; 5.82 ff.). Like Kant, he believed that the clue for arriving at the categories was to be found in logic. Peirce fails to demonstrate that the categories are necessary, sufficient, and nonreducible in all the uses that he makes of them. I do not think that this is a serious failure of his philosophy. On the contrary, it helps us to see how the categorial scheme actually functions. The dominant spirit of Peirce's use of the categories is reflected in the passage cited from the letter to Lady Welby. There is a descriptive, empirical, pragmatic temper manifested in Peirce's use of the categories.[15] The "proof" or, more accurately, the adequacy of the categories is to be found in the ways in which Peirce uses them to illuminate fundamental similarities and differences in everything we encounter.

It is in phenomenology or what Peirce calls "phaneroscopy" that he makes the most suggestive and detailed use of the categories. "Phaneroscopy is the description of the *phaneron*; and by the *phaneron* I mean the collective total of all that is in any way or in any sense present to the mind, quite regardless of whether it corresponds to any real thing or not" (1.284). Phenomenology or

. . . *phaneroscopy* is that study which, supported by the direct observation of phanerons and generalizing its observations, signalizes several very broad classes of phanerons; describes the features of each; shows that although they are so inextricably mixed together that no one can be isolated, yet it is manifest that their characters are quite disparate; then proves, beyond question, that a certain very short list comprises all of these broadest categories of phanerons there are; and finally proceeds to the laborious and difficult task of enumerating the principal subdivisions of those categories (1.286).

Firstness is characterized as "the unanalyzed total impression made by any manifold not thought of as actual fact, but simply as a quality, as simple positive possibility of appearance" (8.329). Firstness is that which is qualitative and immediate; "quality is the monadic element of the world" (1.426). Qualities *per se* are neither subjective nor objective. Consider the following examples that Peirce offers as illustrations of Firstness or immediate quality: "the scarlet of your royal liveries, the quality itself independently of its

15. Cf. Richard Rorty's discussion of Peirce's categories in "Pragmatism, Categories, and Language," *The Philosophical Review* 70 (April 1961).

being perceived or remembered" (8.329); "the quality of the emotion upon contemplating a fine mathematical demonstration, the quality of feeling of love" (1.304); "a vague, unobjectified, still less unsubjectified, sense of redness, or of salt taste, or of an ache, or of grief or joy, or of a prolonged musical note" (1.303). We can easily mistake Peirce's meaning if we think of these qualities as subjective feelings that are somehow locked up in the privacy of our minds. Everything has its distinctive quality. "The tragedy of King Lear has its Firstness, its flavor *sui generis*" (1.531). The poetic mood comes closest to that state in which we are most directly aware of qualitative immediacy. (Cf. 5.44).

What is Peirce "up to" in calling attention to this variety of qualities and dubbing them all "Firstness"? What is the point of the claim that this is a nonreducible aspect of all phenomena? First, it should be noted how Peirce departs from traditional discussions of quality. In traditional philosophy, the quality or the "whatness" of something has been thought of as a basic epistemological unit, as the primary object of knowledge.[16] However, what Peirce means by quality in the context of his phenomenology is something that is felt or had. We, of course, know that we are aware of qualities, but this "knowledge that" is not to be confused with the actual awareness or direct experience of qualities. Second, Peirce includes far more under the category of Firstness than is to be found in standard classifications of primary and secondary qualities. There are unique, pervasive, ineffable qualities such as the quality of fear or the quality of *King Lear*. Peirce's phenomenological exploration of the diversity of qualities and his claim that it is an aspect of every experience can be understood as an attempt to give proper due to a feature of experience that has been neglected in the tradition of Western philosophy. In this respect, Peirce is representative of many late nineteenth- and twentieth-century philosophers, including Bergson, James, Dewey, and Whitehead, who reacted against what they took to be the "intellectualistic" temper of Western philosophy. All of these philosophers emphasized the concreteness and qualitative

16. In speaking of "traditional philosophy" I have in mind the traditional discussions of primary and secondary qualities. Peirce's conception of quality, however, is very close to Hegel's analysis of quality in his *Logic,* especially Hegel's emphasis on the immediacy of quality and the way in which quality is logically more "primitive" than the concept of essence.

immediacy of experience. But unlike Bergson, for example, Peirce did not claim that the direct awareness of qualitative immediacy provides us with direct, intuitive, infallible knowledge of reality itself. All knowledge, according to Peirce, involves Thirdness and is essentially fallible.

Immediate quality or Firstness is mere unattached possibility. We never really encounter qualities as mere possibilities but only qualities embodied in some concrete form. The aspect of quality is abstracted or prescinded from the complex total experience; it is not something distinct and separable from the rest of experience. This brings us to Peirce's category of Secondness. It is under this category that action (as distinguished from conduct) falls. The phenomenological manifestation of Secondness is to be found in the "sense of shock," surprise, struggle, or wherever there is "as much a sense of resisting as of being acted upon" (5.45). By "struggle" Peirce means "mutual action between two things regardless of any sort of third or medium, and in particular regardless of any law of action" (1.322). Secondness is essentially dyadic, just as Firstness is monadic. When Secondness is used to focus our attention on a nonreducible feature of experience, it signifies that *"not mere twoness but active oppugnancy is in it"* (8.291).

You get this kind of consciousness in some approach to purity when you put your shoulder against a door and try to force it open. You have a sense of resistance and at the same time a sense of effort. There can be no resistance without effort; there can be no effort without resistance. They are only two ways of describing the same experience. It is a double consciousness. We become aware of ourself by becoming aware of the not-self. The waking state is a consciousness of reaction; and as the consciousness *itself* is two-sided, so it has also two varieties; namely action, where our modification of other things is more prominent than their reaction on us, and perception, where their effect on us is overwhelmingly greater than our effect on them. . . . The idea of other, of *not*, becomes a very pivot of thought. To this element I give the name of Secondness. (1.324)

Peirce's fertile imagination is at work here. His use of the categories highlights basic similarities which have frequently been ignored. Secondness is prominent in both the notions of experience and existence. "It is the compulsion, the absolute constraint upon us to think otherwise than we have been thinking that constitutes experience"

(1.336). "Experience is that determination of belief and cognition generally which the course of life has forced upon a man. One may lie about it; but one cannot escape the fact that some things *are* forced upon his cognition. There is an element of brute force, existing whether you opine it exists or not" (2.138). As for existence, Peirce tells us that "*existence* means reaction with the environment, and so is a dynamic character" (5.503). "The *existent* is that which reacts against other things" (8.191).

Once again we may feel uneasy about this imaginative grouping of phenomena and concepts as manifesting Secondness. But consider the suggestiveness of this classification. For example, we can view Peirce's claim that Secondness is the dominant characteristic of experience from the perspective of traditional empiricism. The essential insight of empiricism is that all ideas and hypotheses must ultimately be brought to the test of experience. But why is experience the touchstone for testing all knowledge claims? This is because of the brute compulsion of experience itself. "Experience" refers "to that which is forced upon a man's recognition, will-he nill-he" (5.613). There is a deep irony in the development of the empiricist tradition. The basic insight into the essential compulsive ingredient in experience that is so prominent in Locke's philosophy was eventually betrayed, as empiricism became more subjectivistic and phenomenalistic. What seemed so clear to Locke and was the starting point of his philosophy, viz., that our observation of external sensible objects and the internal operations of the mind "are the fountains of knowledge, from whence all the ideas we have, or can naturally have, do spring"[17] became more and more problematic as empiricism became more subjective and skeptical. From Peirce's point of view, we can say that the subjectivistic and phenomenalistic varieties of empiricism smothered the original insight that experience is nonreducibly compulsive and dyadic, that it exhibits Secondness. Empiricists tended to confuse the noncognitive nonreducible compulsiveness of experience with the notion that what experience forces upon us has absolute authority.

We can appreciate the significance of Peirce's use of the category of Secondness from an entirely different orientation. Peirce is calling our attention to the "over againstness" or facticity in all experience

17. John Locke, *An Essay Concerning Human Understanding*, ed. by A. C. Fraser, Vol. 1, p. 122.

and existence that has been a key emphasis in the existentialist tradition. The internal oppositional tension of human existence is the
basis for Kierkegaard's claim that concrete, individual, human existence can never be *aufgehoben*. When the existentialists speak of the
bruteness of human existence and its resistance to being taken up in
a system of thought, when they insist on the inescapable facticity of
human life, they are emphasizing what Peirce calls Secondness. The
existentialists have also claimed that the "waking state is a consciousness of reaction" (Peirce, quoted above); and the statement that
"the idea of other, of *not,* becomes a very pivot of thought" might
well have appeared in Sartre's *Being and Nothingness*. Peirce's use
of the categories shows us a revealing way of linking up existentialism with a tradition that many have thought to be alien to the spirit
of existentialism—empiricism. If one of the functions of categorial
analysis is to articulate new ways of "seeing" the world, whose
fruitfulness is to be assessed by their power to illuminate, then we
can begin to see the point of Peirce's categorial analysis.

The final category, Thirdness, is at once the most intriguing and
difficult to understand. Habits, laws, rules, potentiality, intentions,
concepts, signs, meaning, and conduct are all classified as Thirds.
Peirce's favorite example of a triadic relation is "giving." "A *gives*
B to C. This does not consist of A's throwing B away and its acci-
dentally hitting C. . . . If that were all, it would not be a genuine
triadic relation, but merely one dyadic relation followed by another.
There need be no motion of the thing given. Giving is a transfer of
the right of property. Now right is a matter of law, and law is a matter
of thought and meaning" (1.345). We cannot present an adequate
account of the concept of giving by describing it in terms of physical
(or even mental) juxtaposition. What is characteristic about giving
is that there are some conventions, rules, or customs by virtue of
which an act is *giving* and not just physical displacement. These conventions, rules, or customs are essential constituents of the type of
action or conduct that is properly designated "giving." Giving is a
form of conduct and we cannot understand giving if we restrict ourselves to analyzing it in terms of Firstness and Secondness. Consider
the closely related example of A making a contract with C. "To say
that A signs the document D and C signs the document D, no matter
what the contents of that document, does not make a contract. The
contract lies in the intent. And what is the intent? It is that certain

conditional rules shall govern the conduct of A and of C" (1.475).

We can gain a firmer grasp of what he is maintaining by noting a similarity between Peirce's discussion of Thirdness and recent analytic philosophy. The distinction between happening and doing, or between movement and action, which has been so prominent in recent analytic investigations, is reflected in Peirce's distinction of Secondness and Thirdness.[18] Although Peirce uses the term "conduct" for what more recent philosophers have called "action," he is making the same basic distinction. The reason why "giving" or "signing a contract" exemplifies Thirdness is that such practices exist only insofar as there exist rules, habits, norms that provide the criteria for identifying and classifying instances of these practices. If one restricted himself to trying to give an account of "signing a contract" in terms of physical or psychical movements (Seconds), one would not be able to account for the activity involved. A specific instance of signing a contract could not take place without the background of "conditional rules" that define this practice. These general elements that constitute the practice cannot be analyzed in terms of Seconds. This is, of course, not to deny that a physical movement takes place in the signing of a contract, but rather to emphasize that the physical movements count as an instance of the activity, practice or conduct, because of the role these movements play.[19]

18. Cf. the discussion of the distinction between action and movement in Part IV, pp. 264-266.

19. The type of triadic analysis that Peirce presents for "giving" and "signing" a contract is generalized and applied to a wide variety of epistemological and metaphysical issues. Peirce's claims bear a close resemblance to the anti-reductionist arguments of many contemporary analytic philosophies. This similarity is illustrated by Rorty when he writes, "One might explain what makes a batch of sense data a cat by saying either that it *means* a cat to somebody, or that somebody *intends* to take it to be a cat, or that somebody follows a *rule* in terms of which it represents a cat, or that somebody has a *habit* of saying 'cat' when he encounters it, or that somebody expects the usual *laws* describing the behavior of such sense data to hold. Peirce's point is that all these italicized terms are names for Thirdness, and that consequently any of them may be analyzed in terms of another but that none of them can be reduced either to sense data themselves (Firsts) or to the merely dyadic relations which hold among sense data (for example, such Seconds as spatio-temporal nextness and sheer similarity). Any 'reduction' of cats to patches will, therefore, miss the reference to a logical interpretant which makes the cat a cat. It will lose the same kind of thing that gets lost when we 'reduce' giving to handing over and taking." "Pragmatism, Categories, and Language,"

Action and Conduct

Brute action is perfectly determinate; there is no indeterminateness or vagueness in brute action.[20] Action insofar as it approximates pure Secondness is singular and antigeneral; it exhibits what Duns Scotus called *hic et nunc*. I have spoken of action insofar as it approximates pure Secondness, because we must keep in mind that elements distinguished by all three categories are manifested in every experience. There is no such thing as an experience of pure brute action or Secondness, but there is an element of bruteness that can be prescinded or abstracted in the analysis of experience. "There is nothing at all that is absolutely confrontial; although it is quite true that the confrontial is continually flowing in upon us" (7.653).

Conduct, as distinguished from brute action, is essentially general. While brute action is singular, conduct is a type or kind of activity. Conduct is closely related to Peirce's central notion of habit. "[Readiness] to act in a certain way under given circumstances and when actuated by a given motive is a habit; and a deliberate, or self-controlled, habit is precisely a belief" (5.480). Though Peirce speaks of habit here in a context in which it is appropriate to speak of "motive" and "control," the notion of habit plays a much broader role in Peirce's philosophy. He argues that everything, whether animate or inanimate, manifests habits. "Habit" in its wider sense "denotes such a specialization, original or acquired, of the nature of a man, or an animal, or a vine, or a crystallizable chemical substance, or anything else, that he or it will behave, or always tend to behave, in a way describable in general terms upon every occasion (or upon a considerable proportion of the occasions) that may present itself of a generally describable character" (5.538). Peirce's thesis that everything manifests habits—"What we call a Thing is a cluster or

---

The Philosophical Review 70 (1961), 202–203. While the above illustration shows the similarity of Peirce's Thirdness to recent epistemological claims, Peirce's strategy is also reflected in contemporary discussions of action, especially in the centrality of the concepts of "practice" and "rule." Cf. John Rawls, "Two Concepts of Rules," *The Philosophical Review* 64 (1955); and Wilfrid Sellars, "Some Reflections on Language Games" in *Science, Perception and Reality*.

20. For a discussion of the meaning of "generality," "vagueness," and "indeterminateness," see 5.446 ff; 5.505 ff.

habit of reactions" (4.157)—is a way of calling attention to the fact that everything in the universe is governed by or exhibits laws, and that this lawfulness is to be understood in terms of the conditional generality characteristic of Thirdness. It also calls attention to the continuity that Peirce claims is exhibited throughout all of nature. There are important differences between the habits manifested by a crystallizable chemical substance and those exhibited in rational behavior, but there is also continuity in this lawfulness exhibited throughout nature.

Conduct, or more generally, habit consists of what Peirce calls "would-be's." To say that a person or a thing has a habit means that it "*would* behave (or usually behave) in a certain way *whenever* a certain occasion should arise" (8.380). Although conduct, habits, or "would-be's" issue in action, "no agglomeration of actual happenings can ever completely fill up the meaning of a 'would-be' " (5.467). We can now see why Peirce insists that Thirds involve reference to the future. While the past is the "storehouse of knowledge" and "whenever we set out to do anything, we 'go upon,' we base our conduct on facts already known" (5.460), the laws, habits, and conduct that we come to know are not exhausted by past or even future regularities. The conditional generality of Thirdness is not exhausted by any finite set of past, present, or future happenings. Furthermore, "future facts are the only facts that we can, in a measure control; and whatever there may be in the Future that is not amenable to control are the things that we *shall* be able to infer, or *should* be able to infer under favorable circumstances" (5.461). When Peirce adds that thinking itself is a "kind of action" or conduct (8.191), that intelligence consists of "acting in a certain way" (6.286) and that "all thought . . . must necessarily be in signs" (5.251), many of his most important and interesting theses fit together into a comprehensive, coherent perspective.

The pragmatic maxim itself is primarily concerned with conduct, deliberate conduct, not with actions as discrete happenings. In its original form Peirce states the maxim as follows: "Consider what effects, that might conceivably have practical bearings, we conceive the object of our conception to have. Then, our conception of these effects is the whole of our conception of the object" (5.402). At a later date, commenting on what appears to be a clumsy formation, Peirce pointed out that the

. . . employment five times over of derivates of *concipere* must then have had a purpose. In point of fact it had two. One was to show that I was speaking of meaning in no other sense than that of *intellectual purport.* The other was to avoid all danger of being understood as attempting to explain a concept by percepts, images, schemata, or by anything but concepts. I did not, therefore, mean to say that acts, which are more strictly singular than anything, could constitute the purport or adequate proper interpretation, of any symbol. . . . Pragmaticism makes thinking to consist in the living inferential metaboly of symbols whose purport lies in conditional general resolutions to act. (5.402, fn. 3)

Peirce identifies the intellectual purport or meaning of a proposition with habits and conduct, and these are essentially general and conditional.[21] The pragmatic maxim is intended to single out from "the myriads of forms into which a proposition may be translated . . . that form in which the proposition becomes applicable to human conduct" (5.427). In clarifying the meaning of his pragmaticism, Peirce is acutely conscious of the categorial difference between Thirdness and Secondness and he seeks carefully to distinguish his position from those who attempt to characterize the meaning of a proposition or a concept in terms of a set of discrete deeds, observations, or facts. "To say that I hold that the import, or adequate ultimate interpretation, of a concept is contained, not in any deed or deeds that will ever be done, but in a habit of conduct, or general moral determination of whatever procedure there *may come to be,* is no more than to say that I am a pragmaticist" (5.504). We can now see even more clearly why Peirce called himself a pragmaticist, for there are sharp differences between his position and more common varieties of pragmatism and positivism. "Vulgar" pragmatism and positivism have (unsuccessfully) sought to identify the meaning of a proposition with some determinate set of consequences or observations: in this respect these positions have been nominalistic. But Peirce called himself a scholastic (and sometimes a Scotistic) realist. He also claimed that pragmatism and realism entail each other (Cf. 5.453, 5.470, 5.503).[22] We cannot explore in depth what

21. Cf. George Gentry, "Habit and Logical Interpretant," *Studies in the Philosophy of Charles Sanders Peirce,* ed. by P. Wiener and F. Young; and John F. Boler, "Habits of Thought," *Studies in the Philosophy of Charles Sanders Peirce, Second Series.*

22. Cf. John F. Boler, *Charles Peirce and Scholastic Realism.*

Peirce means by realism, but the cash value of Peirce's realism is that there are real laws, generals, habits—in short, Thirds. Pragmaticism rests on the claim that there are real generals which cannot be logically reduced to singular elements, and that these generals constitute the very meaning of concepts.[23]

Rational Control and Criticism

In our discussion of conduct, we have begun to see the importance of controlled conduct. There are aspects of experience that are beyond or below the level of control. The shock or surprise of experience is something over which we have no control. "The 'hardness' of fact lies in the insistency of the percept, its entirely irrational insistency—the element of Secondness in it" (7.659). Furthermore, "even after the percept is formed" Peirce notes that "there is an operation which seems to me quite uncontrollable. It is that of judging what it is that the person perceives" (5.115). We must not draw the wrong conclusion from this and similar claims. One of Peirce's most brilliant insights is a careful distinction between *compulsion* and *authority*. A failure to make this distinction leads to the paradoxes of intuitionism where the insistency of a percept, perceptual judgment, or belief is mistakenly taken as evidence of its unquestioned validity. A consequence of this mismating of concepts is the

23. In light of recent discussion of realism, one can easily miss Peirce's point and mistake his position for one that he critically attacks. In recent discussions, "realism" has frequently been interpreted as a doctrine of one who countenances "abstract entities" as part of his ontology. More precisely, if one admits "abstract entities" as values of the bound variables of an articulated conceptual framework, then such a framework is committed to these abstract entities; this is "realism" or "platonism" in the new way of words. Frequently an "abstract entity" is thought of as something which has a determinate character like a particular or individual. This is the sort of view that Peirce called "platonism"; he claimed that to identify realism with platonism leads to the gravest confusions. Thirds for Peirce are not sharp-edged entities; they are essentially vague and indeterminate. Thirds are not a variation on Seconds; Thirdness is a different and nonreducible category. Peirce's realism is intended as a critique and alternative to all forms of platonism. For a detailed working out of the implications of Peirce's realism and its similarity to recent developments in analytic philosophy, see Rorty, "Pragmaticism, Categories, and Language," *The Philosophical Review* 70 (1961), 204 ff.

mistaken conclusion that there are basic, infallible, self-authenticating epistemological episodes that serve as the foundation of knowledge. This is the error that Peirce claims lies at the core of modern intuitionism whether it is of the rationalist or empiricist variety.[24] Peirce warns us, "We all know, only too well, how terribly insistent perception may be; and yet, for all that, in its most insistent degrees, it may be utterly false,—that is, may not fit into the general mass of experience" (7.647). And even those propositions and beliefs which are indubitable and which "we cannot but regard . . . as perfectly true and perfectly certain" may turn out to be false (5.498).

Although there are operations of the mind that are uncontrollable, and indeed uncontrollable operations "logically exactly analogous to inferences," inference itself "is essentially deliberate, and self-controlled. . . . Reasoning as deliberate is essentially critical, and it is idle to criticize as good or bad that which cannot be controlled" (5.108). "To criticize as logically sound or unsound an operation of thought that cannot be controlled is not less ridiculous than it would be to pronounce the growth of your hair to be morally good or bad. The ridiculousness in both cases consists in the fact that such a critical judgment may be *pretended* but cannot really be performed in clear thought, for on analysis it will be found absurd" (5.109). But what is controlled in reasoning? It is our habits or conduct. Reasoning involves the use of logic, and "whenever a man reasons, he thinks that he is drawing a conclusion such as would be justified in every analogous case" (5.108). More specifically, all reasoning involves the use of what Peirce calls "leading" or "guiding" principles. "That which determines us, from given premises, to draw one inference rather than another, is some habit of mind. . . . The particular habit of mind which governs this or that inference may be formulated in a proposition whose truth depends on the validity of the inferences which the habit determines; and such a formula is called a *guiding principle* of inference" (5.367). These guiding principles can be formal principles essential for all reasoning as well as material principles based on experience. Moreover, these guiding principles are involved in warranting the transition from premises to conclusions regardless of whether the type of rea-

24. Cf. Karl Popper, "On the Sources of Knowledge and of Ignorance," *Conjectures and Refutations;* and Wilfrid Sellars, "Empiricism and the Philosophy of Mind," *Science, Perception and Reality,* especially pp. 164 ff.

soning is deductive, inductive, or "abductive," the term Peirce uses for the form of reasoning that leads to new ideas and scientific discovery.

With this conception of rationality as self-controlled conduct, we approach the heart of Peirce's philosophy. The concept of self-controlled conduct provides the mediating link between the traditional dichotomies of theory and practice, thought and action. Man as knower or inquirer is viewed as an agent who has and can control his habits and is not a passive spectator of reality. Reality itself is characterized as that which corresponds to the true judgments arrived at by the ideal community of inquirers. We have no direct, intuitive cognitive access to reality. Though there is a bruteness in reality (Secondness) which limits and conditions inquiry, our knowledge claims about the real are warranted by the self-corrective process of inquiry, not by a direct appeal to what is immediately before us. "A rational person . . . not merely has habits, but also can exert a measure of self-control over his future actions" (5.418). He exerts this control by shaping and modifying his conduct which on appropriate occasions issues in specific actions. Self-control is not a matter of "all-or-nothing"; there are degrees of self-control.

There are inhibitions and coordinations that entirely escape consciousness. There are, in the next place, modes of self-control which seem quite instinctive. Next, there is a kind of self-control which results from training. Next, a man can be his own training-master and thus control his self-control. When this point is reached much or all the training may be conducted in imagination. When a man trains himself, thus controlling control, he must have some moral rule in view, however special and irrational it may be. But next he may undertake to improve this rule; that is, to exercise a control over his control of control. To do this he must have in view something higher than an irrational rule. He must have some sort of moral principle. This, in turn, may be controlled by reference to an esthetic ideal of what is fine. There are certainly more grades than I have enumerated. Perhaps their number is indefinite. The brutes are certainly capable of more than one grade of control; but it seems to me that our superiority to them is more due to our greater number of grades of self-control than it is to our versatility. (5.533)

This rich passage provides a clue for understanding one of Peirce's most tantalizing suggestions, viz., that there is a hierarchy of the normative sciences such that logic is dependent on ethics and ethics is dependent on esthetics. But before turning to a consideration of the hierarchy of the normative sciences, there are further questions to be answered concerning the type of self-control characteristic of rationality.

How are we to analyze self-control? What are its distinctive features? Self-control "consists (to mention only the leading constituents) first, in comparing one's past deeds with standards, second in rational deliberation concerning how one will act in the future, in itself a highly complicated operation, third, in the formation of a resolve, fourth, in the creation, on the basis of the resolve, of a strong determination, or modification of habit" (8.320). Self-control demands constant self-criticism which is "the very life of reasoning" (2.123). But self-criticism does not take place in a vacuum; self-criticism requires an active community of inquirers, a community that is not completely identified with any existing community, but a community "without definite limits, and capable of a definite increase of knowledge" (5.311). The community of inquirers, which is ultimately the basis for distinguishing the real from the unreal, and the true from the false, functions as a regulative ideal in Peirce's philosophic scheme (see 5.311).

Peirce always emphasizes the social character of the individual. The very nature of the individual is determined by his forms of participation in community life. "A person is not absolutely an individual. His thoughts are what he is 'saying to himself,' that is, is saying to that other self that is just coming into life in the flow of time. When one reasons, it is that critical self that one is trying to persuade; and all thought whatsoever is a sign, and is mostly of the nature of language" (5.421).

The claim that thought is a form of internal dialogue, and that dialogue presupposes a community in which there are effective standards and norms of discourse, is one of Peirce's fundamental tenets. The upshot of his theory of signs is that all signification, which includes all language and thought, is essentially social in nature. This emphasis on the social or communal nature of man reflects Peirce's strong anti-subjectivistic bias. If all reasoning, even when it is internalized in an individual, has an intrinsically social character and the very life of reasoning is self-criticism, then we see more clearly why constant criticism, conflict with alternative hypotheses and theories, is so vital for achieving warranted beliefs through inquiry. Peirce's understanding of the nature and role of the self-critical community prefigures the critical rationalism developed by Popper.[25]

Norms

Throughout this discussion of conduct, control, criticism and community, one issue stands out as prominent, the status of norms. There can be no self-control of conduct or self-criticism unless there are norms by which we distinguish the true from the false, the right from the wrong, the correct from the incorrect. All reasoning exists in a logical space of norms. Peirce came to appreciate this point more and more clearly in his mature philosophic outlook. He sought to delineate the essential characteristics of the normative sciences. This is certainly one of the most fascinating and unsatisfactory aspects of Peirce's philosophy, for he never worked out in detail what he frequently promised us—a detailed explication of the normative sciences. Nevertheless, we can grasp the point of what he was attempting to show and see how it helps to complete the line of inquiry we have been following.

A normative science is *theoretical* and "studies what ought to be" (1.281). Peirce thought that the normative sciences could be exhaustively classified into logic, ethics, and esthetics. The thesis that logic is dependent on ethics may strike us as odd: this seems to be a complete reversal of the order that we might normally attribute to these disciplines. The further claim that ethics is dependent on esthetics may strike us as downright absurd. I want to suggest that Peirce's hierarchy of normative sciences not only embodies a profound insight, but that understanding what he means by this ordering is the key for grasping the import of rationality as self-control. Finally, we will be able to answer the question: What according to Peirce, is the end or goal of life?[26]

25. Cf. Karl Popper, "Conjectures and Refutations" in *Conjectures and Refutations*.

26. A good guide for interpretating Peirce is to take seriously his own self-criticism and claims about what he is "up to." Writing to William James in 1902, Peirce says: "But I seem to myself to be the sole depositary at present of the completely developed system, which all hangs together and cannot

Reasoning is a deliberate form of voluntary conduct involving the use of logical norms. Although logic can be divided into different branches, logic is the critique of arguments and leading principles. Logic "not only lays down rules which ought to be, but need not be followed; but it is the analysis of the conditions of attainment of something of which purpose is an essential ingredient" (1.575). If logic is to lay down rules that ought to be followed in reasoning, then there must be an appeal to an end or purpose by which we can justify the rules that ought to be followed. "Logic is a study of the means of attaining the end of thought" and "it is Ethics which defines that end" (2.198). The dependence of logic on ethics is expressed in other ways. "Thinking is a kind of action, and reasoning is a kind of deliberate action; and to call an argument illogical, or a proposition false, is a special kind of moral judgment" (8.191). "The whole operation of logical self-control takes precisely the same quite complicated course which everybody ought to acknowledge is that of effective ethical self-control" (5.533).

It should be clear that Peirce is redefining "Ethics," at least when we consider some of the traditional meanings of this term. But there is a "core" of its traditional meaning that he wants to preserve. The substantive point that Peirce is emphasizing is that logic is essentially normative; it is concerned with laying down rules that ought to be followed in reasoning. But the imperatives or rules that logic lays down are not categorical, they are hypothetical; they are laid down in light of some goal, end, or purpose to be achieved. The understanding and critique of these ends of logic is what Peirce labels "Ethics." We must not think that Peirce is advocating that logic ought to be moralistic or made subservient to psychological factors; these are tendencies he deplored. But he does believe that the fundamental question of ethics is "What am I prepared deliberately to

---

receive any proper presentation in fragments. My own view in 1877 was crude. [The "Fixation of Belief" was published in November, 1877 and "How to Make Our Ideas Clear" in January, 1878.] Even when I gave my Cambridge lectures [1898] I had not really got to the bottom of it or seen the unity of the whole thing. It was not until after that that I obtained the proof that logic must be founded on ethics, of which it is a higher development. Even then, I was for some time so stupid as not to see that ethics rests in the same manner on a foundation of esthetics. . . ." (8.255)

accept as the statement of what I want to do, what am I to aim at, what am I after?" And logic (broadly conceived) demands answers to these questions; "it is, therefore, impossible to be thoroughly and rationally logical except on an ethical basis" (2.198). We see here Peirce's own version of the primacy of practical reason.

Once it is realized that conceptual thought is essentially normative, and that the norms of inquiry are the source of the authority of knowledge claims, then inquiry as a self-corrective process requires a critique of these very norms.[27] Furthermore, criticism presupposes the possibility of control. "Any operation which cannot be controlled, any conclusion which is not abandoned, not merely as soon as *criticism* has pronounced against it, but in the very act of pronouncing that decree, is not the nature of rational inference—is not reasoning." Reasoning as deliberate is essentially critical, and it is idle to criticize as good or bad that which cannot be controlled. "Reasoning essentially involves *self-control,* so that the *logica utens* is a particular species of morality" (5.108).

When we grapple with the claim that ethics is ultimately based on esthetics, the issue seems to be more perplexing. Not only does this appear to be a more problematic suggestion, but Peirce himself tells us very little about what he means, and what he does say is not always consistent. The supremacy of esthetics is emphasized only in some of Peirce's late papers. Yet I want to suggest that the general line of argument that leads him to this conclusion is incisive and crucial for understanding his entire philosophy.

Once again if we think of "esthetics" with many of its normal connotations we are sure to be misled. By "esthetics" Peirce means a science of ends, and the business of the esthetician "is to say what is the state of things which is most admirable in itself regardless of any ulterior reason" (1.611). The problem of esthetics is "to determine by analysis what it is that one ought deliberately to admire *per se* in itself regardless of what it may lead to and regardless of its bearing upon human conduct" (5.36). From this initial characterization it should be evident that Peirce's view of the object with which esthetics is concerned is closely related to Plato's concep-

27. Cf. Wilfrid Sellars' discussion of the logical space of conceptual thought, "Empiricism and the Philosophy of Mind" and "Some Reflections on Language Games" in *Science, Perception and Reality.*

tion of the Good, and Kant's Ideas of Pure Reason. The type of argument he offers to show that there is such an ultimate end is similar to arguments developed by Plato and Kant.

Let us try to bring out the significance of the primacy of esthetics by what might seem to be a devious route. I have suggested that there is a parallel between Peirce's claim that logic is based on ethics and recent epistemological investigations of rules and norms. But consider for a moment the state of ethical and legal philosophy among Anglo-Saxon philosophers. Peirce already saw all too clearly what many linguistic analysts have failed to see. After the demise of orthodox positivism, and under the inspiration of the later Wittgenstein, we detect a new approach to the problems of ethics and law. Whereas orthodox positivism condemns "ethical judgment" as nonsense, or at best the expression or evincing of noncognitive emotions and attitudes, the newer approach that has replaced positivistic emotivism has exposed its hidden and unjustified presupposition, that is, that science, or rather what the positivists mistakenly thought of as the nature of science, is the measure of all legitimate meaning. Once we saw that the emperor had no clothes, that the positivists were telling us what few philosophers had ever doubted—that ethical discourse is different from scientific discourse—a new temper emerged. It was now proclaimed that ethical discourse is autonomous and that the philosopher's task is to describe the logic of our actual moral discourse with all its intrinsic subtlety and complexity. A tremendous amount of intellectual energy has gone into the exploration of the so-called logic of moral discourse, the ways in which we do argue about moral issues, and the criteria used for distinguishing good and bad reasons in moral arguments. But one of the nagging and persistent questions has been: How are we to provide an ultimate justification for the rules, principles, practices, and norms that we actually employ? There are some who suggested that to ask this question is to exceed the bounds of linguistic propriety. Others recognize this as a legitimate issue but claim that the philosopher's task is done when he has described moral discourse. Still others, who reveal a hidden affinity with the existentialists, have suggested that in the end, Decision is king. Even here there has been disagreement about whether such a decision is completely arbitrary (because there are no further standards by which we can evaluate these decisions) or whether such an ultimate decision is the most "rational"

decision that a man can make. The entire discussion has floundered
because there has been a failure to acknowledge what Peirce saw
so clearly. We cannot be content with a description of our actual
moral discourse. No matter how we may attempt to avoid the issue,
the question of ultimate justification is crucial. To answer this question we must critically investigate our ultimate goals and purposes;
we must find out what it is that we *ought* ultimately to admire and
seek. It is in this sense that ethics is dependent on esthetics, or to put
the issue more neutrally, the criteria of right and wrong in logic as
well as in ethics ultimately depend on the ends of all human activity.

An ultimate end of action *deliberately* adopted, that is to say, *reasonably*
adopted—must be a state of things that *reasonably recommends itself
in itself* aside from any ulterior consideration. It must be an *admirable
ideal,* having the only kind of goodness that such an ideal *can* have;
namely, esthetic goodness. From this point of view the morally good
appears as a particular species of the esthetically good. (5.130)

Now it must be frankly admitted that Peirce's love of architectonic
and classification of the various sciences tends to obscure the main
thrust of his argument. For, while one will find a great deal in
Peirce's corpus concerning the science of logic, he never develops
for us in any detail the structure and procedures of the theoretical
"normative sciences" of ethics and esthetics. He certainly promises
much more than he delivers. But if we cut through the elaborate hierarchy of "sciences" we can detect the strands of a single line of
argument. All reasoning is essentially normative and therefore presupposes some standards by which we assess better and worse arguments; these standards are themselves open to critical investigation,
but all criticism itself presupposes an ideal. We must therefore
implicitly or explicitly acknowledge some ultimate ideal as that
which ought to govern human activity. And it is clear from the above
passage that we must not only acknowledge such an ideal but deliberately or reasonably adopt it.

Even if we go this far with Peirce, we still don't know what
he takes to be the ultimate ideal, the good, the highest regulative
principle. What is it that is admirable in itself and has this intrinsic
esthetic quality? If action is not the end or goal of human life, what
is the end? Peirce answers:

So, then, the essence of Reason is such that its being never can have been completely perfected. It always must be in a state of incipiency, of growth. It is like the character of a man which consists in the ideas that he will conceive and in the efforts that he will make, and which only develops as the occasions actually arise. . . . The development of Reason requires as a part of it the occurrence of more individual events than can ever occur. It requires, too, all the coloring of all qualities of feeling, including pleasure in its proper place among the rest. The development of Reason consists, you will observe, in embodiment, that is, in manifestation. The creation of the universe, which did not take place during a certain busy week in the year 4004 B.C., but is going on today and never will be done, is this very development of Reason. *I do not see how one can have a more satisfying ideal of the admirable than the development of Reason so understood. The one thing whose admirableness is not due to an ulterior reason is Reason itself comprehended in all its fullness, so far as we can comprehend it. Under this conception, the ideal of conduct will be to execute our little function in the operation of the creation by giving a hand toward rendering the world more reasonable wherever, as the slang is, it is "up to us" to do so.* (1.615; my italics)

Peirce is not only giving expression to his cosmic vision of the growth of "concrete reasonableness" as *the* ultimate ideal of human life, but also revealing his own deepest personal convictions. This is the ideal by which Peirce himself lived and which enabled him to suffer the pain, misery, and isolation that marred his life. This passage, written in 1903, is a conscious formulation of an ideal that Peirce praised much earlier in 1871 when, speaking of the spirit of Duns Scotus and the scholastics, he said:

Nothing is more striking in either of the great intellectual products of that age, than the complete absence of self-conceit on the part of the artist or philosopher. . . . His work is not designed to embody *his* ideas, but the universal truth. . . . The individual feels his own worthlessness in comparison with his task, and does not dare introduce his vanity into the doing of it. . . . Finally, there is nothing in which the scholastic philosophy and the Gothic architecture resemble one another more than in the gradually increasing sense of immensity which impresses the mind of the student as he learns to appreciate the real dimensions and cost of each. (8.11)

We have come to the very coping-stone of Peirce's thought—the ultimate ideal of self-control—the commitment to the growth of concrete reasonableness as the *summum bonum*. We have tried to show one path that weaves through an apparent disarray of ideas and themes to this culmination. What initially appears to be confused, chaotic, and even inconsistent, turns out upon analysis to be systematic, coherent, and powerful. One of the most exciting features of Peirce's work is that the more we try to think out the problems with which he was concerned—problems central to all philosophy—the more we can detect his systematic power. Our primary focus has been upon the concepts of action and conduct, but a full-scale analysis of Peirce's thought would have to explore the systematic connection of his ultimate ideal of the growth of concrete reasonableness with his metaphysical and cosmological speculations about the growth of law, synechism, tychism, and evolutionary love.[28] In delineating the connections among the concepts of action, conduct, habit, criticism, community, and control, we have come to the central theme of rationality as critical self-control, a self-control manifested in a hierarchy of normative sciences where our ultimate ideal, the *summum bonum,* is the continued growth of concrete reasonableness. The subtlety of Peirce's discussions is evidenced at every turn in this thorny path. And yet, if the systematic network of interlacing concepts that we have sketched is correct, difficulties that we find here in his concept of self-control will reverberate throughout his entire philosophy.

What Peirce's analysis demands at this point is a coherent theory of the self which would make sense of the idea of "self-control." After all, what is it that exercises the control and is capable of reasonably adopting an ultimate end? Wherein are we to find the identity, unity, and continuity of individual selves? Peirce does not really answer these questions with the same incisiveness that we find in other regions of his philosophy. Despite many important hints, Peirce has failed to work out an adequate theory of the self. Indeed, I believe that this was not only his failure, but the failure of the entire pragmatic movement.[29] We might try to excuse this by recalling the dialectical context in which pragmatism developed. The movement rebelled against the excesses of subjectivism and "mentalism" characteristic of so much of modern epistemology. This is

28. For a detailed exploration of Peirce's conception of the normative sciences and their relation to his cosmological and metaphysical theories, see Vincent G. Potter, S.J., *Charles S. Peirce, On Norms and Ideals.*

29. For a criticism of Dewey's theory of the self, see my book, *John Dewey,* pp. 176 ff.

not really an excuse, but a way of calling attention to a pervasive failure of this movement. More specifically, there is a serious incoherence in what Peirce does say about the self. The nature of human individuality always seemed to be a source of intellectual embarrassment for Peirce. Peirce went so far as to claim that "individual man, since his separate existence is manifested only by ignorance and error, so far as he is anything apart from his fellows, and from what he and they are to be, is only a negation" (5.317). Or again, disparaging individuality, he declares, "now you and I—what are we? Mere cells of the social organism. Our deepest sentiment pronounces the verdict of our own insignificance. Psychological analysis shows that there is nothing which distinguishes my personal identity except my faults and my limitations—or if you please, my blind will, which it is my highest endeavor to annihilate" (1.673). There are traces of American transcendentalism that appear in these passages. Peirce is betraying his own insight that there is a dimension of individuality or positive Secondness that distinguishes the individual self. More important, such a conception of the self makes a mockery of the ideal of individual self-control or the adoption of the ultimate ideal of concrete reasonableness by an individual. If my separate existence is manifested only by ignorance and error, if I differ from my fellow man only by being a negation, then "where" and "what" is the "I" that controls and adopts ultimate ideals?

There are many difficulties and lacunae in Peirce's investigations. His claim in 1902 that he seems to himself to be the "sole depositary" of the "completely developed system" (8.255) is more the expression of a hope or aspiration than a solid achievement. Much of what Peirce himself considered most central and important in his philosophy has not been taken up by other philosophers. His cosmological speculations strike the modern reader as an oddity and few philosophers have developed Peirce's categorial scheme. Nevertheless, many of the strategies and arguments that are involved in Peirce's categorial distinctions find their counterparts in recent analytic philosophy. What has become a vital part of our philosophic heritage is Peirce's overall view of inquiry and the role of man as an active, critical agent in developing inquiry. Before Peirce, when philosophers turned their attention to science, it was primarily the results of the scientific process that preoccupied them. Or they approached empirical science with a set of independent epistemological biases which they set out to vindicate by an appeal to science. But Peirce, himself a practicing scientist, sought to generalize from the process of scientific investigation. It is the spirit of science as an activity that he sought to articulate and clarify. He developed a general theory of inquiry as a critical activity for discovering and warranting "truths" which he believed could and should be generalized to all areas of investigation. Genuine scientific problems arise against an extensive background of beliefs, methods, techniques, etc., which set the problem to be confronted. In such a context there is real doubt which must be dissociated from the "feigned doubt" of the Cartesian tradition. No serious inquiry can begin without making many complex assumptions, and the attempt to secure a firm foundation for inquiry which does not make any assumptions is idle and misguided. What validates our knowledge claims is not the "origins" of knowledge, but the techniques, methods, and norms we use in testing these claims. The essential fallibility of all inquiry is no cause for despair, but rather an incentive for openness and for testing as rigorously and critically as we can all hypotheses and theories. Because of the essential social and public nature of all signification, meaning, and knowledge, we must not only countenance, but seek out intersubjective criticisms of all hypotheses. The establishment of a free, open, self-critical community of inquirers is an ideal to be striven for and it is an ideal that Peirce advocated in all his work. This is the way in which we can aid the growth of "concrete reasonableness." The cardinal principle for Peirce is: Do not block the road to inquiry! If we take the pragmatic spirit seriously, we will be suspicious of all attempts to fix once and for all boundaries between what we can know and what we cannot know, between what is to be taken as meaningful and what is meaningless, between what is presumably known a priori and what is known a posteriori. All basic distinctions are relative to the stage of the development of inquiry and there is no conceptual distinction that cannot be revised, modified, or even abandoned in light of further inquiry. Man from this perspective is seen as an active inquirer, and Peirce's theory of inquiry stands as one of the great attempts to show how the classic dichotomies between thought and action, or theory and *praxis* can be united in a theory of a community of inquirers committed to continuous, rational, self-critical activity.

John Dewey: Reconstruction of Experience[30]

The philosophic relationship between Peirce and Dewey is a complex and subtle one. Textbook descriptions of American pragmatism suggest a direct linear continuity from Peirce to James to Dewey. Dewey was a graduate student at Johns Hopkins (1882–1884) during the brief period when Peirce taught there and it is commonly assumed that the seeds of Dewey's own pragmatism were sown during this early stage of his intellectual career. But the more closely one studies the intellectual development and preoccupations of Peirce and Dewey, the more one realizes the falsity of this simplistic picture. Dewey did come into contact with Peirce at Johns Hopkins. Peirce had already developed the outlines of his theory of inquiry, but Dewey was primarily influenced by the idealist and Hegelian tradition represented by his teacher G. S. Morris. Only as Dewey moved away from Hegelianism to a more naturalistic and instrumentalistic position did he come to appreciate the significance of Peirce's work. Dewey was much more generous in acknowledging the importance of Peirce's investigations than Peirce was in commending Dewey's work. One of the sharpest criticisms of Dewey's *Studies in Logical Theory* (1903) was written by Peirce.[31] Much later, when Dewey reviewed the collection of Peirce's articles edited by Morris R. Cohen as well as the volumes of Peirce's *Collected Papers,* Dewey encountered the full range of Peirce's philosophy.[32] With the publication of Dewey's *Logic: The Theory of Inquiry* (1938), the influence of Peirce and the acknowledgement of this influence is quite explicit.

Peirce's and Dewey's differences of style, concern, and approach are striking. Yet, despite these differences, there is also a convergence of point of view. It is as if Dewey had taken an independent

30. Parts of the following discussion of Dewey are based on my book, *John Dewey.*

31. See Peirce's review of *Studies in Logical Theory* and his letters to Dewey in the *Collected Papers of Charles Sanders Peirce,* 8.188–8.190; 8.239–8.244.

32. See "The Pragmatism of Peirce," *Journal of Philosophy* 21 (1916); "The Founder of Pragmatism," *The New Republic* 81 (1935); "Peirce's Theory of Quality," *Journal of Philosophy* 32 (1935); and "Peirce's Theory of Linguistic Signs, Thought and Meaning," *Journal of Philosophy* 43 (1946).

philosophic journey and only late in his own career did he fully discover that Peirce's quite different development had led him to insights and conclusions that harmonized and at the same time complemented Dewey's views.

Peirce's primary sources of philosophical inspiration were logical. Peirce always preferred to think of himself as an exact logician. His reflections on the nature of science and inquiry were stimulated by his knowledge of and participation in the hard sciences of physics and chemistry. Although Peirce wrote perceptively about the entire range of the history of philosophy, he chiefly admired the work of the medieval philosophers. Peirce was suspicious of the demand that philosophy should become practical in the sense of dealing with current social and political issues. In his voluminous writings, there is scarcely any serious concern with the important social and political events of his time. Even though Peirce stressed the importance of ethics in the hierarchy of normative sciences, it was ethics as a *theoretical* science that was the primary object of his interest.

Dewey had little knowledge of the complexities of the physical sciences. The scientific disciplines that most influenced Dewey were biology and the social sciences. He lacked Peirce's creative logical genius. Unlike Peirce who believed that the only proper entry into philosophy was through exact logic, Dewey shared the bias of many idealists who were skeptical of the tendency to generalize about the nature of philosophy on the basis of work in formal logic. "Formal logic," especially in Dewey's early days was taken to be the name of a misguided form of static epistemology. Dewey was relatively indifferent to medieval philosophy. In his mature writings he felt a much greater affinity with the naturalism of Greek philosophy. Dewey was not only intimately involved in the primary educational, social, and political developments of his time, he advocated a conception of philosophy in which it would become a form of social criticism.

But as I hope to show, these basic differences between Peirce and Dewey had a creative influence on the development of a pragmatic outlook and led to a richer conception of the nature of human action. Peirce supplied the intellectual backbone to pragmatism, but Dewey perceived the ways in which Peirce's ideal of a self-critical community of inquirers had important consequences for education, social reconstruction, and a revitalization of democracy.

With the passing of time, Peirce, who was a relatively unknown and obscure figure during his life, has come to be appreciated for the intellectual giant that he is. Many of Peirce's leading ideas are being rediscovered, appreciated, and explored by contemporary philosophers. Dewey, who enjoyed enormous popularity and influence, is scarcely taken seriously today by contemporary philosophers. But recently, there are signs that philosophers are discovering what Dewey articulated so well. Philosophy isolated from the rest of life can become sterile. When philosophers deal exclusively with the problems of philosophers they can lose contact with the problems of men. Dewey did have a deep belief in the possibility of making intelligence effective in all modes of human life. He was skeptical of utopianism and thought that it was frequently an excuse for not facing the hard tangled realities that confront us. He advocated an ideal of shared intelligent activity in the life of a democratic community by which men could eliminate social evils, enrich their experience, and achieve desirable goods. Dewey has been accused of being overly optimistic and naive in his faith in the power of intelligence. But he argued that the only alternative to developing the social institutions and habits that cultivate creative intelligence is to allow ourselves to be misshapen and dehumanized by powerful social forces. Dewey's understanding of intelligent activity comes into focus within the context of his theory of experiential situations.

Dewey begins *Experience and Nature* by citing the claim that "experience is a weasel word."[33] Every major philosophic position in the history of Western philosophy has had something to say about what experience really is. But Dewey believes that the concept is too valuable for us to abandon it and he seeks to articulate a new theory of experience which is appropriate for our time.

Although there is scarcely a work of Dewey's in which he does not discuss experience, one of his boldest statements is found in "The Need for a Recovery of Philosophy."[34] He lists five contrasts between his view of experience and what he dubs the "orthodox" or "traditional" view of experience. By commenting on each of these five contrasts, we can indicate what Dewey meant by experience

33. John Dewey, *Experience and Nature,* first edition, p. 1.

34. "The Need for a Recovery of Philosophy," in *Creative Intelligence, Essays in the Pragmatic Attitude.* Reprinted in *John Dewey: On Experience, Nature and Freedom.* All page references are to this latter volume.

and see how it sets the context for his understanding of human action.

(i) In the orthodox view, experience is regarded primarily as a knowledge-affair. But to eyes not looking through ancient spectacles, it assuredly appears as an affair of the intercourse of a living being with its physical and social environment.[35]

In the history of philosophy, especially in modern philosophy since Descartes, the primary question has been: What kind of knowledge, if any, does experience yield? Or what is the role of experience in our knowledge of the world. For example, although empiricism and rationalism have been thought of as opposing philosophies, both movements have been primarily concerned with experience as a "knowledge-affair"—empiricists maintaining that experience is the only source of knowledge of the world, while rationalists have argued that experience is never *sufficient* to yield genuine knowledge. Part of the basis of the disagreement stems from differing conceptions of experience and reason. But the concern with experience has been epistemologically oriented. This is also true of Dewey's own early, idealistic interpretation of experience. A major shift took place in Dewey's development when he came to appreciate that there is more to experience than knowledge. To approach the nature of experience from an exclusively epistemological orientation results in a distortion of experience. Furthermore, "knowing" as systematic inquiry can be properly understood only when we realize its *function* within the larger context of experience.

What does it mean to insist that there is more to experience than knowing, and what is the significance of this claim? It is not difficult to grasp what Dewey means, in fact it is quite obvious. But philosophers have a way of forgetting or neglecting the obvious. When Dewey speaks of "nonreflective" or "noncognitive" experience, he means the type of experience in which knowing or inquiry is not the primary objective. "Anyone [who] recognizes the difference between an experiencing of quenching thirst where the perception of water is a mere incident, and an experience of water where knowledge of what water is, is the controlling interest; or between the enjoyment of social converse among friends and a study deliberately made of the character of the participants; between esthetic appreciation of a picture and an examination by a connoisseur to

35. "The Need for a Recovery of Philosophy," p. 23.

establish the artist"[36] recognizes the difference between noncognitive or nonreflective experiences and experiences in which knowing is primary. Dewey is not denying that there is thinking or conscious awareness in all human experiences. But we distort our experience as *lived* if we think that the paradigm for all experience is *knowing*.

Every experience involves an interaction (or as he later said, a transaction)[37] between a living organism and its environment. In every experience there is both suffering or undergoing and activity. These aspects of experience are mutually related and are interdependent.

Insofar as we identify anything as *an* experience, there is a pervasive quality that unifies the experience and sets it off from other experiences. A memorable evening at the theater involves an enormous complexity of interacting factors including my own attitudes, beliefs, habits, reactions, as well as the theater, the performance, actors, etc. But although an indefinite number of features can be discriminated in such an experience, there is a unity and integrity that pervades all these features. Philosophers have claimed that such complex experiences are nothing but aggregates of basic simples that make up the experience. Dewey argues that we must not mistake distinctions and discriminations instituted for specific purposes with the experience as it is lived.

Another distinguishing feature of experiences, whether nonreflective or reflective, is that there is a dominant focus and an indefinite horizon in every experience. There is "brilliancy and obscurity, conspicuousness or apparency, and concealment or reserve, with a constant movement of redistribution."[38] At one stage in the development of an experience one factor may dominate our attention, while as the experience develops this factor may pass into the background or horizon.

Most of our lives consist of experiences which are not primarily cognitive or reflective. We are biological creatures continually involved in doing, enjoying, suffering. Inquiry arises as the "dominant trait of a situation when there is something seriously the matter, some trouble, due to active discordance, dissentiency, conflict among

36. John Dewey, *Essays in Experimental Logic*, p. 2.
37. See John Dewey and Arthur F. Bentley, *Knowing and the Known* for a discrimination of "action," "interaction," and "transaction."
38. *Essays in Experimental Logic*, p. 6.

the factors of a prior non-intellectual experience: when . . . a situation becomes tensional."[39] The purpose of the specific inquiry is to locate the difficulty and to devise a method for coping with it. Every specific inquiry is itself controlled and guided by the wider context of experience within which it occurs. Dewey wants to bring us back from the highly abstract and artificial ways in which philosophers have discussed experience to the concrete contexts of life itself.

(ii) According to tradition experience is (at least primarily) a psychical thing, infected throughout by "subjectivity." What experience suggests about itself is a genuinely objective world which enters into the actions and sufferings of men and undergoes modifications through their responses.[40]

This second contrast with "tradition" is already implicit in what we have said, but it is sufficiently important to deserve special attention. Dewey is referring to the "subjectivistic turn" that philosophy took after Descartes. Descartes' dualism of mind and body, together with his conception of mind as a thinking substance which "contains" ideas by which the mind knows "external objects," led to an epistemological preoccupation with what is "in" or "before" the mind. Experience as subjective experiencing became a dominant concern of philosophers. When this subjectivistic bias was followed to the bitter end, some philosophers came to the conclusion that man is trapped in the privacy of the acts and contents of his mind and that he lacks any adequate evidence for believing that there is an objective world "outside" his private, subjective experience. Dewey, like the other pragmatists, argued that the steps leading to the conclusion that experience is exclusively mental, private, and subjective consist of a tissue of fallacies. It is of course true that there is no experience without an experienc*er* and experienc*ing*. But there is no warrant for holding that experience is exclusively private and subjective. The "thicker" conception of experience that Dewey is advocating, which is truer to our ordinary ways of understanding experience, recognizes that subjectivity is a pole or dimension within experience. But all experience also includes an objective dimension. "Subjectivity" and "objectivity" are names for changing functional distinctions within experience. In this respect, Dewey cannot only

39. *Essays in Experimental Logic,* p. 11.
40. "The Need for a Recovery of Philosophy," p. 23.

draw support from the analyses of Peirce and James, but also from continental phenomenology with its emphasis on the *Lebenswelt* and from Wittgensteinian analysis with its concern for *Lebensform*. In differing ways, all of these philosophic tendencies have been reacting against the misguided subjectivism of so much modern philosophy.

(iii) So far as anything beyond a bare present is recognized by established doctrine, the past exclusively counts. Registration of what has taken place, reference to precedent, is believed to be the essence of experience. Empiricism is conceived of as tied up to what has been, or is "given." But experience in its vital form is experimental, an effort to change the given; it is characterized by projection, by reaching forward into the unknown; connection with a future is its salient trait.[41]

While we may have critical reservations about the fairness of Dewey's characterization of "established doctrine," we can grasp what he has in mind. A dominant tendency in traditional empiricism has been to identify experience with what is now presented to us or what is the result of past observations. We detect this tendency in Hume's description of experience.

The nature of experience is this. We remember to have had frequent instances of the existence of one species of objects; and also remember, that the individuals of another species of objects have always attended them, and have existed in a regular order of contiguity and succession with regard to them. . . . In all these instances, from which we learn the conjunction of particular causes and effects, both the causes and effects have been perceiv'd by the senses and are remember'd: But in all cases where we reason concerning them there is one perceiv'd or remember'd, and the other supply'd in conformity to our past experience.[12]

Hume sought to explain how it is that when we are presented with an instance of the species of an object, we imagine the effect associated with it and *believe* that it will reoccur. To this extent Hume is concerned with the relation of past experience to the future. But note how easily Hume slides from the nature of experience to *past* experience. And note too how Hume's description of experience is oriented by his primary epistemological concern.

41. "The Need for a Recovery of Philosophy," p. 23.

42. David Hume, *A Treatise of Human Nature,* ed. by L. A. Selby-Bigge, p. 87.

When we shift our perspective to a biological-anthropological orientation and take seriously the experimental attitude so fundamental to modern scientific inquiry, we realize that within experience "anticipation is . . . more primary than recollection; projection than summoning of the past; the projective than the retrospective."[43] The primary situations of life are those where there is something to be done, where we manipulate the world in order to achieve desired ends, where we actively seek to transform the situations within which we find ourselves. Like the existentialists, Dewey always underscores that man "lives forward," although he draws very different consequences from this. In maintaining that experience in its "vital form is experimental," Dewey also indicates the dominant role that activity plays in human experience. Philosophers have frequently written as if our primary attitude toward the world is that of the spectator who passively observes and records what is happening and what has happened. But man for Dewey is essentially an agent, or more accurately, an agent-patient. He is not a spectator looking into reality or nature from the outside. Man is a part of nature and his activity conditions and is conditioned by the entire range of his cognitive activities. The very nature of sensation, perception, and knowledge have been misunderstood because of the failure to appreciate the ways in which these processes themselves function within human activity. Dewey's point is echoed in Stuart Hampshire's recent claim when he says:

The deepest mistake in empiricist theories of perception, descending from Berkeley and Hume, has been the representation of human beings as passive observers receiving impressions from 'outside' of the mind, where the 'outside' includes our own bodies. In fact I find myself from the beginning able to act upon objects around me. In this context to act is to move at will my own body, that persisting physical thing, and thereby to bring about perceived movements of other physical things. I not only perceive my body, I also control it: I not only perceive external objects, I also manipulate them. . . . . It is therefore wrong to represent experience of the external world as some synthesis of impressions of each of the five senses. A physical object is recognized as a potential obstruction, or as something to be manipulated, occupying a definite position in relation to me at the moment of perception.[44]

43. "The Need for a Recovery of Philosophy," p. 27.
44. Stuart Hampshire, *Thought and Action,* pp. 47–48.

Once we realize that experience is primarily an active transaction between a living organism and its environment, then our understanding of the entire range of man's cognitive functions is transformed. They are properly located as functions in the life activity of an individual; "we are active beings from the start and are naturally . . . engaged in redirecting our action in response to changes in our surroundings."[45]

Dewey placed so much stress on the active projective dimension of experience that there is a danger of misinterpreting him. There has been a shallow criticism of Dewey that he conceives of man as a restless agent who is always concerned with a future that eludes him. This common criticism ignores that Dewey was just as concerned with the moments of completeness and fulfillment that take place within the rhythm of experience. He was highly critical of those doctrines which sacrificed the present to some far-off future. In his *Art as Experience,* Dewey analyzes the consummatory phase of experience which is dominated by "esthetic quality that rounds out an experience into completeness and unity. . . ." "Life is no uniform uninterrupted march or flow. It is a thing of histories, each with its own plot, its own inception and movement toward its close, each having its particular rhythmic movement; each with its own unrepeated quality pervading it throughout."[46]

(iv) The empirical tradition is committed to particularism. Connections and continuities are supposed to be foreign to experience, to be byproducts of dubious validity. An experience that is an undergoing of an environment and a striving for its control in new directions is pregnant with connections.[47]

Dewey is reiterating the point so eloquently made by William James in his criticism of traditional empiricism and his demand for a "radical empiricism." In the history of British empiricism, there has been a strong particularistic and atomistic tendency. Experience consists of aggregates of discrete and separable perceptions. Dewey, like the other pragmatists and like Bergson and Whitehead, accuses past philosophers of foisting upon us a highly abstract and artificial

45. John Dewey, "The Reflex Arc Concept in Psychology," *Psychological Review* 3 (1896), p. 239.
46. John Dewey, *Art as Experience,* p. 41; pp. 36–37.
47. "The Need for a Recovery of Philosophy," p. 23.

analysis of experience, one that mistakes an abstraction for the concreteness of experience itself. Once one accepts an atomistic view of experience then there are insoluble problems in accounting for the order and objectivity that are characteristic of our experience. Kant seized upon limitations of an atomistic theory of experience and claimed that our understanding supplies the categories and principles by which we order experience. But for Dewey and the pragmatists, the problem here is a pseudo-problem and the various "solutions" offered are pseudo-solutions. They are based on a misrepresentation of experience. "Some things are relatively insulated from the influence of other things; some things are easily invaded by others; some things fiercely attracted to conjoin their activities with those of others. Experience exhibits every kind of connection from the most intimate to mere external juxtaposition."[48] Connections and relations are as much a part of experience as the particulars that we isolate within experience. Dewey's view of experience is essentially holistic, not in the sense that there is a single absolute experience, but in the more empirical and pluralistic sense where there are a plurality of overlapping experiences, each having internal complexity and integrity. Dewey's theory of experiential situations is intended to avoid the excesses of extreme atomistic empiricism and block universe monisms.

. . . every experience in its direct occurrence is an interaction of environing conditions and an organism. As such it contains a fused some*what* experienc*ed* and some processes of experienc*ing*. In its identity with a life-function, it is temporally and spatially more extensive and more internally complex than a single thing like a stone, or a single quality like red. For no living creature could survive, save by sheer accident, if its experiences had no more reach, scope and content, than the traditional particularistic empiricism provided for. On the other hand, it is impossible to imagine a living creature coping with the entire universe at once. In other words, the theory of experiential situations which follows directly from the biological-anthropological approach is by its very nature a *via media* between extreme atomistic pluralism and block universe monisms.[49]

Each of the preceding four contrasts between Dewey's theory of

48. "The Need for a Recovery of Philosophy," p. 29.
49. John Dewey, "Experience, Knowledge and Value: A Rejoinder," *The Philosophy of John Dewey*, ed. by Paul Arthur Schlipp, p. 544.

experiential situations and the "orthodox" or "traditional" view reinforces each other. Collectively they indicate the alternative perspective that Dewey is developing for understanding human life. But Dewey indicates a fifth contrast which is the most important for him and which is based on the previous four.

(v) In the traditional notion experience and thought are antithetical terms. Inference, so far as it is other than a revival of what has been given in the past, goes beyond experience; hence it is either invalid, or else a measure of desperation by which, using experience as a springboard, we jump out of a world of stable things and other selves. But experience taken free of the restrictions imposed by the older concept, is full of inference. There is, apparently, no conscious experience without inference; reflection is native and constant.[50]

"Experience" in many of its characteristic philosophic uses has been used as a contrast term with "thought," or "inference," or "reason." Underlying this use is a fundamental epistemological doctrine that experience is limited to what is sensed, perceived, or remembered. Experience supplies the input and reason is the faculty or capacity by which we order, arrange, and draw inferences from this input. Here too Dewey challenges a dogma that has infected traditional philosophy. Experience *can* be nonrational and irrational, but it can also be *funded* with intelligence and controlled inference. The proper contrast, according to Dewey, is not between experience and reason, but between experience which is funded by the procedures and results of intelligent activity and experience which is not.

In stressing that experience is not primarily a "knowledge-affair" Dewey intends to highlight inquiry as a mode of discourse which is located in and controlled by a wider context of experience. Furthermore, experience and inquiry are not limited to what is mental, private, and subjective. As a living organism, man continually acts and reacts within an objective world. The fundamental issue for Dewey is always what will be the quality and nature of our interactions and transactions. "Any reaction is a venture; it involves risk. . . . But the organism's fateful intervention in the course of events is blind, its choice is random, except as it can employ what happens to it as a basis for inferring what is likely to happen later. In the degree in which it can read future results in present on-goings,

50. "The Need for a Recovery of Philosophy," p. 23.

its responsive choice, its partiality to this condition or that, become intelligent."[51] This leads directly to the point of Dewey's third contrast where he emphasizes that "experience in its vital form is experimental, and is oriented toward the future." The connection with the future is the basis for intelligent activity. Because experience "contains" connections and continuities, we can learn from experience and evolve standards and norms for guiding future behavior.

Dewey's exploration of the five contrasts culminates with a plea for the realization of intelligence in all phases of human life; not intelligence that is "the faculty of intellect honored in textbooks and neglected elsewhere," but intelligence that is "the sum-total of impulses, habits, emotions, records, and discoveries which forecast what is desirable and undesirable in future possibilities, and which contrive ingenuously in behalf of imagined good."[52]

The theory of experiential situations is the central motif of Dewey's philosophy. He stated the essentials of this theory as early as 1896 in "The Reflex Arc Concept in Psychology" where he criticized a mechanistic interpretation of stimulus-response interactions and argued for a functional interpretation of stimulus-response within an "organic coordination."[53] "Stimulus" and "response" signify changing, organically related functions that play a role in maintaining and reconstructing a situation. It is the "organic coordination" that is the basic unit of behavior.

In his *Studies in Logical Theory* (1903) and again in *Logic: The Theory of Inquiry* (1938), he analyzed the nature of systematic knowing or inquiry from the perspective of its role within the wider context of experience—as it arises out of a specific problematic situation, and is guided by this situation. When successful, inquiry reconstructs this situation. Late in his career when Dewey set out to state succinctly his conception of inquiry, he returned once again to this central point.

. . . the unsettled, indecisive character of the situation with which inquiry is compelled to deal affects all the subject matters that enter into all inquiry. It affects, on the one hand, the observed existing facts that are

51. "The Need for a Recovery of Philosophy," p. 34.
52. "The Need for a Recovery of Philosophy," p. 68.
53. John Dewey, "The Reflex Arc Concept in Psychology," *Psychological Review* 3 (1896).

taken to locate and delimit the problem; on the other side, it affects all of the suggestions, surmises, ideas that are entertained as possible solutions of the problem.[54]

One of the most fascinating and important aspects of Dewey's theory of experiential situations is his thesis that situations possess unique pervasive qualities which unify experiential situations and set them apart from other situations. He came to realize the affinity of this claim with Peirce's analysis of the Firstness characteristic of all experiences. Such pervasive qualities are not to be confused with mere subjective feelings; they are properly predicated of situations.[55] The importance of this qualitative immediacy is the clue for understanding the fundamental role that esthetic categories play in Dewey's theory of experiential situations. The consummatory phase in the rhythm of experience is one that is dominated by esthetic wholeness, integrity, and fulfillment. Esthetic experience is not the name of a special type of experience which differs in kind from other experiences. Esthetic quality can and ought to be a characteristic of all experiences.

The enemies of the esthetic are neither the practical nor the intellectual. They are the humdrum; slackness of loose ends, submission to convention in practice and intellectual procedure. Rigid abstinence, coerced submission, tightness on one side and dissipation, incoherence, aimless indulgence on the other, are deviations in opposite directions from the unity of experience.[56]

In Dewey's educational and social philosophy, he also emphasizes the esthetic consummatory dimension of experience. He criticizes educational and social institutions and practices for neglecting this esthetic dimension of experience. This is evidenced in the separation of means and ends in our educational and social thinking. The quality and content of the ends-in-view which we strive to attain depend upon the quality of the means that we use to attain them. When we separate ends and means, when we think of means as *mere* means

54. Letter to Albert George Adam Balz, *Journal of Philosophy* 46 (1949). Reprinted as "In Defense of the Theory of Inquiry," in *John Dewey: On Experience, Nature and Freedom,* p. 136.

55. See John Dewey, "Peirce's Theory of Quality," *Journal of Philosophy* 32 (1935); and "Qualitative Thought," in *Philosophy and Civilization.*

56. *Art as Experience,* p. 40.

to some distant goal, we are in danger of destroying the efficacy of our means and the potency of our ends. Means and ends, whether in education, moral, or political life designate the same experience viewed from different perspectives. Our task is to strive to make all experience more esthetic, funded with meaning, and fulfilling.

Although human experience has distinctive qualities and functions which are most significantly indicated by the capacity for discourse and communication, experience consists of natural transactions continuous with other natural transactions. In *Experience and Nature,* Dewey develops a comprehensive naturalism in which he explores the ways in which experience is both continuous with the rest of nature and he indicates the features of human experience which distinguish it from other natural transactions. Dewey's naturalism is not a mechanistic materialism. Nature *has* mechanism, but it is not a mechanism. There are regularities within nature. It is only by discovering these regularities that we can exercise some control over our natural and social environment. A primary characteristic of human experience is its purposiveness. We are creatures who can imaginatively construct new possibilities and by intelligent inquiry we can reconstruct our experience so that the goods that we most deeply desire can be achieved and made stable.

Man as Craftsman

At the heart of Dewey's theory of experiential situations and his comprehensive naturalism is an understanding of man as an organic agent-patient. Like all natural beings, man's responses to his environment are selective. These selective responses characterize his individuality. In acting we are always choosing. Our choices can be blind, motivated by impulse, convention, or rigid habit, but our choices and actions can also be intelligent. "A choice which intelligently manifests individuality enlarges the range of action, and this enlargement in turn confers upon desires greater insight and foresight, and makes choices more intelligent."[57] Whatever area or problem Dewey explored, it is this perspective that sets the context for his investigation.

57. John Dewey, "Philosophies of Freedom," *Philosophy and Civilization,* p. 286.

When for example, Dewey considers the problems of moral life, it is always the perspective of man as a moral agent that is dominant, not man as a moral spectator, critic, or judge. A great deal of misunderstanding has resulted from a failure to appreciate that Dewey is calling for a shift of emphasis from the way in which most modern post-Kantian moral philosophers have treated problems of ethics. This shift recalls the spirit of Aristotle's approach to the problems of moral and political life. The paradigm of a moral situation is one in which there are conflicts and our task is to decide what is to be done. In such situations, we are called upon to make a practical judgment, "a judgment of what to do, or what is to be done: a judgment respecting the future termination of an incomplete and in so far indeterminate situation."[58] Dewey would fully agree with Stuart Hampshire's indictment of modern (post-Kantian) moral philosophy when he declares:

Suppose . . . one is confronted with a difficult and untrivial situation in which one is in doubt what one ought to do, and then, after full consideration of the issues involved, one arrives at the conclusion. One's conclusion, reached after deliberation, expressed in the sentence 'x is the best thing to do in these circumstances,' is a pure or primary moral judgment (the solution of a practical problem). It is misleading to the point of absurdity to describe this sentence, as used in such a context, as meaningful only in the sense in which an exclamation is meaningful, or as having no literal significance, or as having the function merely of expressing and evoking feeling. It is also misleading to describe it as a statement about the agent's feeling or attitude; for such a description suggests that the judgment would be defended if attacked, primarily by an appeal to introspection. It is surely misleading to describe the procedure by which a judgment or decision is re-established as right as one of comparing degrees of moral emotion towards alternative courses of action. I am supposing (what is normal in such cases) that the agent has reasoned and argued about the alternatives, and am asserting that he would then justify his conclusion, if it were attacked, by reference to these arguments. . . .[59]

58. John Dewey, "The Logic of Judgments of Practise," *Journal of Philosophy* 12 (1915), 514.

59. Stuart Hampshire, "Fallacies in Moral Philosophy," *Mind*, n.s., 58 (1949). Hampshire also emphasizes the importance of dealing with moral philosophy from the perspective of the moral agent, and he also draws attention to the analogy between the moral agent and the craftsman or artist.

Enlightened moral judgment necessitates criticism, but the primary contexts of such criticism are the indeterminate situations which require choice and action on our part.

Moral judgments are themselves one type of practical judgments which can be expressed in a variety of ways: "M.N. should do thus and so; it is better, wiser, more prudent, right, advisable, opportune, expedient, etc. to act thus and so."[60] Dewey singles out a number of characteristics of practical judgments. In the first place, practical judgments are made in the context of an incomplete situation that requires completion—something must be done. The logic of such judgments cannot be understood if we abstract these judgments from the typical contexts in which they occur. Second, the judgment itself is a factor in the completion of the situation, it is "*a determining factor in the outcome*"[61] of the situation. Third, the subject matter of such judgments "implies that it makes a difference how the given is to be terminated."[62] A practical judgment "affects the subject-matter for better or worse."[63] Fourth, practical judgments involve essential reference to both means and ends. They single out the obstacles to be confronted in a specific situation, the means employed to surmount these obstacles, and the ends to be achieved in completing the specific situation. The subject matter of a practical judgment is not exhausted by what is "given" in a specific situation, but neither can a practical judgment be oblivious to what is "given." "The given is undoubtedly just what it is; it is determinate throughout. But it is the given of something to be done. The survey and inventory of present conditions (facts) are not something complete in themselves; they exist for the sake of an intelligent determination of what is to be done, what is required to complete the given."[64] Fifth, practical judgments are hypothetical; they claim that the "facts which constitute the statement of the given are relevant and adequate for the purpose in hand—the determination of a possibility to be accomplished in action."[65] Finally, practical

60. "The Logic of Judgments of Practise," *Journal of Philosophy* 12 (1915), 505.

61. "The Logic of Judgments of Practise," p. 506.

62. "The Logic of Judgments of Practise," p. 507.

63. "The Logic of Judgments of Practise," p. 507.

64. "The Logic of Judgments of Practise," p. 508.

65. "The Logic of Judgments of Practise," p. 510.

judgments can be validated or invalidated by the state of affairs that they bring about. "The determination of the end-means which constitutes the content of the practical proposition is hypothetical until the course of action indicated has been tried."[66] I think that Dewey misrepresents his point when he says "The event or issue of such action *is* the truth or falsity of the judgment."[67] But we can unscramble the point that Dewey is making. Practical judgments are tentative and hypothetical. They are made on the basis of the assessment of the situation, what we judge to be the relevant conditions influencing the situation and the relevant possibilities to be achieved. No matter how careful and accurate we have been in our assessment of the situation, there is no way of absolutely guaranteeing the correctness of our practical judgments. We may, and frequently do, discover when we act that we have been mistaken, that we have misjudged what is to be done. This can occur for a variety of reasons; we may have misjudged the relevant facts, or overlooked other facts that turn out to be relevant, or we may have misjudged the best course of action to be followed, etc. Clearly, what does happen is relevant to the assessment of our original practical judgment. In this respect, the actual consequences which issue from our practical judgments can validate or invalidate these judgments.

It should be clear that the range of practical judgments has a much greater scope than what is normally considered the domain of moral and political life, for we make practical judgments in a variety of everyday life situations as well as in our most advanced and sophisticated inquiries. What may not be obvious is the extent to which Dewey seeks to generalize from this analysis.

Traditionally, theory has been contrasted with practice, and theoretical judgments have been sharply distinguished from practical judgments. To the extent that these two types of judgment have been assimilated, philosophers have written as if practical judgments were a degenerate form of theoretical judgments. Dewey moves in the opposite direction. His claim is that theoretical judgments have been misunderstood precisely because of the failure to appreciate how they share the characteristics of practical judgments which have been outlined above. This is one of Dewey's most important

66. "The Logic of Judgments of Practise," p. 510.
67. "The Logic of Judgments of Practise," p. 510.

and most misunderstood claims. He did not mean that theoretical judgments are justified only insofar as they serve some "practical" ends, or that we must always have our sights set on the "practical" uses of knowledge. On the contrary, theoretical inquiry gains its systematic explanatory power in the degree to which it abstracts from the demands of immediate existential situations. Unless we have a disinterested concern with developing theoretical inquiry for its own sake, we cripple the systematic explanatory power of our theories. Speaking of theories as they are used in scientific inquiry, Dewey says that they are "matters of systematic abstraction. Like ideas, they get away from what may be called the immediately given facts in order to be applicable to a much fuller range of relevant facts. A scientific theory differs from ideas which, as we say, 'pop into our heads,' only in its vast and systematic range of applicability. The peculiarity of *scientific* abstraction lies in the degree of its freedom from *particular* existential adhesions."[68]

While acknowledging the genuine differences between the varieties of theoretical and practical judgments and inquiries, Dewey is primarily concerned to focus on their similarities and continuities. All of the characteristics of practical judgments are applicable to theoretical judgments. These judgments too are made in the context of indeterminate situations; they are factors in resolving and determining the outcome of these situations; they are essentially hypothetical and prescribe courses of action to be followed to test and validate these judgments; and they can be confirmed or disconfirmed by the consequences which issue from these judgments.

We have noted that in analyzing our moral and political life, Dewey advocated that we focus on the moral agent as he confronts a situation of conflict in which something must be done. Dewey is advocating a similar change of perspective when we consider all inquiry, including theoretical inquiry. The cash value of Dewey's attack on the spectator theory of knowledge can be seen here. Just as moral and political philosophy has been led astray by focusing on the end products of our deliberations and neglecting the process of deliberation itself, Dewey makes the same indictment against traditional epistemology. It has been excessively preoccupied with a logic of proof and results rather than the process by which we discover,

68. "In Defense of the Theory of Inquiry," *John Dewey: On Experience, Nature and Freedom,* p. 140.

test, and modify our hypotheses. It has failed to focus on the status of our knowledge claims as they function within the process of inquiry itself. Like Peirce, Dewey argued that the lesson to be learned from experimental science is that what distinguishes genuine knowledge from fancy and mere speculation is precisely the procedures within inquiry by which we discover, test, and warrant our knowledge claims. When we focus on discovering and inquiring, we are led to very different conclusions concerning knowledge itself. We become aware of the essentially hypothetical nature of all knowledge claims; we look to consequences rather than "origins" of knowledge; we realize that the norms of inquiry are not supplied from some source "outside" of inquiry, but are arrived at, refined, and modified in the course of the process of inquiry. "Knowledge, as an abstract term, is a name for the product of competent inquiries. . . . The 'settlement' of a particular situation by a particular inquiry is no guarantee that *that* settled conclusion will always remain settled. The attainment of settled beliefs is a progressive matter; there is no belief so settled as not to be exposed to further inquiry. It is the convergent and cumulative effect of continued inquiry that defines knowledge in its general meaning. . . . When knowledge is taken as a general abstract term related to inquiry in the abstract, it means 'warranted assertibility.' "[69]

Dewey's primary project, his fundamental end-in-view, is to bring the problems and procedures of our moral and social life into closer harmony with the dramatic advances made in experimental scientific inquiry. He believed that when we focused on man as an agent-patient we had a perspective from which we could detect the important similarities and continuities among these various dimensions of human experience. He argued that an analysis of scientific inquiry as a process is not value neutral. There are important moral lessons to be learned from the attitudes, dispositions, and habits required for open experimental inquiry. And he believed that these lessons could be applied to the entire range of our moral, political and social life.

Philosophers are frequently loath to admit how much of their thinking is shaped by basic metaphors and analogies. Dewey was not, and by appreciating the basic analogy that pervades his thought, we can understand the basic change of orientation that he sought to

69. John Dewey, *Logic: The Theory of Inquiry,* pp. 8–9.

bring about in philosophy. Like Peirce, he argued that past philosophy, especially post-Cartesian philosophy, had been dominated by the metaphor of the fixed "mental eye." Sensing, perceiving, and knowing had been analyzed in terms of the model of mental seeing. Disputes arose concerning what sees, what is seen, and what is the relation of what we see to "external reality." But the analogy that Dewey believes is more appropriate for understanding human life, including our cognitive processes, is the esthetic analogy of the craftsman or artist involved in doing and making. This is an analogy that was taken seriously by the Greek philosophers, especially Aristotle. According to Dewey, Greek philosophy limited the application of this analogy to our ethical and political life, to *praxis* as contrasted with *theoria*. With the development of modern experimental scientific inquiry, Dewey maintained that this analogy could now be extended to what had been traditionally classified as *theoria*. Experimental knowing is essentially an art that involves, like all arts, a conscious directed manipulation of objects and situations. In the process of experimental inquiry, there is a reconstruction involving a continuous interaction between the craftsman and the subject matter that he is transforming. The craftsman perfects his art, not by comparing his product to some "ideal" model, but by the cumulative results of experience—experience which benefits from tried and tested procedures, but always involves risk and novelty. There are significant differences between the art of inquiry and other arts, and Dewey is sensitive to these. The analogy is intended to be suggestive and heuristic, not a literal straightjacket. The use of this analogy suggests the way in which Dewey sought to bring the range of our practical activities and judgments into closer connection with our cognitive activities and judgments.

Education in the Democratic Community

There is a thematic continuity that runs through Dewey's investigations. Dewey tells us that a practical judgment is a proposal concerning what is to be done in a specific indeterminate situation. The judgment itself makes a difference in the way in which the situation is resolved. Dewey extends his analysis of practical judgments to theoretical judgments and his theory of inquiry and valuation is essentially practical in this sense. The aim of this theory is to enlighten us about how we ought to inquire and deliberate. This proposal for the development of creative intelligence is based on what Dewey considers to have been the most effective, intelligent procedures for ascertaining and warranting knowledge and for resolving situations in which there is a conflict of values. The theory of inquiry and valuation has been developed against the background of Dewey's understanding of our cultural situation, for he believed that the deepest conflicts of our times arise from the divorce of science and practical life, or theory and practice.

The same theme is evidenced in the way in which Dewey conceives of the task of philosophy. Dewey would agree with Marx that past philosophers have been primarily concerned with interpreting the world. He would also agree that the point is to change it. However, for Dewey this does not mean abandoning philosophy or overcoming it, but reconstructing philosophy.

There are human difficulties of an urgent, deep-seated kind which may be clarified by trained reflection, and whose solution may be forwarded by the careful development of hypotheses. When it is understood that philosophic thinking is caught up in the actual course of events, having the office of guiding them toward a prosperous issue, problems will abundantly present themselves. Philosophy will not solve these problems; philosophy is vision, imagination, reflection—and these functions apart from action, modify nothing and hence resolve nothing. But in a complicated and perverse world, action which is not informed with vision, imagination, and reflection, is more likely to increase confusion and conflict than to straighten things out. . . . Philosophy recovers itself when it ceases to be a device for dealing with the problems of philosophers and becomes a method, cultivated by philosophers, for dealing with the problems of men.[70]

If action is to be informed by vision, if we are to make the ideal of critical intelligence a living reality, then radical steps must be taken. A thorough reconstruction of social institutions is required. Man's social environment exerts a decisive influence on the type of creature he is to become. We were drifting toward a situation in which the very ideal of shared intelligence is being undermined. Man is becoming dehumanized, his activities routinized, and his esthetic life cheapened and degraded. Long before the present prophets of doom,

70. "The Need for a Recovery of Philosophy," pp. 66–67.

Dewey warned against the pernicious consequences of an uncontrolled technological industrial society. What then is to be done? For Dewey the answer was clear. If philosophy really is to become practical, if it really is to help in fostering a society which is freer, more humane, more satisfying, and more intelligent, then we must turn our critical attention to the educative effect of all social institutions.

This is why "philosophy of education is not a poor relation of general philosophy even though it is often so treated even by philosophers. It is ultimately the most significant phase of philosophy."[71] Or, "if we are willing to conceive of education as the process of forming dispositions, intellectual and emotional, toward nature and fellow men, philosophy may even be defined *as the general theory of education*."[72] Education is taking place all the time in our transactions with the world. All social institutions influence the education of the individual. Consequently, Dewey proposed a reconstruction of all social institutions including political and economic institutions. "When self-hood is perceived to be an active process, it is also seen that social modifications are the only means of changed personalities."[73] The social institution that is the primary object of Dewey's concern is the school. It is the school that most desperately needs reconstruction. Educational reform offers the best chance for developing creative intelligence.

We cannot explore the details of Dewey's philosophy of education, but it has been so badly misunderstood that it is necessary to touch upon some of its highlights. Dewey criticized the artificiality and externality of traditional approaches to education that stressed the structure and content of the curriculum, and conceived of education as a joyless process of imposing these studies upon a recalcitrant child. But Dewey was just as critical—and this point cannot be overemphasized, since it is still popularly thought of as Dewey's view—of the excesses of progressive education insofar as it is child-oriented and stresses the role of the child in determining what he wants to study. Such a view sentimentalizes and idealizes the child, and fails to appreciate the extent to which a child's experience is

71. John Dewey, "The Relation of Science and Philosophy as the Basis of Education," *Problems of Men,* p. 165.
72. John Dewey, *Democracy and Education,* p. 383.
73. *Reconstruction in Philosophy,* p. 154.

immature and crude. "Doing as one pleases signifies a release from truly *intellectual* initiative and independence," and when unlimited free expression is allowed, children "gradually tend to become listless and finally bored, while there is an absence of cumulative, progressive development of power and of actual achievement in results."[74] In opposition to this view, Dewey argues for the necessity of deliberate guidance, direction, and order. Education ought to be a continuous process of reconstruction in which there is a progressive movement away from the child's immature experience to experience that becomes more pregnant with meaning, more systematic and controlled. What Dewey means by this must be viewed against the background of this theory of experiential situations and inquiry. The goal of education is the development of creative intelligence, but we must keep in mind the distinctive meaning that this concept has for Dewey. Intelligence is not to be identified with a narrow concept of reason considered as the ability to make inferences and draw conclusions from explicitly stated premises. Intelligence consists of a complex set of flexible and growing habits that involve sensitivity; the ability to discern the complexities of situations; imagination that is exercised in seeing new possibilities and hypotheses; willingness to learn from experience; fairness and objectivity in judging and evaluating conflicting values and opinions; and the courage to change one's views when it is demanded by the consequences of our actions and the criticisms of others. All education is moral education, when we understand "moral" in the broad sense which involves intelligent evaluation. Another way of making this point is to say that the function of education is to bring about the effective realization of the experimental spirit in all phases of human life. Education must be concerned with all aspects of the individual's intellectual and emotional development. The point of the slogan "learn by doing" is that a sound education must encourage and cultivate the active experimental dimension of the child's experience. There is no simple or mechanical way of achieving the goal of creative intelligence, for it depends on the subtle transactions with social environment that the child encounters. "It is the business of the school environment to eliminate, so far as possible, the unworthy features of the existing environment from influence upon mental

74. John Dewey, *Construction and Criticism*, p. 11; "Individuality and Experience," *Journal of the Barnes Foundation* 2 (1926), 1.

habits and attitudes. It establishes a purified medium of action. . . .
As a society becomes more enlightened, it realizes that it is responsible *not* to transmit and conserve the whole of its existing achievements, but only such as to make a better future society. The school
is the chief agency for the accomplishment of this end."[75] Dewey
did not advocate acquiescence to the status quo, or adjustment to existing institutions, as some critics have charged. It has become fashionable to criticize American education for being unduly influenced
by Dewey's ideas. However, insofar as our schools have failed to
develop the tough-minded habits of intelligence, insofar as they have
failed to make education a more joyous and fulfilling experience,
they have failed to be influenced by what is most basic for Dewey.

The type of educational reform that Dewey advocated is one
needed for social reconstruction and for a revitalization of democracy. Here too Dewey argued that there were lessons to be learned
from the experimental scientific inquiry.

It is of the nature of science not so much to tolerate as to welcome diversity of opinion, while it insists that inquiry brings the evidence of observed facts to bear to effect a consensus of conclusions—and even to
hold the conclusion subject to what is ascertained and made public in
further new inquiries. I would not claim that any existing democracy has
ever made complete or adequate use of scientific method in deciding
upon its policies. But freedom of inquiry, toleration of diverse views,
freedom of communication, the distribution of what is found out to every
individual as the ultimate intellectual consumer, are involved in the
democratic as in the scientific method.[76]

Democracy is more than a form of government, it is a way of life
and a moral ideal. Dewey's views on experience, inquiry, and education shape his faith in democracy.

Democracy as compared with other ways of life is the sole way of living
which believes wholeheartedly in the process of experience as end and
as means; as that which is capable of generating the science which is the
sole dependable authority for the direction of further experience and
which releases emotions, needs, and desires so as to call into being the
things that have not existed in the past. For every way of life that fails
in its democracy limits the contacts, the exchanges, the communications,

75. *Democracy and Education,* p. 24.
76. John Dewey, *Freedom and Culture,* p. 102.

the interactions by which experience is steadied while it is also enlarged and enriched. The task of this release and enrichment is one that has to be carried on day by day. Since it is one that can have no end till experience itself comes to an end, the task of democracy is forever that of the creation of a freer and more humane experience in which all share and to which all contribute.[77]

Dewey dedicated his life to this ideal and task. It is based on the change of perspective that he sought to bring about in our understanding of man and the task of philosophy. The primary issue for man is not whether or not to act, but *how* he shall act. Philosophy has the role of clarifying the nature of man as an agent-patient and of showing the ways in which creative intelligence can be developed. When we realize that life itself is an art, that man can play a decisive role in shaping his own environment and thereby shaping himself, we turn our attention to the best and most enlightened ways in which this can be done. Man is neither a plaything of forces beyond his control, nor an agent who can bring about a better future by willing it. Nothing much can be accomplished without a significant change of the social institutions which are the medium of human life. Unless we turn our attention to the tasks of social reconstruction, life will become more mechanical, routinized, dull, and alienated. The proper response to the poignant conflicts of our present cultural situation is not to retreat into the self, nor to lose ourselves in utopian thinking, but to apply ourselves completely and passionately to the task "of the creation of a freer and more humane experience in which all share and to which all contribute."

Pragmatists are open to criticism from a variety of perspectives and they have been (especially Dewey) severely criticized. In an age that places a high value on clarity, subtlety, and rigor, Dewey's reflections seem primitive and rough hewn. Philosophers trained in the techniques of analytic philosophy find it almost impossible to pin down the precise meaning or meanings of Dewey's key concepts. Dewey praised the virtues of specificity and careful analysis, but he certainly didn't practice them. In his desire to overcome all hard-and-fast dichotomies, important analytic distinctions are blurred. It

77. John Dewey, "Creative Democracy—The Task Before Us," *Classic American Philosophers,* ed. by Max Fisch, p. 394.

may be laudable to attempt to overcome the dichotomies of the "is" and the "ought," "fact" and "value," the "descriptive" and the "prescriptive," but if this is to be accomplished in a careful and convincing manner, then we must meticulously discriminate the meanings of these complex concepts. Even more fundamental, the very spirit of Dewey's conception of philosophy has been out of joint with the conception of philosophy that has been dominant for most analytic philosophers. The primary emphasis in analytic philosophy, especially recent linguistic philosophy, has been on the description, analysis, and understanding of our complex web of concepts. It is not the *basic* objective of philosophy to recommend, prescribe, or to propose. The history of philosophy is filled with confusions, ambiguities, and fallacies because philosophers have not paid sufficient attention to the nuances of the language in which we do our thinking. The contribution that philosophy can make to human understanding is to clear away the underbrush that leads us into philosophic perplexity, to dissolve pseudo-problems, and to enlighten us by clarifying the logic of our concepts. In Part IV, we shall see that even when the concept of action became a dominant focal point for analytic philosophy, the essential concern has been with the clarification of the meaning of this and related concepts. Dewey, of course, would agree that all intelligent activity depends upon careful, meticulous analysis. Insofar as analytic philosophy has performed this task, he would welcome its contributions. But Dewey is advocating a very different role for philosophy, one which is based on his understanding of man as an agent-patient. Philosophy is or ought to become the criticism of criticisms directed toward fostering enlightened change and social reconstruction. Philosophy's main task is to become practical, where this means addressing itself to the basic issues and conflicts that confront us, and making practical judgments about what is to be done.

We cannot turn our backs on the enormous sophistication and refinement that has been brought about by analytic philosophy. We can admit the legitimacy of criticism of the pragmatists insofar as it is a demand for more careful and subtle analysis. But this should not blind us to the contribution of the pragmatists and the challenge that they present to the aims of analytic philosophy. One of the saddest chapters in analytic philosophy has been its treatment of political and social philosophy. These disciplines have even been pronounced "dead." Even analytic moral philosophy is rapidly becoming a form of scholasticism that has only the most tangential relation with the moral problems that men are actually experiencing today. There are signs that some analytic philosophers, especially younger ones, are realizing the dangers of a narcissistic scholasticism that can result from the obsessive concern with the "problems of philosophers," and are searching for ways to make philosophy practical in the sense which Dewey advocated. The aim of developing "practical wisdom" which was once taken to be a primary goal of philosophic reflection has played almost no role in analytic philosophy. Dewey not only reminds us of the importance of this goal, but shows us new ways in which it can be revitalized.

There is another lesson that analytic philosophers can, and are beginning to, learn from the pragmatists. Central to both Peirce's and Dewey's philosophy is the theory of inquiry as a continuous self-corrective process. Every distinction, every knowledge claim is itself open to further criticism and modification. Many analytic philosophers, especially those engaging in conceptual analysis, have been guilty of one of the oldest sins in philosophy—seizing upon important distinctions and reifying them into rigid dichotomies. The older way of commiting this sin was to claim that basic distinctions reveal metaphysical or epistemological dichotomies. The newer way has been to speak of conceptual, a priori, distinctions. In the analysis of the concept of action in Part IV, we will see how prevalent and misguided have been the attempts to settle complex issues by a priori fiat, issues which can be properly resolved only in the continuing process of inquiry itself.

Existentialist philosophers and those sympathetic with them have developed another line of criticism against the pragmatists. Taking seriously the claim that philosophy ought to deal with the "problems of men," their charge is that the pragmatic thinkers have failed to do this. They would agree with Dewey that the primary issue for man is not whether to choose or act, but *how* to choose and act. Men are choosing and acting all the time and in doing so they are choosing what they are to become. But in speaking of the problems of *men,* we already move away from the burden that each unique existing individual faces. Pragmatists with their emphasis on the public, the community, and the social are guilty of the same type of "forgetfulness" characteristic of the Hegelians. They fail to confront honestly the absurdity and futility of the human situation. They are blind to the existential dilemmas posed by human consciousness itself and human inwardness.

It is certainly true that the problems and issues that have been so central to Kierkegaard and Sartre have been peripheral to the main concerns of Peirce and Dewey (although this is not so for William James). The power and attraction of existentialist thought is owed to the fact that it speaks to problems that many contemporary individuals deeply feel. Peirce's belief in the growth of "concrete reasonableness" and Dewey's concern for the growth of "creative intelligence" seem a bit old fashioned and irrelevant to the poignant conflicts of contemporary life. Kierkegaard and Sartre have described and dissected forms of internal conflict, self-deception, despair, anxiety, and choice that are almost totally neglected by Peirce and Dewey. But the more sensitively we appreciate the analysis of the human condition as described by existentialist thinkers, the more we can appreciate what is most basic and vital in the pragmatist tradition. Both sides agree that the main problem for men is *how* we will choose and act. Kierkegaard and Sartre have shown us that we deceive ourselves when we think that there is a firm, objective, fixed, ground that we can rely on in making our choices and in acting. The pragmatists agree. The search for a "foundation" for moral choice and action is a part of the same misguided search for a "foundation" of knowledge. Once we give up the quest for certainty, once we recognize the impossibility of an "absolute" justification, and the fallibility of all beliefs, including our moral beliefs, we need not despair. We may never solve the problems of human alienation, but it is within our power to alleviate and ameliorate alienation. If we are serious about this task, then we must direct our activity toward the realization of a genuine community of inquirers in which all share and all participate. We must engage in those forms of *praxis* that can effect a genuine social reconstruction in which the quality of each unique individual's life is transformed.

It is this last point that is the main target of the attack by Marxist critics. They recognize how close in spirit the pragmatists are to Marx himself. Social *praxis* becomes the dominant category for Dewey as it does for Marx. Dewey also maintains that our practical activity shapes the entire range of our human activities, including our cognitive functions, and that this practical activity is itself shaped by social institutions in which we participate. Like Marx, Dewey believed that the only way to bring about a freer, more humane society in which creative individuality can flourish is by the transformation of objective social institutions. Like Marx, Dewey calls for a criticism of criticisms that is directed toward controlled change. And both agree that action which is not informed by correct understanding becomes futile and self-defeating. From a Marxist perspective, these similarities between Marx and Dewey are not a basis for praising Dewey's philosophy, but for condemning it. Dewey's main failure is the failure to be genuinely radical, to get at the "roots." His faith in creative intelligence is naive because he underestimates the powerful social, political, and economic forces that distort and corrupt this "ideal." Despite Dewey's intention, the consequence of his own philosophy is to perpetuate the social evils that it seeks to overcome. To believe, for example that it is possible to bring about reconstruction of all social institutions through educational reform is to be completely unrealistic about the extent to which our schools are and will continue to be a reflection of a larger society in which they function. No capitalist society will tolerate a school system that is designed to overthrow it. A Marxist critic would claim that all this might have been known if Dewey had a correct understanding of the dynamics of existing society. If one wants further confirmation, we need only look at the failure of Dewey's ideas to be effective and their impotence in light of the basic conflicts in our society. The social conflicts that even Dewey perceived have not been ameliorated, they have been worsened. Where in American society can one find evidence of the growth of "creative intelligence" and the realization of the ideal of a democratic community of shared experience? Despite the influence of Dewey, our school system is even more chaotic and confused in its practices, aims, and objectives than it was during Dewey's lifetime. If Dewey was alarmed about what was happening to our social and natural environment during the first half of the twentieth century, look at the rapid deterioration since then. Even science has not become, as Dewey hoped, the beacon for intelligent activity, but a terrifying means for destruction. And the esthetic quality of our daily lives continues to be degraded and dehumanized.

These are strong indictments. I believe that they are essentially correct in the deficiencies they highlight and in the charge that

Dewey was unrealistically optimistic about what could and would be achieved by social reform. Even granted the thrust of these and other related criticisms, it would be disastrous if we discarded what stands at the center of the pragmatic tradition. This tradition, especially in the central position that it assigns to the theory of inquiry, has developed a critical understanding of the norms by which any idea or hypothesis is to be tested and evaluated. Radical thinking is rightly sensitive to the ways in which the demand for objective inquiry can become a disguise for impotence and can become corrupted. Radical thinking itself can all too easily degenerate into uncritical dogmatism. Marx called for the radical criticism of all existing social institutions. But it is the pragmatists who have perspicuously and forcefully delineated the norms of critical inquiry.

PART FOUR

THE CONCEPT
OF ACTION

ANALYTIC PHILOSOPHY

MARXISM, EXISTENTIALISM, AND PRAGMATISM are all deeply rooted in nineteenth-century philosophy. One who is unfamiliar with this philosophic tradition—especially as developed during the period from Kant to Hegel—would be at a severe disadvantage in making sense of the primary concerns and fundamental thrusts of these movements. Each of the thinkers we have examined thus far was struggling with the issues raised by this tradition, appropriating what he took to be sound, rejecting what he thought to be misleading and false, and developing his own point of view against the background of this thought. But when we approach analytic philosophy, the situation appears to be totally different. It is almost as if the nineteenth century had never existed—at least the main tradition of German thought—and we initially discover a much deeper affinity with the type of philosophizing characteristic of traditional empiricism and rationalism. This seeming lack of continuity is, in part, responsible for the failure of significant communication between analytic philosophers and continental philosophers working in the mainstream of European philosophy. With Marxism and existentialism, despite all their differences, there is at least a common universe of discourse within which we can compare and contrast these positions. And with pragmatism—for all its attempt to break with its nineteenth-century roots—we can locate its point of departure from this tradition. Philosophers working in these movements felt the inadequacies of Hegelianism, and each in his distinctive way focused on human activity as the means for "going beyond" Hegel. But with the analytic movement there is both ignorance and revulsion against the type of philosophizing that provided the intellectual sources of these other three movements. Hegel is not even a philosopher who has to be taken seriously, and who must be answered. He represents

230

what is worst and most irresponsible in traditional philosophy: he is obscure, confused, vague, and inconsequential. One cannot underestimate the fervor with which early analytic philosophers rejected traditional philosophy, especially that of the nineteenth century. They found their inspiration in the sciences and in the great advances in logic, not in philosophy. There were, of course, some favored "historical" philosophers such as Hume and there was a recognition of affinities with nineteenth-century empiricism and positivism. But even here the value placed on such positions was because of their approximation to new analytic techniques. The time had come—so the original members of the Vienna Circle believed— to be rid of the nonsense that was characteristic of so much of traditional philosophy, and finally to put philosophy on a sound, rigorous, scientific basis. Almost to a man, the members of the Vienna Circle were trained as scientists, not as philosophers, and they exhibited a missionary spirit in their desire to make philosophy legitimate and respectable. The early positivists celebrated the end of metaphysics and speculative philosophy; they condemned to historical curiosity the meaninglessness, mistakes, and superstitions of two thousand years of philosophy.

The situation was slightly different in England where English philosophers, along with the Vienna Circle, provided the fountainhead of the analytic movement. Russell and Moore, two central figures in the analytic movement, started with heavy doses of English absolute idealism. But they soon reacted against this imposing doctrine and quickly came to share the sentiments expressed by William James when he declared at the opening of his lectures delivered at Oxford in 1908, "Fortunately, our age seems to be growing philosophical again—still in the ashes live the wonted fires. Oxford, long the seed-bed, for the English world, of the idealism inspired by Kant and Hegel, has recently become the nursery of a very different way of thinking. . . . It looks as if the ancient English empiricism, so long put out of fashion here by nobler sounding germanic formulas, might be repluming itself and getting ready for a stronger flight than ever."[1] James could hardly have realized how prophetic his words were. Today, one would be amused that anyone could speak of Oxford as the "seed-bed, for the English world, of the idealism inspired by Kant and Hegel." This was a brief and

1. William James, *A Pluralistic Universe,* p. 3.

unfortunate chapter—a temporary aberration—in the ancient tradition of British empiricism.

The above picture is oversimplified but it was one that would be accepted by most practicing analytic philosophers. One of the parts of the picture that doesn't quite fit is the role that the Viennese philosopher Wittgenstein played in twentieth-century British philosophy. Wittgenstein had an enormous influence on two generations of British philosophers. But it was *not* the tormented, spiritual figure struggling with the disease of philosophic questioning and the significance of *"Das Mystische"* that exerted this influence. It was a "domesticated" Wittgenstein that was taken to be influential. His *Tractatus* was interpreted (today we realize it was misinterpreted) as laying the foundations for logical positivism and logical atomism which was so attractive to early analytic philosophers. And his later lectures delivered at Cambridge in the 1930's and 1940's together with his posthumous *Philosophical Investigations* were taken as laying the groundwork for the new "ordinary language analysis." Recent studies have shown us how badly Wittgenstein has been distorted by some of his "followers," and have revealed his spiritual affinities with nineteenth-century thought, especially that of Kierkegaard and Schopenhauer.[2]

There are other significant qualifications to the view of analytic philosophy as representing a total break with nineteenth-century philosophy. The more closely we study the early Moore and Russell, the more we can appreciate how even their rebellion against idealism was tainted with, and shaped by, the idealism that they were reacting against. Although there is far more continuity with the past than is frequently realized, this does not alter the fact that most of the early analytic philosophers conceived of themselves as making a radical break with the past. The centrality of the concern with the concept of action which has become the dominant focus of so much of post-Wittgenstein philosophy did not arise because of a desire to answer or to "go beyond" Hegel. To appreciate the importance of the concept of action and the aspects of this concept that have been investigated, we will have to recreate the dialectic of analytic

2. See Eddy Zemach, "Wittgenstein's Philosophy of the Mystical," *The Review of Metaphysics* 18 (September 1964); and Stanley Cavell, "The Availability of Wittgenstein's Later Philosophy," *The Philosophical Review* 71 (1962).

philosophy. I use the term "dialectic" deliberately, for as I shall try to show, it is helpful to view the development of analytic philosophy as a grand philosophic dialogue that illustrates the stages of what Hegel himself considered to be a typical dialectical process. I want first to establish the general outlook characteristic of early analytic philosophers and to explore why the concept of action played an insignificant role in their thinking. I will then discuss the reaction to this early reductionism and the antithesis that emerged in response to the one-sidedness and "falsity" of this orientation. But we will see how this response by ordinary language philosophers or conceptual analysts is itself guilty of exaggerations and distortions. Finally, we will sketch the beginnings of a "synthesis" of these antithetical poles within analytic philosophy that is now in the process of emerging.

As I suggested much earlier, I believe that analytic philosophy has passed through a series of stages that closely parallels a dialectical movement of epistemological positions adumbrated for us by Hegel in his *Phenomenology*.[3] This transition is illustrated in the way in which Kant has replaced Hume as the "hero" of analytic philosophy. But I want to go further and suggest that with recent developments, the possibility of a rapprochment with Hegel now exists. It is not that I am advocating a "return" to Hegel, or even that analytic philosophers would benefit by a serious encounter with Hegel (although I do believe this would be healthy), but rather that the type of concerns and perspectives that are so central to Hegel and those post-Hegelian philosophers influenced by Hegel have become relevant to the internal dialectic of analytic philosophy itself. It is risky to make predictions about the direction that philosophy—or a philosophic movement—will take, for these may be little more than an expression of one's own hopes and expectations. But I do believe that in the Anglo-Saxon world there is an increasing interest in Hegel and the Hegelian tradition. While there are many reasons for this, one reason is that philosophers—especially younger philosophers—are beginning to feel uneasy about the scholasticism that threatens analytic philosophy. They are beginning to realize that questions and issues which they have been told are illegitimate, meaningless, or nonphilosophical, are among the most important philosophic issues.

3. See p. 24 n.

The critique of analytic philosophy developed in this chapter is both "internal" and "external." It is "internal" insofar as I will follow the critical twists and turns within analytic philosophy in regard to the concept of action. I will isolate and criticize the tendency to resolve complex conceptual and empirical issues by a priori fiat. But it is "external" insofar as I want to show that the self-imposed limitations that analytic philosophy has set for itself are no longer warranted, and that there are vital issues that have been taken to fall "outside" the domain of analytic philosophy which it can no longer ignore. Analytic philosophy can no longer ignore the questions and challenges presented by the other philosophic movements we have investigated.

Let us imagine the situation of a future historian of philosophy who wants to tell the story of the development of analytic philosophy from the period of the 1920's (when some of the most important "classics" of this movement were published) until the present. To begin his task, he might acquaint himself with the philosophic literature that was most influential at these two terminal points in order to discover what were the central issues preoccupying philosophers. A cursory glance at the philosophical periodicals and books published in the 1960's would reveal that the status and nature of action, and such related concepts as intention, purpose, teleology, motive, and reasons were in the very foreground of philosophic discussion. Examining the literature that was foundational to the development of analytic philosophy, he might be surprised to discover that there is scarcely any direct concern with the nature of human action as a philosophic problem. Why was the investigation of action on the periphery of philosophic discussion in the early days of analytic philosophy? What difficulties, problems, insights, and strategies led to its growing importance? These questions can be asked in different ways. We may want to know the specific historical influences and the chronological sequence of these changes. Or we may want to focus on the philosophic story or dialectic involved—the problems and issues that led to a changing orientation. Without claiming to have the perspective of a future philosophic historian, it is this philosophic story that I want to tell. My ultimate aim is to understand and assess the contribution of analytic philosophy to the study of human action.

But first, it is helpful to jump into the middle of the discussion in order to gain a general idea of the issues that have been in the foreground of recent investigations. In *A Hundred Years of Philosophy,* Passmore presents a generalized sketch of an argument that has been repeated and developed with variations in the post-Wittgensteinian literature in philosophical psychology and the philosophy of mind.

It runs like this: there is a distinction between motions of the body, such as the knee reflex, and activities of the person, or 'behavior.' Behavior can never be defined in terms of movements of the body, since the very same set of movements can be present in quite different kinds of behavior. For example, the same movements of the body can take place in signaling that one is about to turn left or in pointing to an article in a shop-window, and yet these are quite different pieces of behavior. The physiologist can explain the motions of a body in terms of causes, but he cannot explain human behavior. Indeed behavior has no causes.

To explain a piece of behavior, on this view, is to give a reason for it, to mention its aim or purpose, or to point to the rules that govern it. (These are, of course, different but related procedures). Since behavior is essentially normative, the new teleologists argue, it is logically impossible to explain how men behave if we restrict ourselves to the purely descriptive language available to physical science. There is no way of deducing from a knowledge of physiology, however thorough, that there is a rule in our society to the effect that an extended hand means 'I am about to turn to the right.' So it is impossible to explain in physiological terms a particular piece of behavior which takes place in order to accord with that rule.[4]

Every major concept and move in the above passage demands further analysis and justification. Later I shall examine the claims made here in greater detail, but I want to note that this argument and others closely related to it have been used to support such claims as: there is a sharp dichotomy between the physical world of motions and the human world of actions or behavior; that the types of explanations and descriptions required to account for human action are categorically different from those used in the physical sciences; and, that the ideal of a unity of science envisioned by physicalists, materialists (and other varieties of reductionists)—a unity whereby all psychological concepts and laws needed to account for human

4. John Passmore, *A Hundred Years of Philosophy,* Rev. ed., p. 530.

behavior can be reduced or translated into the language of physical science—is illusory. This "ideal" is based on a misconception of the distinctive nature of human action and the conceptual framework in which we describe and explain human action. The mistake of the reductionists, it is claimed, is not simply to advance a false empirical hypothesis, but to advocate an ideal that is "logically impossible." Among some of the more militant defenders of this "new" orientation, the very possibility of social science has been called into question.

I want to examine these ambitious claims carefully. If they are correct, they challenge one of the most powerful and influential paradigms in philosophy—one which has played a prominent role in the history of modern philosophy and has been articulated with great vigor, clarity, and persuasiveness by most of the philosophers whose work laid the foundations for the analytic movement. We may call this the "reductionist" paradigm. The world, language, meaning, or knowledge (depending on which point of view we select) is conceived of as consisting of a complex of ultimate basic, simple elements. The task of philosophical analysis is to isolate and categorize the basic simples and to show how everything that is legitimate in what appears to be complex and unanalyzed can be reduced to (or translated into) the basic simples. I call this a "paradigm" because I want to isolate its most general and abstract features which have taken ontological, epistemological, and linguistic forms in the history of philosophy.[5]

The argument presented by Passmore challenges one variety of the reductionist paradigm, the belief that "ideally" everything that we can legitimately describe and explain about human behavior or action can, in principle, be described and explained in terms of "motions of the body," or "the purely descriptive language available to physical science." But the point of the passage quoted is to challenge not only *this* variation of reductionism, but any variation of the reductionist paradigm that is applied to the description and explanation of human action. Many of the new teleologists do not

5. The precise meaning of "reduction" and the variations in the types of reduction have proved to be one of the most complex and elusive issues in analytic philosophy. For a helpful survey of the problems involved, especially as it pertains to psychology, see Merle B. Turner, *Philosophy and the Science of Behavior,* Chapters 11, 12.

simply object to the reduction of genuine psychological explanations to physiological explanations, but to any attempt to reduce or translate the language of action, intention, purpose, etc. to a logically more primitive language.[6] Such a reduction, it is maintained, is "logically impossible." Positively, the new teleologists claim that there is something nonreducible and distinctive about the nature of human action and agency such that it requires a conceptual framework which is radically different from, but no less legitimate than, those employed in the physical sciences.

It has been said that analytic philosophers are not concerned with the "big" or primary questions that have preoccupied traditional philosophers. In the tangle of subtle issues concerning the status of human action, we catch a glimpse of what has certainly been a primary issue for philosophy: Just what sort of creature is man? If it is possible, even in principle, to give a fully adequate account of man in terms of concepts and laws available to the physical sciences— ideally to tell the complete story of what man is in the language of physics—then one need not countenance any special types of concepts or new types of laws in order to describe and explain human action. Such a view is a necessary (although not yet a sufficient) condition to support the thesis of the mechanistic materialist that man is *nothing but* a complex physical mechanism, differing in degree of complexity but not in kind from other physical mechanisms. But if the new teleologists can make out their case—in particular, that

6. The expressions, "the new teleologists" and "post-Wittgensteinian philosophers" are used to designate a loosely related group of philosophers who have been deeply influenced by Wittgenstein's *Philosophical Investigations*. Many of these were either educated at or have taught at Oxford. With the spread of analytic philosophy, representatives of this group of philosophers are found throughout the English-speaking world. Not all philosophers influenced by Wittgenstein have been concerned with the concept of action, and among those concerned with the concept of action, not all have been interested in teleology. Nevertheless, the term "new teleologists" is helpful in calling attention to a distinctive orientation that has emerged in analytic philosophy during the past twenty years.

In speaking of the "language of action, intention, purpose, etc.," we intend to call attention to the claim that the conceptual framework or language that involves these concepts forms a distinctive linguistic stratum. One of the major issues for post-Wittgensteinian philosophers has been the clarification of the logical grammar of this language of action and a specification of what concepts essentially belong to this language.

teleological concepts are not reducible to mechanistic concepts and are essential to account for human action—then the thesis that man is nothing but a complex physical mechanism is false, and we can know a priori that it is false.

The above characterization of the battle between the reductionists and the new teleologists is intended to be a first approximation of the issues to be confronted. In the technical discussions which we will be exploring, a basic or primary issue is at stake: what, if anything, is distinctive about man, and especially about human action? Thus far we have relied on our preanalytic or intuitive understanding of the key concepts involved in the debate. We need to sharpen our understanding of these key concepts, and in particular, the concept of reduction. We can do this by taking a close look at the way in which this concept functioned in one of the early classics of the analytic movement, Carnap's *Der Logische Aufbau der Welt*.

Constructionalism and the Aufbau

In the preface to the first edition of the *Aufbau* (1928), Carnap presents what he himself might have called a poetic description of the mood that pervades his early work as well as that of many of the other thinkers of the famous Vienna Circle.

We feel that there is an inner kinship between the attitude on which our philosophical work is founded and the intellectual attitude which presently manifests itself in entirely different walks of life; we feel this orientation in artistic movements, especially in architecture, and in movements which strive for meaningful forms of personal and collective life, of education, and of external organization in general. We feel all around us the same basic orientation, the same style of thinking and doing. It is an orientation which demands clarity everywhere, but which realizes that the fabric of life can never quite be comprehended. It makes us pay careful attention to detail and at the same time recognizes the great lines which run through the whole. It is an orientation which acknowledges the bonds that tie men together, but at the same time strives for free development of the individual. Our work is carried by the faith that this attitude will win the future.[7]

7. Rudolf Carnap, *Der Logische Aufbau der Welt;* translated as *The Logical Structure of the World* by Rolf A. George, p. xviii. All references are to the English translation which has been written in consultation with Carnap.

This passage is revealing for a variety of reasons. It reflects how Carnap, early in his philosophic career, was inspired by an ideal of what philosophy can and ought to be. It shows the fervor and the excitement of the "new" demand for clarity of structure and form, and the optimism about the successes to be achieved when "this attitude will win the future." The allusions to the artistic movements of the day, especially architecture, are striking because they suggest the type of clarity, form, and structure that Carnap was seeking. There is strong similarity between the ideology expressed here and that of the *Bauhaus*. There is the same emphasis on clean lines and reduction to basic forms and elements. Carnap's *Aufbau* is dominated by architectural metaphors.

Specifying the way in which such clarity is to be achieved in philosophy, Carnap tells us that the aim of the book is "to establish a 'constructional system,' that is, an epistemic-logical system of objects or concepts."[8] He begins his first chapter with a quotation from Russell: "The supreme maxim in scientific philosophizing is this: Wherever possible, logical constructions are to be substituted for inferred entities."[9] A constructional system attempts a "step-by-step derivation or 'construction' of all concepts from certain fundamental concepts."[10] To understand what is involved in such a deriva-

---

This passage from the preface to Carnap's *Aufbau* takes on added significance when viewed against the background of Hegel, and especially the Hegelian influence on continental philosophy which was the object of attack and derision by the early logical positivists. Hegel had explicitly attacked in the preface to his *Phenomenology* the ideal of philosophy and philosophic method that Carnap delineates in this passage. From the time of Hegel until the founding of the Vienna Circle, German philosophy was dominated by a deep suspicion of modeling philosophy after the natural sciences or the formal sciences. There were counter tendencies to this trend, most notably in the work of Frege, but only with the Vienna Circle did this counter tendency come to full fruition. One of the common attitudes that united the early positivists was their revulsion against the obscurantism, speculative excesses, and lack of common agreement among continental philosophers whose own lineage could be traced to Hegel. It is as if—and this is the spirit of Carnap's *Aufbau*—one had to start all over again and demand clarity, precision, and rigor, if philosophy was to be "saved" from muddles and confusions that resulted from the pernicious influence of Hegel and his intellectual descendents.

8. *Aufbau*, p. 5.
9. *Aufbau*, p. 5.
10. *Aufbau*, p. 5.

tion or construction, we must specify what is meant by "reduction." Carnap gives the following preliminary characterization of "reduction": "An object (or concept) is said to be *reducible* to one or more other objects if all statements about it can be transformed into statements about these other objects."[11] A constructional system will, therefore, consist of basic elements and relations (or perhaps a single relation) out of which we can construct other more complex concepts. We need more than a list of basic elements and relations; we must also specify the rules by which reductive transformations can be carried out. Carnap is careful to emphasize that the formal requirements of a constructional system do *not* dictate what elements are to be taken as basic. On the contrary, he argues that different types of elements can serve as a basis, and consequently different types of constructional systems can be articulated. Selecting one set of elements as the basic one is a matter of choice dictated more by practical considerations than by theoretical ones. Already in the *Aufbau,* we can detect the seeds of Carnap's ontological and linguistic neutralism which is expressed later in his principle of tolerance and his distinction between internal and external questions.[12]

But what is the purpose of developing constructional systems? It is in this way (and sometimes Carnap writes as if this is the *only* way) that philosophy can become scientific and achieve the type of clarity, rigor, and objectivity that are characteristic of the best scientific explanations. Constructional systems lay bare the structural relations that obtain among different levels of concepts. It is possible, Carnap maintains in the *Aufbau,* to take psychological elements as the basic elements, and it is also possible to take physical elements as basic. Consequently we can say that relative to one constructional system C, physical concepts are reducible to psychological concepts, while relative to C_1, it is possible to reduce all psychological concepts to physical concepts.

It cannot be exaggerated—despite Carnap's claim to be an empiricist—how rationalistic his program really is. The conviction that

11. *Aufbau,* p. 6. Carnap gives a more exact definition of reduction on page 60.

12. See Rudolf Carnap's *The Logical Syntax of Language,* and "Empiricism, Semantics, and Ontology," *Revue Internationale de Philosophie* 11 (1950).

such reductions *must* be possible and can be performed has the status of an a priori commitment. Consider his argument designed to show that "all physical objects are reducible to psychological ones":

Statements about physical objects can be transformed into statements about perceptions (i.e., about psychological objects). For example, the statement that a certain body is red is transformed into a very complicated statement which says roughly that, under certain circumstances, a certain sensation of the visual sense ("red") occurs.

Statements about physcal objects which are not immediately about sensory qualities can be reduced to statements that are. If a physical object were irreducible to sensory qualities and thus to psychological objects, this would mean that there are no perceptible indicators for it. Statements about it would be suspended in the void; in science, at least, there would be no room for it. *Thus, all physical objects are reducible to psychological ones.*[13]

Initially this may seem to be a clear, rigorous argument, but it harbors many difficulties, ambiguities, and suppressed assumptions. The first premise asserts that "Statements about physical objects can be transformed into statements about perceptions." One might think that the way to justify such a claim (if it can be justified) is to examine statements about physical objects to see if such a transformation can actually be carried out. But Carnap does no such thing. It is a problem for him—and a difficult one—to specify in detail what such a construction or reduction would look like, but it doesn't appear to be at all problematic for Carnap to question whether such transformations are possible. This premise is not based on a careful examination of cases, but is stated as if it were an obvious truth. Or consider the move, "If a physical object were irreducible to sensory qualities and thus to psychological objects, this would mean that there were no perceptible indicators for it." Why? Is there any logical or empirical absurdity in maintaining that there are perceptible indicators for physical objects, but that not all statements about physical objects can be transformed into statements about psychological objects? My point here is not to criticize in detail the sort of argument that Carnap has presented; it has been

13. *Aufbau,* p. 92.

severely criticized by many analytic philosophers.[14] Rather, I want
to underscore the a priori commitment to the possibility of reduction
that pervades his book and which dominates logical atomism, logical
positivism, and logical constructionalism. This commitment to
reductionism is crucial for understanding the neglect of the concept
of action in the early days of analytic philosophy. The reductionist
paradigm of explanation which was taken to be *the* ideal of philosophic explanation, so dominated philosophic thinking at this time
that the issue of whether one could perform reductions of such
concepts as action, intention, motive, etc. to more basic simples
(regardless of whether these "simples" were taken to be physical
or psychological) was not a problem for Carnap and other reductionists. The primary issue was to state the formal requirements for
a constructional system and to develop alternative systems. From
the perspective of those who claim that the conceptual framework
of action is nonreducible, Carnap's program begs the central issue,
viz., whether we have any good reasons for thinking that such a
reduction is possible.

We can see this a priori bias functioning even more clearly if we
follow the outlines of the constructional system that Carnap develops
in the *Aufbau*. Having established to his satisfaction that there is a
"mutual reducibility," between psychological and physical concepts,
the question arises of which elements should be taken as basic. According to Carnap, such a decision does not involve any metaphysical
or ontological issues. It is determined by the specific purposes guiding
our construction. Carnap points out "that from the standpoint of
empirical science the constructional system with a physical basis
constitutes a more appropriate arrangement of concepts than any
other."[15] But at this early stage of his development Carnap thinks
that if we want to express the epistemic order of concepts or objects,
a psychological basis or more specifically, an autopsychological
basis is appropriate.

Carnap begins his construction by taking "elementary experi-

14. For a detailed critique of phenomenalism, the philosophic position that
claims that our physical object language can be translated or reduced into the
language of sense data, see Wilfrid Sellars, "Phenomenalism," in *Science,
Perception and Reality*. For a general review of the difficulties with phenomenalism, see J. O. Urmson, *Philosophical Analysis*.

15. *Aufbau*, p. 95.

ences" to be the basic elements. Relative to the system being constructed, these basic elements are unanalyzable. The techniques that Carnap introduces to adumbrate this constructional system are extremely complex, but we can follow the general direction of his inquiry. His route proceeds from introducing the basic relation ("recollection of similarity") and the basic elements ("elementary experiences") through the construction of "physical space," "my body," "the world of perception," and "the world of physics." Finally he discusses the "upper levels": heteropsychological and cultural objects. These include "customs" and "social habits" as well as the "state." It is at this stage in his investigation that Carnap discusses the type of example that has been seized upon by many post-Wittgensteinian philosophers as paradigmatic of what is non-reducible in the language of action. Carnap offers the following example of what such a reduction might look like:

EXAMPLE: The custom of greeting through lifting of one's hat would perhaps have to be constructed in the following form: "The custom of 'greeting through lifting of one's hat' is present in a society (or in some other sociological grouping) at a certain time, if, among the members of the society at that time, there is present a psychological disposition of such a kind that, in situations of such and such a sort, a voluntary act of such and such a sort takes place."[16]

This example of "greeting through lifting of one's hat" is very close to the favorite example of "signaling" cited earlier in the passage from Passmore. A post-Wittgensteinian philosopher might argue that there is no description or explanation of the motions involved in such a gesture that would be adequate to account for this practice of greeting. In order for a series of motions to be a "greeting," there must be "a rule in our society to the effect" that lifting a hat *means* "I am greeting you," and this sort of rule cannot be reduced or translated into concepts that do not presuppose the concept of a rule. The reductive move via the "world of physics" that Carnap's constructional system requires cannot be carried out. The critic might also subject to careful scrutiny the notion of a "psychological disposition." Certainly this sounds like a scientific concept and we do use dispositional concepts in describing and explaining physical phenomena. But a great deal is packed into the

16. *Aufbau*, p. 231.

use of "psychological disposition" in this example. The custom of greeting—in normal circumstances—not only presupposes that there is someone to be greeted, but that the person performing the act knows or believes that there is someone to be greeted and intends to extend a greeting. Moreover, a particular act of greeting by lifting one's hat presupposes the institution or practice in order to be a greeting. A person might conceivably have a disposition to lift his hat in a society in which this is not a way of greeting someone; then the event of lifting one's hat would not be an act of greeting. Finally, Carnap's example uses the concept of a "voluntary act," without giving us a clue as to how this concept can be reduced (ultimately) to "elementary experiences." The upshot of these criticisms is that Carnap has presented us with a sham reduction: he has evaded the crucial issues. A close examination reveals the speciousness of his attempt to reduce the cultural practice of greeting by lifting one's hat to "elementary experiences."

We are not yet in a position to evaluate the claims and counter-claims in this debate. But we can see even more clearly why the nature of action, or to put the matter linguistically, the status of the linguistic framework in which we describe and explain human actions, was so peripheral to Carnap's program. He did not see any important or interesting philosophic problem here. Why? Because he never seriously doubted that the concept of human action and its related concepts would ideally become part of a constructional system whereby all statements concerning action could be transformed into statements about more basic elements. Why wasn't the possibility of such a reduction seriously questioned? What was the justification for the supreme confidence that such a reduction could, in principle, be performed? It certainly was not a conclusion based on careful description and investigation of the relevant concepts. It was rather an a priori regulative principle that such reductions *must* be possible if the concepts are legitimate.

The demand that such reductions must be possible was closely linked with Carnap's view of what constitutes knowledge, and especially science as "the system of conceptual knowledge":

The aim of science consists in finding and ordering the true statements about the objects of cognition. . . .

In order to be able to approach this aim, that is, in order to be able to make statements about objects at all, we must be able to construct these objects (for, otherwise, their names have no meaning). *Thus, the formation of the constructional system is the first aim of science.* It is the first aim, not in a temporal, but in a logical, sense.[17]

While the insistence on construction and reduction did function as an a priori commitment, it would be misleading to think that this ideal was completely arbitrary. To Carnap, and others affected by the reductionist spirit, the major breakthroughs in scientific knowledge, whether in the empirical or formal disciplines, appeared to have resulted from the discovery of how concepts, relations, and laws could be reduced to some more basic conceptual framework. Reduction embodied the very ideal of scientific clarity, rigor, precision, and explanation. Even if we accepted this view of the success of reductionist paradigms in scientific inquiry, it is a significant extrapolation to demand that every legitimate concept must have a definite place in a (nontrivial) constructional system. For Carnap this becomes the very criterion of its legitimacy. As we shall soon see, the growth of philosophic interest in the concept of action goes hand-in-hand with the metaphilosophical questioning of the nature, status, and legitimacy of the demand for reduction.

The Spirit of Reductionism

Thus far, we have focused on Carnap's *Aufbau* in our attempt to show the commitment to the reductionist paradigm that influenced the early stages of analytic philosophy. Historically, it would be inaccurate to suggest that the *Aufbau* was *the* major foundational work of the analytic movement, or that Carnap's early work affected the tone, goals, and approach of all analytic philosophy. Carnap's work is representative. It is almost an "ideal type" of the spirit that pervaded much of the work of analytic philosophy during the 1920's and 1930's. We might have focused on Russell's "Philosophy of Logical Atomism," Wittgenstein's *Tractatus,* or Ayer's polemical *Language, Truth and Logic* to make the same general point. We know today that these several works reveal striking differences of emphasis, content, method, and doctrine. But there is a similar spirit that pervades all of them. In their concern with

17. *Aufbau,* p. 288.

the foundations of knowledge, or with the perspicuous representation of the logical grammar of meaningful sentences and propositions, there never was any serious confrontation with the tangle of issues in understanding, describing, and explaining human action. In these philosophers too, as in the case of Carnap, there is an a priori conviction that there is nothing meaningful or important about human action that can not (in principle) be reduced or translated into a more elementary and basic language. What cannot be so reduced is illegitimate, nonsensical, or ineffable.

Wittgenstein tells us in the *Tractatus* that "The world is the totality of facts, not of things" (1.1) and further that "The world is independent of my will" (6.373), so that "even if all that we wish for were to happen, still this would only be a favor granted by fate, so to speak: for there is no *logical* connection between the will and the world, which would guarantee it, and the supposed physical connection itself is surely not something that we could will" (6.374).[18] Furthermore, Wittgenstein claims that belief in a causal nexus is a superstition. Something very strange seems to have happened to the concept of human action (insofar as we think of it as a manifestation of the human will). It has no place *in* the world. This is not an inadvertent awkward consequence that follows from what Wittgenstein says. It is precisely the doctrine that he self-consciously affirms. We see this in the tantalizing proposition 6.43.

> If good and bad acts of will do alter the world, it can only be the limits of the world that they alter, not the facts, not what can be expressed in language.
> In short their effect must be that it becomes an altogether different world. It must so to speak, wax and wane as a whole. . . .

There does not seem to be any place in the world for acts of will or human action. Or more accurately, the only status that human action can have *in the world* is to be part of the totality of independent atomic facts that make up the world. If we think that the concept of human action requires the minimal idea of an agent who is causally efficacious, there is no such agent in the world; the belief in any type of causal nexus is a superstition. The only way in which acts of will can alter the world is by altering the *limits* of the world, not

18. Ludwig Wittgenstein, *Tractatus Logico-Philosophicus,* translated by D. F. Pears and B. F. McGuinness. All references are to this translation.

what is in the world (the facts). The more rigorously one follows out this line of thought, the clearer it becomes that acts of will "belong" to what Wittgenstein calls the "transcendent"—about which we cannot speak and which we must consign to silence. From a Tractarian point of view, anything concerning human action that is not reducible to independent propositions that picture states of affairs is ineffable.

We discover still another variety of the reductionist spirit in the popular and fashionable logical positivism of Ayer. As adumbrated in *Language, Truth, and Logic,* there are only two types of legitimate sentences or propositions—analytic and synthetic propositions. An analytic proposition is linguistic in character and devoid of factual content; "a proposition is analytic when its validity depends solely on the definitions of the symbols it contains."[19] Synthetic propositions are empirical and their meaning is determined by the verifiability criterion of meaning. What then are we to say about descriptions and explanations of human actions, intentions, purposes, etc.? Insofar as we are not just defining terms, or uttering nonsense, we are asserting empirical propositions which, in principle, are verifiable. There is no epistemological or linguistic difference between statements concerning agents or actions and any other common sense or scientific statements. There is no knowledge of man that is not empirical knowledge and all empirical knowledge can be scientific knowledge consisting of verifiable synthetic propositions. Any knowledge of man's psychological characteristics including his activities is properly the subject matter of empirical psychology. To think that there is some special feature or aspect of human activity that we can know about in some manner which is not part of empirical psychology or reducible to empirical psychology is a mistake. Again, this is a conclusion affirmed on the basis of an a priori commitment to what *must* be the character of any statement that is cognitively significant, and *not* on the basis of a careful examination of the concepts pertaining to human action.

Lest one think that it is only in the philosophers that one finds the reductionist spirit dominant, it is helpful to take a look at the ideology of some of the "classical" behavioral psychologists. We find the same ideal of what is to be a proper scientific explanation, one which is to guide the development of behaviorism. The lines of

19. A. J. Ayer, *Language, Truth and Logic,* p. 78.

influence are complex, for some of the spokesmen for behaviorism were influenced by positivist doctrines, and the work of the behaviorists provided additional support for the positivist program of reduction. One of the boldest and most articulate champions of the virtues of behaviorism was Clark Hull. In a passage that has been singled out for criticism by several post-Wittgensteinian philosophers, he tells us:

An ideally adequate theory of even so-called purposive behavior ought, therefore, to begin with colorless movement and mere receptor impulses as such, and from these build up step by step both adaptive and maladaptive behavior. The present approach does not deny the molar reality of purposive acts (as opposed to movement), of intelligence, of insight, of goals, or intents, or strivings, or of value; on the contrary, we insist upon the genuineness of these forms of behavior. We hope ultimately to show the logical right to the use of such concepts by deducing them as secondary principles from more elementary objective primary principles. Once they have been derived we shall not only understand them better but be able to use them with more detailed effectiveness, particularly in the deduction of the movements which mediate (or fail to mediate) goal attainment, then would be the case if we accepted teleological sequences at the outset as gross, unanalyzed (and unanalyzable) wholes.[20]

Hull sketches for us what an ideal science of human behavior would look like. In Carnap's terminology, the *basic elements* would be objective "colorless movement and mere receptor impulses." Such a science would provide us with basic principles (postulates) from which we could derive complex theorems. Ideally the theorems would be well confirmed by experimental evidence and we could make novel predictions based on this system. Furthermore, the primary principles would be mechanistic, for Hull considers an organism to be a "self-maintaining mechanism." By "mechanism," he means *"a physical aggregate whose behavior occurs under ascertainable conditions according to definitely statable rules or laws."*[21] The greatest obstacle that Hull sees to the attainment of full behavioral objectivity is the "unfortunate" tendency to "anthropomorphic subjectivism," where there is an inadvertent substitution of ourselves in place of a legitimate theoretical construct, and where we naively

20. Clark L. Hull, *Principles of Behavior*, pp. 25-26.
21. *Principles of Behavior*, p. 384.

project our knowledge onto a situation that calls for rules of functional relationships. The prophylaxis that he recommends for this temptation is to think of a behaving organism as a "completely self-maintaining robot."[22] He concludes his *Principles of Behavior* on a note of great optimism that echoes Carnap's own prophecy in the Preface to the *Aufbau*.

. . . there is reason to hope that the next hundred years will see an unprecedented development in this field. One reason for optimism in this respect lies in the increasing tendency, at least among Americans, to regard the "social" or behavioral sciences as genuine natural sciences rather than *Geisteswissenschaft*. Closely allied to this tendency is the growing practice of excluding the logical, folk, and anthropomorphic considerations from the list of the presumptive primary behavioral explanatory factors. Wholly congruent with these tendencies is the expanding recognition of the desirability in the behavioral sciences of explicit and exact systematic formulation, with empirical verification at every possible point. If these three tendencies continue to increase, as seems likely, there is good reason to hope that the behavioral sciences will presently display a development comparable to that manifested by the physical sciences in the age of Copernicus, Kepler, Galileo, and Newton.[23]

The problem of whether it is really possible to deduce purposive acts, intelligence, insight, etc. from "elementary objective primary principles" is not an issue that Hull seriously confronts. Like other reductionists, it is Hull's conviction that such reductions or deductions *must* be possible. And like Carnap, this is *the way* to legitimize, "to show the logical right," of the gross molar concepts of purposive acts. This is the only way in which we can understand, explain, and show the credibility of these concepts. The possibility that there might be levels of nonreducible conceptual frameworks, or that perhaps it is not logically or empirically possible to perform such reductions, or that there can be legitimate nonscientific knowledge of purposive acts, is not even seriously considered. The alternatives for him are between what he takes to be the canons of tough-minded scientific objectivity or the unfortunate tendency to "anthropomorphic subjectivism."

We can appreciate how sharp the conflict is between this be-

22. *Principles of Behavior,* p. 27.
23. *Principles of Behavior,* p. 400.

havioral expression of the ideal of reduction and that of the new teleologists when we realize that what Hull takes to be "an ideally adequate theory" is precisely what his opponents consider to be a "logical impossibility." (Compare Hull's statements with the passage cited earlier from Passmore.) What is particularly relevant for our inquiry is the tendency of both sides to attempt to resolve the issue by a priori fiat: the reductionists arguing that it *must* be possible to perform such reductions, the teleologists arguing that it is logically or conceptually impossible to perform these reductions. For neither position (at least in its extreme formulations) does the issue of reducibility or nonreducibility appear to be the type of empirical issue that might be resolved by further empirical inquiry. We are already anticipating the central issue which we will have to encounter: What are the ground rules for deciding between reductionists and antireductionists?

A Metaphilosophical Interlude

Thus far I have spoken as if analytic philosophy were a relatively well-defined philosophic movement. It is roughly true that there is a consensus about the philosophers, problems, and procedures that are characteristic of analytic philosophy. However, any attempt to state precise criteria or common underlying presuppositions of this movement is likely to lead to gross oversimplification. Analytic philosophers themselves are distrustful of such attempts and skeptical of their value. There has, of course, been a dominant concern with language and a commitment to the belief that the investigation of linguistic issues is the best way of clarifying, resolving, and dissolving philosophic perplexities. No account of analytic philosophy can neglect the "linguistic turn" in twentieth-century philosophy. But even such a minimal claim is open to ambiguity and dispute. What is meant by "language," "clarification," "analysis," and the very aims of analytic philosophy are subject to wide and conflicting interpretations.[24]

Much more important for our purposes than giving a general

24. For an excellent discussion of these issues, see Richard Rorty's introduction to his book, *The Linguistic Turn*.

characterization of analytic philosophy is to realize that within this movement there have been basic differences which are as extreme as any found in the history of philosophy. The growth of interest in philosophical psychology and the philosophy of mind, where the investigation of the concept of action has been central, is intimately tied up with a revolution that has taken place within the analytic movement. Like other revolutions, the steps leading up to it were gradual and piecemeal, but after the revolution nothing has been quite the same. The nature of a philosophic problem, the subject matter and methods employed for investigating issues and settling controversies, even what is considered to be a good philosophic argument, have altered.

An indication of the radical nature of the change has already been suggested. The very ideal of reductive analysis has recently been challenged as not only a false ideal, but one that is logically or conceptually impossible. If we are to understand how such a reversal has taken place in such a comparatively short span of time, we need to appreciate just what sort of revolution has occurred.

We know that in some areas of scientific research there are times when a specific area of research is in the foreground while others lie fallow. The reasons and causes for this are complex and can involve scientific as well as nonscientific factors. While techniques, hypotheses, and theories are developed that provide breakthroughs—such as the recent breakthrough in molecular biology—scientists can and do recognize other legitimate problems and areas of research which need investigation. In biology there are also well recognized problems concerning evolutionary theory and ecology. These areas can become "alive" when techniques and hypotheses are developed for novel types of experimentation and observation.

It would be misleading, however, to think of the case of the concept of action according to this analogy. A more appropriate analogy is the sort of scientific revolution that Kuhn explores, where there is a revolutionary change in the very paradigm of description and explanation.[25] New ways of observing, describing, and explaining arise. What was not even considered problematic according to the old paradigm now comes into the focus of investigation. This is the sort of revolution that has taken place within analytic philosophy

25. Thomas Kuhn, *The Structure of Scientific Revolutions*.

(although we shall see that what is "revolutionary" has a strong affinity with what is traditional).

The revolution that I have been speaking about has been identified with the rise of "ordinary language philosophy," but for reasons which will become clear, I consider this label is a misnomer which has generated a great deal of confusion. As a heuristic device for understanding this revolution, let us sketch the ideal of systematic knowledge that has been proposed by the mechanistic materialist. As scientific inquiry advances, he tells us, we are becoming clearer and clearer about the basic microphysical elements and processes that make up the world and the functional regularities exhibited by these basic elements and processes. Furthermore, scientific inquiry is leading to a unity of science resulting from the convergence of the independent investigations of physicists, chemists, biologists, psychologists, etc. There is an overall direction in this inquiry, for although there is a proliferation of subsciences and we are becoming increasingly aware of the complexity of the universe, the general outline of a scientific image of man and the universe is emerging whereby all manifest phenomena can be explained in terms of more basic elements and laws, and ultimately in terms of physical elements and laws. When this view is applied to the study of man, the mechanistic materialist tells us that man is *nothing but* a complex physical mechanism.

But if we compare this "scientific image of man" with the "manifest image of man"—the way in which we ordinarily think of ourselves in the universe, something seems to be out of joint.[26] We certainly appear to ourselves as beings who have intentions and motives, who sometimes act for reasons and achieve goals, whose life is regulated by standards, norms, and ideals. For a large part of our lives, we offer and consider as perfectly satisfactory explanations in terms of our purposes and goals. Why are you running across the campus? Because I want to get to my class on time. Why are you studying chemistry? Because I want to satisfy the requirements for getting into medical school. There does not seem to be anything controversial or startling in this; we certainly talk and act in this

26. The terms "scientific image of man" and "manifest image of man" are taken from Wilfrid Sellars. For his discussion and resolution of the clash of these two images, see "Philosophy and the Scientific Image of Man" in *Science, Perception and Reality*.

manner. The most committed reductionist doesn't want to deny these manifest facts. The interesting problems and tensions arise when we try to interpret such facts and to assess their significance. Some of the more extreme reductionists have talked as if our ordinary ways of talking and thinking about such matters are confused, vague, and objectionable. We would presumably have a much more perspicuous and accurate representation of what we are saying if we could reform and reconstruct such talk into an "ideal" language —one where the systematic interrelations of our molar concepts were clearly structured. Others, like Hull, acknowledge the "molar reality of purposive acts," but claim that "legitimate" talk about such acts must be justified. The correct way of doing this is to "show the logical right of the use of such [teleological] concepts by deducing them as secondary principles from more elementary objective primary principles."

The felt tension between the claims of the "scientific image" and that of the "manifest image" has led a number of philosophers to question the nature and appropriateness of reductive analysis. Ambitious claims had been made about the possibility of reduction and what could be done *in principle*. But when it came down to showing, *in fact,* how concepts of the manifest image could be reduced or translated, the achievements have been extremely disappointing. Furthermore, all sorts of difficulties became evident in the very attempt to carry out reductions.[27] Philosophers even questioned what was to be gained by reductive analysis. It would be very difficult to find a philosophic consensus today about the success of any reduction, translation, or construction other than those restricted to the formal and scientific disciplines.

Philosophers began to question what appeared to be "an absolute presupposition" of an earlier stage of analytic philosophy, viz., that reductive analysis was *the* method to achieve clarity. To declare oneself against this paradigm was to declare oneself to be allied with the forces of darkness, vagueness, and obscurantism. But the critics of reductive analysis argued that the unlimited use of this paradigm was itself responsible for philosophic confusion, technical obscurity, and irrelevance. They accused the early reductionists of foisting upon us an a priori model of what must be the structure of language,

27. For a survey of the difficulties with reductive analysis, see J. O. Urmson, *Philosophical Analysis.*

meaning and knowledge, instead of looking and seeing what is actually the case. They charged that reductionists, with all their pretentions to being empirical, were in truth manqué rationalists imposing a priori categories on a recalcitrant, tangled empirical reality.

The most important figure in this revolution is Wittgenstein. As we follow his development from his Tractarian period through his lectures in the 1930's to his *Philosophical Investigations,* we can witness the revolution in the making. Much more important than anything that Wittgenstein *said* is what he *showed.* More effectively than any other contemporary philosopher, he helped exorcise the deep philosophic bias characteristic of so much early analytic philosophy, including his own *Tractatus*—that language, meaning, knowledge must conform to a reductionist model if it is to be legitimized.

Consider the following passage from his *Philosophical Investigations:*

F. P. Ramsey once emphasized in conversation with me that logic was a 'normative science.' I do not know exactly what he had in mind, but it was doubtless closely related to what only dawned on me later: namely, that in philosophy we often *compare* the use of words with games and calculi which have fixed rules, but cannot say that someone who is using language *must* be playing such a game. But if you say that our languages only *approximate* to such calculi you are standing on the very brink of misunderstanding. For then it may look as if what we were talking about were an *ideal* language. As if our logic were, so to speak, a logic for a vacuum.—Whereas logic does not treat of language—or of thought— in the sense in which a natural science treats of a natural phenomenon, and the most that can be said is that we *construct* ideal languages. But here the word "ideal" is liable to mislead, for it sounds as if these languages were better, more perfect, than our everyday language; and as if it took the logician to show people at last what a correct sentence looked like.

All this, however can only appear in the right light when one has attained greater clarity about the concepts of understanding, meaning, and thinking. For it will then also become clear what can lead us (and did lead me) to think that if anyone utters a sentence and *means* or *understands* it he is operating in a calculus according to definite rules.[28]

Although Wittgenstein's remarks are about the use of words, lan-

28. Ludwig Wittgenstein, *Philosophical Investigations,* p. 38e.

guage, logic and calculi, they have important consequences for the range of issues that we have been considering. The early logical positivists and logical atomists were on the "very brink of misunderstanding." Implicit in Carnap's program of constructionalism, Russell's logical atomism, and even Hull's ideal of a behavioral science is a model similar to the one that Wittgenstein is exposing. The primary question is not the value of "ideal" systems or languages, but the precise *role* that such an ideal plays. According to many of the early analytic philosophers, the ideal language to be constructed would be a "better," "more perfect" language than the one we now use. And there was a belief that our ordinary ways of talking and thinking only "approximate such calculi." The issue is not one of clarity and determinateness versus obscurity and vagueness, or analysis versus some more questionable method, but rather what is the best way to achieve clarity and what are the appropriate analytic techniques.

If one is skeptical of the reductionist urge of philosophers who favor the development of artificial languages and constructional systems, what is the alternative to be adopted? There is less unanimity about the proper alternative than there has been about what is wrong with the varieties of reductive analysis. Analytic philosophers since the World War II have been exploring a variety of techniques and approaches, but we can use P. F. Strawson's sketch of an alternative to reductive analysis as a starting point for examining the new philosophic mood.

After all, we are seeking to gain an understanding of the concepts and categories in terms of which we carry on our thinking; not only, or primarily, our advanced and technical thinking, but our common, daily thinking. For it is the most general, most fundamental, most ordinary ideas which give rise to the major problems of philosophy. Is it, after all, so reasonable to think that our ordinary use of language blurs and distorts these ordinary ideas? For common speech is subjected to the severest of all tests for efficiency, as a medium for the expression and communication of our thoughts—the test of constant use. If we want to understand the habits and way of life of an animal, we must carefully observe his behavior in natural surroundings; it is no good turning our backs on his actual behavior, constructing a clockwork model from an engineer's designs and then studying that. So with our concepts. If we want to know how they work, we must watch them at work. As for the failure of the original program of analysis, as applied to the sentences in common speech, the fault there lay not in common speech, but in a too rigid and too narrow conception of analysis. Why would it be supposed that the only way to gain understanding of the words which express the philosophically puzzling concepts was to translate sentences in which they occurred into sentences in which they did not occur? The belief in the exclusive efficacy of this method is just the troublesome legacy of discredited theories. It is too rigid a conception of analysis, because it supposes the existence of exact quasi-definitional relations between classes of concepts, which do not in fact obtain. It is too narrow, because it neglects altogether very many quite different features of the functioning of language, which it is of the first importance accurately to note and describe, if our philosophical problems are to be resolved. . . . So, for the old, limited and theory-ridden program of analysis, we are to substitute a different aim: that of coming to understand philosophically puzzling concepts by carefully and accurately noting the ways in which the related linguistic expressions are actually used in discourse. Of course, not all features of the use of these expressions will be relevant to the philosopher's task. It is his special skill to discern *which* are relevant, and *how* they are relevant.[29]

Strawson's eloquent statement might serve as a manifesto for what rapidly became the dominant attitude of a new generation of analytic philosophers. The chief representatives of this new approach were centered in Oxford, but their influence has spread throughout the English-speaking world. But why, we may ask, should there be a special interest in ordinary language? Think for a moment of the ways in which such an apology might have inhibited the development of the technical, artificial languages so fundamental for the advancement of scientific understanding. Or the ways in which such a defense can be abused to sanction the superstitions and prejudices that have crept into our ordinary ways of speaking and thinking throughout history. If ordinary language is our concern, why not turn to the science of linguistics for illumination rather than to armchair philosophic reflection? All of these questions have been asked of the champions of ordinary language analysis, and one of the keenest issues in analytic philosophy today centers about the

29. P. F. Strawson, "Construction and Analysis" in *The Revolution in Philosophy* by A. J. Ayer, W. C. Kneale, G. A. Paul, D. F. Pears, P. F. Strawson, G. J. Warnock, R. A. Wollheim, with an introduction by Gilbert Ryle, pp. 103-104.

controversy between those who favor rational reconstruction of our concepts and those who favor "carefully and accurately noting" the complex relations of "our ordinary use of language."[30]

Strawson's statement of an alternative to reductive analysis indicates the more fundamental issue at stake here and suggests how he would answer the above polemical questions. He tells us that "we are seeking to gain an understanding of the concepts and categories in terms of which we carry on our thinking." Like his philosophic opponents whose views have also been shaped by the "linguistic turn," Strawson shares the belief that the proper way of getting clear about our thinking is to get clear about the ways in which we speak— the language which expresses our thoughts. This is one reason why he and others sympathetic to his approach favor the label "conceptual analysis," rather than "ordinary language analysis." When conceptual analysis is directed to identifying, classifying, and describing the most general features of our conceptual structure, then we are engaged in "descriptive metaphysics": the description of the most basic concepts used in thinking about the world. The possibility of such a descriptive metaphysics does presuppose that "there is a massive central core of human thinking which has no history—or none recorded in the histories of thought; there are categories and concepts which, in their most fundamental character, change not at all. . . . They are commonplaces of the least refined thinking; and are yet the indispensable core of the conceptual equipment of the most sophisticated human beings. It is with these, their interconnections, and the structure that they form, that a descriptive metaphysics will be primarily concerned."[31]

We can detect how the "revolution" which we have been describing in analytic philosophy connects up with traditional philosophy. The concern with the basic concepts and categories used in thinking about ourselves and the universe is as old as philosophy itself. There are basic similarities between this "new" program and that of such philosophers as Aristotle and Kant. It is no accident that while an earlier generation of analytic philosophers drew inspiration

30. See Rorty's discussion of the issues involved in this debate in his introduction to *The Linguistic Turn*.

31. P. F. Strawson, *Individuals. An Essay in Descriptive Metaphysics*, p. 10.

from Hume, especially those aspects that were interpreted as supporting a program of reductive analysis, the newer generation of analytic philosophers have "rediscovered" Aristotle and Kant.

Although our metaphilosophical interlude may appear to be a digression, it has direct relevance to the investigation of action. It is in the exploration of the concepts pertaining to action that many practitioners of conceptual analysis claim to have located concepts that are "of the most fundamental character," and belong to the "indispensible core of conceptual equipment of the most sophisticated human beings." These concepts, so it is claimed, defy reductive analysis. Consequently, since the concept of action is a fundamental one, and since it cannot be reduced or translated into a language that is exclusively mechanistic, it turns out to be a conceptual truth—and one of the most important results of conceptual analysis—that it is false to think of man as nothing but a "complex physical mechanism." The new interest in action is itself part of the changing philosophic orientation that we have been exploring. But the investigation of the concept of action arose only when the blinders imposed by the demands of reductive analysis were removed. It is not, as we have emphasized, that philosophers suddenly noticed an important cluster of problems that had been neglected by earlier analytic philosophers. With the growing skepticism concerning the methods and aims of reductive analysis and the development of alternative procedures for describing and analyzing the conceptual framework that we employ in our daily lives, a new way of treating and investigating issues arose. A problem which did not exist for the first generation of analytic philosophers now became the major philosophic problem to be confronted.

Before examining what post-Wittgensteinian philosophers have been attempting to tell us about the concept of action, there is one further metaphilosophical issue that must be kept in mind. It has extremely important consequences in understanding and assessing these investigations. After we have explored the discussion of the concept of action, we will return to an examination of this issue. It is one of the most important and basic issues confronting analytic philosophy today.

Suppose we grant with Strawson that there is a massive core to the conceptual structure of human beings that has no history, and that it is possible by a sensitive analysis to exhibit the main characteristics of this core. Suppose too that we discover that the category of persons as agents or human actors is indeed a basic category of our ways of thinking about ourselves. And let us also suppose that we can show that there is a conceptual structure involving such concepts as action, intention, and purpose that logically or conceptually cannot be reduced, translated, or even partially interpreted into a more basic nonteleological framework. What would we have succeeded in showing? There are those who think that if we can show all this, and show that such conclusions follow from conceptual analysis rather than from empirical considerations, then we have the strongest possible grounds for claiming that the ideal of a complete, adequate description of man in mechanistic terms is a false ideal—that indeed we have hit rock bottom in the description of man. If we think of metaphysics as a discipline that elucidates the most general and basic concepts that we use in understanding ourselves and the world, then we have a proper metaphysical understanding of man which may be *supplemented* by scientific inquiry, but can never be challenged by it—precisely because scientific inquiry, like all inquiry, presupposes what our conceptual analysis has revealed. If there is an apparent clash between what our conceptual analysis reveals and what presumably is the result of the "scientific image of man," then we have gone wrong someplace in understanding what a scientific analysis reveals. It is logically or conceptually impossible for there to be a fundamental incompatibility here; it is self-contradictory to hold that scientific thinking at once presupposes the truth of what our descriptive metaphysics says and shows the falsity of this descriptive metaphysics.

Now as strong as this argument for the necessary truth of the results of conceptual analysis may appear, it is *not* sound and has been seriously questioned by a number of philosophers. It may be that everything that the conceptual analyst wants to maintain about the distinctive and nonreducible nature of the language of action is true for the way in which man normally conceives of himself. Yet nevertheless, it is theoretically possible to question the entire "manifest" framework, to argue *not* that such a conceptual framework can be *reduced,* but that it can be *replaced.* We may have good reasons for saying that even though the conceptual framework or language of action is nonreducible, it can be replaced by a better scientific

(and even mechanistic) framework. The articulation and justification of this view strikes at the very heart of the program of conceptual analysis. It challenges the logical right of claiming that
any conceptual analysis, no matter how sensitive, sophisticated, and
convincing, is sufficient to draw metaphysical conclusions about
what man really is.[32]

The New Teleology
and Its Dualistic Consequences

I have already referred to the work of Wittgenstein and Strawson
in fostering the revolution that has taken place in analytic philosophy. Ryle, Hampshire, and Austin, all of whom lectured at Oxford,
also played key roles in carrying out the critique of reductive analysis
and developed new approaches to conceptual and linguistic analysis.[33] A consequence of the liberation from the narrow restrictions
of early analytic philosophy has been the emergence of new areas of
study including most prominently philosophy of mind, or philosophical psychology. In the 1930's when the ideology of logical positivism
was still dominant, there simply was no place for philosophical
psychology. All the legitimate issues concerning "mind" or psychology (which were not definitional) were thought of as empirical
issues and belonged properly to the empirical science of psychology.
But by the end of the 1940's the outlines of philosophical psychology
began to take shape. From that time until today there has been
virtually a deluge of contributions to this area. A series of short
monographs edited by R. F. Holland entitled *Studies in Philosophical Psychology* signaled the new directions to be explored in the
philosophy of mind. Many of these monographs focused on the
new approach to the concept of action.[34] Using some of the works

32. See my discussion of the "displacement hypothesis," pp. 281 ff.
33. See Gilbert Ryle, *The Concept of Mind;* Stuart Hampshire, *Thought
and Action;* J. L. Austin, *Philosophical Papers,* ed. by J. O. Urmson and
G. J. Warnock.
34. This series has been published by Routledge and Kegan Paul. It includes
monographs by P. T. Geach, D. W. Hamlyn, Alaisdair MacIntyre, R. S.
Peters, Peter Winch, Norman Malcolm, A. I. Meldon, David Armstrong,
Peter Alexander, Anthony Kenny, and Jonathan Bennett. In addition to the

in this series as a source (and supplementing them with other important studies of action) I want to sketch the outlines of the theory of action that has developed. As we follow the dialectic of analytic philosophy, we will see that many of the a priori "conceptual truths" announced in these works have been severely criticized. The criticism has taken two interrelated forms. Every major dichotomy and distinction that was boldly set forth has been challenged. What we might call the "first generation" of philosophical psychologists saw clear and distinct major conceptual dichotomies where a more skeptical and cautious "second generation" has seen only differences of degree. But we will also discover as we indicated in the conclusion of our preceding section, a critique of the program of conceptual analysis and a fortiori, a critique of some of the major claims made about the nature of human action.

In *The Concept of Motivation,* R. S. Peters argues for two characteristic theses concerning the concept of action. There is a negative or critical thesis in which he attacks "the tradition stemming from Hobbes that there can be an all-inclusive theory of human behavior from whose basic postulates answers to all forms of questions, 'Why does Jones do X?' will eventually be deduced."[35] In order to justify his thesis, Peters wants to show that there are different ways in which the question, "Why does Jones do X?" can be asked and that the sorts of answers that can be given to this question are "logically different and sometimes logically exclusive."[36] If he can substantiate this latter claim and show us the legitimacy of logically exclusive types of answers, then there certainly would be a strong presumptive basis for claiming that there can't be a unified all-inclusive theory in which we can answer all forms of the question, "Why does Jones do X?"

Suppose the action we are investigating is Jones crossing the

---

monographs published in the series, *Studies in Philosophical Psychology,* three recent anthologies of articles are helpful for gaining an overview of the variety of issues and approaches involved in the theory of action: *Readings in the Theory of Action,* ed. by Norman S. Care and Charles Landesman; *Human Action,* ed. by Theodore Mischel; and *The Human Agent, Royal Institute of Philosophy Lectures,* Vol. 1 (1966/7). See also the special double issue of *Inquiry* 13 (Summer 1970) dedicated to articles on "Action."

35. R. S. Peters, *The Concept of Motivation,* p. 148.

36. *Concept of Motivation,* p. 148.

street and we want to know why he does this. In normal circumstances, we would be asking "what was his *reason* for doing that or
what was the *point* of it, what *end* he had in mind?"[37] If we ask Jones
why he crossed the street, it would be perfectly appropriate for him
to say "To buy some tobacco," or because "I wanted some tobacco."
And although there may be special circumstances in which we might
be dubious about this particular explanation, we normally consider
it to be a complete and adequate explanation of why Jones crossed
the street. In response to our question there is nothing further to be
said. The fact that we offer and accept this sort of explanation is so
obvious and noncontroversial, one may wonder what philosophic
interest it can generate. We do *explain* many instances of human
action by noting the reason, point, end, or goal that the agent had
in mind, or in *redescribing* the action: he was going to buy some
tobacco. But it is also clear that even in such simple situations we
are making many complex assumptions which need not normally be
called into question. For example, we are assuming that walking
across the street is an efficient way of getting to the tobacco shop
and that Jones knows or believes this. We are also assuming that
there is an intimate connection between Jones' desire or intention to
get tobacco and his walking across the street. The latter activity
doesn't just contingently happen after one forms an intention, although there can be circumstances where he intends to buy some
tobacco and something happens to prevent him from doing so.

Furthermore, even such a simple action as buying some tobacco
presupposes the complex social institution or practice of buying
and selling. There are no social institutions that characterize such a
basic act as raising one's arm, but it would make no sense to speak
of buying something unless the social institution of buying and selling existed. There are also actions which may not be done in order
to achieve a goal or end, but nevertheless conform to social standards and conventions. Dancing, for example, might not be done for
any end, but it is an activity that requires knowledge of the rules
and conventions that characterize the particular dance (knowing
how to dance). There are also some actions where "norms enter
into and often entirely define the end"[38] such as passing an examination or getting married. One couldn't get married or pass an examina-

37. *Concept of Motivation*, p. 4.
38. *Concept of Motivation*, p. 5.

tion unless there were conventions, rules, and norms defining these practices and laying down criteria (no matter how vague) for what is to count as a performance of this activity. The pattern into which we fit our commonsense explanations of such actions is labeled by Peters, "the rule-following" purposive model.[39] He stresses the importance of this pattern for two reasons. First he wants to point out that "most of our explanations are couched in terms of this model and our predictions of people's behavior presupposes it."[40] It is Peters' second reason for emphasizing this model that introduces a controversial thesis and provides the cutting edge for what he wants to claim about the concept of action. The rule-following purposive model is the basis for understanding human action, and this model shows "that human actions cannot be sufficiently explained in terms of causal concepts like 'colorless movements.' "[41] This is a direct challenge to the program of a science of behavior envisioned by Hull whom I have quoted as claiming: "An ideally adequate theory even of so-called purposive behavior ought . . . to begin with colorless movement and mere receptor impulses as such, and from these build up step by step both adaptive behavior and maladaptive behavior."[42]

It isn't quite clear from the passage we have quoted whether Peters is ruling out the possibility of causal explanations of human actions or only those causal explanations in terms of "colorless movements." But he clears up this ambiguity when he makes the stronger claim "If we are in fact confronted with a case of a genuine action (i.e., an act of doing something as opposed to suffering something), then causal explanations are *ipso facto* inappropriate as sufficient explanations."[43] This latter claim is not offered as an empirical hypothesis which is subject to confirmation, but as a logical or conceptual truth: "There cannot therefore be a sufficient explanation of actions in causal terms because . . . there is a logical gap between nature and convention."[44]

But how are we to account for the dramatic reversal which has

39. *Concept of Motivation*, pp. 5 ff.
40. *Concept of Motivation*, pp. 6-7.
41. *Concept of Motivation*, p. 8.
42. *Principles of Behavior*, p. 25.
43. *Concept of Motivation*, p. 12.
44. *Concept of Motivation*, p. 14.

taken place here and for Peters' seemingly dogmatic claims? What Peters thinks he has uncovered is a radical difference between two types of explanation: reason explanations and causal explanations. It is the former that is appropriate for explaining actions. Reason explanations are of a different type than, and logically incompatible with, causal explanations. While Peters presents us with a rough idea of what is a reason explanation (it is the type of explanation where knowing the reason, point, or end of the action is sufficient to account for why the action was performed), it is not entirely clear what he means by a causal explanation. If we examine what Peters himself says about causal explanations, it is difficult to see why reason explanations are not a variety of causal explanations. "To give a causal *explanation* of an event involves at least showing that other conditions being presumed unchanged a change in one variable is a *sufficient* condition for a change in another."[45] But in the very example that Peters gives us of a "genuine action"—a man crossing the street to get some tobacco—a change in one variable "is a sufficient condition for a change in another." Suppose Jones sets out to buy some tobacco in a situation that is like the former one. Only this time, just as he is about to cross the street, he hesitates and remembers he has a dentist's appointment and so sets off hurriedly in the opposite direction. "Other conditions being presumed unchanged," the sudden realization that he has a dentist's appointment (which he wants to keep) explains why he hesitated and walked in the opposite direction.

It is not causal explanation *per se* that is logically incompatible with reason explanation, but a specific theory or type of causal explanation. This becomes clear in the passage that immediately follows his characterization of causal explanation. "In the mechanical conception of 'cause' it is also demanded that there should be spatial and temporal contiguity between the movements involved. Now the trouble about giving this sort of explanation of human actions is that we can never specify an action exhaustively in terms of movements of the body or within the body."[46] Here we touch upon a second major dichotomy that has pervaded much of the post-Wittgensteinian exploration of action: the dichotomy between action and movement or physical motion. But before passing on to

45. *Concept of Motivation*, p. 12.
46. *Concept of Motivation*, p. 12.

the significance of this dichotomy, note how glibly Peters passes from the generic notion of causation to the specific notion of mechanical causation. Much of the polemical force of Peters' argument and other variations of this argument results from the easy way in which causation is identified with a specific theory of causation, viz., variations on Hume's theory. It is difficult to find in any of the early advocates of philosophical psychology a detailed and careful analysis of causation and causal explanation. They have frequently written as if the concept of causation were perfectly clear and the important point was to clarify the nature of reason explanations and show how these are not what they take to be the paradigm (more frequently the caricature) of causal explanation. This glib treatment of causation has been one of the main targets of their critics.

The contrast between action and movement is intimately related to the distinction between reason explanations and causal explanations. The example, signing a contract, that Peters gives to clarify this second dichotomy is a favorite one of post-Wittgensteinian philosophers. (Compare this with "signaling" discussed in the passage cited above by Passmore.) If we restrict the concept of movement to that of physical displacement we can see why movements and actions must be distinguished. One might make the same movements, or the same types of movement and yet be performing very different actions. I may make the same type of movements when signing my name in two different instances, but in one case the act that I am performing is showing someone what a signature is, while in another situation, the same bodily movements may count as legally binding me to a contract. Furthermore, Peters claims that in the case of signing a contract, "it would be impossible to stipulate exhaustively what the movements *must* be. For if this is a case of human action the agent must be presumed to be intelligent and he will, accordingly, vary his movements in a great variety of ways. He may hold the pen slightly differently, vary the size of his writing according to the space available, and so on, depending on the sort of ink, paper, and pen available. But provided that he produces a signature which confirms to rough and ready criteria—e.g., it must not be typed—more or less *any* movements will do."[47] The point of these observations is to show us how different are the concepts of movement and action. There can be actions—or at least acts—that

47. *Concept of Motivation,* p. 13.

do not involve movements.[48] If ordinary language is our guide, it is perfectly appropriate to ask what did Jones do when he was struck by a policeman. To answer that he refrained from striking back because Jones practices nonviolence might be a satisfactory answer. Here there is an *act* of nonviolence without any movement. While it is not difficult to understand this distinction between action and movement, one may wonder about its philosophic import. This dichotomy dovetails with the distinction between causal explanations and reason explanations. Peters (and others) seem to think that causal explanation is restricted to explaining variations in movement (not action). To give a causal explanation of an action would require that it be possible to reduce or translate action concepts into movement concepts. But since this cannot be done (because action concepts and movement concepts are logically different types of concepts), we cannot hope to give causal explanations of actions. We may, of course, be able to give a causal account of the movements involved in a specific action, but this is not to give a causal account of the action. As Peters says, "So we could never give a sufficient explanation of an action in causal terms because we could never stipulate the movements which would have to count as dependent variables. A precise functional relationship could never be established."[49] Peters' claims are striking, but the philosophic conclusions that he draws from the distinction between action and movement reveal as much about his assumptions concerning the nature of causation as it does about this distinction. Peters assumes, without arguing the point, that the legitimate domain of causal explanation is movement—physical displacement—not action. We will see how questionable this assumption is.

Implicit in our discussion thus far is still another dichotomy that has been a touchstone for the new teleologists—and this is a dichotomy that has an ancient philosophic lineage—between doing and happening, or between agency and suffering (undergoing). Peters speaks of a case of "genuine action" as one of "an act of doing some-

48. Some analytic philosophers have distinguished "actions" and "acts," but this distinction is not directly relevant to the main thrust of Peters' argument. See David Sachs, "A Few Morals About Acts," *The Philosophical Review* 75 (1966).

49. *Concept of Motivation*, p. 13.

thing as opposed to suffering something."[50] Melden, who also uses this distinction, writes:

A very great number of physiological events take place, happen, get done when one raises one's arm; but it not only makes sense to ask whether these things are things that one does, it is in fact questionable that this is the case. If so, we cannot identify what happens, gets done, with what a person does.[51]

Richard Taylor has made extensive use of this distinction, tracing it back to the notion of efficient causation articulated by Aristotle. (We can appreciate how treacherous discussions of philosophical psychology are when we realize that Peters, Melden, and others clearly have in mind some variation of Humean causation when they declare that we cannot give causal explanations of actions. Richard Taylor, who shares a similar outlook on a number of fundamental issues, attacks the prevalent Humean notion of causation and defends a modified form of the Aristotelian notion of efficient causation.) In this sense of "cause," *I* am sometimes the cause of my actions.[52] Once we understand the way in which Richard Taylor is using "cause," Peters and Melden might well agree with the spirit, if not the letter, of the following:

A true interpreted statement of the form "A was the cause of B" means, in light of the foregoing, that both A and B are conditions or sets of conditions that occurred; that each was, given all other conditions that occurred, but only those, both necessary and sufficient for the occurrence of the other; that B did not precede A in time; *and* that A made B happen by virtue of its power to do so. But this final qualification, *alas!* renders the whole analysis empty. For to say that A made B happen obviously means that A *caused* B, and to say that it did this by virtue of its efficacy as a *cause*—or, in short, that A caused B. To say of anything, then, that it was the cause of the thing in question, means simply and solely that *it was* the cause of the thing in question, and there is absolutely no other conceptually clearer way of putting the matter except by introduction of mere synonyms for causation. Positively, what this means is that causation is a philosophical category, that while the concept of causation can perhaps be used to shed light upon other problems or used

50. *Concept of Motivation*, p. 12.
51. A. I. Melden, *Free Action*, p. 56.
52. Richard Taylor, *Action and Purpose*.

in the analysis of other relationships, no other concept can be used to analyze it.[53]

It doesn't seem very satisfactory to be told that to say of anything that it was a cause of something else "means simply" that it was the cause of the thing in question. But this should not blind us to the point of this tautology. In the history of philosophy and science the concept of causal efficacy did not prove particularly successful in advancing scientific inquiry. No one ever succeeded in specifying criteria for distinguishing genuine cases of causal efficacy from pseudo-cases. Without such criteria the concept can and did lend itself to abuse resulting in unilluminating pseudo-explanations. In the seventeeth and eighteenth centuries, we find the articulation of a different concept that did prove much more fruitful. It too was labeled "causation" and was intended as a replacement for the older Aristotelian concept of efficient cause which entailed the treacherous references to "efficacy" and "power." The new concept of causation focused on the regularities of similar types of events. There is a direct lineage from this concept of regularity and the contemporary search for functional relationships that is so fundamental to all sciences, including the natural and the social sciences. Many tough-minded scientists and philosophers of science have come to hold that this is the only legitimate concept of causation. There has been enormous sophistication and subtlety in refining a crude regularity thesis, but at the heart of even the most refined analyses stands the functional correlation of variables as the quintessence of scientific causation.

Post-Wittgensteinian philosophers have been challenging the claim that there is nothing more to causation than nomological functional correlations and have been urging that we need another concept of "causation" in order to give an account of human behavior. These philosophers are not denying the success of the natural sciences, nor are they advocating that the practice of scientific inquiry requires a concept of causal efficacy. They are arguing that in the enthusiasm with the achievements of the natural sciences, we have lost sight of a profound insight that was articulated by Aristotle and is fundamental to our most basic ways of thinking about man. No matter how difficult it may be to specify

53. *Action and Purpose,* p. 39.

criteria for what is to count as agency, and granted that there are many difficult borderline cases—where it is unclear whether X *did* something or something *happened* to X—the concept of agency is basic to our understanding of what sort of creature man is. In law, morals, politics, social behavior, and psychological disorders, and in many ordinary contexts, we do make the distinction between doing and suffering or undergoing; we assume that we are genuine agents capable of causal efficacy. Post-Wittgensteinian philosophers argue that not only is it impossible to reduce or analyze this concept of agency in terms of the regularity of events, we cannot even conceive what it would mean to abandon such a concept in the understanding of ourselves and others; it is fundamental to our conceptual framework. Richard Taylor's tautology is a way of calling attention to the primitiveness and fundamental character of our concept of causal agency.

Although there are sharp internal differences among many of the new teleologists, there is a consensus that the concept of personal agency, or the distinction between genuine doing and suffering, is fundamental to *our* conceptual framework. Sellars underscores this point when he says, "Thus the conceptual framework of persons is the framework in which we think of one another as sharing the community intentions which provide the ambience of principles and standards (above all, those which make meaningful discourse and rationality itself possible) within which we live our own individual lives. A person can almost be defined as a being that has intentions."[54]

This last point suggests still another concept that has been used to pin down the difference between action and nonaction, viz., intention or intentionality. Charles Taylor presents a typical argument concerning the role of intention in action, and its consequences for distinguishing action from nonaction.

. . . the distinction between action and non-action hangs not just on the presence or absence of the corresponding intention or purpose, but on this intention or purpose having or not having a role in bringing about the behavior. With action, we might say the behavior occurs because of the corresponding intention or purpose; where this is not the case, we are not dealing with action. But to use the expression 'because of' here might mislead. For we could not say that the intention was the causal

54. *Science, Perception and Reality*, p. 40.

antecedent of the behavior. For the two are not contingently connected in the normal way. We are not explaining the behavior by the 'law,' other things being equal, intending X is followed by doing X, for this is part of what we mean by 'intending X,' that, in the absence of interfering factors, it is followed by doing X. I could not be said to intend X if, even with no obstacles or other countervailing factors, I still didn't do it. Thus my intention is not a causal antecedent of my behavior.[55]

There are some respects in which "intentions" are like causes, and Taylor is willing to say that "we can treat . . . intentions very much as causal antecedents as far as prediction and control are concerned, even though they necessarily tend to bring about the actions we explain, predict or bring about by them."[56] Nevertheless, there is a "strong sense" of (Humean) causation in which intentions are not truly causal antecedents of behavior. Charles Taylor has sought to uncover the epistemological biases that are presupposed by and give rise to such a regularity theory of causation. He argues that such a theory presupposes an atomistic view of the world where events are separable and independent of each other.[57] Consequently, it is a requirement of the regularity theory of causation that we should be able to describe the antecedents and consequents of a causal functional law independently. There must be no *essential* reference to the consequent in describing the antecedent of such a causal law,

55. Charles Taylor, *The Explanation of Behaviour,* p. 33. When Charles Taylor claims that "my intention is not a causal antecedent of my behavior," he has in mind the regularity theory of causation. Here he follows most of the new teleologists and differs from Richard Taylor's use of the concept of cause. As we noted earlier, Richard Taylor's point is similar to that of the other new teleologists. But he is critical of a Humean analysis of cause and argues for a neo-Aristotelian analysis of (efficient) cause.

56. Charles Taylor, "Relations Between Cause and Action," *Proceedings of the Seventh Inter-American Congress of Philosophy* (Quebec, 1967), p. 249. In a reply to criticism by J. Margolis, Charles Taylor clarifies his position as follows: "The interesting thing here seems to be that intentions, desires, etc., while non-contingently linked with the actions that flow from them, nevertheless function in other ways like causes, e.g., we can think of them as bringing about these actions. If we focus on the requirement that cause and effect be contingently linked, we will still say that desires aren't causes. This is the language I used in the book [*The Explanation of Behaviour*]. But it is misleading, and I'd prefer not to put it this way now, just because of all the misunderstandings which arise." "A Reply to Margolis," *Inquiry* 11 (1968), 128.

57. See Chapter 4 of *The Explanation of Behaviour.*

and no *essential* reference to the antecedent in describing the consequent. A causal functional law asserts a contingent regularity between antecedents and consequents. But these requiremets cannot be satisfied in explaining an action. The relation between an intention and an action is *not* a relation of contingent regularity. "We have to identify, as it were, an 'antecedent' which is non-contingently linked with its consequent."[58] Explanation by reference to intention violates the basic condition of functional causal explanations whereby all relations between antecedents and consequents are considered to be contingent regularities. Taylor offers the following example to elucidate his point.

Why did he hit him? He had framed an intention long ago to do so: this serves to rule out other possibilities, *e.g.*, that he did it by accident, or completely on impulse; but it cannot be construed as giving a cause. For when we focus on the intention as a causal antecedent we are forced to recognize that we specify it by the action which we use it to explain, in this case, hitting the man.[59]

But what precisely is an intention? The analysis of this concept has proved to be one of the trickiest in the repertoire of philosophical psychologists.[60] We cannot explore all its ramifications, but it is worthwhile to explore one significant point where recent trends in analytic philosophy link up with that of contemporary continental phenomenology. The concept of intention—or more generally, intentionality—has been at the very heart of continental phenomenology. Charles Taylor who, more than most analytic philosophers, is aware of this affinity, has himself been influenced by Merleau-Ponty. To appreciate what is distinctive about human action, we need to uncover what lurks behind a metaphor that is prevalent in our thought of ourselves as personal agents. It is the metaphor of the "inside" or "center" of activity.

What is essential to this notion of an 'inside' . . . is the . . . notion of consciousness in the sense of intentionality. To speak of an 'intentional description' of something is to speak not just of any description which this thing bears, but of the description which it bears for a certain person,

58. *Explanation of Behaviour*, p. 44.
59. "Relations Between Cause and Action," *Proceedings of the Seventh Inter-American Congress of Philosophy*, p. 246.
60. Cf. G. E. M. Anscombe, *Intention*.

the description under which it is subsumed by him. Now the notion of an action as directed behavior involves that of an intentional description.[61]

If we accept this characterization of "intentional description" and the claim that it is essential for understanding action (or even *some* human actions), then we can see in one fell swoop the inadequacies of a behaviorism which would reject this notion as unnecessary and eliminable. If such a behaviorism restricted itself to behavior in the sense of what is physically observable (and didn't consider self-avowals as a form of behavior) then it would not have any adequate means for capturing what Taylor characterizes as "intentional description." Paradoxically, we would be forced to conclude that such a behaviorism does not account for human action. Furthermore, we can see how basic this notion of "intentional description" is to the whole range of our moral behavior (including legal, political, and social behavior). Whether we take the position of a spectator or that of an agent, crucial legal and moral distinctions depend upon what we accept as "the description which it bears for a certain person, the description under which it is subsumed by him." This is our basis for distinguishing different types of murder, or even coming to the conclusion that murder was or was not committed when confronted with what (from an external point of view) may be the "same" event.

According to Charles Taylor, the crucial difference between teleological explanations and mechanical explanations is that the former require the use of a premise which violates the formal requirements for mechanical explanations. In a teleological explanation, we will explain the event that occurs by saying that it is *required* for an end or goal.

. . . when we say that an event occurs for the sake of an end, we are saying that it occurs because it is the type of event which brings about this end. This means that the condition of the event's occurring is that a state of affairs obtain such that it will bring about the end in question, or such that this event is required to bring about that end. To offer a teleological explanation of some event or class of events, e.g., the behavior of some being, is then, to account for it by laws in terms of which an event's occurring is held to be dependent on that event's being required for some end.[62]

61. *Explanation of Behaviour*, p. 58.
62. *Explanation of Behaviour*, p. 9.

The scope of teleological explanations is not restricted to explanations of human action. Taylor shows how teleological explanations *may* be applied to animal behavior. Our ordinary explanations of human actions are, so Charles Taylor claims, teleological. Furthermore he argues that a proper science of human behavior will most likely take a teleological form. I say "most likely," because while Charles Taylor argues that mechanical explanation and teleological explanation are incompatible, there is no a priori reason to believe that we will not some day be able to *replace* teleological explanations by mechanical explanations of human behavior. The details of Charles Taylor's argument are complex and we cannot explore them in detail here. For our purposes, we simply want to note that in the distinction between mechanical and teleological explanations, the claim that these are competing forms of explanation, and that explanation of action is essentially teleological, we find one more way in which the new teleologists have sought to articulate what is distinctive about human action.

Throughout our discussion, we have detected a suspicion of the claims of empirical psychology, and more generally of the possibility of giving scientific explanations of human actions. Actually we can discriminate at least *three* main attitudes toward the possibility of an empirical science of human action. To complete the general picture of the theory of action developed by the new teleologists, we need to explore the ways in which they understand and assess the possibilities of an empirical science of human behavior.

The first position does not question the viability and contribution of the sciences, but maintains that a scientific view of man provides us with a limited perspective. If we think of the distinction between movement and action, where the former member of this distinction is the legitimate domain of science, then we may conclude as Peters and Melden at times seem to suggest, there is nothing intrinsically wrong with attempting to give scientific causal explanations of human "behavior." But such explanations will be restricted to the movements that take place (internally or externally) in human organisms and are categorically different from genuine reason, motive, or intention explanations of human action. It is not science, or even a science of behavior that is under attack, but rather an *ideology* that is being severely criticized. This is the ideological claim (not the scientific claim) that a science of behavior can, in principle, answer *all* legitimate questions about human behavior including those about human action. This is what Peters and Melden are claiming is impossible. This is the point of Peters' negative thesis that the tradition stemming from Hobbes is mistaken in claiming that "there can be an all-inclusive theory of human behavior from whose basic postulates answers to all forms of the question 'Why does Jones do X?' will eventually be deduced," and his positive thesis that the different sorts of legitimate answers that can be given to this question are "logically different and sometimes logically exclusive."

The position that emerges from Charles Taylor's investigations is much more subtle. He basically agrees with Peters and Melden in noting a sharp conceptual difference between action and movement, reason explanation and causal explanation, doing and happening. But he draws different consequences from these conceptual distinctions. In the first place, he attacks the bias that scientific explanation must take a mechanical causal form. The issue for Charles Taylor is not whether or not it is possible to develop a scientific all-inclusive theory of human behavior, but rather what will be the ultimate *form* of the laws of such a science. There is no a priori reason to believe that it is impossible to develop such a science whose basic laws are teleological in form. And there are good reasons to think that this will be the form of laws in a scientific theory of human behavior. But even though Charles Taylor is sympathetic with the general thrust of many post-Wittgensteinian philosophers, he is much more cautious and sophisticated in drawing unsupportable ontological conclusions. Although he criticizes in detail various behavioristic approaches which rely on a notion of causation that consists of regularities among independent antecedents and consequents, he holds out the possibility that eventually some mechanical theory of human behavior might prove to be the best sort of theory for describing and explaining human behavior. If such a theory were to be developed, then we would be forced to admit that teleological laws can be replaced by mechanical laws. More strikingly, we would have to admit that even though the *concept* of action is not reducible to the *concept* of movement, we may nevertheless dicover that our behavior may be accounted for by a mechanistic theory. In effect, this means that our *present* concept of action, which is so basic to our conceptual structure, would be abandoned. And consequently, this would effect a radical transformation of our present conceptual structure. But no matter how unlikely or preposterous such a possibility may seem, it cannot be ruled out a priori.

For Peters and Melden, causal (scientific) explanations and reason explanations are compatible once we realize that we are asking and answering different sorts of questions. For Charles Taylor, mechanical and teleological explanations are rival types of explanation, but it is an open question what will be the form of the laws in an adequate scientific theory of man. Louch, however, advocates a much more extreme position.

In the preface to his *Explanation and Human Action,* he announces that "My main intent has been to show that the idea of a science of man or society is untenable. I defend this view by developing a philosophical thesis as to the nature of explanation, contrary to that which would be required to support scientific claims of psychologists and sociologists."[63] One by one he takes up the various social sciences—including psychology, sociology, anthropology, political science, and economics—to show just why they are untenable as scientific disciplines. But all of his attacks are based on, and develop in a variety of ways, insights which he shares in common (although he sometimes radically departs from) other post-Wittgensteinian philosophers. His central thesis is that

when we offer explanations of human behavior, we are seeing that behavior as justified by the circumstances in which it occurs. Explanation of human action is moral explanation. In appealing to reasons for acting, motives, purposes, intentions, desires and their cognates, which occur in both ordinary and technical discussions of human doings, we exhibit an action in the light of circumstances that are taken to entitle or warrant a person to act as he does.[64]

Moral explanations are not scientific explanations and they are incompatible with scientific explanations. To think that such moral explanations can be assimilated to scientific explanations is to commit the grossest sort of category mistake, but it is precisely this

63. A. R. Louch, *Explanation and Human Action,* p. viii.
64. *Explanation and Human Action,* p. 4.

mistake that is the basis for thinking that a science of man is viable.

But what does Louch mean by "moral explanations"? His clearest characterization is the following:

On the procedural view [of morality], a man whose actions are guided by his assessments, and his understanding of his own and others' actions by the grounds he finds for those actions in the situation of the actor, is looking at behavior morally. So long as he describes his own and others' conduct as doing something well or poorly, effectively or clumsily, appropriately or mistakenly, he is a moral agent or observer. It may be that the grounds he discovers as the end products of his diagnoses shock or offend various moral sensibilities; but this is relatively unimportant. The point is, he thinks in terms of grounds. He acts or describes actions not by seeking temporal antecedents or functional dependencies, but by deciding that the situation *entitles* a man to act in the way he did or is likely to do.[65]

The point that Louch is making (although he uses it in a different way) bears a close resemblance to Charles Taylor's discussion of "intentional description."[66] It is not the case that there is some substratum in action that is value-neutral and to which we apply value-laden predicates (which presumably, in principle, could be isolated from the value-neutral substratum). Terms of appraisal enter *essentially* in our very descriptions and explanations of actions.

. . . values do not enter descriptions of human affairs as disruptive influences; rather, they allow us to describe human behavior in terms of action. Inasmuch as the units of examination of human behavior are actions, they cannot be observed, identified, or isolated except through categories of assessment and appraisal. There are not two stages, an identification of properties and qualities in nature and then an assessment of them, stages which then could become the business of different experts. There is only one stage, the delineation and description of occurrences in value terms.[67]

65. *Explanation and Human Action*, p. 51.

66. Louch's book is highly polemical, especially in his attack on the claims made by the various social sciences. At times one wishes there were more sustained argument instead of polemic. But it is striking to realize that the cluster of insights that are central to his study—the ways in which we perceive and understand the world in terms of categories of assessment and evaluation—is very close in spirit to the cluster of insights that have been central to continental phenomenology.

67. *Explanation and Human Action*, p. 56.

But if categories of assessment and appraisal enter essentially into our description of actions, these categories will also enter essentially into our explanations of these actions—otherwise we are not explaining what we are describing. Louch doesn't think that there is a single paradigm for our moral explanations of human action. Most of our explanations of actions are ad hoc, shifting their form depending on the context, but the family of different types of moral explanations cannot be reduced to scientific explanations. They do not fit the hypothetical deductive model that is characteristic of the natural sciences. Because most of our explanation of human action is typically moral explanation—in this extended sense of "moral"—and because the social sciences have neglected this truth and sought to "force" the explanations of behavior into the alien paradigms of the natural sciences, "most of psychological and social inquiry . . . has been vitiated by methodological concerns that have no bearing upon the puzzles and problems that arise within a view of man as an agent."[68]

Peters, Melden, Charles Taylor, and Louch all agree that recent behavioristic tendencies in the social sciences reflect deep conceptual confusions. All agree that the hope expressed by Hull that behavioral psychology holds out the promise of a comprehensive and adequate science of human behavior is illusory. They disagree in their assessment of the possibilities of a science of man. Peters and Melden, at least some of the time, argue that while we can gain a scientific causal account of the movements involved in human action, we do not thereby explain human *action*. Human actions are not caused, and for them this seems to be a sufficient reason to conclude that it is impossible scientifically to explain human actions. Charles Taylor agrees that actions are not caused in the "strict" mechanical sense of causation, but he argues that teleological explanations and laws are empirical. Consequently there is no a priori or conceptual reason to believe that it is impossible to develop a comprehensive science of man. The primary issue for Charles Taylor is what types of explanations and laws will prove most fruitful in the study of human behavior. Although he is sharply critical of the various forms of behaviorism which have been advocated, and persuasively argues that it is likely that the science of man will take a teleological form, he leaves open the possibility that some

68. *Explanation and Human Action*, pp. 237-238.

form of mechanistic theory may replace our teleological explanations of human behavior. Louch argues for the most extreme position. Because explanation of human action is moral explanation, and because moral explanation is not scientific explanation, he attacks the possibility of developing a social science of man. He argues that existing "social sciences" are shot through with conceptual confusions and that the influence of so-called "social sciences" has been more pernicious than beneficial in the understanding of man as agent.

A Critique of the New Dualism

In the previous section I explored some of the major distinctions and dichotomies of the conceptual analysis of action. Even though there have been serious internal differences among philosophical psychologists, all of these distinctions fall into place in the major strategy of dealing with human action. The cumulative result of these many inquiries has been to reveal (or to remind us) how different the grammar or logic of action is from some of the simplistic accounts that emerged from reductive analysis. One positive result of these investigations has been to expose epistemological prejudices and to show how difficult it is to come up with satisfactory reductions or translations of our action concepts in a language that does not itself contain the distinctive features of our action talk. Whatever metaphysical conclusions we draw, it is undeniable that these distinctions and concepts are fundamental to the ways in which we think about ourselves and others. The concepts of action, intention, goals, agency and person are not peripheral to our conceptual scheme; they are absolutely central, and without them it would be difficult to make intelligible sense of the world in which we find ourselves. But the claims of many philosophical psychologists have been much more ambitious. When I discussed reductive analysis, I was concerned to show that the demand for reduction, and the belief that action concepts can be reduced or translated into an atomistic and mechanical framework functioned as an a priori principle. In a curious way, the conceptual analysis of action has been a mirror image of reductive analysis. Its practitioners have exhibited a tendency to settle the issue of the status of action concepts by a priori fiat. It is ironic that conceptual analysis, which was originally characterized not only as a rebellion from reductive analysis, but as a revolt against the dualism of the Cartesian tradition that has dominated so much of modern philosophy, has resulted in a "new" dualism.[69] This dualism is not a dualism of two types of substance, mind and body, but a dualism of two different, nonreducible, and logically incompatible conceptual schemes or languages; the language of action and reason explanations versus the language of movement and mechanical causal explanation. For many of the more extreme philosophical psychologists this is an unbridgeable chasm, a rigid dichotomy claimed to be a conceptual, a priori, necessary truth. Although conceptual analysts phrase their points in terms of language, it is apparent that they are drawing some very strong metaphysical conclusions from this dichotomy, which presumably tells us the way things really are. Man cannot be exhaustively characterized in a language restricted to mechanistic concepts; consequently it is false to believe that man is nothing but a complex physical mechanism. To say that the category of action or agency is basic to our conceptual framework is to say man is a being who really acts, really does things, is sometimes really motivated by reasons and not by causes. But we hope to show that the apriorism implicit in conceptual analysis is just as unwarranted as the apriorism implicit in reductive analysis.

We can put this point in a slightly different way. Pervading the claims and counterclaims concerning the reducibility or nonreducibility of the concept of action, there have been two false pictures that have been responsible for much of the polemic. From the side of tough-minded reductionists, there has been a suspicion that their opponents are trying to resurrect some sort of obscure subjectivistic anthropomorphism. But anti-reductionists have accused their adversaries of begging the hard issues and refusing to open their eyes to the pervasiveness of real and fundamental distinctions. Philosophical psychologists have sometimes written as if the only alternative to showing a logical or conceptual dichotomy between two strata of language or two conceptual schemes is to claim that man must be

69. Cf. Charles Landesman, "The New Dualism in the Philosophy of Mind," *The Review of Metaphysics* 19 (1965).

conceived of as nothing but a complex physical mechanism. We want to show that this either/or—either anthropomorphic subjectivism or reductive mechanism—is unwarranted.

I stated earlier that two main (interrelated) tendencies can be discerned in the criticisms of what the "first generation" of philosophical psychologists claimed to be the necessary, a priori truths yielded by conceptual analysis. The first trend has been a serious questioning of the dichotomies between reason explanations and causal explanations, action and movement, doing and happening, teleological and mechanical laws and explanations. The thrust of this line of criticism has not been to deny that there are important distinctions to be drawn, but to show that these distinctions do not have the hard and fast rigidity claimed for them and that many of the important philosophic conclusions based on these distinctions are highly dubious. Since the types of criticisms developed have been extremely diverse and complex, it would be tedious to discuss all this material.[70] But it is the second, more radical type of criticism that I want to explore.

70. The following is a selection from the many articles that have criticized the more ambitious claims of the new teleologists: C. G. Hempel, "Rational Action," *Proceedings and Addresses of the American Philosophical Association* 35 (1962); R. Hancock, "Interpersonal and Physical Causation," *Philosophical Review* 71 (1962); R. Brandt and J. Kim, "Wants as Explanations of Actions," *Journal of Philosophy* 60 (1963); B. Goldberg, "Can Desire be a Cause?" *Analysis* 15 (1965); Charles Landesman, "The New Dualism in the Philosophy of Mind," *The Review of Metaphysics* 19 (1965); W. D. Gean, "Reasons and Causes," *The Review of Metaphysics* 19 (1966); W. P. Alston, "Wants, Actions, and Causal Explanation," in *Intentionality, Minds, and Perception,* ed. by H. Castañeda; W. P. Alston, "Do Actions Have Causes?" and J. J. Thomson, "Comments" in *Proceedings of the Seventh Inter-American Congress of Philosophy* (Quebec, 1967); R. Macklin, "Doing and Happening," *The Review of Metaphysics* 22 (1968); Jerry A. Fodor, *Psychological Explanation.* For a more complete listing of material dealing with the theory of action, see the "Selected Bibliography" in *Readings in the Theory of Action,* ed. by N. Care and C. Landesman.

Donald Davidson's article, "Action, Reasons, and Causes," *The Journal of Philosophy* (1963), which has received extensive discussion, is representative of what I have called the "first trend" of criticism. In this article, Davidson agrees with a good deal of what conceptual analysts have claimed about the structure of our "reason explanations." But he argues that such explanations are not incompatible with causal explanations, but rather represent one *type* of causal explanation. His strategy, however, is to argue that the "new dual-

The Displacement Hypothesis

The investigation of the concept of action in analytic philosophy has been intimately related to a cluster of metaphilosophical issues. In the early days of analytic philosophy, the claims made about the nature of human action reflected the intellectual bias in favor of reductive analysis as *the* proper method of philosophical analysis. In the revolution against the excesses of reductive analysis, a newer, more flexible approach to conceptual analysis emerged in which the concept of action became a focal point. I cited Strawson's explication and defense of conceptual analysis where he maintains that "if we want to understand the habits and way of life of an animal, we must carefully observe his behavior in natural surroundings; it is no good turning our backs on his actual behavior, constructing a clockwork model from an engineer's designs and then studying that."[71] Strawson's view, shared by many other linguistic philosophers, is that there is a basic core of concepts that are fundamental to our way of thinking about ourselves and the world and that the task of descriptive metaphysics is to lay bare and reveal the structure of these basic concepts and categories. To the extent that we are successful in our descriptive metaphysics, it makes little sense to ask whether this is the way things really are—for the very point of descriptive metaphysics is to articulate the "categories and concepts, which, in their most fundamental character, change not at all."[72] Strawson's defense seems eminently plausible. Whatever the excesses of some of the proponents of conceptual analysis, they certainly

---

ists" have misconceived the nature of causal statements. When causal statements are properly understood—especially singular causal statements—then we can see (so Davidson argues) that "reason explanations" or what he labels "rationalizations" are causal explanations. Once again, we can see how important a proper analysis of causal statements is for the controversies concerning the status of action.

For a critical discussion of Davidson's paper, see Robert J. Richman, "Reasons and Causes," *Australasian Journal of Philosophy* 47 (1969); Charles Landesman, "Actions as Universals: An Inquiry into the Metaphysics of Action," *American Philosophical Quarterly* 6 (1969); Joseph Margolis, "Reasons and Causes," *Dialogue* 8 (1969); Ruth Macklin, "Norm and Law in the Theory of Action," *Inquiry* 11 (1968).

71. "Construction and Analysis," in *The Revolution in Philosophy,* p. 103.
72. *Individuals,* p. 10.

have succeeded in making us much more aware of the distinctive character of the ways in which we do think about ourselves and the world.

Recently, the entire program of conceptual analysis, insofar as it is supposed to yield conceptual, necessary truths has been called into question in a most radical fashion. A critique has developed that has significant consequences for assessing the program of conceptual analysis, and more generally, for understanding the philosophic enterprise.

Briefly and boldly stated, champions of the displacement hypothesis do *not* question the possibility that by conceptual analysis we can isolate "categories and concepts, which in their fundamental character" are central to the ways in which we ordinarily describe, explain, and understand ourselves and the world. Nor do they question that this conceptual framework may be incompatible with and consequently nonreducible to scientific frameworks. Nevertheless, they maintain that the conceptual framework in which we now think of ourselves and others as agents can be displaced by a radically different scientific framework. Consequently, the picture of man that emerges from conceptual analysis of our ordinary ways of thinking and speaking is a *false* picture. It does not reveal the way things really are or the type of creature that man really is. If these critics are right, then no matter how successful and sophisticated a conceptual analysis is carried out, it can at best reveal our (human) *beliefs* about the way things are. Descriptive metaphysics by conceptual analysis—insofar as metaphysics aims at describing the way things really are—is a futile enterprise. To use an older terminology, conceptual analysis is a logic of appearance, not of reality. The most pugnacious and polemical champion of the displacement hypothesis is Paul Feyerabend, who acknowledges that he is building on ideas suggested by Karl Popper. Wilfrid Sellars and Richard Rorty have developed more sophisticated explications and defenses of the hypothesis and J. J. C. Smart is a recent convert to this perspective. Some remarks by Charles Taylor indicate that he can also be classified with this group of philosophers, although he differs in some important ways.[73]

73. The displacement hypothesis has been developed primarily in regard to discussion of the mind-body problem and scientific materialism. But the arguments developed are relevant to the status of our concepts of action and

I indicated earlier that conceptual analysis, with all its revolutionary overtones, bears a very close resemblance to some traditional philosophic approaches. One persistent strain in philosophy,
most notably represented by Aristotle and Kant, has been the search
for and explication of our basic concepts and categories. With all the
differences in method, style, and content between Anglo-Saxon conceptual analysis and continental phenomenology, both movements
share the aim of revealing the basic ways in which man thinks about
himself and the world. All of these approaches have focused on what
Sellars calls the "manifest image" of man in the world. But they go
further in *endorsing* this image as the true image of what man really
is, or (in the case of Kant) what man can legitimately hope to know
about himself.[74] However, displacement theorists are questioning
whether this entire approach is one that can reveal the way things
really are. According to them, the manifest image of man is a *false*
picture of man in the world. They are therefore questioning what has
been one of the most perennial strains in the history of philosophy, a
strain also evidenced in the varieties of contemporary philosophy.
But their critique goes even further. They question a presupposition
that has been common to reductive analysts, conceptual analysts, and
even critics such as Davidson. All of these philosophers have presupposed that many of the statements which we ordinarily make about
ourselves, especially in regard to action concepts, are meaningful
and true. Carnap doesn't reject such assertions as false and Hull

---

agency. See Paul Feyerabend, "Explanation, Reduction, and Empiricism,"
Minnesota Studies in the Philosophy of Science, Vol. 3, ed. by Herbert Feigl
and Grover Maxwell; "Materialism and the Mind-Body Problem," *The Review
of Metaphysics* 17 (1963); "Problems of Empiricism," in *Beyond the Edge of
Certainty: Essays in Contemporary Science and Philosophy,* ed. by Robert
Colodny; Wilfrid Sellars, *Science, Perception and Reality;* Richard Rorty,
"Mind-Body Identity, Privacy, and Categories," *The Review of Metaphysics*
19 (1965); J. J. C. Smart, "Conflicting Views about Explanation," *Boston
Studies in the Philosophy of Science,* Vol. 2, ed. by R. Cohen and M. Wartof-
sky; Charles Taylor, *The Explanation of Behaviour.* Stephen Körner's papers
on transcendental deductions are also relevant to the status of the displace-
ment hypothesis. See "Transcendental Tendencies in Recent Philosophy,"
Journal of Philosophy 63 (1966) and "The Impossibility of Transcendental
Deductions," *The Monist* 53 (1967).

74. Cf. Wilfrid Sellars, "Philosophy and the Scientific Image of Man" in
Science, Perception and Reality.

doesn't deny "the molar reality of purposive acts," but both are committed to programs of reductive analysis in order to clarify the meaning and truth of these claims. And, of course, the quarrel of the philosophical psychologists with the reductionists has not been about the meaningfulness and truth of our characteristic claims about action concepts, but whether these can be possibly reduced or translated into a more "basic" language. The displacement theorists take a radical turn: they maintain that, despite our strong convictions to the contrary, the most pervasive and basic types of assertions we make about our intentions, actions, reasons, motives are (or, may be) *false*.

The displacement hypothesis has been developed in a controversy concerning the nature of scientific explanation and reduction. It has been applied to more general philosophic issues, especially to the mind-body problem, and is directly relevant to our discussion of the concept of action. I cannot explore the controversy in all its ramifications, but I do need to touch on some of the highlights.[75]

75. Although Feyerabend, Rorty, and Sellars all subscribe to some version of the displacement hypothesis, there are important differences among them. Feyerabend's version is the crudest of the three. Roughly speaking, Feyerabend seems to hold that any language system or conceptual scheme is a "theory" and any theory can be displaced by a better theory which is incompatible with the original theory. "Ordinary language" for Feyerabend turns out to be a very poor theory and he is convinced that it will some day be displaced by a better theory. Rorty, although close to Feyerabend, wants to emphasize the *possibility* of displacement rather than the prediction that our ordinary language *will* be displaced. In a recent answer to critics of his position, he says: ". . . I am not in any sense claiming that the customary vocabulary of introspection is 'illegitimate.' Rather, I am merely claiming the same legitimacy for the neurological vocabulary—where 'legitimacy' means the right to be considered a report of experience. My attitude is not that some vocabularies are 'illegitimate,' but rather we should let a thousand vocabularies bloom and then see which survive. The materialist predicts that the neurological vocabulary will triumph. He may be right, but if he is, it is not because of some special feature of this vocabulary which consists in its having originated in theoretical science. Given different cultural conditions, one can imagine the neurological vocabulary having been the ordinary familiar one and the mentalistic one the 'scientific' alternative." ["In Defense of Eliminative Materialism," *The Review of Metaphysics* 24 (September, 1970).] Sellars has directly criticized Feyerabend and indirectly criticized Rorty's approach. (For his criticism of Feyerabend, see his article, "Scientific Realism or Irenic Instrumentalism," in *Boston Studies in the Philosophy of Science*, Vol. 2, ed. by

From the work of the early logical positivists and later logical empiricists a coherent generalized picture has emerged of the nature of scientific explanation and especially the relation of theory and observation. Our observation language is our basic language. It is the language in which we describe phenomena. Observation statements are to be explained, and observation statements also serve as the basis for testing and confirming scientific hypotheses and theories. Although there have been many controversies concerning the precise nature of the observation language and most champions of the "classical approach" now readily admit that the distinction between an observation language and a theoretical language is a changing and variable one, they do insist that there is an important functional distinction between these two languages. Our theoretical language will consist of nonobservable concepts, postulates, transformation rules, etc. It is the language that we use to explain observation statements. In order to bridge theory and observation, there must also be correspondence rules by which we specify partial interpretations of *some* of our theoretical concepts and statements in terms of observation sentences. Hypothetical-deductive theories together with the correspondence rules enable us to derive and predict observation statements. When alternative scientific theories and hypotheses are developed, we will normally adopt the theory which best explains and predicts our observations. As we develop more comprehensive theories, we can also derive less comprehensive theories from them. Thus, for example, Newtonian mechanics is a theory that not only enables us to explain and predict a wide variety

---

Robert Cohen and Marx Wartofsky.) The following statement concerning "the nature and status of sensory consciousness" would be applicable for Sellars to the puzzles concerning the concept of action, and indicates what he thinks must be done if one is to make out the case for displacement: "But 'neurophysiology' contains many promissory notes (what science does not!) and these are not just matters of detail. Everything hinges on the terms in which they are drawn. It is surely obvious that to appeal to a theory-sketch of human behavior which makes essential use of such place-holders as 'central state' and 'bodily process,' without exploring the conditions which an adequate explanatory framework of behavior must satisfy, is to provide purely verbal solutions to serious puzzles in the philosophy of mind and, in particular, puzzles concerning the nature and status of sensory consciousness." ["Science, Sense Impressions, and Sensa: A Reply to Cornman," *The Review of Metaphysics* 24 (March 1971), 398–399.]

of observations, it also enables us to derive from its postulates other theories and laws such as Kepler's.

The above is a simplification of an analysis that has been developed in great detail and with enormous technical sophistication, but it is sufficient to present a generalized view of what is under attack by Feyerabend and others.[76] According to Feyerabend, this picture is not only false to the actual historical development of scientific inquiry, it also harbors faulty methodological assumptions. Feyerabend challenges the notion of an observation language that is relatively independent of a theoretical language and can serve as a basis for testing it. A theoretical language contains its own observation language. And any observation language contains theoretical assumptions. There is no set of observations or observation statements that remains constant and serves as a touchstone for evaluating theories. What counts as an observation or a description from the perspective of one theory is not only different from (despite what appears to be the same use of key terms) other theories, the two sets of observations and descriptions are typically incompatible. We do not "measure" a proposed scientific theory against a common set of observations or descriptions. The great advances in science come when we invent or discover new theories that are inconsistent with accepted theories. The familiar story that Newtonian mechanics can be derived from a more comprehensive relativity theory is false, for the two theories are actually incompatible. Not only has science developed by the clash of incompatible theories, Feyerabend advocates as a regulative principle a *"principle of proliferation: Invent, and elaborate theories which are inconsistent with the accepted point of view, even if the latter should happen to be highly confirmed and generally accepted."*[77]

76. For a good succinct characterization of this "classical picture," see Carl G. Hempel, *Philosophy of Science*. A detailed sophisticated articulation and defense of this view is developed by Ernest Nagel, *The Structure of Science*.

77. P. K. Feyerabend, "Reply to Criticism," *Boston Studies in the Philosophy of Science*, Vol. 2, pp. 223–224. Thomas Kuhn has developed a similar theory of the nature of scientific revolutions in *The Structure of Scientific Revolutions*. Despite the antipathy of many contemporary philosophers and historians of science to Hegel, the central theme that science develops by the clash and conflict of incompatible theories bears a strong resemblance

The epistemological kernel of Feyerabend's position which enables him to draw these conclusions is his attack on two principles which lie at the heart of the accepted theory of explanation. These are (1) the consistency condition: "Only such theories are . . . admissible in a given domain which either *contain* the theories already used in this domain, or which are at least *consistent* with them inside the domain"; (2) the condition of meaning invariance: "Meanings will have to be invariant with respect to scientific progress; that is, all future theories will have to be framed in such a manner that their use in explanations does not affect what is said by the theories, or factual reports to be explained."[78]

The two principles are intimately related and both, according to Feyerabend, are mistaken. If we closely examine the nature of scientific change we discover that the basic scientific theories such as Newton's and Einstein's are in fact inconsistent. Furthermore, this is not a defect; it is because Einsteinian relativity theory is inconsistent with Newtonian mechanics that we can displace Newtonian mechanics. Einstein's theory is not a better theory for explaining the same set of observations. What counts as an observation, description, or fact has also changed. Feyerabend is not maintaining that inconsistency is a *sufficient* condition for displacing one theory by another and thereby "advancing" scientific criteria. But he does maintain that it is a *necessary* condition characteristic of major advances in scientific explanation. Feyerabend sums up his argument against the condition of meaning invariance in the following way:

Our argument against meaning invariance is simple and clear. It proceeds from the fact that usually some of the principles involved in the determination of the meaning of older theories or points of view are inconsistent with the new, and better, theories. It points out that it is natural to resolve this contradiction by eliminating the troublesome and unsatisfactory older principles and to replace them by principles, or theorems, of the new and better theory. And it concludes by showing

---

to Hegel's own analysis of the *dialectical* development of theories. Feyerabend acknowledges and explores this similarity in his essay "Against Method," *Minnesota Studies in the Philosophy of Science,* Vol. IV, ed. by Michael Radner and Stephen Winokur.

78. "Problems of Empiricism," *Beyond the Edge of Certainty,* p. 164.

that such a procedure will also lead to the elimination of the old meanings and thereby to the violation of meaning invariance.[79]

Even such straightforward descriptions as "This liquid has a temperature of 50°C" will have a different meaning when stated by a theorist of classical mechanics and when stated by a theorist of statistical mechanics. Furthermore, these different meanings are, strictly speaking, incompatible because the theoretical considerations that enter into the definition of the meaning of temperature in these two theories are incompatible. A statement like "This liquid has a temperature of 50°C" is not a neutral observation statement independent of the two theories.

There is and ought to be the perpetual conflict of inconsistent and incompatible theories.[80] We will adopt one theory as a better theory for a variety of complex reasons, but the classical reason, viz., that the better theory is one that better explains the same set of observations that the older theory explains is not a good reason because we cannot attach any sense to the expression the "same set of observations."

But how, one may ask, are these claims and the disputes that have arisen among philosophers of science related to the concept of action? "Inconsistency," "incompatibility," and "conflict," are not pejorative terms, but the terms that signal genuine advance in inquiry. When confronted with a well-established theory or way of thinking or speaking, our task is to invent new theories and ways of speaking that are "factually adequate" and incompatible with existing modes. Feyerabend applies these considerations directly to ordinary language analysis or conceptual analysis. To labor the point, as Feyerabend thinks conceptual analysts have, that our ordinary ways of speaking are incompatible with our scientific modes of discourse does show the nonreducibility of our ordinary ways of speaking, but this has *no* bearing on the truth or correctness of ordinary language. Reducibility or nonreducibility isn't the essential issue (for neither is caloric theory reducible to kinetic theory);

79. "Explanation, Reduction, and Empiricism," *Minnesota Studies in the Philosophy of Science,* Vol. 3, p. 82.

80. Feyerabend thinks this condition ought to prevail not only in scientific inquiry, but in all aspects of life. See his discussion of the role of the modern theater. "The Theater as an Instrument of the Criticism of Ideologies," *Inquiry* 10 (1967).

it is rather whether we can replace our ordinary ways of speaking with better ways of explaining and describing. Disputes between reductionists and nonreductionists have centered about the possibility and acceptability of various forms of translation of expressions from one framework into terms of another framework. But, according to Feyerabend, this has been a fruitless and perverse enterprise, based on false methodological and epistemological views. There are *no* good reasons to think that we cannot come up with a radical alternative to our ordinary language which will provide us with a better way of understanding and explaining ourselves, our "actions," "intentions," "reasons." And we can be sure that even if these words are preserved in the new theory, they will have a radically different meaning. In short, for Feyerabend, our ordinary language is nothing but a bad theory, one which he thinks is empirically inadequate. He defends the possibility and the necessity of developing alternative theories to the conventional ways in which we think and speak about ourselves and the world. Speaking of our "common idioms," Feyerabend says that

such idioms are adapted not to *facts,* but to *beliefs.* If these beliefs are widely accepted; if they are intimately connected with the fears and hopes of the community in which they occur; if they are defended, and reinforced with the help of powerful institutions; if one's whole life is somehow carried out in accordance with them—then the language representing them will be regarded as most successful. At the same time it is clear that the question of the truth of the beliefs has not been touched.[81]

Or expressing his views on the status of linguistic arguments, Feyerabend says:

For if my belief is correct, and if it is indeed possible to develop a "materialistic" theory of human beings, then we shall of course be forced to abandon the "mental" connotations of the mental terms, and we shall have to replace them by physical connotations. According to the point of view which I am defending in the present paper, the only legitimate way of criticizing such a procedure would be to criticize this new materialistic theory by either showing that it is not in agreement with the experimental findings or pointing out that it possesses some undesirable formal features (for example, by pointing out that it is *ad hoc*).

81. "Materialism and the Mind-Body Problem," *The Review of Metaphysics,* 17 (1963), 51–52.

Linguistic counter arguments have, I hope, been shown to be completely irrelevant.[82]

The relevance of the displacement hypothesis to the conceptual analysis of action should now be clear. If Feyerabend is right, then even if the strongest claims of conceptual analysts are accepted, these analysts are nevertheless still basically mistaken. It may be true that the concept of action and related concepts are fundamental to the ways in which we now think about ourselves and others. It may be true that these concepts *have been* so fundamental to our ordinary ways of thinking that they have not significantly changed in the recorded history of mankind. It may be true that the "logic" of our action talk is incompatible with existing or even imagined scientific discourse. It may be that the conceptual analysts are right in their claims that it is impossible to translate or reduce action concepts to a language restricted to the mechanical regularities of movements. But even if all this were true, even if we conceded the most ambitious claims of the philosophical psychologists, we would have an analysis only of idioms that are "adapted not to *facts,* but to *beliefs.*" There is nothing in the program of conceptual analysis that can rule out the real possibility that we might come up with a radically incompatible theory which would replace our present ways of speaking and thinking. For Feyerabend, if our aim is to advance inquiry and our knowledge of man, then we ought to develop radical alternatives.

Feyerabend has been severely criticized on a number of points, especially his challenge to "meaning invariance." To make his thesis stick, Feyerabend needs to develop a theory of meaning which indicates the criteria for sameness of meaning and difference of meaning. Although there are hints and suggestions, he certainly hasn't provided a successful analysis. Furthermore, critics have noted some of the paradoxical consequences that follow from his position. If the meaning of basic concepts in different theories is as different as he says, then it is difficult to see what sense can be given to the claim that the theories are inconsistent or incompatible.[83] Putnam

82. "Explanation, Reduction, and Empiricism," *Minnesota Studies in the Philosophy of Science,* Vol. 3, p. 91.

83. For detailed criticisms of Feyerabend's views, see Peter Achinstein, "On the Meaning of Scientific Terms," *Journal of Philosophy* 61 (1964),

points out that Feyerabend's strategy is "to minimize and deny the extent to which science is the *cumulative* acquisition of knowledge about Nature, in order to enhance the plausibility of his own curious view, which is that the best we can hope for (indeed, all it makes sense to hope for) is to arrive, not at correct explanations of phenomena, but alternative explanations by means of false theories."[84] Even sympathetic admirers such as Smart have wondered if Feyerabend's differences with the classical picture of scientific explanation are as dramatic and extreme as he suggests. If we understand Nagel's depiction of the relation of older theories to newer better theories as one where the "approximate correctness of the old theory must be deducible from the new one,"[85] then many of Feyerabend's objections turn out to be beside the point.

But despite many weaknesses in Feyerabend's position, I do think that there is one point that is very important and effective. For Feyerabend challenges the deep a priori bias of many ordinary language philosophers. He warns against easy and glib claims that something is a conceptual truth, or an a priori necessary truth. No matter how basic, useful, and practical many of our present ways of speaking are, no matter how inconceivable it may seem that there could be significant changes and revisions, one can't produce any good reasons a priori for ruling out change and alteration which can be influenced by further empirical research. In this respect he challenges the dichotomy between conceptual analysis and empirical inquiry which lies at the heart of so much recent linguistic philosophy.

We need not deny that there is a distinction to be made between conceptual analysis and empirical inquiry, but we are on the very

---

Concepts of Science, Chapters 3 and 4; Dudley Shapere, "Meaning and Scientific Change," *Mind and Cosmos;* Hilary Putnam, "How Not to Talk About Meaning," *Boston Studies in the Philosophy of Science,* Vol. 2; See also Paul K. Feyerabend's replies, "On the 'Meaning' of Scientific Terms," *Journal of Philosophy* 61 (1964); "Reply to Criticism," *Boston Studies in the Philosophy of Science,* Vol. 2.

84. "How Not to Talk About Meaning," *Boston Studies in the Philosophy of Science,* Vol. 2, p. 207.

85. "Conflicting Views about Explanation," *Boston Studies in the Philosophy of Science,* Vol. 2, pp. 161 ff.

brink of misunderstanding when we reify this distinction into a hard-and-fast dichotomy. There has been a misguided tendency in recent linguistic philosophy to do this, to stop further investigation by declaring that we have arrived at a "conceptual truth" or to rule out claims by labeling them as conceptual confusions or category mistakes. This is an example of what Peirce spoke of as blocking the road of inquiry. And I do think that the displacement theorists have been successful in exposing this tendency to resolve complex issues once and for all by (faulty) a priori claims. As Rorty says, it is not statements that are confused but people. The deviance of an expression from our commonly accepted ways of speaking is never sufficient to condemn the deviant expression as meaningless or a category mistake. Further, no matter how we are struck by differences in kind in our different conceptual schemes, every difference in kind "is always capable of being softened into a difference of degree by further empirical inquiry."[86] All of this should serve as a warning to linguistic philosophers that they should not "think that they can do better what metaphysicians did badly—namely, prove the irreducibility of entities."[87] We might add that conceptual analysts, especially those interested in philosophical psychology, are fooling themselves if they think that they can progress far in understanding what man is, what it is to have intentions, emotions, moods, etc. unless their subtle conceptual distinctions are significantly related to empirical psychological investigations.

In *this* respect, the upshot of our discussion of the displacement hypothesis harmonizes with the conclusions reached in an independent way by Charles Taylor. Throughout our discussion of the status of action in analytic philosophy, I have argued against the possibility of resolving the issue of just what sort of creature man is by any a priori argument. I have attempted to expose the aprioristic bias of both reductionists and conceptual analysts. Although Charles Taylor does argue that teleological explanation and mechanistic explanation are rival types of explanation and that the concept of action is not reducible to the concept of movement, these conceptual dichotomies do not settle the issue of what is or will be the proper

86. "Mind-Body Identity, Privacy, and Categories," *The Review of Metaphysics* 19 (1965), 51.
87. "Mind-Body Identity, Privacy, and Categories," p. 54.

concepts and explanations pertaining to human behavior.[88] But there is one crucial point where Taylor lapses into the type of thinking he is exposing. It is worthwhile to focus on this point because it provides a hint for evaluating the claims and counter claims of reductionists and nonreductionists and for gaining some perspective of the contribution of analytic philosophy to our understanding of human action.

After arguing that a teleological concept of action is basic to our ordinary ways of thinking and speaking, Charles Taylor asks whether this means that a nonteleological explanation of human behavior is impossible. For many philosophical psychologists, demonstrating that such a concept is basic to our ordinary ways of thinking and speaking is *sufficient* to answer the question affirmatively: it is impossible to give a nonteleological explanation of human behavior. But Charles Taylor argues that drawing such a conclusion is too hasty. "The fact that a distinction is made and agreed on does not show that it has been properly understood, that the criteria on which it is putatively made are valid."[89] We must distinguish the fact that we do make fundamental distinctions from the ways in which we characterize these distinctions. "If a systematic nonteleological explanation is correct, then we shall be shown to have mischaracterized the distinction between action and non-action. It will not hang on the role of intention as we now understand it, but rather on laws by

88. To appreciate Charles Taylor's subtle position it is important to distinguish two different *types* of issues. The first concerns the compatibility and/or reducibility of teleological and mechanistic explanations. Charles Taylor argues that these are ultimately "rival" forms of explanation. The second concerns the *conceivability* of displacing teleological explanations of human behavior by mechanistic explanations. Charles Taylor argues that such a displacement is conceivable. Such a displacement would involve a conceptual and an empirical revision of our present conceptual framework. Taylor has been criticized on both counts. See Denis Noble, "Charles Taylor on Teleological Explanation," *Analysis* 27 (1967); Joseph Margolis, "Taylor on the Reduction of Teleological Laws," and Taylor's reply, *Inquiry* 11 (1968); Judith J. Thomson's comments on Taylor's "Relations Between Cause and Action," *Proceedings of the Seventh Inter-American Congress of Philosophy*. On the issue of the conceivability of mechanism, see Norman Malcolm, "Explaining Behavior," *The Philosophical Review* 76 (1967), and "Conceivability of Mechanism," *The Philosophical Review* 77 (1968).

89. *Explanation of Behaviour,* p. 46.

which different sorts of behavior are explained."[90] The analogy that Charles Taylor uses to illustrate his meaning is the Aristotelian distinction between natural and violent movement.

Thus we can all understand the Aristotelian distinction between 'natural' and 'violent' movement, and will all admit that the things distinguished here really do fall into different categories, but this does not mean that we can accept the criteria on which it was putatively made, can accept that it is really the 'natural' and the 'violent' that are being distinguished. What happened here is that a distinction was in fact made on certain criteria which were wrongly characterized, and the wrong characterization was linked with certain very deeply rooted features of the conceptual scheme of the day.[91]

Taylor suggests that this is what someday may happen to our distinction between action and nonaction. It is not that we will discover that there is no distinction where we now think there is a basic distinction, but rather the criteria for making this distinction and the significance that we now attach to it may alter drastically. Consequently, it is possible that one day we may discover that our behavior may be accounted for by a mechanistic theory despite the present serious failure of all mechanistic theories to do so. Even if this turns out to be the case, it does not mean that "we may one day find that we have been talking nonsense all our lives."[92] However, Charles Taylor obscures an equally paradoxical consequence of his analysis. For although we may not discover that we have been talking nonsense all our lives, we would discover that we have been making false claims all our lives. This is entailed by his own analysis. Taylor claims to have shown that the teleological concept of action is basic to our ordinary ways of thinking, and furthermore, that the type of descriptions and explanations that we give for actions are not translatable or reducible to a mechanistic framework. To entertain seriously the possibility that we might some day be able to explain human behavior in mechanistic terms (which, Taylor argues rivals teleological explanation) means that we might discover that our present concept of action and intention has *no* application. Or to put the point ontologically, we would discover that there are *no*

90. *Explanation of Behaviour*, p. 46.
91. *Explanation of Behaviour*, p. 46.
92. *Explanation of Behaviour*, p. 100.

actions (only complex movements). But if it is conceivable that we might discover that as a matter of fact there are no actions, then surely our present descriptions and explanations of actions in terms of intentions would be false. When we draw out the consequences of Charles Taylor's position in this way, we can see more clearly why conceptual analysts have boggled at the suggestion that we might some day abandon our present conceptual scheme in which action descriptions and explanations are so fundamental and adopt a mechanistic framework that is incompatible with present deeply embedded concepts and categories.[93]

I think we can give a more sympathetic reading of what Taylor *intends*—one which militates against the possibility that we might some day discover that all our claims about action are false.

Let us consider Sartre's theory of emotions against the background of the program of conceptual analysis. Although philosophical psychologists have been sharply critical of traditional empiricist and rationalist philosophies of mind, they nevertheless have accepted the basic distinction between suffering or experiencing something and doing something. Traditionally, passions have been understood as something that an individual suffers or experiences, not something that he chooses or something that he does. According to Sartre, this traditional dichotomy is mistaken and he argues that passions and emotions are indeed the results of choice, although not the results of voluntary deliberation. I am not concerned in this context with whether or not Sartre is right, but only with claiming that he *might* be right (which of course, requires a detailed specification of the meaning of choice and the cluster of concepts involved in clarifying what it means to choose and to act). To rule out Sartre's theory because we do not normally think of passions as chosen is to adopt a misguided attitude of linguistic conservatism in the face of a challenging alternative. One reason why we might want immediately to reject Sartre's theory is because of our recognition that there is a deep conceptual difference between the paradigm of passions and the paradigm of actions. Sartre is not denying this distinction, but arguing that the *criteria* that have been used to make this distinction are misguided. It is not the case that actions are chosen while passions are not. If his theory is to have any plausibility he can't explain

93. Cf. Norman Malcolm, "Conceivability of Mechanism," *Philosophical Review* 77 (1968).

away the phenomena of our conceptual distinctions; he must explain them. And this is what he certainly attempts to do.

The distinction between what we *now* call passions and actions is not denied; it is conceptually relocated. For Sartre, the distinction is not between something chosen and something not chosen, but a distinction of different *types* of choice. If Sartre's theory is correct or if a theory like Sartre's came to be accepted because of its explanatory value, then we would have a new way of characterizing a basic distinction that we now make.

I want to reiterate that I am not here defending the correctness of Sartre's theory. There are difficult issues which I do not think Sartre has satisfactorily confronted.[94] But I am defending the claim that whether or not we accept a theory like Sartre's will depend on its explanatory value and this is an issue that cannot be settled simply by ordinary language or conceptual analysis. What would we say if a Sartrean type theory came to be accepted? We *could* say that insofar as we previously characterized passion as something that passively happened to a person, we were uttering falsehoods. We *could* also say with Feyerabend that the meaning of "passion" in Sartre's theory and the meaning of "passion" in ordinary language are incompatible. But these would be misleading ways of characterizing what has happened. It is not that we would no longer distinguish between what we now call "passions" and "actions," but we would characterize this distinction in a different way.

The point of the above illustration is to emphasize a semantical feature concerning sameness and difference of meaning, and what is involved in a shift of meaning. The theory of meaning has been one of the main concerns of analytic philosophers and it certainly has been one of the most tangled and confused areas of investigation. We can all too easily fall into the trap of thinking that there are, or ought to be, fixed and clear-cut criteria that would enable us to say that an expression used in one context or conceptual scheme has the same or a different meaning from when it is used in another context (and in many specific instances there are such criteria). But it is an illusion to think that there always are criteria that enable us to distinguish sameness and difference of meaning. Much of the "shock" value of Feyerabend's position depends on the idea of meaning

94. For a critique of Sartre's theory of emotions, see Joseph P. Fell's *Emotion in the Thought of Sartre*, pp. 113 ff.

invariance which is a caricature of the way in which we (and the scientific community) speak about sameness and difference of the meaning of our fundamental concepts. We need to be reminded again of a point that Wittgenstein makes so effectively in his *Philosophical Investigations* when he shows us that there are cases in which we can change the criteria used in employing an expression (and even adopt new criteria which are incompatible with the criteria formerly employed) and yet we will continue to say that we are using the same expression. Sometimes what is called for is a decision where we could say that we are still using the same expression or that we have a new and different expression.

This semantical point about the sameness and difference of meaning has important consequences for understanding the concept of action when we realize that it is precisely new empirical discoveries or theoretical advances that can provide the warrant for changing the criteria concerning our language of action. As Rorty says in a statement that we have already cited, every difference in kind "is always capable of being softened into a difference of degree by further empirical inquiry."

Displacement theorists sometimes write as if we might someday wake up and discover that there are no "actions," "reasons," "intentions," "sensations," etc., or that the statements that we have been making when we use these concepts all turn out to be false. When the issue is put this way, it strikes us as quite fanciful and absurd. But when we carefully analyze what they mean in suggesting such claims, we discover that they are making a much more modest but a no less important point. There is no a priori reason to think that it is impossible to change the criteria for the employment of these central expressions, or even to give up some of them as no longer perspicuous. But any "new" theory or conceptual scheme that is offered as a serious candidate for replacement must be able to give a satisfactory answer to questions like, "Well, what was I talking about when I said that I did x for the following reasons?" And, furthermore, we must be able to give "good reasons" why this new way of speaking is better, more adequate, or more perspicuous.

We can now evaluate the issue between conceptual analysts and advocates of the displacement hypothesis. Conceptual analysts have performed an important function in calling our attention to and describing the subtle sorts of distinctions that we make and the concepts that we use in describing and explaining human actions. To the extent that we are more self-conscious of the nature of the concepts that we use, to that extent we are in a better position to understand these concepts and the type of creature who uses them. Conceptual analysts have also exposed the inadequacies of simplistic reductivist analyses of our langauge of action. I have been most critical of conceptual analysts insofar as they have been too ready to jump to unwarranted conclusions about conceptual, a priori, necessary truths. In this respect, advocates of the displacement hypothesis have played an extremely important role. It is just this tendency that they have vehemently attacked. They have reminded us of a tendency which is as old as philosophy itself, to mistake some important or fundamental distinction for being an a priori, categorical, or ontological dichotomy. Champions of the displacement hypothesis (at their best) are not condemning conceptual analysis but providing us with a perspective for evaluating the program of the conceptual analysis of action. It is an important task, one which is necessary but not *sufficient* to tell us the way things are, and in particular, what man really is. In the process of doing this, advocates of the displacement hypothesis have frequently, especially in the case of Feyerabend, overstated their case, or stated it in a misleading way. In part this is due to a faulty theory of "meaning invariance" and "change of meaning." If we characterize sameness of meaning in such a way that if there is *any* change of meaning of concepts owing to new theories and empirical discoveries, we are forced to say that we are no longer dealing with the same concepts, we are faced with all sorts of odd paradoxes. Feyerabend and even Taylor are misleading in suggesting that someday we might discover that we never really performed an action, or did anything intentionally, or ever did something because we had good reason for doing it. As our example from Sartre illustrates, this is a dramatic and misleading way of making the correct point that deeply embedded conceptual distinctions may be relocated and modified in light of the challenge of new theories and discoveries.

There is an important lesson to be learned (again) from the pragmatists with their emphasis on inquiry as a self-corrective rational process, their insistence on fallibilism, and their general suspicion of ontological, epistemological, and even linguistic dichotomies. Ever since the rise of modern science there have been philosophers who

have attempted—once and for all—sharply to demarcate philosophy
from the scientific disciplines. In our own time this was reflected
first in the sharp dichotomy between analytic propositions and
empirical propositions. Despite the criticism of logical positivism by
conceptual analysts, they too have been guilty of the same type of
tendency in their attempts sharply to demarcate conceptual analysis
from empirical analysis. In part, this tendency is a reaction against
scientism, where it is proclaimed that "finally" the issues that have
preoccupied philosophers can now be solved by empirical science.
The lesson that we should have learned, a lesson that stands in the
foreground of the pragmatic contribution to philosophic inquiry, is
that we can recognize differences without falling into the trap of
reifying dichotomies and that the relation of philosophy and science
is and ought to be dialectical. Without falling prey to scientism we
can recognize that there is no philosophic claim that cannot be
altered, modified, or softened in light of further scientific investigation. This doesn't mean that philosophy must wait upon the developments of science, for it has the perennially important task of clarifying what we know and what we do not know, of articulating the
present landscape of human knowledge and providing us with a way
of "knowing our way about." This has significant consequences for
the study of human action. We do as a result of the detailed work
of conceptual analysts have a much better idea of what is involved
in the description and explanation of human action, but we should
also be sensitive to how much we do not understand about ourselves
as agents and how much can be contributed to our understanding by
further scientific investigation as well as by alternative philosophic
approaches to the clarification of the nature, role, and context of
human action.

Some Open Questions

The argument developed in Part IV has been sufficiently complex
that it may be helpful to summarize some of its main stages. We began by delineating the reductionist paradigm that pervaded so much
of early analytic philosophy. Not only did these philosophers believe
that some form of reductive analysis was *the* proper philosophic
method, they shared a strong a priori bias that, *in principle,* the

language of action—or what was sound, legitimate, and meaningful in this language—could be reduced to a more primitive language. The concept of action was not an important philosophic problem because they were convinced it would "yield" to reductive analysis. There was no serious attempt to "look and see" if such a reduction could be performed; rather, they "knew" that such a reduction *must* be possible.

We then considered the dialectical reaction to this early position and sketched the metaphilosophical doubts that arose concerning the possibility, necessity, and perspicacity of reductive analysis. The challenge to reductive analysis went hand-in-hand with the increasing interest in the concept of action (and related concepts). The logical grammar of these concepts suggested a linguistic stratum that could not be reduced or translated into a more primitive atomistic and mechanistic language. Although issues were explored primarily in terms of language, some very important metaphysical issues were lurking in the background. If the strong claims of the conceptual analysts were correct concerning the nonreducibility and centrality of our language of action, then it would seem that we have convincing a priori reasons to assert that man is not just a complex physical mechanism, but rather a being capable of a whole range of activity that could not be adequately described and explained in the language of the physical sciences.

While conceptual analysts made us sensitive to the shortcomings of reductive analysis and exposed the "falsity" of their sham reductions, they were also guilty of reifying distinctions into "a priori necessary truths." They too sought (unsuccessfully) to resolve complex issues concerning the nature and status of action by a priori fiat.

The a priorism of conceptual analysis has been attacked in two different ways. First, every one of the major conceptual or "logical" dichotomies that conceptual analysts claimed to have discovered has been severely criticized. The result of this critical endeavor has been to soften these dichotomies, and to reveal that the distinctions we make are more complex, subtle, and indefinite than were originally claimed. Consequently, many of the grandiloquent transcendental conclusions that were originally made by conceptual analysts on the basis of their meager linguistic analyses have been deflated.

The second line of attack on conceptual analysts has come from advocates of the displacement hypothesis. Feyerabend seems to be saying concerning reductive analysis and conceptual analysis—a plague on both your houses. Both approaches are faulty and mis-guided. If we wish to advance philosophic and scientific inquiry, then we are under the constant obligation to come up with new, radical, incompatible theories that challenge and can displace exist-ing theories. But, in the hands of a much more subtle dialectician like Wilfrid Sellars, we can see how the displacement hypothesis represents a self-conscious dialectical attempt—one which is very Hegelian in spirit—to incorporate what he takes to be the "truth" implicit in these antithetical approaches and to reject what is false in them.[95] Conceptual analysts must be given their just due for the illumination they have provided in revealing the complexity, dis-tinctiveness, and logical character of the ways in which man con-ceives of himself, and in particular in illuminating the centrality of the concept of a person who is capable of intentional action. They are also right in showing that the language of the manifest image of man in the world is not reducible to a language that does not reflect the distinctive features of the manifest image. But Sellars goes on to argue, they have been hasty in drawing unwarranted ontological conclusions from their linguistic analyses. They have described the appearances that must be "saved" in any adequate account of man in the world. But they have failed to realize that it is possible to raise critical questions about the *entire* manifest image and to argue that it may be replaced by a more adequate scientific image of the world. It is here that Sellars thinks that the reductive analysts had a genuine insight. For they—especially Wittgenstein of the *Tractatus*—had a grasp on the formal structure of what such an ideal language might look like. Their mistake, according to Sellars, was to think that we must first begin by constructing or reconstructing such a perspicuous language. This is not the beginning of philosophy, but the end of philosophy, the goal toward which it is striving. Sellars is particu-larly sensitive to the need not just to assert the possibility of displace-

95. Sellars is one of the few analytic philosophers who has had profound grasp of the history of philosophy and has used his appreciation for the philosophic tradition in his creative philosophizing. In particular, Sellars is aware of the similarity of his dialectical approach to the Hegelian conception of dialectic. See my study of his philosophy, "Sellars' Vision of Man-in-the-Universe," *The Review of Metaphysics* 20 (1966).

ment, but to sketch in detail what such a synoptic view of man in the world would be like. A comprehensive synoptic scheme must be able to account for just those features of the manifest image that we take to be essential and distinctive. One of the most central features is that we conceive of ourselves as persons capable of intentional action.

When we put the issues in this perspective, then some of the "shock value" of the displacement hypothesis is dissipated. What first looked like extreme claims that we might someday discover that we never have performed an action—and especially an intentional action—because there are no such "entities," turns out to have a very different import. Not only are philosophers under an obligation to come to a clearer and firmer understanding of the manifest image and the nature and status of action and persons who perform such actions, they must be constantly open to the novel and unexpected ways in which further empirical inquiry can and will alter our understanding of the status of the manifest image.

But where does this leave us? I suggested at the beginning of this part that only now has the rapproachment between analytic investigations and Hegelian concerns become a real possibility. I can now explain what I meant. In order to gain the clarity, rigor, and precision that analytic philosophers have valued so highly, they have imposed severe limitations on what is and is not the proper business of philosophy and philosophic analysis. This is no less true for conceptual analysts than it has been for reductive analysts. In the early stages of both these developments there was a strong conviction that methods and techniques had been developed which would soon put an end to philosophy by resolving or dissolving all philosophic puzzles. There are very few voices today who would subscribe to these ambitious claims. On the contrary, the dialectic of analytic philosophy itself has brought us to a renewed sense of the complexity and variety of philosophic issues that need to be confronted. Concerning the concept of action, we are becoming aware of how inadequate our grasp is of the complexity of this concept and its interrelationships with other concepts. But even more important, we are becoming aware of questions that must be raised which analytic philosophers have scarcely begun to ask. Many different lines of inquiry in analytic philosophy have brought us to an appreciation of how deeply man's language and action is embedded in and conditioned by social practices and institutions. We cannot even begin to make sense of what we mean by action unless we consider how specific instances of actions are embodied in the social practices and institutions that shape our lives. This has not only been a central motif in recent analytic philosophy, it is central to Hegel, Marx, and the pragmatists. But in the past, analytic philosophers have not pressed their inquiries concerning the social context of action and practice. They have not paid much attention to the dynamics of social change and to the factors that shape those practices and institutions which are the medium of our lives. Nor have they paid much attention to the critical question of what ought to be the direction of social change. The biases which once existed against considering such issues as legitimate philosophic questions no longer carry much conviction. There are some signs that philosophers trained in analytic techniques are beginning to raise such questions and to see how important they are for confronting issues that have been central to a number of disputes within analytic philosophy itself. In short, some younger analytic philosophers are bringing to their investigation a sense of history, development, and social change that has too frequently been lacking in analytic work.[96] It is too early to tell whether this is only a passing interest or the beginnings of a new direction in analytic philosophy. If this direction is pursued (and I believe that it ought to be), then analytic philosophers may rediscover how much they can learn from the Hegelian and post-Hegelian tradition which they have so long considered to be anathema.

We may recall that in the early days of analytic philosophy Carnap

96. Two recent articles may be singled out as illustrating this new perspective: Alison Knox, "The Polemics of 'Descriptive Meaning,'" *The Review of Metaphysics* 24 (1971); and, Amelie Rorty, "Naturalism and the Ideology of Paradigmatic Moral Disagreements," *The Review of Metaphysics* 24 (1971). Both of these articles are concerned with disputes in analytic discussions of ethics. But both attempt to show how a sensitivity to the dynamics of social change can alter our understanding and evaluation of issues in analytic philosophy that bear on the concept of action. As indicated previously, Jürgen Habermas is a young German philosopher from the "Frankfurt School" of critical theory who has become increasingly concerned with analytic philosophy. The confrontation that he is encouraging between German thought and analytic philosophy is one that brings into focus problems of social change and historical development that have been so central to the Hegelian and post-Hegelian tradition. See the Bibliography for Habermas' works.

spoke of the "new" orientation as one "which acknowledges the bonds that tie men together, but at the same time strives for free development of the individual."[97] This theme has not been a central concern of analytic philosophy, but perhaps the ground has been prepared and the time is ripe for this to become a dominant theme in the analytic inquiry into human action.

97. *Aufbau*, p. 5.

EPILOGUE

IN APPROACHING THE END of this inquiry, I have arrived only at a beginning. My primary concern has been to present fair, sympathetic, although critical interpretations of each of the four positions discussed: Marxism, existentialism, pragmatism, and analytic philosophy. In each case I sought to "enter" into the distinctive perspective and to be true to the insight and idiom characteristic of these different approaches. I have argued that the concepts of *praxis* and action are central to these positions and I have attempted to explore how they became dominant, what problems they were intended to resolve, what aspects have been emphasized, and what each approach contributes to the ongoing inquiry into human activity.

I warned the reader at the outset that it would be naive to think that there is some easy or eclectic synthesis of the variety of views examined, and I hope that there is now an appreciation not only of similarities and resemblances, but also of sharp differences. It is my own conviction that our understanding of *praxis* and action is enhanced when we take each of these positions seriously and seek to meet the challenges presented by them. The time is ripe for philosophers to take off the blinders that have prevented them from learning from each other and to escape the provincialism that has cramped philosophizing in the recent past. I am acutely aware that this inquiry is a prolegomenon only to the job of critical encounter and synthesis that needs to be done. It is in this sense that I have arrived at a beginning. There is a new mood of openness and receptivity that is emerging on the philosophical scene. I believe that the spirit of critical appreciation which I have attempted to bring to this inquiry is shared by a growing number of younger philosophers—even though many may sharply disagree with some of my interpretations and conclusions. While recognizing that the work of systematic encounter and synthesis is a future project not only for myself but for the community of philosophers concerned with furthering our understanding of human activity, I want to review briefly what

I take to be the strengths and limitations of each of the four positions examined.

Unlike those who look upon Marxism as some sort of historical curiosity, or a nineteenth-century intellectual movement that is now "dead," I think that the Marxist perspective—especially concerning the significance and ramifications of *praxis*—is one of the most "alive" and powerful orientations of our time. And against those who do not think there is anything in Marxism that ought to be of concern to the serious philosopher, I think that Marxism is relevant to the most basic philosophic and practical issues of our time. Marxists and critics of Marx have paid a great deal of attention to Marx's specific understanding (and sometimes, misunderstanding) of the dynamics of capitalist society, his theory of class conflict, his expectations of the coming revolution and the role that the proletariat would play in this revolution, and the validity (or lack of validity) of Marx's supposed "predictions." These investigations are important. Marx constantly insisted that we must get to the "roots" and down to "hard facts," and his own theories and hypotheses must meet the rigorous tests that he set for others. But I do think that the smugness with which some defenders of Marx have insisted that he is right on all essential points (if only we understand him correctly) and the glibness with which some critics of Marx have dismissed him without any serious confrontation, can divert us from appreciating the core of Marx's thought, what I have called his "radical anthropology." Marx had a profound understanding of the ways in which men *are* what they *do,* of how their social *praxis* shapes and is shaped by the complex web of historical institutions and practices within which they function and work. Marx revealed to us and focused his attention on the "paradox" of human activity in its social forms. For it is man, or rather classes of men who constantly and continuously create and reinforce the social institutions that pervade human life. These are the objectifications of social *praxis*. And yet these institutions—especially when understood in terms of political economy—have the consequence not of freeing *praxis* and creating those conditions which allow for the enjoyment of free individuality, but of enslaving man, dehumanizing and alienating him. One reason why I believe that Marx is so alive and relevant today is that this "paradox" of alienation has not lessened in the past hundred years, it has become more poignant and subtle. We increasingly feel that there is almost a demonic logic in the development of technology itself, a "logic" that is misshaping man, increasing his alienation and his growing impotence in the face of what seem to be impersonal forces. Few thinkers have had Marx's profound understanding of how this changing political economy affects every dimension of human life—our political convictions, religious beliefs, ideology, and especially the way in which we treat other men. But Marx's fundamental conviction, from beginning to end, is that the situation in which we find ourselves is not ultimately an ontological or existential one from which there is no escape. It is an historical state of affairs, which while it has its "own necessity," is nevertheless the resultant of human activity and can be changed by revolutionary *praxis*. The more deeply we penetrate this situation, the more concretely and critically we understand the dynamics of our historical condition, the closer we can come to the real possibility of radical transformation. The reason why such critical understanding can be efficacious is because it speaks to man's deepest desires and needs—his search for liberation and emancipation where freedom becomes a concrete reality. I do not believe that Marx ever achieved the unity of theory and practice that is the dominant theme of his investigations. But no thinker has so vividly and dramatically held before us this challenge and goal.

At the heart of Marx's theorizing is a "radical anthropology" which seeks to overcome the dichotomies that have plagued modern thought and life: the dichotomies between the "ought" and the "is," the descriptive and the prescriptive, fact and value. These are not just artificial distinctions introduced by philosophers—they pervade and shape our lives. We are much more secure when we are dealing with the "facts," with what we can describe. We have an uneasy suspicion that when we turn to questions of value, whether they be personal or social, we are dealing with issues that are ultimately a matter of individual preference and bias. A dominant positivist orientation affects most of our intellectual life and has the consequence of making it difficult or impossible to deal with the vital issues of choice and action that we confront all the time.

Marx's "experiment" is a bold one. He clearly saw the disastrous social consequences that follow from such an attitude and how deeply it is rooted in social life. He attempted to bring a new perspective to the human condition. By analyzing the forms and roots of alienation and exploitation we could discover the real possibilities for transformation. We could resolve the "paradox" of social *praxis* by discovering the ways to create institutions that would no longer alienate us, but foster the rational, free, creative development of *individuals*. Marx himself was aware that thinking about man and society in this way where our end or *telos* is human emancipation affects every dimension of our understanding of what man is and can be. Marx, we might say, was articulating a new paradigm for describing, understanding, and eventually changing the quality of human life. It is a paradigm shaped by his understanding of the nature, dynamics, and consequences of human activity—*praxis*. I have indicated in my discussion of Marx that recognizing what Marx sought to achieve, grasping his essential project, is not yet to judge its success or lack of success. The viability of approaching all of human life from the perspective of social *praxis* is still an open issue demanding further development and specification. But I am convinced that at the root of the recent international concern with Marx and Marxism is the appeal of this paradigm in providing a perspective for comprehending and coming to grips with the conflicts and irrationalities of contemporary life.

It should be clear that I do not look upon Marxism as an ideology, dogma, secular religious creed, closed system, or final "science of man." I think that those who do are missing what is most vital to Marx himself, his commitment to constant critique. Rather, I understand Marxism as a basic orientation, as a way of asking new sorts of questions, as a set of insights that make us sensitive to conflicts and contradictions within existing society, and as posing for us deep and disturbing challenges. In saying this, it is the openness of Marxism that I want to emphasize and the demand, indeed the necessity of "going beyond" Marx himself.

At the same time that we appreciate what is still "alive" in a Marxist orientation, we must be scrupulously careful about its limitations. Although I have emphasized throughout that Marx himself was constantly engaging in self-criticism, this is not a characteristic that has always played a fundamental role in many of his followers and disciples. Orthodox Marxism has tended to become a closed system and an unquestioned dogma. What is lacking even in Marx himself is a firm understanding of what ought to be the norms of critical inquiry by which it can continually refine and correct itself.

Even Marx's conception of "science" bears the traces of a nineteenth-century conception of *"Wissenschaft"* which supposedly reveals the way things are with finality and necessity. It is this tendency in Marx's thought that can and has led to turning Marxism into a form of absolute dogmatism that has disastrous intellectual and political consequences.

Further, we know that Marx's end-in-view is a communist or humanist society in which the individual can truly enjoy his freedom and in which his *praxis* becomes an expression of this freedom rather than the process by which he alienates himself. We know too that Marx became increasingly skeptical and suspicious of any program or ideology that promised individual salvation without the radical transformation of social institutions and practices. But here too the delicate tension and balance that is so characteristic of Marx himself has not been maintained by many who consider themselves his followers. There is always the danger that we will lose sight of the end of "revolutionary praxis"—the creation of a society in which there is the full creative and rational development of human individuality. There is a danger too that in the name of human freedom, we betray this very freedom. These are not just "abstract" possibilities, they are what has happened in the history of our times by those who have cited Marx as their "authority." What is so attractive about Marxism is precisely what is so dangerous about it—its demand for totality. The relentless criticism of all existing institutions is not in the name of economic or political freedom, but total human emancipation in which there will be the historical creation of a new society and a new man. Marxism promises not just amelioration of obvious injustices, but the end of all social exploitation and alienation. Many commentators have remarked about the messianic and salvific themes that run through Marx's thought. We know that these must be qualified by Marx's tough-minded realism. But I don't think that it can be denied that the appeal and power of Marxism is because it speaks to what men so desperately want to believe. Marx fuses themes that have been basic to the entire tradition of Western civilization. Explicitly or implicitly, he tells us that the perennial dream and hope of Western man—that he will achieve freedom, that he will finally overcome the alienation and suffering that has plagued him, that he will achieve complete emancipation—is not only a real historical possibility, but one which is imminent. He tells us too that this emancipation will be achieved not by faith, but by scientific knowledge—a scientific knowledge that is no longer divorced from practice, but becomes the guide for *praxis*. This too has been one of man's most cherished hopes, that through knowledge freedom will be achieved. Marx is not only telling us that this is a viable ideal or norm, but that the proper understanding of the history of man reveals that this is the end or *telos* of history (or rather prehistory). It is no wonder that for many Marxism has become a faith, a doctrine to be followed by "true believers." But once we make this transition, once we believe that Marxism *must* be true because we *want* it to be true, we have turned Marxism into a secular faith that all too easily can be used to justify mass murder and human enslavement. We thereby turn Marxism into its dialectical opposite; it no longer serves as an orientation for guiding the free development of *praxis,* but a doctrine of repression. Marxism (at least the Marxism of Marx) must be thought of as a grand experiment, the attempt to develop a new perspective and orientation for understanding man, one that focuses on *praxis* as the key for this understanding. Conceived of in this manner, Marxism demands further development and critique. It is more valuable for the questions that it forces us to ask than for the "definitive" solutions it provides. It has already changed our conception of man as a human agent and its promise for furthering our understanding of *praxis* is not yet fulfilled or exhausted.

My attitude toward existentialism—especially the prominent place it assigns to individual freedom, choice, commitment, and action as inwardness or authenticity—is ambivalent. No other philosophic orientation has contributed as much to our understanding and appreciation of the fragility of human inwardness. Existential thinkers have been relentless and brilliant in unmasking the subtle ways in which we deceive ourselves, attempt to escape from our freedom, and seek some ground or foundation that lies "outside" of ourselves. In their phenomenological investigations of our internal life, they have revealed the forms of despair and anxiety that men experience. Much of the philosophy of mind and philosophical psychology of traditional philosophy pales in comparison to the richness of existential analysis. When we read Kierkegaard and Sartre, we feel that these men are speaking to us in ways which few other thinkers have done. They have captured for us the depth and significance of unhappy consciousness that is characteristic of so much contemporary life. They make us acutely and painfully aware of the freedom that we are and what it means to choose oneself. And they call upon us to act, to commit and engage ourselves with authenticity and passionate inwardness. At the core of existential reflection is always the plight of the human existing individual. Existentialists have appreciated how easy it is to lose sight of ourselves and how many contemporary intellectual and social forces tempt us to forget or smother the existing individual. We know that, "in principle" Hegelianism and Marxism are concerned with the full realization of the individual and that for both these orientations, there is an ultimate harmony and unity of the individual and the universal. But existentialists have been wary of this synthesis, and of how readily it can become a "lunatic postulate," or a form of bad faith. They have suggested and argued that although it is man's deepest desire to achieve the unity of the for-itself-in-itself, to achieve final fulfillment and wholeness, this is an impossible ideal. They have told us that man must have the courage and honesty to realize that this is the human situation. In the final analysis, we can count on no doctrine, faith, meaning, value that lies "outside" ourselves in making the decisions and choices of what we are to do and become. We are brought back to the realization that human freedom, action, and decisiveness have no ultimate foundation outside of ourselves.

I believe that the existentialists have had a deep insight into the many intellectual and social forces that can conspire against the self-consciousness of our own freedom and inwardness. In part, this is the basis of their indictment against traditional philosophy, and especially against the Hegelians. But they have been acutely aware of how the forms of social life, whether it be the church, the state, the party, or the class conspire to the same result. When Kierkegaard turns his polemic against the contemporary church and when Sartre attacks "orthodox" Marxists for reifying social categories, it is the uniqueness and autonomy of the existing individual that they are defending—an existing individual who can never be "mediated" or absorbed in a "higher synthesis." The forces and temptations leading us to forget what it means to be such an individual are becoming ever more widespread, pernicious, and pervasive as our advanced technological society continues its march of "progress." The temptation to forget what it means to be an existing individual is not only manifested by the champions and defenders of this "progress" but by many of those who consider themselves its archenemies. We are capable of creating a society in which there is no longer any passionate inwardness and authenticity, and the existentialists are profoundly aware of this possibility. In the end they stand as a *negation,* a refusal to countenance the reduction of man to the world of objects.

What I find so distressing about existentialism is the logic of its dialectic—the existential solipsism and nihilism that threatens it. This nihilism threatens to undermine precisely that which they have so dramatically sought to underscore. As I have already suggested, I believe that Kierkegaard saw this, and that this is the clue to understanding the morbidity, hopelessness, and black despair of his latest journal entries. And while Sartre has at times realized that this is where his early phenomenological ontology was leading him, he has desperately sought to avoid this "conclusion." For if nihilism is the "final chapter" of the existential dialectic, then it is pointless to think that authentic existence or passionate inwardness is any better, more valuable, or more desirable than a life of forgetfulness and bad faith. We may try to console ourselves with the thought that it is at least within our power to choose what we are to become, but this is rather hollow if all ultimate choices, decisions, and actions are without any foundation and justification.

I do not think that the nihilism that threatens to undermine existentialism is an "accidental" or "incidental" conclusion of the existential dialectic—a conclusion that can be conveniently avoided without altering the "essentials" of the existential perspective. It is traceable to the very "beginnings" of this dialectic. If, for example, we accept Sartre's ontological analysis of the "in itself" and the "for itself," then I fail to see how nihilism is escapable; it follows directly from this analysis. This is why we must return to "beginnings," something which Sartre claims to have done in his later writings, although I do not think he has ever really done this (or, at least, not done it successfully). I do think, however, that Sartre has displayed a shrewd insight in returning to Marx (and through Marx, to Hegel) in his attempt to escape from this impasse. For what is demanded is a rethinking and reappraisal of what it means to be a man, and specifically what is involved in human *praxis.* We need to incorporate the Hegelian and Marxist insight that there are historical ways in which the existing individual can be "mediated," that there are forms of alienation and exploitation that can be overcome. Marx, and especially Hegel saw that any dialectic of the existing individual that cuts him off from the social character of his individuality is doomed to failure. Human freedom (as Sartre himself has recently emphasized) makes no sense unless we grasp the concrete ways in which our own freedom is bound up with other men. The project of the later Sartre, to effect a synthesis between Marxism and existentialism, is an important one. My accusation is that Sartre has not been radical enough in the Marxist sense of getting to the "roots." He has failed to provide us with the "radical anthropology" which would successfully integrate the delicate balance between the forms and dynamics of social *praxis* and the individual freedom and activity that stands at the center of existential thought.

When we turn to the pragmatists, we are initially struck by the difference of mood, emphasis, and concern. There is nothing in Peirce or Dewey that is comparable to the emphasis on, and subtle analysis of, human inwardness. They were suspicious of the "subjectivist" bias that colors so much of existential thought, and which they claimed lies at the foundation of so much of modern philosophy. An appreciation of, and sensitivity to, the nature of scientific inquiry played a much greater role for them than it did for either Marx or the existentialists. But they were sharply critical of the understanding of the nature and significance of scientific inquiry provided by traditional philosophy. Not only did the advocates of rationalism and empiricism fail to understand the quintessence of scientific inquiry, this failure had crippling consequences for the metaphysical and epistemological doctrines of these positions. It was the "experimental spirit" of science that was prominent for the pragmatists, science as inquiry, as a perpetual, critical, and self-corrective process. The image of man that emerges from the pragmatic point of view is man as a craftsman, as an active manipulator advancing new hypotheses, actively testing them, always open to ongoing criticism, and reconstructing himself and his environment. Practice and activity informed by reason and intelligence became central to their vision of man in the universe, and like Hegel and Marx they appreciated the essential social nature of this practice and activity. We have seen in our discussion of the pragmatists that this new understanding of man demanded a rethinking of the entire range of philosophic problems—including the appeal to foundations and origins to secure our knowledge, the role of the "myth of the given," the analysis of perception, cognition, universals, and even the meaning of "reality" itself. Peirce was aware of the task of reconstruction that is required to develop a philosophic orientation that at once captures and reflects the "experimental habit of mind." The effect of this reconstruction, to which he dedicated his intellectual life, has been a revolution in our conception of what inquiry is and ought to be—one which is echoed and further developed in contemporary philosophy of science and analytic philosophy. The ideal of a critical community of inquirers has significant consequences for our understanding of human activity. If such a community is to be approximated, then it requires that we develop in ourselves and others those critical habits and modes of rational conduct by which we can advance concrete reasonableness. Taking the pragmatists seriously means purging ourselves of the quest for absolute certainty in our intellectual and moral lives. It means giving up absolutism or dogmatism in all of its crude and sophisticated forms. The alternative that the pragmatists present us with is not one of despair or skepticism. There is rather the clear imperative never to block the road to inquiry, to realize that any of our beliefs, no matter how cherished and fundamental they may seem to be, are open (and indeed require) further criticism. If we are to secure and warrant our knowledge claims, we do not do this by searching for absolute foundations or origins, but by cultivating those habits and forms of conduct that further the realization of the critical spirit. Dewey was particularly sensitive to the moral and social consequences of this new understanding of critical inquiry. If Peirce's ideal is not to remain just an ideal, but is to become actualized, then we must begin with reconstructing our social, and especially our educational institutions. People do not become effectively rational by being told to do so or by reading books alone. All social institutions have educational consequences, whether for better or worse. There is no point in paying "lip service" to the ideal of critical intelligence if this is not a living reality in men's lives. For Dewey, what we have learned about critical inquiry is not morally or socially neutral. It demands the creation of a community in which there are shared values of openness and fairness, the courage and willingness to change our minds in light of further criticism. It also demands the cultivation of imagination which is not bound by what has been but is able to project new hypotheses and alternatives, and the realization that it is only by mutual criticism that we can advance our knowledge and reconstruction of human experience so that it becomes funded with meaning, freer, and esthetically coherent.

I believe that the pragmatists present us with a badly needed corrective to the excesses that threaten both Marxism and existentialism. Marx called for constant and relentness critique. But I do not think that he always appreciated the norms of critical inquiry. If critique is not to degenerate into invective and dogmatism (as it has in the hands of some of his followers), then it requires that we take seriously what the pragmatists have been telling us. No position or point of view has an "exclusive" hold on the truth. Critique requires the openness and mutual criticism that is central to the pragmatic conception of a community of inquirers. I believe too, that if Marx had a deeper appreciation of this central theme, that if he had broken more radically than he had with a nineteenth-century German understanding of knowledge and science as revealing once and for all the nature of the way things are and their inner necessity, then he might have protected himself against some of the abuses and crimes committed in his name.

So too does an existentialist orientation need to be corrected by a healthy appreciation for what the pragmatists have been telling us. It is certainly true that the pragmatists have virtually ignored the inwardness which has always been the focal point of existential reflection. And it is also true that this insensitivity has resulted in neglecting a vital dimension of freedom, choice, and decisiveness. But the danger of existentialism is to retreat into a subjectivism that becomes solipsistic and nihilistic. No matter how much we emphasize human inwardness and the despair and anxiety that men suffer, this does not exhaust the richness of human activity. Man lives in a social and natural world, as even the existentialists have emphasized. But their primary attitude toward these dimensions of human life has been that they present man with a temptation and a threat—for he is constantly in danger of forgetting that he is an existing individual. They have failed to pay sufficient attention to the *opportunities* that man's natural and social environment present. If "freedom," "choice," and "action" are not to become empty abstractions; if we are to avoid falling into the trap where human individuality becomes devoid of any concrete determination, then an adequate account of human activity must incorporate the concrete social dimensions of practice and conduct that are so fundamental for the pragmatists.

Analytic philosophers have frequently prided themselves in bringing about the most dramatic revolution in the history of philosophy. "The linguistic turn" has been held out to us as the "final solution" to the problem of philosophic method. Once this turn has been taken, it is supposedly within our grasp to resolve or dissolve all "philosophic" problems and perplexities. But curiously, if one looks at this movement with historical perspective, it appears to be the most traditional and tradition-bound movement of the four positions we have examined. We have seen that Marxism, existentialism, and pragmatism have all attempted—in strikingly different ways—to "go beyond" Hegel. Each attempt focuses on human activity in this endeavor. But the end or *telos* of these movements has not been just a theoretical understanding of *praxis* and action, but rather a form of activity itself.

We can return to our own starting point. The end or *telos* of the practical disciplines or *praxis*, according to Aristotle, is not theoretical knowledge (although such knowledge is important for the practical disciplines). It is rather a distinctive type of activity. For Aristotle, ethics and politics are *not* metaethics or metapolitics, the *descriptive* study of how men conduct their moral and political lives and the types of reasoning they employ in arriving at moral and political positions. The *telos* of the practical disciplines is to change our forms of activity and to bring them into closer approximation to the full ideal of free human activity. However, for Aristotle, there is still a sharp distinction between the theoretical and the practical disciplines, and philosophy as the study of first principles is a theoretical not a practical discipline. Using Aristotle's paradigm of *praxis*, we can say that Marxism, existentialism, and pragmatism have, in radically different ways, attempted to extend this paradigm to the entire range of man's cognitive and practical life. It is not only Marx who thinks that the point of understanding is no longer just to "interpret" but to "change"; this basic orientation is shared by both existentialists and pragmatists. This, of course, does not diminish their differences concerning what is to be changed, how it is to be changed, and why change is so vital.

In the above sense, analytic philosophy does not represent an attempt to "go beyond" Hegel or to remake philosophy into "practical philosophy" which would, as Cieszkowski proclaimed in the 1840's, exercise "a direct influence on social life and developing the future in the realm of concrete activity." Ironically, despite the contempt and the low esteem that many analytic philosophers have for Hegel, they agree with Hegel that the primary object of philosophy is to describe and comprehend what is. Consequently, when analytic philosophers turned their attention to the study of human action, it was not with the primary end-in-view of changing human action, but rather of understanding the concept of action, the ways in which it is intimately linked with other concepts, and the ways in which it can be reduced or not reduced to other basic forms of discourse. I see no reason to denigrate this concern. I have argued that following the complex dialectic of analytic philosophy has brought us to a more perspicuous and subtle understanding of the status and ramifications of the concept of action. In a more careful and rigorous manner than has been performed by other movements in the history of philosophy, analytic philosophers have shown us the speciousness and fallaciousness of simplistic attempts to reduce the concept of action to a more basic atomistic and mechanistic framework. Conceptual analysts have shown us the deficiencies of traditional theories of mind in providing an adequate analysis and understanding of the concept of action (and its related concepts). They have exerted a therapeutic function in reminding us that in talking about actions, explaining them, justifying particular actions, we are operating in a linguistic stratum that has a distinctive "logical grammar." No philosophic theory or scientific theory can provide us with an adequate account of action if it ignores or is insensitive to the "logical grammar" of the concept of action. I have been critical of both reductive analysts and conceptual analysts for the apriorism that runs through these positions—for their attempts to resolve complex issues by a priori fiat. A penetrating examination of these approaches reveals that they have been guilty of the sin which they have accused traditional philosophy of committing—drawing unwarranted ontological and metaphysical conclusions from their linguistic analyses. This is why, despite the excesses of enthusiasts of the displacement hypothesis, I believe that they represent a healthy development in analytic philosophy. At their best,

they root out the easy road of "a priori" solutions to complex philosophic and human issues, and have brought to analytic philosophy
an appreciation of the pragmatic principle that any belief, category,
or conceptual scheme is subject to further revision and criticism
in the development of ongoing inquiry.

What I find most objectionable in the analytic movement is not
what analytic philosophers do—I have insisted upon its importance—but rather the *ideology* that has surrounded this movement.
In the early days of both reductive analysis and conceptual analysis,
there was an absolute conviction that for the "first time" philosophers had hit upon the right method and approach for dissolving or
resolving all philosophic problems. Both approaches held out the
promise that within a short time, the job of philosophy would be
finished and we would be "done" with our philosophizing. We have
already discovered how hollow these "promises" were. While it
would be difficult to find many such "enthusiasts" around, the
ideology lingers on and there are still many practicing analytic
philosophers who believe that their primary function is to clear up
the confusions and muddles of others. Presumably, when and if this
job is completed, there will be nothing more for philosophers to do.

Early advocates of analytic philosophy did maintain (as Carnap
did) that the "new" spirit and the "new" approach would have
dramatic consequences for the entire range of human activities.
To the extent that we became clearer about what we really know
and can know, and what is only pseudo-knowledge; what the boundaries are between the meaningful and the meaningless; what are clear
ways of talking and confused ways, then presumably we would be
able to live better lives uncluttered by superstitions and false beliefs.
But the fact is that this end-in-view has played an insignificant role
in the development of analytic philosophy. Analytic philosophy has
tended to become more professional, more technical, and more
remote from human concerns. Analytic philosophy is threatened by
a scholasticism in which philosophers will only be able to talk to
other philosophers trained in the same school. There are some who
are not afraid of this tendency and indeed praise this direction. It
may be that philosophy can contribute very little to our understanding of human life, but at least (so they claim) we will "finally" secure
real knowledge of what we can and cannot do in philosophy and

thereby escape the "amateurism" and false starts characteristic of so much of traditional philosophy.

Fortunately, there are counter tendencies. There are some analytic philosophers, like Wilfrid Sellars, who have the wisdom to realize that there is more in common between analytic philosophy and traditional philosophy than has been acknowledged by many analytic philosophers, and that indeed analytic philosophy still has a great deal to learn from this tradition. And further, that it is important to reaffirm in new ways the perennial attempt of philosophy to gain a synoptic vision of man in the universe. There are many analytic philosophers who are growing restless with the provincialism and exclusiveness that has been characteristic of so much analytic endeavor. They are beginning to realize that the dialectic of analytic philosophy itself, especially in the recent concern with action, is leading us to issues and problems that have not been seriously considered by analytic philosophers and that these issues and problems are closely related to those considered by the other philosophic movements we have examined. There are even signs that some younger analytic philosophers are becoming skeptical of the injunction that the exclusive job of the philosophy is to describe, and they think that perhaps philosophy, once again (informed by the care and sophistication of analytic techniques) can reaffirm the ideal of being a critical guide to the development of *praxis*. It is too early to tell whether these new tendencies are the signs of a new direction or only passing fashions. But I do believe that analytic philosophy is presently confronted with a crucial decision. It can kill itself under the weight of its own demand for ever-increasing technical mastery and its tendency to become scholastic in the pejorative sense of this term. But it can also be rejuvenated, and come alive in its confrontation with the ever-present "problems of men." It can extend its horizons and become a critical guide in the development of *praxis*.

Throughout this inquiry, I have struck a note of cautious optimism. I know that there are many—both within and without the field of philosophy—who despair of the philosophic endeavor and the current philosophic scene. They are overwhelmed by what strikes them as the chaos and the babble of voices in the philosophic "community." There are philosophers who themselves think that philosophy can no longer (if it ever did) offer anything vital to our comprehension of man and the directions to be taken in bringing about freer, more creative, and more humane individual and social activity. But I hope that this book, in some measure, shows that there is not sufficient cause for this despair. The perennial issues of philosophy have new and devious ways of reasserting themselves at times when they seem most moribund. The ancient and modern questions of what is the nature of man and his activity and what ought to be the directions pursued in this activity are once again being reaffirmed as primary issues for reflective men.

BIBLIOGRAPHY

Achinstein, Peter, *Concepts of Science*. Baltimore: The Johns Hopkins Press, 1968.

———, "On the Meaning of Scientific Terms," *Journal of Philosophy* 61 (September 17, 1964).

Allison, Henry, "Christianity and Nonsense," *The Review of Metaphysics* 19 (March 1966).

Alston, W. P., "Do Actions Have Causes?" *Proceedings of the Seventh Inter-American Congress of Philosophy*. Quebec: Les Presses de l'Université Laval, 1967.

———, "Wants, Actions, and Causal Explanation," *Intentionality, Minds, and Perception,* ed. by H. Castañeda. Detroit: Wayne State University Press, 1966.

Althusser, Louis, *For Marx*. New York: Vintage Books, 1969.

Anderson, Thomas C., "Is a Sartrean Ethics Possible?," *Philosophy Today* 14 (Summer 1970).

Anscombe, G. E. M., *Intention*. Oxford: Basil Blackwell, 1958.

Arendt, Hannah, *The Human Condition*. Chicago: University of Chicago Press, 1958.

Aristotle, *The Basic Works of Aristotle,* ed. by Richard McKeon. New York: Random House, 1941.

Austin, J. L., *Philosophical Papers,* ed. by J. O. Urmson and G. J. Warnock. London: Oxford University Press, 1961.

Avineri, Shlomo, "The Hegelian Origins of Marx's Political Thought," *The Review of Metaphysics* 21 (September 1967).

———, *The Social and Political Thought of Karl Marx*. Cambridge: Cambridge University Press, 1968.

Ayer, A. J., *Language, Truth and Logic*. New York: Dover Publications, 1946.

Barion, J., *Hegel und die marxistische Staatslehre*. Bonn: H. Bouvier, 1963.

Belkind, Allen J., *Jean-Paul Sartre in English*: A Bibliographical Guide. Kent, Ohio: The Kent State University Press, 1970.

Berlin, Isaiah, *Karl Marx*: *His Life and Environment,* 2nd edition. London: Oxford University Press, 1948.

Bernstein, Richard J., "Action, Conduct and Self-Control," *Perspectives on Peirce,* ed. by Richard J. Bernstein. New Haven, Conn.: Yale University Press, 1965.

————, *John Dewey*. New York: Washington Square Press, 1966.

————, "Peirce's Theory of Perception," *Studies in the Philosophy of Charles Sanders Peirce,* Second Series, ed. by E. C. Moore and R. S. Robin. Amherst: University of Massachusetts Press, 1964.

————, "Sellars' Vision of Man-in-the-Universe," *The Review of Metaphysics* 20 (September, December 1966).

Boler, John F., *Charles Peirce and Scholastic Realism.* Seattle: University of Washington Press, 1963.

————, "Habits of Thought," *Studies in the Philosophy of Charles Sanders Peirce,* Second Series, ed. by E. C. Moore and R. S. Robin. Amherst: University of Massachusetts Press, 1964.

Brandt, R., and Kim, J., "Wants as Explanations of Actions," *Journal of Philosophy* 60 (July 18, 1963).

Brazill, William J., *The Young Hegelians.* New Haven: Yale University Press, 1970.

Calvez, Jean-Yves, *La pensée de Karl Marx.* Paris: Editions du Seuil, 1956.

Care, Norman S., and Landesman, Charles (eds.), *Readings in the Theory of Action.* Bloomington: Indiana University Press, 1968.

Carnap, Rudolf, *Der Logische Aufbau der Welt,* trans. as *The Logical Structure of the World* by Rolf A. George. Berkeley and Los Angeles: University of California Press, 1967.

————, *The Logical Syntax of Language.* London: Kegan Paul Trench, Trubner & Co., 1937.

————, "Empiricism, Semantics, and Ontology," *Revue Internationale de Philosophie* 11 (1950). Reprinted in *The Linguistic Turn,* ed. by Richard Rorty. Chicago: University of Chicago Press, 1967.

Cavell, Stanley, "The Availability of Wittgenstein's Later Philosophy," *The Philosophical Review* 71 (January 1962).

Cieszkowski, A. V., *Prolegomena zur Historiosophie.* Berlin: Veit, 1838.

Contat, Michel and Rybalka, Michel, *Les escrits de Sartre.* Paris: Gallimard, 1970.

Cornu, Auguste, *Karl Marx, l'homme et l'oeuvre. De l'hegelianisme au materialisme historique.* Paris: F. Alcan, 1934.

————, *Karl Marx et Friedrich Engels: leur vie et leur oeuvre,* Vols. I-III. Paris: Presses universitaires de France, 1955–1962.

Davidson, Donald, "Action, Reasons, and Causes," *The Journal of Philosophy* 60 (November 7, 1963).

Desan, Wilfrid, *The Marxism of Jean-Paul Sartre.* New York: Doubleday, 1965.

Dewey, John, *Art as Experience.* New York: Minton, Balch & Co., 1934.

———, *Characters and Events*. New York: Henry Holt and Co., 1929.

———, *Construction and Criticism*. New York: Columbia University Press, 1930.

———, "Creative Democracy—The Task before Us," *Classic American Philosophers,* ed. by Max Fisch. New York: Appleton-Century-Crofts, 1951.

———, *Democracy and Education*. New York: The Macmillan Co., 1916.

———, "The Development of American Pragmatism," *Philosophy and Civilization*. New York: Minton, Balch & Co., 1931.

———, *Essays in Experimental Logic*. Chicago: University of Chicago Press, 1916.

———, *Experience and Nature,* 1st ed. Chicago: Open Court Publishing Co., 1926.

———, "Experience, Knowledge and Value: A Rejoinder," *The Philosophy of John Dewey,* ed. by Paul Arthur Schlipp. Evanston, Ill., and Chicago: Northwestern University Press, 1939.

———, *Freedom and Culture*. New York: G. P. Putnam's Sons, 1939.

———, "From Absolutism to Experimentalism," *John Dewey: On Experience, Nature and Freedom,* ed. by Richard J. Bernstein. New York: The Liberal Arts Press, 1960.

———, "The Founder of Pragmatism," *The New Republic* 81 (January 30, 1935).

———, "Individuality and Experience," *Journal of the Barnes Foundation* 2 (January 19, 1926).

———, Letter to Albert George Adam Balz, *Journal of Philosophy* 46 (May 26, 1949). Reprinted as "In Defense of the Theory of Inquiry," in *John Dewey: On Experience, Nature and Freedom,* ed. by Richard J. Bernstein. New York: The Liberal Arts Press, 1960.

———, *Logic: The Theory of Inquiry*. New York: Henry Holt and Co., 1938.

———, "The Logic of Judgments of Practise," *Journal of Philosophy* 12 (September 16, September 30, 1915).

———, "The Need for a Recovery of Philosophy," *Creative Intelligence: Essays in the Pragmatic Attitude,* reprinted in *John Dewey: On Experience, Nature and Freedom,* ed. by Richard J. Bernstein. New York: The Liberal Arts Press, 1960.

———, "Peirce's Theory of Linguistic Signs, Thought and Meaning," *Journal of Philosophy* 43 (February 14, 1946).

———, "Peirce's Theory of Quality," *Journal of Philosophy* 32 (December 19, 1935).

———, "Philosophies of Freedom," *Philosophy and Civilization*. New

York: Milton, Balch & Co., 1931.

————, "The Pragmatism of Peirce," *Journal of Philosophy* 21 (December 21, 1916).

————, "Qualitative Thought," *Philosophy and Civilization*. New York: Minton, Balch & Co., 1931.

————, *The Quest for Certainty*. New York: Minton, Balch & Co., 1929.

————, *Reconstruction in Philosophy*. New York: New American Library, 1950.

————, "The Reflex Arc Concept in Psychology," *Psychological Review* 3 (July 1896).

————, "The Relation of Science and Philosophy as the Basis of Education," *Problems of Men*. New York: Philosophical Library, 1946.

————, and Bentley, Arthur F., *Knowing and the Known*. Boston: The Beacon Press, 1949.

Dove, Kenley R., "Hegel's Phenomenological Method," *The Review of Metaphysics* 23 (June 1970).

Dupré, Louis K., *The Philosophical Foundations of Marxism*. New York: Harcourt, Brace and World, 1966.

Easton, Loyd D., *Hegel's First American Followers*. Athens, Ohio: Ohio University Press, 1967.

Edie, James, "William James and Phenomenology," *The Review of Metaphysics* 23 (March 1970).

Fell, Joseph P., III, *Emotion in the Thought of Sartre*. New York: Columbia University Press, 1966.

Feuerbach, Ludwig, *The Essence of Christianity*, trans. by George Eliot and with an introduction by Karl Barth. New York: Harper & Brothers, Harper Torchbooks, 1957.

Feyerabend, Paul K., "Against Method: Outline of an Anarchistic Theory of Knowledge," *Minnesota Studies in the Philosophy of Science*, Vol. 4, ed. by Michael Radner and Stephen Winokur. Minneapolis: University of Minnesota Press, 1970.

————, "Explanation, Reduction, and Empiricism," *Minnesota Studies in the Philosophy of Science*, Vol. 3, ed. by Herbert Feigl and Grover Maxwell. Minneapolis: University of Minnesota Press, 1962.

————, "Materialism and the Mind-Body Problem," *The Review of Metaphysics* 17 (September 1963).

————, "On the 'Meaning' of Scientific Terms," *Journal of Philosophy* 62 (December 16, 1964).

————, "Problems of Empiricism," *Beyond the Edge of Certainty*, ed. by Robert Colodny. Englewood Cliffs, N.J.: Prentice-Hall, 1965.

————, "Reply to Criticism," *Boston Studies in the Philosophy of Science*, Vol. 2, ed. by Robert S. Cohen and Marx W. Wartofsky. New

York: Humanities Press, 1965.

————, "The Theater as an Instrument of the Criticism of Ideologies," *Inquiry* 10 (Autumn 1967).

Findlay, J. N., *Hegel: A Re-examination*. London: George Allen and Unwin Ltd., 1958.

Fodor, Jerry A., *Psychological Explanation: An Introduction to the Philosophy of Psychology*. New York: Random House, 1968.

Garelick, Herbert M., *The Anti-Christianity of Kierkegaard*. The Hague: Martinus Nijhoff, 1965.

Gean, W. D., "Reasons and Causes," *The Review of Metaphysics* 19 (June 1966).

Gentry, George, "Habit and Logical Interpretant," *Studies in the Philosophy of Charles Sanders Peirce,* ed. by P. Wiener and F. Young. Cambridge, Mass.: Harvard University Press, 1952.

Goldberg, B., "Can Desire be a Cause?" *Analysis* 15 (1964–1965).

Gorz, André, *Strategy for Labor*. Boston: Beacon Press, 1968.

Habermas, Jürgen, *Die Strukturwandel der Öffentlichkeit: Untersuchugen zu einer Kategorie der bürgerlichen Gesellschaft.* Neuwied am Rhein und Berlin: Luchterhand, 1962.

————, *Erkenntnis und Interesse*. Frankfurt am Main: Suhrkamp, 1968.

————, *Technik und Wissenschaft als 'Ideologie.'* Frankfurt am Main: Suhrkamp, 1968.

————, *Theorie und Praxis: Socialphilosophische Studien*. Neuwied am Rhein und Berlin: Luchterhand, 1963.

————, *Toward a Rational Society*. Boston: Beacon Press, 1970.

Hampshire, Stuart, "Fallacies in Moral Philosophy," *Mind* n.s., 58 (October 1949).

————, *Thought and Action*. London: Chatto and Windus, 1959.

Hancock, R., "Interpersonal and Physical Causation," *The Philosophical Review* 71 (July 1962).

Hanson, N. R., *Patterns of Discovery*. Cambridge: Cambridge University Press, 1958.

Hartman, Klaus, *Sartre's Ontology: A Study of Being and Nothingness in the Light of Hegel's Logic*. Evanston, Ill.: Northwestern University Press, 1966.

Hegel, Georg W. F., *Grundlinien der Philosophie des Rechts,* ed. by Johannes Hoffmeister. Hamburg: Felix Meiner, 1955.

————, *Phänomenologie des Geistes,* ed. by Johannes Hoffmeister. Hamburg: Felix Meiner, 1952.

————, *Vorlesungen über die Philosophie der Weltgeschichte,* 1. *Die Vernunft in der Geschichte,* ed. by Johannes Hoffmeister. Hamburg: Felix Meiner, 1955.

———, *Sämtliche Werke,* ed. by Georg Lasson; Bd. VIII: *Philosophie der Weltgeschichte.* Leipzig: Felix Meiner, 1920.

———, *Werke.* Vollständige Ausgabe. Bd. VI, *Encyklopädie der philosophischen Wissenschaften im Grundrisse,* 1. Teil *Die Logik,* ed. by Leopold v. Henning. Berlin: Duncker und Humblot, 1843. Bd. IX, *Vorlesungen über die Philosophie der Geschichte,* ed. by Eduard Gans, 2nd printing supervised by Dr. Karl Hegel. Berlin: Duncker und Humblot, 1840.

———, *Hegel's Philosophy of Right,* trans. with notes by T. M. Knox. Oxford: At the Clarendon Press, 1953.

———, *Hegel's Science of Logic,* trans. by A. V. Miller. London: George Allen & Unwin, 1969.

———, *The Logic of Hegel,* trans. by William Wallace, 2nd ed. Oxford: Oxford University Press, 1892.

———, *The Phenomenology of Mind,* trans. with an introduction by J. B. Baillie. 2nd revised ed. London: George Allen and Unwin, 1949.

———, *Reason in History: A General Introduction to the Philosophy of History,* trans. with an introduction by Robert S. Hartman. New York: The Liberal Arts Press, 1953.

Heidegger, Martin, *Sein und Zeit.* Halle a. d. S.: Max Niemeyer, 1927.

Hempel, Carl G., *Philosophy of Science.* Englewood Cliffs, N. J.: Prentice-Hall, 1966.

———, "Rational Action," *Proceedings and Addresses of the American Philosophical Association* 35 (1962).

Hook, Sidney, *From Hegel to Marx.* New York: The Humanities Press, 1950.

Hull, Clark L., *Principles of Behavior.* New York: Appleton-Century-Crofts, 1943.

The Human Agent. Royal Institute of Philosophy Lectures, Vol. I (1966/7). New York: St. Martin's Press, 1968.

Hume, David, *A Treatise of Human Nature,* ed. by L. A. Selby-Bigge. Oxford: At the Clarendon Press, 1888.

Hyppolite, Jean, *Studies on Marx and Hegel,* trans. by John O'Neill. New York: Basic Books, Inc., 1969.

James, William, "A Dialogue," *The Writings of William James,* ed. by John J. McDermott (The Modern Library) New York: Random House, 1967.

———, *A Pluralistic Universe.* London: Longmans, Green, and Co., 1909.

Kaufmann, Walter, *Hegel: Reinterpretation, Texts, and Commentary.* Garden City, N.Y.: Doubleday & Co., 1965.

Kelly, George Armstrong, "Notes on Hegel's 'Lordship and Bondage,' "

The Review of Metaphysics 19 (June 1966).

Kierkegaard, Søren, *Concluding Unscientific Postscript,* trans. by David F. Swenson, completed after his death and provided with Introduction and Notes by Walter Lowrie. Princeton: Princeton University Press, 1944.

———, *Either/Or,* trans. by David F. Swenson and Lillian M. Swenson. Princeton: Princeton University Press, 1944.

———, *Philosophical Fragments or A Fragment of Philosophy,* by Johannes Climacus (pseudonym), trans. and with an introduction by David F. Swenson, new introduction and commentary by Niels Thulstrup, translation revised and commentary translated by Howard V. Hong. Princeton: Princeton University Press, 1962.

———, *The Sickness Unto Death,* trans. by Walter Lowrie. New York: Doubleday & Co., Doubleday Anchor Books, 1954.

Knox, Alison, "The Polemics of 'Descriptive Meaning,' " *The Review of Metaphysics* 24 (March 1970).

Kojève, Alexandre, *Introduction à la lecture de Hegel,* ed. by Raymond Queneau. Paris: Gallimard, 1947.

———, *Introduction to the Reading of Hegel,* ed. by Allan Bloom and trans. by James H. Nichols, Jr. New York: Basic Books, 1969.

Kolakowski, Leszek, "Karl Marx and the Classical Definition of Truth," *Toward a Marxist Humanism,* trans. by Jane Zielonko Peel. New York: Grove Press, 1968.

Körner, Stephen, "The Impossibility of Transcendental Deductions," *The Monist* 53 (July 1967).

———, "Transcendental Tendencies in Recent Philosophy," *Journal of Philosophy* 63 (October 13, 1966).

Kuhn, Thomas, *The Structure of Scientific Revolutions.* Chicago: University of Chicago Press, 1962.

Landesman, Charles, "Actions as Universals: An Inquiry into the Metaphysics of Action," *American Philosophical Quarterly* 6 (July 1969).

———, "The New Dualism in the Philosophy of Mind," *The Review of Metaphysics* 19 (December 1965).

Lefebvre, Henri, *The Sociology of Marx.* New York: Vintage Books, 1969.

Lévi-Strauss, Claude, *La pensée sauvage.* Paris: Plon, 1962.

Lichtheim, George, "Oriental Despotism," *The Concept of Ideology.* New York: Vintage Books, 1967.

———, *Marxism in Modern France.* New York: Columbia University Press, 1966.

———, "Sartre, Marxism, and History," *The Concept of Ideology.* New York: Vintage Books, 1967.

Linschoten, Hans, *On the Way Toward a Phenomenological Psychology*: *The Psychology of William James,* trans. by Amedeo Giorgi. Pittsburgh: Duquesne University Press, 1968.

Lobkowicz, N. (ed.), *Marx and the Western World.* South Bend, Indiana: University of Notre Dame Press, 1967.

————, *Theory and Practice: History of a Concept from Aristotle to Marx.* Notre Dame: University of Notre Dame Press, 1967.

Locke, John, *An Essay Concerning Human Understanding,* ed. by A. C. Fraser. Oxford: Oxford University Press, 1894.

Louch, A. R., *Explanation and Human Action.* Berkeley and Los Angeles: University of California Press, 1966.

Lowenberg, J., *Hegel's Phenomenology: Dialogues on the Life of Mind.* LaSalle, Ill.: Open Court Publishing Co., 1965.

Lukács, Georg, *Geschichte und Klassenbewusstsein.* Berlin: Der Malik-verlag, 1923.

MacIntyre, Alasdair, "The Idea of a Social Science," in *Proceedings of the Aristotelian Society,* Supplementary Volume XLI, 1967.

————, *Marxism and Christianity,* rev. ed. New York: Schocken Books, 1968.

Mackey, Louis, "Kierkegaard and the Problem of Existential Philosophy," *The Review of Metaphysics* 9 (March, June 1956).

————, "The Poetry of Inwardness," in *Existential Philosophers: Kierkegaard to Merleau-Ponty,* ed. by George Alfred Schrader, Jr. New York: McGraw-Hill, Inc., 1967.

Macklin, Ruth, "Doing and Happening," *The Review of Metaphysics* 22 (December 1968).

————, "Norm and Law in the Theory of Action," *Inquiry* 11 (Winter 1968).

Malcolm, Norman, "Conceivability of Mechanism," *The Philosophical Review* 77 (January 1968).

————, "Explaining Behavior," *The Philosophical Review* 76 (January 1967).

Marcuse, Herbert, *One-Dimensional Man.* Boston: Beacon Press, 1964.

Margolis, Joseph, "Reasons and Causes," *Dialogue* 8 (June 1969).

————, "Taylor on the Reduction of Teleological Laws," *Inquiry* 11 (Spring 1968).

Marx, Karl, *Capital,* ed. by Frederick Engels and trans. by Samuel Moore and Edward Aveling, three volumes. New York: International Publishers, 1967.

————, *Frühe Schriften,* I. Stuttgart: Cotta-Verlag, 1962.

————, *Grundrisse der Kritik der politischen Ökonomie.* Berlin: Dietz Verlag, 1953.

————, *Karl Marx on Colonialism and Modernization,* ed. with an Introduction by Shlomo Avineri. New York: Doubleday, 1968.

————, *Pre-Capitalist Economic Formations,* trans. by Jack Cohen, ed. and with an introduction by E. J. Hobsbawm. London: Lawrence & Wishart, 1964.

————, *Writings of the Young Marx on Philosophy and Society,* ed. by Loyd D. Easton and Kurt H. Guddat. Garden City, N.Y.: Doubleday & Co., Anchor Books, 1967.

————, and Engels, Friedrich, *Historisch-kritische Gesamtausgabe,* ed. by D. Rjazanov and V. Adoratskij. Frankfurt-Berlin: Marx-Engels-Verlag, 1927-32. Referred to as *MEGA.*

————, *Werke,* Vols. I-XXXIX. Berlin: Dietz Verlag, 1956–.

————, *Basic Writings on Politics and Philosophy,* ed. by Lewis S. Feuer. New York: Doubleday and Co., Anchor Books, 1959.

McLellan, David, "Marx and the Missing Link," *Encounter* 35 (November 1970).

————, *Marx Before Marxism.* New York: Harper & Row, 1970.

————, *The Young Hegelians and Karl Marx.* London: Macmillan, 1969.

McLeod, Norman, "Existential Freedom in the Marxism of J. P. Sartre," *Dialogue* 7 (June 1968).

McMahon, Joseph H., *Humans Being: The World of Jean-Paul Sartre.* Chicago: University of Chicago Press, 1970.

McTaggart, John McTaggart Ellis, *A Commentary on Hegel's Logic.* Cambridge: Cambridge University Press, 1910.

Melden, A. I., *Free Action.* London: Routledge & Kegan Paul, 1961.

Mészáros, István, *Marx's Theory of Alienation.* London: Merlin Press, 1970.

Mischel, Theodore (ed.), *Human Action.* New York: Academic Press, 1969.

Müller, Gustav Emil, "The Hegel Legend of 'Thesis-Antithesis-Synthesis,'" *Journal of the History of Ideas* 19 (June 1958).

Murdoch, Iris, *Sartre: Romantic Rationalist.* New Haven: Yale University Press, 1953.

Nagel, Ernest, *The Structure of Science.* New York: Harcourt, Brace & World, 1961.

Nicholaus, Martin, "Proletariat and Middle Class in Marx: Hegelian Choreography and the Capitalistic Dialectic," *For a New America,* ed. by James Weinstein and David W. Eakins. New York: Vintage Books, 1970.

————, "The Unknown Marx," *The New Left Reader,* ed. by Carl Oglesby. New York: Grove Press, 1969.

330   BIBLIOGRAPHY

Noble, Denis, "Charles Taylor on Teleological Explanation," *Analysis* 27 (January 1967).

Olafson, Frederick A., *Principles and Persons: An Ethical Interpretation of Existentialism*. Baltimore: The Johns Hopkins Press, 1967.

Passmore, John, *A Hundred Years of Philosophy*, Rev. ed. New York: Basic Books, 1966.

Peirce, Charles Sanders, *Collected Papers of Charles Sanders Peirce*, Vols. I-VI, ed. by Charles Hartshorne and Paul Weiss. Cambridge, Mass.: Harvard University Press, 1931-1935.

————, *Collected Papers of Charles Sanders Peirce*, Vols. VII-VIII, ed. by Arthur W. Burks. Cambridge, Mass.: Harvard University Press, 1958.

Peters, R. S., *The Concept of Motivation*, 2nd ed. London: Routledge & Kegan Paul, 1960.

Petrović, Gajo, "The Development and Essence of Marx's Thought," *Praxis* 3/4 (1968).

Pöggler, Otto, "Hegel-Editing and Hegel Research," to be published in the forthcoming proceedings of the 1970 Hegel Symposium sponsored by Marquette University.

Popper, Karl, "Conjectures and Refutations," *Conjectures and Refutations*. New York: Basic Books, 1962.

————, "On the Sources of Knowledge and of Ignorance," *Conjectures and Refutations*. New York: Basic Books, 1962.

Potter, Vincent G., S. J., *Charles S. Peirce, On Norms and Ideals*. Amherst: University of Massachusetts Press, 1967.

Putnam, Hilary, "The Analytic and the Synthetic," *Minnesota Studies in the Philosophy of Science*, Vol. 3, ed. by Herbert Feigl and Grover Maxwell. Minneapolis: University of Minnesota Press, 1962.

————, "How Not to Talk About Meaning," *Boston Studies in the Philosophy of Science*, Vol. 2, ed. by Robert S. Cohen and Marx W. Wartofsky. New York: Humanities Press, 1965.

————, "Minds and Machines," *Dimensions of Mind*, ed. by S. Hook. New York: New York University Press, 1960.

Quine, W. V. O., "Two Dogmas of Empiricism," *From a Logical Point of View*. Cambridge, Mass.: Harvard University Press, 1953.

Rawls, John, "Two Concepts of Rules," *The Philosophical Review* 64 (January 1955).

Reidl, John O., "The Hegelians of Saint Louis, Missouri, and Their Influence in the United States," to be published in the forthcoming proceedings of the 1970 Hegel Symposium sponsored by Marquette University.

Richman, Robert J., "Reasons and Causes," *Australasian Journal of Phi-*

losophy 47 (May 1967).

Rorty, Amelie, "Naturalism and the Ideology of Paradigmatic Moral Disagreements," *The Review of Metaphysics* 24 (June 1971).

———, *Pragmatic Philosophy*. Garden City, N.Y.: Doubleday & Co., Anchor Books, 1966.

Rorty, Richard, "In Defense of Eliminative Materialism," *The Review of Metaphysics* 24 (September 1970).

———, *The Linguistic Turn*. Chicago: University of Chicago Press, 1967.

———, "Mind-Body Identity, Privacy, and Categories," *The Review of Metaphysics* 19 (September 1965).

———, "Pragmatism, Categories, and Language," *The Philosophical Review* 70 (April 1961).

Rotenstreich, Nathan, *Basic Problems of Marx's Philosophy*. Indianapolis: Bobbs-Merrill, 1965.

———, "The Essential and the Epochal Aspects of Philosophy," *The Review of Metaphysics* 23 (June 1970).

Rubel, Maximilien, "Contribution à l'histoire de la genèse du 'Capital,' " *Revue d'histoire economique et sociale* 2 (1950).

———, *Karl Marx: essai de biographie intellectuelle*. Paris: M. Rivière, 1957.

Ryle, Gilbert, *The Concept of Mind*. London: Hutchinson, 1949.

Sachs, David, "A Few Morals About Acts," *The Philosophical Review* 75 (January 1966).

Sartre, Jean-Paul, *Critique de la raison dialectique*, Vol. I, *Théorie des ensembles pratiques*. Paris: Gallimard, 1960.

———, *Esquisse d'une théorie des émotions, nouvelle édition*. Paris: Hermann, 1960.

———, *L'être et le néant: Essai d'ontologie phénoménologique*. Paris: Gallimard, 1943.

———, *L'Existentialisme est un humanisme*. Paris: Éditions Nagel, 1960.

———, "Responsé à Albert Camus," *Situations*, IV. Paris: Gallimard, 1964.

———, *Being and Nothingness: An Essay on Phenomenological Ontology*, trans. and with an introduction by Hazel E. Barnes. New York: Philosophical Library, 1956.

———, *The Emotions: Outline of a Theory*, trans. by Bernard Frechtman. New York: Philosophical Library, 1948.

———, *Existentialism*, trans. by Bernard Frechtman. New York: Philosophical Library, 1947.

———, "Reply to Albert Camus," *Situations*, trans. by Benita Eisler.

332　　　　　　　　　　BIBLIOGRAPHY

New York: George Braziller, 1965.

———, *Search for a Method,* trans. by Hazel E. Barnes. New York: Alfred A. Knopf, 1963.

———, *The Words,* trans. by Bernard Frechtman. New York: George Braziller, 1964.

Sellars, Wilfrid, *Science, Perception and Reality.* New York: The Humanities Press, 1963.

———, "Science, Sense Impressions, and Sensa: A Reply to Cornman," *The Review of Metaphysics* 24 (March 1971).

———, "Scientific Realism or Irenic Instrumentalism," *Boston Studies in the Philosophy of Science,* Vol. 2, ed. by Robert Cohen and Marx Wartofsky. New York: Humanities Press, 1965.

Shapere, Dudley: "Meaning and Scientific Change," *Mind and Cosmos.* Pittsburgh: University of Pittsburgh Press, 1966.

Sheriden, James F., Jr., *The Radical Conversion.* Athens, Ohio: Ohio University Press, 1969.

Smart, J. J. C., "Conflicting Views about Explanation," *Boston Studies in the Philosophy of Science,* Vol. 2, ed. by Robert S. Cohen and Marx W. Wartofsky. New York: Humanities Press, 1965.

Spiegelberg, Herbert, *The Phenomenological Movement, A Historical Introduction,* 2 vols. The Hague: Martinus Nijhoff, 1960.

Strawson, P. F., "Construction and Analysis," *The Revolution in Philosophy,* by A. J. Ayer, W. C. Kneale, G. A. Paul, D. F. Pears, P. F. Strawson, G. J. Warnock, and R. A. Wollheim, with an introduction by Gilbert Ryle. London: Macmillan, 1957.

———, *Individuals. An Essay in Descriptive Metaphysics.* London: Methuen & Co., Ltd., 1959.

Taylor, Charles, *The Explanation of Behaviour.* New York: Humanities Press, 1964.

———, "Relations Between Cause and Action," *Proceedings of the Seventh Inter-American Congress of Philosophy.* Quebec: Les Presses de l'Université Laval, 1967.

———, "A Reply to Margolis," *Inquiry* 11 (Spring 1968).

Taylor, Richard, *Action and Purpose.* Englewood Cliffs, N.J.: Prentice-Hall, 1966.

Thompson, Josiah, *The Lonely Labyrinth: Kierkegaard's Pseudonymous Works.* Carbondale and Edwardsville, Ill.: Southern Illinois University Press, 1967.

Thomson, Judith J., "Comments," *Proceedings of the Seventh Inter-American Congress of Philosophy.* Quebec: Les Presses de l'Université Laval, 1967.

Thulstrup, Niels, *Kierkegaards forhold til Hegel og til den spekulative idealisme indtil 1846.* Copenhagen: Glydendal, 1967.

Turner, Merle B., *Philosophy and the Science of Behavior.* New York: Appleton-Century-Crofts, 1967.

Urmson, J. O., *Philosophical Analysis.* London: Oxford University Press, 1956.

Wenley, Robert Mark, *The Life and Work of George Sylvester Morris.* New York: Macmillan, 1917.

White, Morton, *The Origin of Dewey's Instrumentalism.* New York: Columbia University Press, 1943.

Wild, John, *The Radical Empiricism of William James.* New York: Doubleday, 1969.

Wilshire, Bruce, *William James and Phenomenology: A Study of The Principles of Psychology.* Bloomington, Ind.: Indiana University Press, 1968.

Wittgenstein, Ludwig, "A Lecture on Ethics," *The Philosophical Review* 74 (January 1965).

————, *Philosophical Investigations,* trans. by G. E. M. Anscombe. New York: Macmillan, 1953.

————, *Tractatus Logico-Philosophicus,* German text with translation by D. F. Pears and B. F. McGuinness, with the Introduction by Bertrand Russell. London: Routledge and Kegan Paul, 1961.

Zemach, Eddy, "Wittgenstein's Philosophy of the Mystical," *The Review of Metaphysics* 18 (September 1964).

INDEX OF NAMES

INDEX OF SUBJECTS